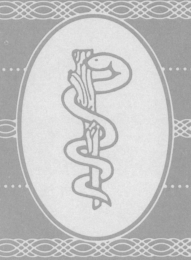

NEW, REVISED, AND EXPANDED EDITION

ON DOCTORING

Stories, Poems, Essays

EDITED BY RICHARD REYNOLDS, M.D.,
AND JOHN STONE, M.D.

Lois LaCivita Nixon Ph.D., M.P.H.,
and Delese Wear Ph.D., Editorial Assistants

Simon & Schuster

New York   London   Toronto   Sydney   Tokyo   Singapore

SIMON & SCHUSTER
ROCKEFELLER CENTER
1230 AVENUE OF THE AMERICAS
NEW YORK, NEW YORK 10020

DESIGNED BY BARBARA MARKS
MANUFACTURED IN THE UNITED STATES OF AMERICA

PERMISSIONS, ACKNOWLEDGMENTS BEGIN ON PAGE 438.

10 9 8 7 6 5 4 3 2 1

LIBRARY OF CONGRESS CATALOGING-IN-PUBLICATION DATA

ON DOCTOR[I]NG : STORIES, POEMS, ESSAYS / EDITED BY RICHARD
   REYNOLDS AND JOHN STONE ; LOIS LACIVITA NIXON, DELESE WEAR,
   EDITORIAL ASSISTANTS.
       P.   CM.
       ON T.P. "[I]" APPEARS AS A CADUCEUS.
       1. PHYSICIANS—LITERARY COLLECTIONS.   2. MEDICINE—LITERARY
   COLLECTIONS.   I. REYNOLDS, RICHARD C., DATE.   II. STONE, JOHN,
   DATE.
   PN6071.P4505   1995   95-16111
            808.8'0356—DC20   CIP
         ISBN 0-684-80255-4

FOR OUR TEACHERS:
OUR STUDENTS, OUR COLLEAGUES, OUR PATIENTS

CONTENTS

INTRODUCTION 11

CAROLA EISENBERG *It Is Still a Privilege to Be a Doctor* 17

THE BIBLE *Naaman Cured of Leprosy, 2 Kings 5:1–14* 20
Ecclesiasticus (or Sirach) 30:14–17 21
Ecclesiasticus (or Sirach) 38:1–15 21

JOHN DONNE *Death Be Not Proud* 22

JOHN KEATS *This Living Hand, Now Warm and Capable* 24

OLIVER WENDELL HOLMES *The Stethoscope Song* 25

EMILY DICKINSON *There's Been a Death* 27
Surgeons Must Be Very Careful 28
I Heard a Fly Buzz 28
"Hope" Is the Thing with Feathers 28

SIR WILLIAM OSLER *Aphorisms* 30

SIR ARTHUR CONAN DOYLE *The Curse of Eve* 34

ANTON CHEKHOV *Misery* 44
A Doctor's Visit 50

ROBERT FROST *"Out, Out—"* 60

W. SOMERSET MAUGHAM Excerpt from *The Summing Up* 62

WILLIAM CARLOS WILLIAMS *The Practice* 68
The Artist 74
Between Walls 74
Le Médecin Malgré Lui 75
The Birth 76
The Last Words of My English Grandmother 77

CONTENTS

	The Girl with a Pimply Face 78
	The Use of Force 89
FRANZ KAFKA	*A Country Doctor* 93
FRANCES CORNFORD	*The Watch* 98
JORGE LUIS BORGES	*The Immortals* 99
ERNEST HEMINGWAY	*Indian Camp* 104
	Hills Like White Elephants 108
ARNA BONTEMPS	*A Summer Tragedy* 112
ZORA NEALE HURSTON	*My Most Humiliating Jim Crow Experience* 121
PABLO NERUDA	*Larynx* 123
SIR JOHN BETJEMAN	*Before the Anaesthetic, or a Real Fright* 126
W. H. AUDEN	*Musée des Beaux Arts* 128
	The Art of Healing 130
EUDORA WELTY	*A Worn Path* 133
JOSEPHINE MILES	*The Doctor Who Sits at the Bedside of a Rat* 141
	Sheep 141
BARBARA PYM	Excerpt from *A Few Green Leaves* 142
EDWARD LOWBURY	*Glaucoma* 147
LEWIS THOMAS	*House Calls* 149
	Leech Leech, et Cetera 154
DYLAN THOMAS	*Do Not Go Gentle into That Good Night* 161
RANDALL JARRELL	*Next Day* 162
JOHN CIARDI	*Washing Your Feet* 164
GWENDOLYN BROOKS	*The Bean Eaters* 166
DORIS GRUMBACH	*Coming into the End Zone* 167
ANATOLE BROYARD	*Doctor, Talk to Me* 175
PHILIP LARKIN	*Faith Healing* 182
FERROL SAMS	*Saba* 184
KURT VONNEGUT	*Fortitude* 201

CONTENTS

GRACE PALEY   *A Man Told Me the Story of His Life*   217

JAMES KIRKUP   *A Correct Compassion*   219

DANNIE ABSE   *X-Ray*   222
Case History   222
Carnal Knowledge   223

JAMES DICKEY   *Diabetes*   227
The Cancer Match   230

DENISE LEVERTOV   *Talking to Grief*   232
Death Psalm: O Lord of Mysteries   233

FLANNERY O'CONNOR   *Everything That Rises Must Converge*   235

L. E. SISSMAN   *A Deathplace*   249

RICHARD SELZER   *Mercy*   251
Imelda   255

MAYA ANGELOU   *The Last Decision*   267

RICHARD C. REYNOLDS   *A Day in the Life of an Internist*   268

ROBERT COLES   Excerpt from *The Call of Stories*   277
Medical Ethics and Living a Life   280

X. J. KENNEDY   *Little Elegy: For a Child Who Skipped Rope*   287

GERALD WEISSMANN   *Auden and the Liposome*   288

MILLER WILLIAMS   *Going*   296
A Day in the Death   297

PATRICIA GOEDICKE   *One More Time*   298

L. J. SCHNEIDERMAN   *The Appointment*   299

LINDA PASTAN   *The Five Stages of Grief*   307
Notes from the Delivery Room   309
Remission   310

JOSEPH HARDISON   *The House Officer's Changing World*   311

FRANK GONZALES-CRUSSI   *On Embalming*   316

JOHN STONE   *Gaudeamus Igitur*   326
Death   330

LUCILLE CLIFTON   *the lost baby poem*   331
poem to my uterus   332

CONTENTS

GHASSAN KANAFANI   *Death of Bed 12*   333

LAWRENCE K. ALTMAN   *Don't Touch the Heart*   346

RAYMOND CARVER   *What the Doctor Said*   360
       My Death   361

MARGARET ATWOOD   *The Woman Who Could Not Live with Her
       Faulty Heart*   362

SHARON OLDS   *35/10*   364
       Miscarriage   365

JACK COULEHAN   *The Knitted Glove*   366
       Good News   367

JAMES TATE   *On the Subject of Doctors*   368

ALICE WALKER   *Medicine*   369

DAVID HILFIKER   *Mistakes*   371

MELVIN KONNER   *The Dawn of Wonder*   383

DAVID RINALDI   *Let's Talk About It*   389

HEATHER MCHUGH   *What Hell Is*   391

RONALD VALDISERRI   *Suffering*   393

DAVID HELLERSTEIN   *Touching*   395

ABRAHAM VERGHESE   Excerpt from *My Own Country*   399

PERRI KLASS   *Invasions*   407

ELSPETH CAMERON RITCHIE   *Hospital Sketchbook: Life on the Ward Through
       an Intern's Eyes*   411

JON MUKAND   *The Son: Returning Home*   420

ETHAN CANIN   *We Are Nighttime Travelers*   423

INDEX OF AUTHORS   446

INTRODUCTION

*It's the humdrum, day-in, day-out, everyday work that is the real
satisfaction of the practice of medicine; the million and a half patients a
man has seen on his daily visits over a forty-year period of weekdays
and Sundays that make up his life. I have never had a money practice;
it would have been impossible for me. But the actual calling on people,
at all times and under all conditions, the coming to grips with the
intimate conditions of their lives, when they were being born, when
they were dying, watching them die, watching them get well when they
were ill, has always absorbed me.*

IN THESE FEW SENTENCES from William Carlos Williams's autobiography, he has captured very well the human splendor of medicine.
We have tried to do the same in compiling this anthology, which contains stories, poems, essays, excerpts, and memoirs. In the process of
caring for their patients, physicians have a unique—and privileged—
window on the full range of human emotions. Literature, too, is rich in
its descriptions of individual illnesses and plagues, in its capacity to
reveal patients' reactions to illness and doctors' dilemmas in providing
care. In its own way, literature defines the medical profession and fits
into the larger society. Legacies and traditions, which are an important
part of medicine, are often best manifested in the literature of a given
period of history. Many of our selections were written by physicians.
Williams and Anton Chekhov, W. Somerset Maugham and Lewis
Thomas are only a few of the physician-writers who have relied on their
medical backgrounds to help them understand better the frailties and
strengths, the wonderment of the human condition. Some carried on a
lifelong practice of medicine while simultaneously achieving literary
recognition. Dr. Williams is a fine example—his work, it seems fair to
say, changed the face of American poetry, even as he carried on a large
medical practice (he delivered over three thousand babies, for example).
Somerset Maugham, although he discontinued his medical practice after

internship, gave full credit to the experience in his autobiographical *The Summing Up:* "I do not know a better training for a writer than to spend some years in the medical profession." Others, so well known for their writing, were also trained in the medicine of their day. It is not generally known, for example, that the Romantic poet John Keats did a five-year apprenticeship with a surgeon. During those years, he delivered so many babies that he was not required to take obstetrics and gynecology during the hospital phase of his training.

Of course, one need not be trained in medicine in order to make cogent and crucial observations about what it is like to be sick, hence vulnerable; to witness and record the isolation and alienation that comes eventually to all of us—finally, we are all patients. Franz Kafka was trained as a lawyer; yet, in his short masterpiece "A Country Doctor," he captures the ambiguity, even the surrealism that sometimes attends the medical encounter. In his compelling short story "The Immortals," Jorge Luis Borges (also not a physician) comments trenchantly and presciently on some of the major ethical dilemmas of our time, those centering on organ transplants and utilization of scarce medical resources.

We have included many poems in this anthology. Poems recommend themselves to the editors of such a work because of their economy of form: in a few words, a poem can communicate a complete experience. Read aloud Margaret Atwood's "The Woman Who Could Not Live with Her Faulty Heart." In its rhythms, one can hear the heart, first regular, then skipping. Or listen to the courage embodied in James Dickey's "The Cancer Match." Read Emily Dickinson's short poems, which transcend time and place to speak to us in completely modern—and human—terms. And share with Patricia Goedicke (in "One More Time") the universal experience of having an X ray taken: "When the technician says breathe/I breathe."

Nor have we neglected the wisdom gathered in essays from major clinical figures and teachers over the years; hence, Lewis Thomas's "House Calls" is included. We begin this book, in fact, with just such an essay, one that impressed us from the first time we encountered it in the pages of *The New England Journal of Medicine:* Carola Eisenberg's "It Is Still a Privilege to Be a Doctor." The reader will find his or her own favorites among the many others we have included.

This new edition of *On Doctoring* provided us the chance to add new voices to those previously included: remarkable writing from Grace Paley and Alice Walker; a provocative essay by Doris Grumbach; an additional story by Ernest Hemingway; a short play by the inimitable Kurt Vonnegut. And many others.

Each one of us, of course, has a vast and vested interest in what goes on in the myriad arenas of medicine—and in the nature of the individual doctor-patient encounters explored within the pages of this book. This is all to the good: physicians and patients must continue to talk and listen together—and literature can help in that exchange.

Henry David Thoreau wrote, "To affect the quality of the day—that is the highest of arts." Both medicine and literature have the capacity to affect the quality of the human day. Resonances between these two disciplines offer us a unique view of the human condition that neither one alone can provide. Read. And enjoy.

RICHARD REYNOLDS
JOHN STONE

One of the essential qualities of the clinician is interest in humanity, for the secret of the care of the patient is in caring for the patient.

—FRANCES WELD PEABODY
(1881–1927)

CAROLA EISENBERG

CAROLA EISENBERG (1917–   ). *American physician and educator. Born in Buenos Aires, Argentina, Dr. Eisenberg received her M.D. from the University of Buenos Aires, then did graduate training in psychiatry at that city's Hospicio de Las Mercedes and at Johns Hopkins Hospital. She has taught both at Johns Hopkins and at Harvard Medical School and was dean of student affairs for six years at Massachusetts Institute of Technology and for twelve years at Harvard Medical School.*

IT IS STILL A PRIVILEGE TO BE A DOCTOR

I have been dean for student affairs at Harvard Medical School for eight years. It is my responsibility and privilege to listen to medical students and to support their personal and professional development. What they have been telling me this year troubles me. It is exemplified by a recent encounter with a third-year student.

The student was distressed. What had sustained him through the preclinical years was the anticipation of learning patient care. Now he had earned the right to wear a white coat and enter the wards. What he had encountered had discouraged him profoundly. The problem was not the work; that was as exciting as he had hoped it would be. It was his interaction with his teachers. Once the formal teaching rounds were over, they talked only about the problems they faced. For some, the talk was about the malpractice crisis, the freeze on Medicare fees, the impact of diagnosis-related groups, and shrinking incomes. For others, it was the endless paperwork in applying for research funding, the competition for the declining number of grants, and the uncertainties of sustaining a research career. Medicine, they said, was no fun anymore. If students were included in the conversations, the faculty reminisced about the good old days, which neither they nor the students would ever see. They wondered aloud whether they would choose medicine if they had it to do all over again.

I have heard perhaps a dozen similar stories from students doing clerkships at some of Boston's leading teaching hospitals. But the lamentations about the woes afflicting medicine are hardly limited to teaching faculty. Almost every week, and sometimes daily, one or the other of the media quotes practitioners who threaten to close their offices if they are not granted relief from what they consider onerous restrictions on their income or their right to practice freely. All this hits students hard because they are already worried about the indebtedness they are incurring, particularly in view of the stories about the doctor glut, declining incomes, and the increasing competition for residency positions. They fear that their debts will force them to choose specialties on the basis of anticipated earnings rather than intrinsic interest. Indeed, some, in the role of tutors for premedical students, have begun to dissuade the college students they advise from choosing medicine, because they consider the prospects to be so bleak.

How absurd! It stands the world on its head to suggest that the liabilities of a career in medicine outweigh the assets. Of course there are major problems in the delivery of medical care, and we ought to be in the vanguard of those seeking solutions to them. But to lose sight of just how lucky we are to have a profession in which we do well for ourselves by doing well for others reflects a puzzling loss of perspective. The satisfaction of being able to relieve pain and restore function, the intellectual challenge of solving clinical problems, and the variety of human issues we confront in daily clinical practice will remain the essence of doctoring, whatever the changes in the organizational and economic structure of medicine.

Although physicians' incomes may have declined in real dollars in the 1980s, they remain in the upper decile of all U.S. incomes. Although the practice of medicine may be increasingly vexed by bureaucratic constraints, doctors still retain a degree of autonomy in their clinical activities that is rarely found in other occupations. Although research support may not have kept up with inflation, the opportunities for young investigators in this country exceed those to be found anywhere else in the world and are several orders of magnitude greater than they were forty years ago.

Let us put first things first. Medicine is still a great profession, one held in high esteem by the majority of the public, despite the increase in malpractice suits. Our students look to us as role models for their careers. What we must make sure they learn from us are the personal gratifications medicine brings and the obligation to public service it entails. Of course there are reasons for concern when cost controls are emphasized to the detriment of clinical care, when the untoward outcomes inevitable even with the best medical practice lead to charges of malpractice, and when false economies jeopardize the very research that can improve those outcomes.

But if we are to reverse these trends, we must mobilize our natural allies—our patients and the public at large. It is they who have the greatest stake in the battle to preserve excellence in medical care. Cutbacks in Medicaid and Medicare threaten the health of the poor and the elderly—far more than they do physician incomes. Given the promise of basic research, which has paid off so handsomely in better medicine, cutbacks in federal support penalize the ill whose suffering would have been prevented by the new knowledge—far more than they do research careers. If we focus on our primary responsibility to serve as advocates for our patients, we will both maintain our professional integrity and provide the leadership for a broad public coalition in defense of health care. As long as we emphasize self-serving complaints—threats to *our* incomes and to *our* freedom to practice as we see fit—we will remain isolated and impotent.

As physicians, we have a moral imperative to sustain the highest aspirations of the students we teach. In taking this position, I do not mean to be a Pollyanna. Our students need to know about the problems facing medicine. But those problems need to be seen in perspective. Medical education does not exist to provide doctors with an opportunity to earn a living, but to improve the health of the public. Let us enlist our students in the campaign for equity and quality in medical care. If that campaign is to succeed, it will need the efforts of the best and the brightest.

What we do as doctors, most of the time, is deeply gratifying, whatever the mix of patient care, research, and teaching in our individual careers. I cannot imagine a more satisfying calling. Let us make sure our students hear that message from us.

THE BIBLE
Old Testament, King James Version

NAAMAN CURED OF LEPROSY, 2 KINGS 5:1–14

Naaman, commander of the army of the king of Syria, was a great man with his master and in high favor, because by him the Lord had given victory to Syria. He was a mighty man of valor, but he was a leper. Now the Syrians on one of their raids had carried off a little maid from the land of Israel, and she waited on Naaman's wife. She said to her mistress, "Would that my lord were with the prophet who is in Samaria! He would cure him of his leprosy." So Naaman went in and told his lord, "Thus and so spoke the maiden from the land of Israel." And the king of Syria said, "Go now, and I will send a letter to the king of Israel."

So he went, taking with him ten talents of silver, six thousand shekels of gold, and ten festal garments. And he brought the letter to the king of Israel, which read, "When this letter reaches you, know that I have sent to you Naaman my servant, that you may cure him of leprosy." And when the king of Israel read the letter, he rent his clothes and said, "Am I God, to kill and to make alive, that this man sends word to me to cure a man of his leprosy? Only consider, and see how he is seeking a quarrel with me."

But when Elisha the man of God heard that the king of Israel had rent his clothes, he sent to the king, saying, "Why have you rent your clothes? Let him come now to me, that he may know that there is a prophet in Israel." So Naaman came with his horses and chariots, and halted at the door of Elisha's house. And Elisha sent a messenger to him, saying, "Go and wash in the Jordan seven times, and your flesh shall be restored and you shall be clean." But Naaman was angry, and went away, saying, "Behold, I thought that he would surely come out to me, and stand, and call on the name of the Lord his God, and wave his hand over the place, and cure the leper. Are not Abana and Pharpar, the rivers of Damascus, better than all the waters of Israel? Could I not wash in them, and be clean?" So he turned and went away in a rage. But his servants came near and said to him, "My father, if the prophet had commanded you to do some great thing, would you not have done it? How much rather, then, when he says to you, 'Wash, and be clean'?" So he went down and dipped himself seven times in the Jordan, according to the word of the man of God; and his flesh was restored like the flesh of a little child, and he was clean.

* * *

Better off is a poor man who is well and strong in constitution
  than a rich man who is severely afflicted in body.
Health and soundness are better than all gold,
  and a robust body than countless riches.
There is no wealth better than health of body,
  and there is no gladness above joy of heart.
Death is better than a miserable life,
  and eternal rest than chronic sickness.

ECCLESIASTICUS (OR SIRACH) 30:14–17

Honor the physician with the honor due him,
  according to your need of him,
  for the Lord created him;
for healing comes from the Most High,
  and he will receive a gift from the king.
The skill of the physician lifts up his head,
  and in the presence of great men he is admired.
The Lord created medicines from the earth,
  and a sensible man will not despise them.
Was not water made sweet with a tree
  in order that his power might be known?
And he gave skill to men,
  that he might be glorified in his marvelous works.
By them he heals and takes away pain;
  the pharmacist makes of them a compound.
His works will never be finished;
  and from him health is upon the face of the earth.

My son, when you are sick do not be negligent,
  but pray to the Lord, and he will heal you.
Give up your faults and direct your hands aright,
  and cleanse your heart from all sin.
Offer a sweet-smelling sacrifice, and a memorial portion of fine flour,
  and pour oil on your offering, as much as you can afford.
And give the physician his place, for the Lord created him:
  let him not leave you, for there is need of him.
There is a time when success lies in the hands of physicians,
  for they too will pray to the Lord
that he should grant them success in diagnosis
  and in healing, for the sake of preserving life.
He who sings before his Maker,
  may he fall into the care of a physician.

ECCLESIASTICUS (OR SIRACH) 38:1–15

JOHN DONNE

JOHN DONNE (1572–1631). *English poet and clergyman. Donne's poetry is noted for its wit and its often startling images, drawn from varied realms of human thought and activity—geography, astronomy, law, alchemy, scripture, and even everyday life. His sermons are characterized by rich complexity of thought and spirit and imbued with the intellectual daring and passionate ingenuity he is best remembered for. Donne's works include the* Songs and Sonnets *and the* Holy Sonnets *(both poetry),* Devotions upon Emergent Occasions *(prose meditations on his own serious illness, from which he recovered), and stunning, sometimes bawdy individual poems such as "A Valediction Forbidding Mourning," "A Fever," "The Sun Rising," "The Flea," and "Elegy: Going to Bed."*

DEATH BE NOT PROUD

Death be not proud, though some have called thee
Mighty and dreadful, for, thou art not so,
For, those, whom thou think'st, thou dost overthrow,
Die not, poor death, nor yet canst thou kill me;
From rest and sleep, which but thy pictures be,
Much pleasure, then from thee, much more must flow,
And soonest our best men with thee do go,
Rest of their bones, and soul's delivery.
Thou art slave to fate, chance, kings, and desperate men,
And dost with poison, war, and sickness dwell,
And poppy, or charms can make us sleep as well,
And better than thy stroke; why swell'st thou then?
One short sleep past, we wake eternally,
And death shall be no more, Death thou shalt die.

Seventeenth-century physicians caring for plague patients wore a strange, almost comical, outfit that covered them completely. The gown was usually made of leather, as was the mask. The mask had glass windows over the eyes; its long beak was filled with antiseptics. In his gloved hand, the plague doctor carried a wand to assess the pulse and to avoid direct contact.

JOHN KEATS

JOHN KEATS (1795–1821). *English poet. After training for six years as a surgeon and apothecary, Keats abandoned medicine for poetry at the age of twenty-one. He is best known for his odes, which represent the peak of his achievement: for "La Belle Dame Sans Merci," a work that is both frightening and magical in its apparent simplicity; and for a number of sonnets that mark him as a major Romantic poet in that form. He died of tuberculosis.*

THIS LIVING HAND, NOW WARM AND CAPABLE

This living hand, now warm and capable
Of earnest grasping, would, if it were cold
And in the icy silence of the tomb,
So haunt thy days and chill thy dreaming nights
That thou wouldst wish thine own heart dry of blood.
So in my veins red life might stream again,
And thou be conscience-calmed—see here it is—
I hold it towards you.

OLIVER WENDELL HOLMES

OLIVER WENDELL HOLMES (1809–1894). *American physician, essayist, and poet. Holmes became the first dean of Harvard Medical School in 1842, and went on to become Parkman professor of anatomy and physiology there until his retirement in 1882. He was a famous medical authority; his two important medical publications,* Homeopathy and its Kindred Delusions *(1842) and* The Contagiousness of Puerperal Fever *(1843), were rivaled only by his frequent contributions to* The Atlantic Monthly, *which he helped found.*

Holmes's apparent delight in physiognomy is illustrated in such poetry as "The Living Temple" (1858), "La Griesette" (1863), and "The Stethoscope Song" (1849), given here.

THE STETHOSCOPE SONG (1848)
A PROFESSIONAL BALLAD

There was a young man in Boston town,
　　He bought him a *stethoscope* nice and new,
All mounted and finished and polished down,
　　With an ivory cap and a stopper too.

It happened a spider within did crawl,
　　And spun him a web of ample size,
Wherein there chanced one day to fall
　　A couple of very imprudent flies.

Now being from Paris but recently,
　　This fine young man would show his skill;
And so they gave him, his hand to try,
　　A hospital patient extremely ill.

Then out his stethoscope he took,
　　And on it placed his curious ear;
Mon Dieu! said he, with a knowing look,
　　Why, here is a sound that's mighty queer!

There's *empyema* beyond a doubt;
　　We'll plunge a *trocar* in his side.
The diagnosis was made out,—
　　They tapped the patient; so he died.

Then six young damsels, slight and frail,
    Received this kind young doctor's cares;
They all were getting slim and pale,
    And short of breath on mounting stairs.

They all made rhymes with "sighs" and "skies,"
    And loathed their puddings and buttered rolls,
And dieted, much to their friends' surprise,
    On pickles and pencils and chalk and coals.

So fast their little hearts did bound,
    That frightened insects buzzed the more;
So over all their chests he found
    The *rale sifflant* and the *rale sonore.*

He shook his head. There's grave disease,—
    I greatly fear you all must die;
A slight *post-mortem,* if you please,
    Surviving friends would gratify.

The six young damsels wept aloud,
    Which so prevailed on six young men
That each his honest love avowed,
    Whereat they all got well again.

This poor young man was all aghast;
    The price of stethoscopes came down;
And so he was reduced at last
    To practice in a country town.

Now use your ears, all that you can,
    But don't forget to mind your eyes.
Or you may be cheated, like this young man.
    By a couple of silly, abnormal flies.

EMILY DICKINSON

EMILY DICKINSON (1830–1886). *American poet. Reclusive and
idiosyncratic, Dickinson lived a retiring small-town life in Amherst,
Massachusetts, where she composed more than 1,700 poems, only a few
of which were published in her lifetime. Like her poems, her letters are
illuminated by startlingly fresh imagery and intensely heartbreaking
insights. Dickinson's voice is vigorous, direct, and wise with
introspection; she is widely celebrated as one of America's greatest
poets.*

THERE'S BEEN A DEATH

There's been a Death, in the Opposite House,
As lately as Today—
I know it, by the numb look
Such Houses have—alway—

The Neighbors rustle in and out—
The Doctor—drives away—
A Window opens like a Pod—
Abrupt—mechanically—

Somebody flings a Mattress out—
The Children hurry by—
They wonder if it died—on that—
I used to—when a Boy—

The Minister—goes stiffly in—
As if the House were His—
And He owned all the Mourners—now—
And little Boys—besides—

And then the Milliner—and the Man
Of the Appalling Trade—
To take the measure of the House—

There'll be that Dark Parade—

Of Tassels—and of Coaches—soon—
It's easy as a Sign—
The Intuition of the News—
In just a Country Town—

EMILY DICKINSON

SURGEONS MUST BE VERY CAREFUL

Surgeons must be very careful
When they take the knife!
Underneath their fine incisions
Stirs the Culprit—*Life*!

I HEARD A FLY BUZZ

I heard a Fly buzz—when I died—
The Stillness in the Room
Was like the Stillness in the Air—
Between the Heaves of Storm—

The Eyes around—had wrung them dry—
And Breaths were gathering firm
For that last Onset—when the King
Be witnessed—in the Room—

I willed my Keepsakes—Signed away
What portion of me be
Assignable—and then it was
There interposed a Fly—

With Blue—uncertain stumbling Buzz—
Between the light—and me—
And then the Windows failed—and then
I could not see to see—

"HOPE" IS THE THING WITH FEATHERS

"Hope" is the thing with feathers—
That perches in the soul—
And sings the tune without the words—
And never stops—at all—

And sweetest—in the Gale—is heard—
And sore must be the storm—
That could abash the little Bird
That kept so many warm—

I've heard it in the chillest land—
And on the strangest Sea—
Yet, never, in Extremity,
It asked a crumb—of Me.

The Gross Clinic (1875) by Thomas Eakins
The American surgeon Samuel Gross, pictured here, did not believe in Lister's principles of antisepsis for the operating room. The surgeons wore no gowns or masks. A relative of the patient's, seated at the left, covers his face in dismay.

SIR WILLIAM OSLER

SIR WILLIAM OSLER (1849–1919). *Physician, writer, and educator. Born in Ontario, Canada, Osler received his M.D. from McGill University in Montreal. His career led him first to the University of Pennsylvania, then to the young Johns Hopkins University, where he organized the department of medicine. In 1904, he became Regius Professor of Medicine at Oxford University. Osler wrote extensively on both medical and nonmedical subjects, and had a great influence on medical education in America and England.*

APHORISMS

It is astonishing with how little reading a doctor can practice medicine, but it is not astonishing how badly he may do it.

To study the phenomena of disease without books is to sail an uncharted sea, while to study books without patients is not to go to sea at all.

The physician needs a clear head and a kind heart; his work is arduous and complex, requiring the exercise of the very highest faculties of the mind, while constantly appealing to the emotions and higher feelings.

Common sense in matters medical is rare, and is usually in inverse ratio to the degree of education.

An old writer says that there are four sorts of readers: "Sponges, which attract all without distinguishing; Howre-glasses, which receive and powre out as fast; Bagges, which retain the dregges of the spices and let the wine escape; and Sieves, which retaine the best onely." A man wastes a great many years before he reaches the "sieve" stage.

The Searcher for Knowledge

He who knows not, and knows not that he knows not, is a fool. Shun him.

He who knows not, and knows that he knows not, is simple. Teach him.

*   *   *

Professors may be divided into four classes. There is, first, the man who can think, but who has neither tongue nor technique. Though useless for the ordinary student, he may be the leaven of a faculty and the chief glory of his University. A second variety is the phonographic professor, who can talk, but who can neither think nor work. Under the old regime he repeated year by year the same lecture. A third is the man who has technique, but who can neither talk nor think; and a fourth is the rare professor who can do all three, think, talk, and work.

While medicine is to be your vocation or calling, see to it that you have also an avocation—some intellectual pastime which may serve to keep you in touch with the world of art, of science, or of letters. Begin at once the cultivation of some interest other than the purely professional. The difficulty is in a selection and the choice will be different according to your tastes and training. No matter what it is, have an outside hobby. For the hard-working medical student it is easier perhaps to keep up an interest in literature. Let each subject in your year's work have a corresponding outside author. When tired of anatomy refresh your minds with Oliver Wendell Holmes; after a worrying subject in physiology, turn to the great idealists, to Shelley or to Keats, for consolation; when chemistry distresses your soul, seek peace in the great pacifier, Shakespeare; ten minutes with Montaigne will lighten the burden.

No man is really happy or safe without a hobby, and it makes precious little difference what the outside interest may be—botany, beetles or butterflies, roses, tulips or irises: fishing, mountaineering or antiquities —anything will do so long as he straddles a hobby and rides it hard.

And, for the sake of what it brings, the grace of humility is a precious gift. When to the sessions of sweet silent thought you summon up the remembrance of your own imperfections, the faults of your brothers will seem less grievous, and in the quaint language of Sir Thomas Browne, you will "allow one eye for what is laudable in them."

The battle against polypharmacy, or the use of a large number of drugs (of the action of which we know little, yet we put them into bodies of the action of which we know less), has not been brought to a finish.

But know also, man has an inborn craving for medicine. Heroic dosing for several generations has given his tissues a thirst for drugs. As I once before remarked, the desire to take medicine is one feature which distinguishes man, the animal, from his fellow creatures. It is really one of the most serious difficulties with which we have to contend. Even in minor ailments, which would yield to dieting or to simple home remedies, the doctor's visit is not thought to be complete without the prescription.

Nothing will sustain you more potently in your humdrum routine, as perhaps it may be thought, than the power to recognize the true poetry of life—the poetry of the commonplace, of the ordinary man, of the plain, toil-worn woman, with their loves and their joys, their sorrows and their griefs.

It is a common error to think that the more a doctor sees the greater his experience and the more he knows. No one ever drew a more skillful distinction than Cowper in his oft-quoted lines, which I am never tired of repeating in a medical audience:

> 'Knowledge and wisdom, far from being one,
> Have oft-times no connexion. Knowledge dwells
> In heads replete with thoughts of other men;
> Wisdom in minds attentive to their own.
> Knowledge is proud that he has learned so much;
> Wisdom is humble that he knows no more.'

I wish I had time to speak of the value of note-taking. You can do nothing as a student in practice without it. Carry a small notebook which will fit into your waistcoat pocket, and never ask a new patient a question without notebook and pencil in hand.

For better or worse, there are few occupations of a more satisfying character than the practice of medicine, if a man can but once get *orientirt* and bring to it the philosophy of honest work, the philosophy that insists that we are here, not to get all we can out of life about us, but to see how much we can add to it. The discontent and grumblings which one hears have their source in the man more often than in the environment.

I have three personal ideals. One, to do the day's work well and not to bother about tomorrow . . . The second ideal has been to act the Golden Rule, as far as in me lay, toward my professional brethren and toward the patients committed to my care. And the third has been to cultivate such a measure of equanimity as would enable me to bear success with humility, the affection of my friends without pride, and to be ready when the day of sorrow and grief came to meet it with the courage befitting a man.

The practice of medicine is an art, based on science.

Nothing in life is more wonderful than faith—the one great moving force which we can neither weigh in the balance nor test in the crucible.

Remember how much you do not know. Do not pour strange medicines into your patients.

In the physician or surgeon no quality takes rank with imperturbability.

Silence is a powerful weapon.

Medicine is learned by the bedside and not in the classroom.

Education is a lifelong process, in which the student can make only a beginning during his college course.

Undoubtedly the student tries to learn too much, and we teachers try to teach him too much—neither, perhaps, with great success.

Though a little one, the master-word looms large in meaning. It is the "Open Sesame" to every portal, the great equalizer in the world, the true philosopher's stone which transmutes all the base metals of humanity into gold. The stupid man among you it will make bright, the bright man brilliant, and the brilliant student steady. With the magic word in your heart, all things are possible, and without it all study is vanity and vexation. . . . And the master-word is WORK.

I desire no other epitaph than the statement that I taught medical students in the wards, as I regard this by far the most useful and important work I have been called upon to do.

SIR ARTHUR CONAN DOYLE

SIR ARTHUR CONAN DOYLE (1859–1930). *British physician and writer. Doyle received his M.D. from the University of Edinburgh, then turned to writing to supplement a meager medical practice. He created the personality of Sherlock Holmes (who owed his last name to Dr. Oliver Wendell Holmes), patterning some aspects of the character after one of his Edinburgh professors, Dr. Joseph Bell. Sherlock Holmes and his colleague, Dr. Watson, became an internationally famous crime-solving duo. Arthur Conan Doyle also wrote poems, historical novels, short stories, and science fiction.*

THE CURSE OF EVE

Robert Johnson was an essentially commonplace man, with no feature to distinguish him from a million others. He was pale of face, ordinary in looks, neutral in opinions, thirty years of age, and a married man. By trade he was a gentleman's outfitter in the New North Road, and the competition of business squeezed out of him the little character that was left. In his hope of conciliating customers he had become cringing and pliable, until working ever in the same routine from day to day he seemed to have sunk into a soulless machine rather than a man. No great question had ever stirred him. At the end of this smug century, self-contained in his own narrow circle, it seemed impossible that any of the mighty, primitive passions of mankind could ever reach him. Yet birth, and lust, and illness, and death are changeless things, and when one of these harsh facts springs out upon a man at some sudden turn of the path of life, it dashes off for the moment his mask of civilisation and gives a glimpse of the stranger and stronger face below.

Johnson's wife was a quiet little woman, with brown hair and gentle ways. His affection for her was the one positive trait in his character. Together they would lay out the shop window every Monday morning, the spotless shirts in their green cardboard boxes below, the neckties above hung in rows over the brass rails, the cheap studs glistening from the white cards at either side, while in the background were the rows of cloth caps and the bank of boxes in which the more valuable hats were screened from the sunlight. She kept the books and sent out the bills. No one but she knew the joys and sorrows which crept into his small life. She had shared his exultation when the gentleman who was going to India had bought ten dozen shirts and an incredible number of collars, and she had been stricken as he when, after the goods had gone, the bill was returned from the hotel address with the intimation that no such person had lodged there. For five years they had worked, building up the business, thrown together all the more closely because their marriage had been a childless one. Now, however, there were signs that a change was at hand, and that speedily. She was unable to come downstairs, and her mother, Mrs. Peyton, came over from Camberwell to nurse her and to welcome her grandchild.

Little qualms of anxiety came over Johnson as his wife's time approached. However, after all, it was a natural process. Other men's wives went through it unharmed, and why should not his? He was himself one of a family of fourteen, and yet his mother was alive and hearty. It was quite the exception for anything to go wrong. And yet in spite of his reasonings the remembrance of his wife's condition was always like a sombre background to all his other thoughts.

Doctor Miles of Bridport Place, the best man in the neighbourhood, was retained five months in advance, and, as time stole on, many little packets of absurdly small white garments with frill work and ribbons began to arrive among the big consignments of male necessities. And then one evening, as Johnson was ticketing the scarves in the shop, he heard a bustle upstairs, and Mrs. Peyton came running down to say that Lucy was bad and that she thought the doctor ought to be there without delay.

It was not Robert Johnson's nature to hurry. He was prim and staid and liked to do things in an orderly fashion. It was a quarter of a mile from the corner of the New North Road where his shop stood to the doctor's house in Bridport Place. There were no cabs in sight, so he set off on foot, leaving the lad to mind the shop. At Bridport Place he was told that the doctor had just gone to Harman Street to attend a man in a fit. Johnson started off for Harman Street, losing a little of his primness as he became more anxious. Two full cabs but no empty ones passed him on the way. At Harman Street he learned that the doctor had gone on to a case of measles, fortunately he had left the address—69 Dunstan Road, at the other side of the Regent's Canal. Johnson's primness had vanished now as he thought of the women waiting at home, and he began to run as hard as he could down the Kingsland Road. Some way along he sprang into a cab which stood by the curb and drove to Dunstan Road. The doctor had just left, and Robert Johnson felt inclined to sit down upon the steps in despair.

Fortunately he had not sent the cab away, and he was soon back in Bridport Place, Doctor Miles had not returned yet, but they were expecting him every instant. Johnson waited, drumming his fingers on his knees, in a high, dim-lit room, the air of which was charged with a faint, sickly smell of ether. The furniture was massive, and the books in the shelves were sombre, and a squat black clock ticked mournfully on the mantelpiece. It told him that it was half-past seven, and that he had been gone an hour and a quarter. Whatever would the women think of him! Every time that a distant door slammed he sprang from his chair in a quiver of eagerness. His ears strained to catch the deep notes of the doctor's voice. And then, suddenly, with a gush of joy he heard a quick step outside, and the sharp click of the key in the lock. In an instant he was out in the hall, before the doctor's foot was over the threshold.

"If you please, doctor, I've come for you," he cried; "the wife was taken bad at six o'clock."

He hardly knew what he expected the doctor to do. Something very energetic, certainly—to seize some drugs, perhaps, and rush excitedly with him through the gaslit streets. Instead of that Doctor Miles threw his umbrella into the rack, jerked off his hat with a somewhat peevish gesture, and pushed Johnson back into the room.

"Let's see! You *did* engage me, didn't you?" he asked in no very cordial voice.

"Oh, yes, doctor, last November. Johnson, the outfitter, you know, in the New North Road."

"Yes, yes. It's a bit overdue," said the doctor, glancing at a list of names in a note-book with a very shiny cover. "Well, how is she?"

"I don't—"

"Ah, of course, it's your first. You'll know more about it next time."

"Mrs. Peyton said it was time you were there, sir."

"My dear sir, there can be no very pressing hurry in a first case. We shall have an all-night affair, I fancy. You can't get an engine to go without coals, Mr. Johnson, and I have had nothing but a light lunch."

"We could have something cooked for you—something hot and a cup of tea."

"Thank you, but I fancy my dinner is actually on the table. I can do no good in the earlier stages. Go home and say that I'm coming, and I will be round immediately afterwards."

A sort of horror filled Robert Johnson as he gazed at this man who could think about his dinner at such a moment. He had not imagination enough to realise that the experience which seemed so appallingly important to him, was the merest everyday matter of business to the medical man who could not have lived for a year had he not, amid the rush of work, remembered what was due to his own health. To Johnson he seemed little better than a monster. His thoughts were bitter as he sped back to his shop.

"You've taken your time," said his mother-in-law reproachfully, looking down the stairs as he entered.

"I couldn't help it!" he gasped. "Is it over?"

"Over! She's got to be worse, poor dear, before she can be better. Where's Doctor Miles?"

"He's coming after he's had dinner."

The old woman was about to make some reply, when, from the half-opened door behind, a high, whinnying voice cried out for her. She ran back and closed the door, while Johnson, sick at heart, turned into the shop. There he sent the lad home and busied himself frantically in putting up shutters and turning out boxes. When all was closed and finished he seated himself in the parlour behind the shop. But he could not sit still. He rose incessantly to walk a few paces and then fall back into a chair once more. Suddenly the clatter of china fell upon his ear, and he saw the maid pass the door with a cup on a tray and a smoking teapot.

"Who is that for, Jane?" he asked.

"For the mistress, Mr. Johnson. She says she would fancy it."

There was immeasurable consolation to him in that homely cup of tea. It wasn't so very bad after all if his wife could think of such things. So light-hearted was he that he asked for a cup also. He had just finished it when the doctor arrived, with a small black-leather bag in his hand.

"Well, how is she?" he asked genially.

"Oh, she's very much better," said Johnson, with enthusiasm.

"Dear me, that's bad!" said the doctor. "Perhaps it will do if I look in on my morning round?"

"No, no," cried Johnson, clutching at his thick frieze overcoat. "We are so glad that you have come. And, doctor, please come down soon and let me know what you think about it."

The doctor passed upstairs, his firm, heavy steps resounding through the house. Johnson could hear his boots creaking as he walked about the floor above him, and the sound was a consolation to him. It was crisp and decided, the tread of a man who had plenty of self-confidence. Presently, still straining his ears to catch what was going on, he heard the scraping of a chair as it was drawn along the floor, and a moment later he heard the door fly open, and some one came rushing downstairs. Johnson sprang up with his hair bristling, thinking that some dreadful thing had occurred, but it was only his mother-in-law, incoherent with excitement and searching for scissors and some tape. She vanished again and Jane passed up the stairs with a pile of newly-aired linen. Then, after an interval of silence, Johnson heard the heavy, creaking tread and the doctor came down into the parlour.

"That's better," said he, pausing with his hand upon the door. "You look pale, Mr. Johnson."

"Oh, no, sir, not at all," he answered deprecatingly, mopping his brow with his handkerchief.

"There is no immediate cause for alarm," said Doctor Miles. "The case is not all that we could wish it. Still, we will hope for the best."

"Is there danger, sir?" gasped Johnson.

"Well, there is always danger, of course. It is not altogether a favourable case, but still it might be much worse. I have given her a draught. I saw as I passed that they have been doing a little building opposite to you. It's an improving quarter. The rents go higher and higher. You have a lease of your own little place, eh?"

"Yes, sir, yes!" cried Johnson, whose ears were straining for every sound from above, and who felt none the less that it was very soothing that the doctor should be able to chat so easily at such a time. "That's to say no, sir, I am a yearly tenant."

"Ah, I should get a lease if I were you. There's Marshall, the watchmaker, down the street, I attended his wife twice and saw him through the typhoid when they took up the drains in Prince Street. I assure you his landlord sprung his rent nearly forty a year and he had to pay or clear out."

"Did his wife get through it, doctor?"

"Oh yes, she did very well. Hullo! Hullo!"

He slanted his ear to the ceiling with a questioning face, and then darted swiftly from the room.

It was March and the evenings were chill, so Jane had lit the fire, but the wind drove the smoke downwards and the air was full of its acrid taint. Johnson felt chilled to the bone, though rather by his apprehensions than by the weather. He crouched over the fire with his thin white hands held out to the blaze. At ten o'clock Jane brought in the joint of cold meat and laid his place for supper, but he could not bring himself to touch it. He drank a glass of beer, however, and felt the better for it. The tension of his nerves seemed to have reacted upon his hearing, and he was able to follow the most trivial things in the room above. Once, when the beer was still heartening him, he nerved himself to creep on tiptoe up the stair and to listen to what was going on. The bedroom door was half an inch open, and through the slit he could catch a glimpse of the clean-shaven face of the doctor, looking wearier and more anxious than before. Then he rushed downstairs like a lunatic, and running to the door he tried to distract his thoughts by watching what was going on in the street. The shops were all shut, and some rollicking boon companions came shouting along from the public-house. He stayed at the door until the stragglers had thinned down, and then came back to his seat by the fire. In his dim brain he was asking himself questions which had never intruded themselves before. Where was the justice of it? What had his sweet, innocent little wife done that she should be used so? Why was Nature so cruel? He was frightened at his own thoughts, and yet wondered that they had never occurred to him before.

As the early morning drew in, Johnson, sick at heart and shivering in every limb, sat with his great-coat huddled round him, staring at the grey ashes and waiting hopelessly for some relief. His face was white and clammy, and his nerves had been numbed into a half-conscious state by the long monotony of misery. But suddenly all his feelings leapt into keen life again as he heard the bedroom door open and the doctor's steps upon the stair. Robert Johnson was precise and unemotional in everyday life, but he almost shrieked now as he rushed forward to know if it were over.

One glance at the stern, drawn face which met him showed that it was no pleasant news which had sent the doctor downstairs. His appearance had altered as much as Johnson's during the last few hours. His hair was on end, his face flushed, his forehead dotted with beads of perspiration. There was a peculiar fierceness in his eye, and about the lines of his mouth, a fighting look as befitted a man who for hours on end had been striving with the hungriest of foes for the most precious of prizes. But there was a sadness too, as though his grim opponent had been overmastering him. He sat down and leaned his head upon his hand like a man who is fagged out.

"I thought it my duty to see you, Mr. Johnson, and to tell you that it is a very nasty case. Your wife's heart is not strong, and she has some symptoms which I do not like. What I wanted to say is that if you would like to have a second opinion I shall be very glad to meet any one whom you might suggest."

Johnson was so dazed by his want of sleep and the evil news that he could hardly grasp the doctor's meaning. The other, seeing him hesitate, thought that he was considering the expense.

"Smith or Hawley would come for two guineas," said he. "But I think Pritchard of the City Road is the best man."

"Oh yes, bring the best man," cried Johnson.

"Pritchard would want three guineas. He is a senior man, you see."

"I'd give him all I have if he would pull her through. Shall I run for him?"

"Yes. Go to my house first and ask for the green baize bag. The assistant will give it to you. Tell him I want the A.C.E. mixture. Her heart is too weak for chloroform. Then go for Pritchard and bring him back with you."

It was heavenly for Johnson to have something to do and to feel that he was of some use to his wife. He ran swiftly to Bridport Place, his footfalls clattering through the silent streets, and the big dark policemen turning their yellow funnels of light on him as he passed. Two tugs at the night-bell brought down a sleepy, half-clad assistant, who handed him a stoppered glass bottle and a cloth bag which contained something which clinked when you moved it. Johnson thrust the bottle into his pocket, seized the green bag, and pressing his hat firmly down ran as hard as he could set foot to ground until he was in the City Road and saw the name of Pritchard engraved in white upon a red ground. He bounded in triumph up the three steps which led to the door, and as he did so there was a crash behind him. His precious bottle was in fragments upon the pavement.

For a moment he felt as if it were his wife's body that was lying there. But the run had freshened his wits and he saw that the mischief might be repaired. He pulled vigorously at the night-bell.

"Well, what's the matter?" asked a gruff voice at his elbow. He started back and looked up at the windows, but there was no sign of life. He was approaching the bell again with the intention of pulling it, when a perfect roar burst from the wall.

"I can't stand shivering here all night," cried the voice. "Say who you are and what you want or I shut the tube."

Then for the first time Johnson saw that the end of a speaking tube hung out of the wall just above the bell. He shouted up it—

"I want you to come with me to meet Doctor Miles at a confinement at once."

"How far?" shrieked the irascible voice.

"The New North Road, Hoxton."

"My consultation is three guineas, payable at the time."

"All right," shouted Johnson. "You are to bring a bottle of A.C.E. mixture with you."

"All right! Wait a bit!"

Five minutes later an elderly, hard-faced man with grizzled hair flung open the door. As he emerged a voice from somewhere in the shadows cried—

"Mind you take your cravat, John," and he impatiently growled something over his shoulder in reply.

The consultant was a man who had been hardened by a life of ceaseless labour, and who had been driven, as so many others have been, by the needs of his own increasing family to set the commercial before the philanthropic side of his profession. Yet beneath his rough crust he was a man with a kindly heart.

"We don't want to break a record," said he, pulling up and panting after attempting to keep up with Johnson for five minutes. "I would go quicker if I could, my dear sir, and I quite sympathise with your anxiety, but really I can't manage it."

So Johnson, on fire with impatience, had to slow down until they reached the New North Road, when he ran ahead and had the door open for the doctor when he came. He heard the two meet outside the bedroom, and caught scraps of their conversation. "Sorry to knock you up—nasty case—decent people." Then it sank into a mumble and the door closed behind them.

Johnson sat up in his chair now, listening keenly, for he knew that a crisis must be at hand. He heard the two doctors moving about, and was able to distinguish the step of Pritchard, which had a drag in it, from the clean, crisp sound of the other's footfall. There was silence for a few minutes and then a curious drunken, mumbling sing-song came quavering up, very unlike anything which he had heard hitherto. All the same time a sweetish, insidious scent, imperceptible perhaps to any nerves less strained than his, crept down the stairs and penetrated into the room. The voice dwindled into a mere drone and finally sank away into silence, and Johnson gave a long sigh of relief for he knew that the drug had done its work and that, come what might, there should be no more pain for the sufferer.

But soon the silence became even more trying to him than the cries had been. He had no clue now as to what was going on, and his mind swarmed with horrible possibilities. He rose and went to the bottom of the stairs again. He heard the clink of metal against metal, and the subdued murmur of the doctors' voices. Then he heard Mrs. Peyton say something, in a tone as of fear or expostulation, and again the doctors murmured together. For twenty minutes he stood there leaning against the wall, listening to the occasional rumbles of talk without being able to catch a word of it. And then of a sudden there rose out of the silence the strangest little piping cry, and Mrs. Peyton screamed out in her delight and the man ran into the parlour and flung himself down upon the horse-hair sofa, drumming his heels on it in his ecstasy.

But often the great cat Fate lets us go, only to clutch us again in a fiercer grip. As minute after minute passed and still no sound came from above save those thin, glutinous cries, Johnson cooled from his frenzy of joy, and lay breathless with his ears straining. They were moving slowly about. They were talking in subdued tones. Still minute after minute passing, and no word from the voice for which he listened. His nerves were dulled by his night of trouble, and he waited in limp wretchedness upon his sofa. There he still sat when the doctors came down to him—a bedraggled, miserable figure with his face grimy and his hair unkept from his long vigil. He rose as they entered, bracing himself against the mantelpiece.

"Is she dead?" he asked.

"Doing well," answered the doctor.

And at the words that little conventional spirit which had never known until that night the capacity for fierce agony which lay within it, learned for the second time that there were springs of joy also which it had never tapped before. His impulse was to fall upon his knees, but he was shy before the doctors.

"Can I go up?"

"In a few minutes."

"I'm sure, doctor. I'm very—I'm very—" he grew inarticulate. "Here are your three guineas, Doctor Pritchard. I wish they were three hundred."

"So do I," said the senior man, and they laughed as they shook hands.

Johnson opened the shop door for them and heard their talk as they stood for an instant outside.

"Looked nasty at one time."

"Very glad to have your help."

"Delighted, I'm sure. Won't you step round and have a cup of coffee?"

"No, thanks. I'm expecting another case."

The firm step and the dragging one passed away to the right and the left. Johnson turned from the door still with that turmoil of joy in his heart. He seemed to be making a new start in life. He felt that he was a stronger and a deeper man. Perhaps all this suffering had an object then. It might prove to be a blessing both to his wife and to him. The very thought was one which he would have been incapable of conceiving twelve hours before. He was full of new emotions. If there had been a harrowing, there had been a planting too.

"Can I come up?" he cried, and then, without waiting for an answer, he took the steps three at a time.

Mrs. Peyton was standing by a soapy bath with a bundle in her hands. From under the curve of a brown shawl there looked out at him the strangest little red face with crumpled features, moist, loose lips, and eyelids which quivered like a rabbit's nostrils. The weak neck had let the head topple over, and it rested upon the shoulder.

"Kiss it, Robert!" cried the grandmother. "Kiss your son!"

But he felt a resentment to the little, red, blinking creature. He could not forgive it yet for that long night of misery. He caught sight of a white face in the bed and he ran towards it with such love and pity as his speech could find no words for.

"Thank God it is over! Lucy, dear, it was dreadful!"

"But I'm so happy now. I never was so happy in my life."

Her eyes were fixed upon the brown bundle.

"You mustn't talk," said Mrs. Peyton.

"But don't leave me," whispered his wife.

So he sat in silence with his hand in hers. The lamp was burning dim and the first cold light of dawn was breaking through the window. The night had been long and dark but the day was the sweeter and the purer in consequence. London was waking up. The roar began to rise from the street. Lives had come and lives had gone, but the great machine was still working out its dim and tragic destiny.

ANTON CHEKHOV

ANTON CHEKHOV (1860–1904). *Russian playwright and fiction writer. Trained as a physician, Chekhov published many stories while still in medical school. His first collection,* The Fairy Tales of Melpomene, *was published in 1884, the year he got his degree. The second,* Motley Tales *(1886), brought him wide recognition, and soon after he was regarded as one of the great exponents of realism in Russian literature. Chekhov is considered one of the great modern dramatists, in large part for his acclaimed plays* The Sea Gull *(1896),* Uncle Vanya *(1899),* The Three Sisters *(1901), and* The Cherry Orchard *(1904); his hundreds of short stories and novellas have also established him as one of the great fiction writers of all time.*

MISERY

"To whom shall I tell my grief?"

The twilight of evening. Big flakes of wet snow are whirling lazily about the street lamps, which have just been lighted, and lying in a thin soft layer on roofs, horses' backs, shoulders, caps. Iona Potapov, the sledge-driver, is all white like a ghost. He sits on the box without stirring, bent as double as the living body can be bent. If a regular snowdrift fell on him it seems as though even then he would not think it necessary to shake it off. . . . His little mare is white and motionless too. Her stillness, the angularity of her lines, and the stick-like straightness of her legs make her look like a halfpenny gingerbread horse. She is probably lost in thought. Anyone who has been torn away from the plough, from the familiar gray landscapes, and cast into this slough, full of monstrous lights, of unceasing uproar and hurrying people, is bound to think.

It is a long time since Iona and his nag have budged. They came out of the yard before dinner-time and not a single fare yet. But now the shades of evening are falling on the town. The pale light of the street lamps changes to a vivid color, and the bustle of the street grows noisier.

"Sledge to Vyborgskaya!" Iona hears. "Sledge!"

Iona starts, and through his snow-plastered eyelashes sees an officer in a military overcoat with a hood over his head.

"To Vyborgskaya," repeats the officer. "Are you asleep? To Vyborgskaya!"

In token of assent Iona gives a tug at the reins which sends cakes of

The Sick Child by Edvard Munch.

snow flying from the horse's back and shoulders. The officer gets into the sledge. The sledge-driver clicks to the horse, cranes his neck like a swan, rises in his seat, and more from habit than necessity brandishes his whip. The mare cranes her neck, too, crooks her stick-like legs, and hesitatingly sets off. . . .

"Where are you shoving, you devil?" Iona immediately hears shouts from the dark mass shifting to and fro before him. "Where the devil are you going? Keep to the r-right!"

"You don't know how to drive! Keep to the right," says the officer angrily.

A coachman driving a carriage swears at him; a pedestrian crossing the road and brushing the horse's nose with his shoulder looks at him angrily and shakes the snow off his sleeve. Iona fidgets on the box as though he were sitting on thorns, jerks his elbows, and turns his eyes about like one possessed, as though he did not know where he was or why he was there.

"What rascals they all are!" says the officer jocosely. "They are simply doing their best to run up against you or fall under the horse's feet. They must be doing it on purpose."

Iona looks at his fare and moves his lips. . . . Apparently he means to say something, but nothing comes but a sniff.

"What?" inquires the officer.

Iona gives a wry smile, and straining his throat, brings out huskily: "My son . . . er . . . my son died this week, sir."

"H'm! What did he die of?"

Iona turns his whole body round to his fare, and says:

"Who can tell! It must have been from fever. . . . He lay three days in the hospital and then he died. . . . God's will."

"Turn round, you devil!" comes out of the darkness. "Have you gone cracked, you old dog? Look where you are going!"

"Drive on! drive on! . . ." says the officer. "We shan't get there till to-morrow going on like this. Hurry up!"

The sledge-driver cranes his neck again, rises in his seat, and with heavy grace swings his whip. Several times he looks round at the officer, but the latter keeps his eyes shut and is apparently disinclined to listen. Putting his fare down at Vyborgskaya, Iona stops by a restaurant, and again sits huddled up on the box. . . . Again the wet snow paints him and his horse white. One hour passes, and then another. . . .

Three young men, two tall and thin, one short and hunchbacked, come up, railing at each other and loudly stamping on the pavement with their galoshes.

"Cabby, to the Police Bridge!" the hunchback cries in a cracked voice. "The three of us, . . . twenty kopecks!"

Iona tugs at the reins and clicks to his horse. Twenty kopecks is not a fair price, but he has no thoughts for that. Whether it is a rouble or whether it is five kopecks does not matter to him now so long as he has a fare. . . . The three young men, shoving each other and using bad language, go up to the sledge, and all three try to sit down at once. The question remains to be settled: Which are to sit down and which one is to stand? After a long altercation, ill-temper, and abuse, they come to the conclusion that the hunchback must stand because he is the shortest.

"Well, drive on," says the hunchback in his cracked voice, settling himself and breathing down Iona's neck. "Cut along! What a cap you've got, my friend! You wouldn't find a worse one in all Petersburg. . . ."

"He-he! . . . he-he! . . ." laughs Iona. "It's nothing to boast of!"

"Well, then, nothing to boast of, drive on! Are you going to drive like this all the way? Eh? Shall I give you one in the neck?"

"My head aches," says one of the tall ones. "At the Dukmasovs' yesterday Vaska and I drank four bottles of brandy between us."

"I can't make out why you talk such stuff," says the other tall one angrily. "You lie like a brute."

"Strike me dead, it's the truth! . . ."

"It's about as true as that a louse coughs."

"He-he!" grins Iona. "Me-er-ry gentlemen!"

"Tfoo! the devil take you!" cries the hunchback indignantly. "Will you get on, you old plague, or won't you? Is that the way to drive? Give her one with the whip. Hang it all, give it her well."

Iona feels behind his back the jolting person and quivering voice of the hunchback. He hears abuse addressed to him, he sees people, and the feeling of loneliness begins little by little to be less heavy on his heart. The hunchback swears at him, till he chokes over some elaborately whimsical string of epithets and is overpowered by his cough. His tall companions begin talking of a certain Nadyezhda Petrovna. Iona looks round at them. Waiting till there is a brief pause, he looks round once more and says:

"This week . . . er . . . my . . . er . . . son died!"

"We shall all die, . . ." says the hunchback with a sigh, wiping his lips after coughing. "Come, drive on! drive on! My friends, I simply cannot stand crawling like this! When will he get us there?"

"Well, you give him a little encouragement . . . one in the neck!"

"Do you hear, you old plague? I'll make you smart. If one stands on ceremony with fellows like you one may as well walk. Do you hear, you old dragon? Or don't you care a hang what we say?"

And Iona hears rather than feels a slap on the back of his neck.

"He-he! . . ." he laughs. "Merry gentlemen. . . . God give you health!"

"Cabman, are you married?" asks one of the tall ones.

"I? He-he! Me-er-ry gentlemen. The only wife for me now is the damp earth. . . . He-ho-ho! . . . The grave that is! . . . Here my son's dead and I am alive. . . . It's a strange thing, death has come in at the wrong door. . . . Instead of coming for me it went for my son. . . ."

And Iona turns round to tell them how his son died, but at that point the hunchback gives a faint sigh and announces that, thank God! they have arrived at last. After taking his twenty kopecks, Iona gazes for a long while after the revelers, who disappear into a dark entry. Again he is alone and again there is silence for him. . . . The misery which has been for a brief space eased comes back again and tears his heart more cruelly than ever. With a look of anxiety and suffering Iona's eyes stray restlessly among the crowds moving to and fro on both sides of the street: can he not find among those thousands someone who will listen to him? But the crowds flit by heedless of him and his misery. . . . His misery is immense, beyond all bounds. If Iona's heart were to burst and his misery to flow out, it would flood the whole world, it seems, but yet it is not seen. It has found a hiding-place in such an insignificant shell that one would not have found it with a candle by daylight. . . .

Iona sees a house-porter with a parcel and makes up his mind to address him.

"What time will it be, friend?" he asks.

"Going on for ten. . . . Why have you stopped here? Drive on!"

Iona drives a few paces away, bends himself double, and gives himself up to his misery. He feels it is no good to appeal to people. But before five minutes have passed he draws himself up, shakes his head as though he feels a sharp pain, and tugs at the reins. . . . He can bear it no longer.

"Back to the yard!" he thinks. "To the yard!"

And his little mare, as though she knew his thoughts, falls to trotting. An hour and a half later Iona is sitting by a big dirty stove. On the stove, on the floor, and on the benches are people snoring. The air is full of smells and stuffiness. Iona looks at the sleeping figures, scratches himself, and regrets that he has come home so early. . . .

"I have not earned enough to pay for the oats, even," he thinks. "That's why I am so miserable. A man who knows how to do his work, . . . who has had enough to eat, and whose horse has had enough to eat, is always at ease. . . ."

In one of the corners a young cabman gets up, clears his throat sleepily, and makes for the water-bucket.

"Want a drink?" Iona asks him.

"Seems so."

"May it do you good. . . . But my son is dead, mate. . . . Do you hear? This week in the hospital. . . . It's queer business. . . ."

Iona looks to see the effect produced by his words, but he sees nothing. The young man has covered his head over and is already asleep. The old man sighs and scratches himself. . . . Just as the young man had been thirsty for water, he thirsts for speech. His son will soon have been dead a week, and he has not really talked to anybody yet. . . . He wants to talk of it properly, with deliberation. . . . He wants to tell how his son was taken ill, how he suffered, what he said before he died, how he died. . . . He wants to describe the funeral, and how he went to the hospital to get his son's clothes. He still has his daughter Anisya in the country. . . . And he wants to talk about her too. . . . Yes, he has plenty to talk about now. His listener ought to sigh and exclaim and lament. . . . It would be even better to talk to women. Though they are silly creatures, they blubber at the first word.

"Let's go out and have a look at the mare," Iona thinks. "There is always time for sleep. . . . You'll have sleep enough, no fear. . . ."

He puts on his coat and goes into the stables where his mare is standing. He thinks about oats, about hay, about the weather. . . . He cannot think about his son when he is alone. . . . To talk about him with someone is possible, but to think of him and picture him is insufferable anguish. . . .

"Are you munching?" Iona asks his mare, seeing her shining eyes. "There, munch away, munch away. . . . Since we have not earned enough for oats, we will eat hay. . . . Yes, . . . I have grown too old to drive. . . . My son ought to be driving, not I. . . . He was a real cabman. . . . He ought to have lived. . . ."

Iona is silent for a while, and then he goes on:

"That's how it is, old girl. . . . Kuzma Ionitch is gone. . . . He said good-bye to me. . . . He went and died for no reason. . . . Now, suppose you had a little colt, and you were mother to that little colt. . . . And all at once that same little colt went and died. . . . You'd be sorry, wouldn't you? . . ."

The little mare munches, listens, and breathes on her master's hands. Iona is carried away and tells her all about it.

A DOCTOR'S VISIT

The Professor received a telegram from the Lyalikovs' factory; he was asked to come as quickly as possible. The daughter of some Madame Lyalikov, apparently the owner of the factory, was ill, and that was all that one could make out of the long, incoherent telegram. And the Professor did not go himself, but sent instead his assistant, Korolyov.

It was two stations from Moscow, and there was a drive of three miles from the station. A carriage with three horses had been sent to the station to meet Korolyov; the coachman wore a hat with a peacock's feather on it, and answered every question in a loud voice like a soldier: "No, sir!" "Certainly, sir!"

It was Saturday evening; the sun was setting, the workpeople were coming in crowds from the factory to the station, and they bowed to the carriage in which Korolyov was driving. And he was charmed with the evening, the farmhouses and villas on the road, and the birch-trees, and the quiet atmosphere all around, when the fields and woods and the sun seemed preparing, like the workpeople now on the eve of the holiday, to rest, and perhaps to pray. . . .

He was born and had grown up in Moscow; he did not know the country, and he had never taken any interest in factories, or been inside one, but he had happened to read about factories, and had been in the houses of manufacturers and had talked to them; and whenever he saw a factory far or near, he always thought how quiet and peaceable it was outside, but within there was always sure to be impenetrable ignorance and dull egoism on the side of the owners, wearisome, unhealthy toil on the side of the workpeople, squabbling, vermin, vodka. And now when the workpeople timidly and respectfully made way for the carriage, in their faces, their caps, their walk, he read physical impurity, drunkenness, nervous exhaustion, bewilderment.

They drove in at the factory gates. On each side he caught glimpses of the little houses of workpeople, of the faces of women, of quilts and linen on the railings. "Look out!" shouted the coachman, not pulling up the horses. It was a wide courtyard without grass, with five immense blocks of buildings with tall chimneys a little distance one from another, warehouses and barracks, and over everything a sort of grey powder as though from dust. Here and there, like oases in the desert, there were pitiful gardens, and the green and red roofs of the houses in which the managers and clerks lived. The coachman suddenly pulled up the horses, and the carriage stopped at the house, which had been newly painted grey; here was a flower garden, with a lilac bush covered with dust, and on the yellow steps at the front door there was a strong smell of paint.

"Please come in, doctor," said women's voices in the passage and the entry, and at the same time he heard sighs and whisperings. "Pray walk in. . . . We've been expecting you so long . . . we're in real trouble. Here, this way."

Madame Lyalikov—a stout elderly lady wearing a black silk dress with fashionable sleeves, but, judging from her face, a simple uneducated woman—looked at the doctor in a flutter, and could not bring herself to hold out her hand to him; she did not dare. Beside her stood a personage with short hair and a pince-nez; she was wearing a blouse of many colours, and was very thin and no longer young. The servants called her Christina Dmitryevna, and Korolyov guessed that this was the governess. Probably, as the person of most education in the house, she had been charged to meet and receive the doctor, for she began immediately, in great haste, stating the causes of the illness, giving trivial and tiresome details, but without saying who was ill or what was the matter.

The doctor and the governess were sitting talking while the lady of the house stood motionless at the door, waiting. From the conversation Korolyov learned that the patient was Madame Lyalikov's only daughter and heiress, a girl of twenty, called Liza; she had been ill for a long time, and had consulted various doctors, and the previous night she had suffered till morning from such violent palpitations of the heart, that no one in the house had slept, and they had been afraid she might die.

"She has been, one may say, ailing from a child," said Christina Dmitryevna in a sing-song voice, continually wiping her lips with her hand. "The doctors say it is nerves; when she was a little girl she was scrofulous, and the doctors drove it inwards, so I think it may be due to that."

They went to see the invalid. Fully grown up, big and tall, but ugly like her mother, with the same little eyes and disproportionate breadth of the lower part of the face, lying with her hair in disorder, muffled up to the chin, she made upon Korolyov at the first minute the impression of a poor, destitute creature, sheltered and cared for here out of charity, and he could hardly believe that this was the heiress of the five huge buildings.

"I am the doctor come to see you," said Korolyov. "Good evening."

He mentioned his name and pressed her hand, a large, cold, ugly hand; she sat up, and, evidently accustomed to doctors, let herself be sounded, without showing the least concern that her shoulders and chest were uncovered.

"I have palpitations of the heart," she said. "It was so awful all night. . . . I almost died of fright! Do give me something."

"I will, I will; don't worry yourself."

Korolyov examined her and shrugged his shoulders.

"The heart is all right," he said; "it's all going on satisfactorily; everything is in good order. Your nerves must have been playing pranks a little, but that's so common. The attack is over by now, one must suppose; lie down and go to sleep."

At that moment a lamp was brought into the bedroom. The patient screwed up her eyes at the light, then suddenly put her hands to her head and broke into sobs. And the impression of a destitute, ugly creature vanished, and Korolyov no longer noticed the little eyes or the heavy development of the lower part of the face. He saw a soft, suffering expression which was intelligent and touching: she seemed to him altogether graceful, feminine, and simple; and he longed to soothe her, not with drugs, not with advice, but with simple, kindly words. Her mother put her arms around her head and hugged her. What despair, what grief was in the old woman's face! She, her mother, had reared her and brought her up, spared nothing, and devoted her whole life to having her daughter taught French, dancing, music: had engaged a dozen teachers for her; had consulted the best doctors, kept a governess. And now she could not make out the reason of these tears, why there was all this misery, she could not understand, and was bewildered; and she had a guilty, agitated, despairing expressing, as though she had omitted something very important, had left something undone, had neglected to call in somebody—and whom, she did not know.

"Lizanka, you are crying again . . . again," she said, hugging her daughter to her. "My own, my darling, my child, tell me what it is! Have pity on me! Tell me."

Both wept bitterly. Korolyov sat down on the side of the bed and took Liza's hand.

"Come, give over; it's no use crying," he said kindly. "Why, there is nothing in the world that is worth those tears. Come, we won't cry; that's no good. . . ."

And inwardly he thought:

"It's high time she was married. . . ."

"Our doctor at the factory gave her kalibromati," said the governess, "but I notice it only makes her worse. I should have thought that if she is given anything for the heart it ought to be drops. . . . I forget the name. . . . Convallaria, isn't it?"

And there followed all sorts of details. She interrupted the doctor, preventing his speaking, and there was a look of effort on her face, as though she supposed that, as the woman of most education in the house, she was duty bound to keep up a conversation with the doctor, and on no other subject but medicine.

Korolyov felt bored.

"I find nothing special the matter," he said, addressing the mother as he went out of the bedroom. "If your daughter is being attended by the factory doctor, let him go on attending her. The treatment so far has been perfectly correct, and I see no reason for changing your doctor. Why change? It's such an ordinary trouble; there's nothing seriously wrong."

He spoke deliberately as he put on his gloves, while Madame Lyalikov stood without moving, and looked at him with her tearful eyes.

"I have half an hour to catch the ten o'clock train," he said. "I hope I am not too late."

"And can't you stay?" she asked, and tears trickled down her cheeks again. "I am ashamed to trouble you, but if you would be so good. . . . For God's sake," she went on in an undertone, glancing towards the door, "do stay to-night with us! She is all I have . . . my only daughter. . . . She frightened me last night; I can't get over it. . . . Don't go away, for goodness' sake! . . ."

He wanted to tell her that he had a great deal of work in Moscow, that his family were expecting him home; it was disagreeable to him to spend the evening and the whole night in a strange house quite needlessly; but he looked at her face, heaved a sigh, and began taking off his gloves without a word.

All the lamps and candles were lighted in his honour in the drawing-room and the dining-room. He sat down at the piano and began turning over the music. Then he looked at the pictures on the walls, at the portraits. The pictures, oil-paintings in gold frames, were views of the Crimea—a stormy sea with a ship, a Catholic monk with a wine-glass; they were all dull, smooth daubs, with no trace of talent in them. There was not a single good-looking face among the portraits, nothing but broad cheekbones and astonished-looking eyes. Lyalikov, Liza's father, had a low forehead and a self-satisfied expression; his uniform sat like a sack on his bulky plebeian figure; on his breast was a medal and a Red Cross Badge. There was little sign of culture, and the luxury was senseless and haphazard, and was as ill fitting as that uniform. The floors irritated him with their brilliant polish, the lustres on the chandelier irritated him, and he was reminded for some reason of the story of the merchant who used to go to the baths with a medal on his neck. . . .

He heard a whispering in the entry; some one was softly snoring. And suddenly from outside came harsh, abrupt, metallic sounds, such as Korolyov had never heard before, and which he did not understand now; they roused strange, unpleasant echoes in his soul.

"I believe nothing would induce me to remain here to live . . ." he thought, and went back to the music-books again.

"Doctor, please come to supper!" the governess called him in a low voice.

He went in to supper. The table was large and laid with a vast number of dishes and wines, but there were only two to supper: himself and Christina Dmitryevna. She drank Madeira, ate rapidly, and talked, looking at him through her pince-nez:

"Our workpeople are very contented. We have performances at the factory every winter; the workpeople act themselves. They have lectures with a magic lantern, a splendid tea-room, and everything they want. They are very much attached to us, and when they heard that Lizanka was worse they had a service sung for her. Though they have no education, they have their feelings, too."

"It looks as though you have no man in the house at all," said Korolyov.

"Not one. Pyotr Nikanoritch died a year and a half ago, and left us alone. And so there are the three of us. In the summer we live here, and in winter we live in Moscow, in Polianka. I have been living with them for eleven years—as one of the family."

At supper they served sterlet, chicken rissoles, and stewed fruit; the wines were expensive French wines.

"Please don't stand on ceremony, doctor," said Christina Dmitryevna, eating and wiping her mouth with her fist, and it was evident she found her life here exceedingly pleasant. "Please have some more."

After supper the doctor was shown to his room, where a bed had been made up for him, but he did not feel sleepy. The room was stuffy and it smelt of paint; he put on his coat and went out.

It was cool in the open air; there was already a glimmer of dawn, and all the five blocks of buildings, with their tall chimneys, barracks, and warehouses, were distinctly outlined against the damp air. As it was a holiday, they were not working, and the windows were dark, and in only one of the buildings was there a furnace burning; two windows were crimson, and fire mixed with smoke came from time to time from the chimney. Far away beyond the yard the frogs were croaking and the nightingales singing.

Looking at the factory buildings and the barracks, where the workpeople were asleep, he thought again what he always thought when he saw a factory. They may have performances for the workpeople, magic lanterns, factory doctors, and improvements of all sorts, but, all the same, the workpeople he had met that day on his way from the station did not look in any way different from those he had known long ago in his childhood, before there were factory performances and improvements. As a doctor accustomed to judging correctly of chronic complaints, the radical cause of which was incomprehensible and incurable, he looked upon factories as something baffling, the cause of which also was obscure and not removable, and all the improvements in the life of the factory hands he looked upon not as superfluous, but as comparable with the treatment of incurable illnesses.

"There is something baffling in it, of course . . ." he thought, looking at the crimson windows. "Fifteen hundred or two thousand workpeople are working without rest in unhealthy surroundings, making bad cotton goods, living on the verge of starvation, and only waking from this nightmare at rare intervals in the tavern; a hundred people act as overseers, and the whole life of that hundred is spent in imposing fines, in abuse, in injustice, and only two or three so-called owners enjoy the profits, though they don't work at all, and despise the wretched cotton. But what are the profits, and how do they enjoy them? Madame Lyalikov and her daughter are unhappy—it makes one wretched to look at them; the only one who enjoys her life is Christina Dmitryevna, a stupid, middle-aged maiden lady in pince-nez. And so it appears that all these five blocks of buildings are at work, and inferior cotton is sold in the Eastern markets, simply that Christina Dmitryevna may eat sterlet and drink Madeira."

Suddenly there came a strange noise, the same sound Korolyov had heard before supper. Some one was striking on a sheet of metal near one of the buildings; he struck a note, and then at once checked the vibrations, so that short, abrupt, discordant sounds were produced, rather like "Dair . . . dair . . . dair. . . ." Then there was half a minute of stillness, and from another building there came sounds equally abrupt and unpleasant, lower bass notes: "Drin . . . drin . . . drin. . . ." Eleven times. Evidently it was the watchman striking the hour.

Near the third building he heard: "Zhuk . . . zhuk . . . zhuk. . . ." And so near all the buildings, and then behind the barracks and beyond the gates. And in the stillness of the night it seemed as though these sounds were uttered by a monster with crimson eyes—the devil himself, who controlled the owners and the workpeople alike, and was deceiving both.

Korolyov went out of the yard into the open country.

"Who goes there?" some one called to him at the gates in an abrupt voice.

"It's just like being in prison," he thought, and made no answer.

Here the nightingales and the frogs could be heard more distinctly, and one could feel it was a night in May. From the station came the noise of a train; somewhere in the distance drowsy cocks were crowing; but, all the same, the night was still, the world was sleeping tranquilly. In a field not far from the factory there could be seen the framework of a house and heaps of building material: Korolyov sat down on the planks and went on thinking.

"The only person who feels happy here is the governess, and the factory hands are working for her gratification. But that's only apparent: she is only the figurehead. The real person, for whom everything is being done, is the devil."

And he thought about the devil, in whom he did not believe, and he looked round at the two windows where the fires were gleaming. It seemed to him that out of those crimson eyes the devil himself was looking at him—that unknown force that had created the mutual relation of the strong and the weak, that coarse blunder which one could never correct. The strong must hinder the weak from living—such was the law of Nature; but only in a newspaper article or in a school book was that intelligible and easily accepted. In the hotchpotch which was everyday life, in the tangle of trivialities out of which human relations were woven, it was no longer a law, but a logical absurdity, when the strong and the weak were both equally victims of their mutual relations, unwillingly submitting to some directing force, unknown, standing outside life, apart from man.

So thought Korolyov, sitting on the planks, and little by little he was possessed by a feeling that this unknown and mysterious force was really close by and looking at him. Meanwhile the east was growing paler, time passed rapidly; when there was not a soul anywhere near, as though everything were dead, the five buildings and their chimneys against the grey background of the dawn had a peculiar look—not the same as by day; one forgot altogether that inside there were steam motors, electricity, telephones, and kept thinking of lake-dwellings, of the Stone Age, feeling the presence of a crude, unconscious force. . . .

And again there came the sound: "Dair . . . dair . . . dair . . . dair . . ." twelve times. Then there was stillness, stillness for half a minute, and at the other end of the yard there rang out:

"Drin . . . drin . . . drin. . . ."

"Horribly disagreeable," thought Korolyov.

"Zhuk . . . zhuk . . ." there resounded from a third place, abruptly, sharply, as though with annoyance—"Zhuk . . . zhuk. . . ."

And it took four minutes to strike twelve. Then there was a hush; and again it seemed as though everything were dead.

Korolyov sat a little longer, then went to the house, but sat up for a good while longer. In the adjoining rooms there was whispering, there was a sound of shuffling slippers and bare feet.

"Is she having another attack?" thought Korolyov.

He went out to have a look at the patient. By now it was quite light in the rooms, and a faint glimmer of sunlight, piercing through the morning mist, quivered on the floor and on the wall of the drawing-room. The door of Liza's room was open, and she was sitting in a low chair beside her bed, with her hair down, wearing a dressing-gown and wrapped in a shawl. The blinds were down on the windows.

"How do you feel?" asked Korolyov.

"Thank you."

He touched her pulse, then straightened her hair, that had fallen over her forehead.

"You are not asleep," he said. "It's beautiful weather outside. It's spring. The nightingales are singing, and you sit in the dark and think of something."

She listened and looked into his face; her eyes were sorrowful and intelligent, and it was evident she wanted to say something to him.

"Does this happen to you often?" he said.

She moved her lips, and answered:

"Often, I feel wretched almost every night."

At that moment the watchman in the yard began striking two o'clock. They heard: "Dair . . . dair . . ." and she shuddered.

"Do those knockings worry you?" he asked.

"I don't know. Everything here worries me," she answered, and pondered. "Everything worries me. I hear sympathy in your voice; it seemed to me as soon as I saw you that I could tell you all about it."

"Tell me, I beg you."

"I want to tell you of my opinion. It seems to me that I have no illness, but that I am weary and frightened, because it is bound to be so and cannot be otherwise. Even the healthiest person can't help being uneasy if, for instance, a robber is moving about under his window. I am constantly being doctored," she went on, looking at her knees, and she gave a shy smile. "I am very grateful, of course, and I do not deny that the treatment is a benefit; but I should like to talk, not with a doctor, but with some intimate friend who would understand me and would convince me that I was right or wrong."

"Have you no friends?" asked Korolyov.

"I am lonely. I have a mother; I love her, but, all the same, I am lonely. That's how it happens to be. . . . Lonely people read a great deal, but say little and hear little. Life for them is mysterious; they are mystics and often see the devil where he is not. Lermontov's Tamara was lonely and she saw the devil."

"Do you read a great deal?"

"Yes. You see, my whole time is free from morning till night. I read by day, and by night my head is empty; instead of thoughts there are shadows in it."

"Do you see anything at night?" asked Korolyov.

"No, but I feel. . . ."

She smiled again, raised her eyes to the doctor, and looked at him so sorrowfully, so intelligently; and it seemed to him that she trusted him, and that she wanted to speak frankly to him, and that she thought the same as he did. But she was silent, perhaps waiting for him to speak.

And he knew what to say to her. It was clear to him that she needed as quickly as possible to give up the five buildings and the million if she had it—to leave that devil that looked out at night; it was clear to him, too, that she thought so herself, and was only waiting for some one she trusted to confirm her.

But he did not know how to say it. How? One is shy of asking men under sentence what they have been sentenced for; and in the same way it is awkward to ask very rich people what they want so much money for, why they make such a poor use of their wealth, why they don't give it up, even when they see in it their unhappiness; and if they begin a conversation about it themselves, it is usually embarrassing, awkward, and long.

"How is one to say it?" Korolyov wondered. "And is it necessary to speak?"

And he said what he meant in a roundabout way:

"You in the position of a factory owner and a wealthy heiress are dissatisfied; you don't believe in your right to it; and here now you can't sleep. That, of course, is better than if you were satisfied, slept soundly, and thought everything was satisfactory. Your sleeplessness does you credit; in any case, it is a good sign. In reality, such a conversation as this between us now would have been unthinkable for our parents. At night they did not talk, but slept sound; we, our generation, sleep badly, are restless, but talk a great deal, and are always trying to settle whether we are right or not. For our children or grandchildren that question— whether they are right or not—will have been settled. Things will be clearer for them than for us. Life will be good in fifty years' time; it's only a pity we shall not last out till then. It would be interesting to have a peep at it."

"What will our children and grandchildren do?" asked Liza.

"I don't know. . . . I suppose they will throw it all up and go away."

"Go where?"

"Where? . . . Why, where they like," said Korolyov; and he laughed. "There are lots of places a good, intelligent person can go to."

He glanced at his watch.

"The sun has risen, though," he said. "It is time you were asleep. Undress and sleep soundly. Very glad to have made your acquaintance," he went on, pressing her hand. "You are a good, interesting woman. Good-night!"

He went to his room and went to bed.

In the morning when the carriage was brought round they all came out on to the steps to see him off. Liza, pale and exhausted, was in a white dress as though for a holiday, with a flower in her hair; she looked at him, as yesterday, sorrowfully and intelligently, smiled and talked, and all with an expression as though she wanted to tell him something special, important—him alone. They could hear the larks trilling and the church bells pealing. The windows in the factory buildings were sparkling gaily, and, driving across the yard and afterwards along the road to the station, Korolyov thought neither of the workpeople nor of lake-dwellings, nor of the devil, but thought of the time, perhaps close at hand, when life would be as bright and joyous as that still Sunday morning; and he thought how pleasant it was on such a morning in the spring to drive with three horses in a good carriage, and to bask in the sunshine.

TRANSLATIONS BY CONSTANCE GARNETT

ROBERT FROST

ROBERT FROST (1874–1963). *American poet. Born in California, Frost studied first at Dartmouth College, then for two years at Harvard before abandoning formal education in 1900 to farm and teach in New Hampshire. In 1912, he and his family moved to England, where his first two collections of poetry were published: A Boy's Will (1913) and North of Boston (1914). Both were quickly republished in the United States; in 1915, Frost returned home to New Hampshire—and to critical acclaim which never abated. He became the most popular of poets, a sought-after speaker, and one of the great teachers and talkers of his age. Over the years, Frost won four Pulitzer prizes for his work.*

"OUT, OUT—"

The buzz saw snarled and rattled in the yard
And made dust and dropped stove-length sticks of wood,
Sweet-scented stuff when the breeze drew across it.
And from there those that lifted eyes could count
Five mountain ranges one behind the other
Under the sunset far into Vermont.
And the saw snarled and rattled, snarled and rattled,
As it ran light, or had to bear a load.
And nothing happened: day was all but done.
Call it a day, I wish they might have said
To please the boy by giving him the half hour
That a boy counts so much when saved from work.
His sister stood beside them in her apron
To tell them "Supper." At the word, the saw,
As if to prove saws knew what supper meant,
Leaped out at the boy's hand, or seemed to leap—
He must have given the hand. However it was,
Neither refused the meeting. But the hand!
The boy's first outcry was a rueful laugh,
As he swung toward them holding up the hand,
Half in appeal, but half as if to keep
The life from spilling. Then the boy saw all—
Since he was old enough to know, big boy
Doing a man's work, though a child at heart—
He saw all spoiled. "Don't let him cut my hand off—

The doctor, when he comes. Don't let him, sister!"
So. But the hand was gone already.
The doctor put him in the dark of ether.
He lay and puffed his lips out with his breath.
And then—the watcher at his pulse took fright.
No one believed. They listened at his heart.
Little—less—nothing!—and that ended it.
No more to build on there. And they, since they
Were not the one dead, turned to their affairs.

W. SOMERSET MAUGHAM

W. SOMERSET MAUGHAM (1874–1965). *English novelist, short-story writer, and playwright. Maugham was trained as a physician at St. Thomas's Hospital in London (where, seventy-five years earlier, John Keats was trained). He wrote more than sixty books, including the autobiographical novel* Of Human Bondage *(1915);* The Moon and Sixpence *(1919), based on the life of Paul Gaugin;* The Summing Up *(1938); and* A Writer's Notebook *(1949), a collection of personal reminiscences reflecting both his skepticism and his philosophy of life.*

Excerpt from THE SUMMING UP

I do not know a better training for a writer than to spend some years in the medical profession. I suppose that you can learn a good deal about human nature in a solicitor's office; but there on the whole you have to deal with men in full control of themselves. They lie perhaps as much as they lie to the doctor, but they lie more consistently, and it may be that for the solicitor it is not so necessary to know the truth. The interests he deals with, besides, are usually material. He sees human nature from a specialized standpoint. But the doctor, especially the hospital doctor, sees it bare. Reticences can generally be undermined; very often there are none. Fear for the most part will shatter every defence; even vanity is unnerved by it. Most people have a furious itch to talk about themselves and are restrained only by the disinclination of others to listen. Reserve is an artificial quality that is developed in most of us but as the result of innumerable rebuffs. The doctor is discreet. It is his business to listen and no details are too intimate for his ears.

But of course human nature may be displayed before you and if you have not the eyes to see you will learn nothing. If you are hidebound with prejudice, if your temper is sentimental, you can go through the wards of a hospital and be as ignorant of man at the end as you were at the beginning. If you want to get any benefit from such an experience you must have an open mind and an interest in human beings. I look upon myself as very fortunate in that though I have never much liked men I have found them so interesting that I am almost incapable of being bored by them. I do not particularly want to talk and I am very willing to listen. I do not care if people are interested in me or not. I have no desire to impart any knowledge I have to others nor do I feel the need to correct them if they are wrong. You can get a great deal of entertainment out of tedious people if you keep your head. I remember being taken for a drive in a foreign country by a kind lady who wanted to show me round. Her conversation was composed entirely of truisms and she had so large a vocabulary of hackneyed phrases that I despaired of remembering them. But one remark she made has stuck in my memory as have few witticisms; we passed a row of little houses by the sea and she said to me: "Those are week-end bungalows, if you understand what I mean; in other words they're bungalows that people go to on Saturdays and leave on Mondays." I should have been sorry to miss that.

I do not want to spend too long a time with boring people, but then I do not want to spend too long a time with amusing ones. I find social intercourse fatiguing. Most persons, I think, are both exhilarated and rested by conversation; to me it has always been an effort. When I was young and stammered, to talk for long singularly exhausted me, and even now that I have to some extent cured myself, it is a strain. It is a relief to me when I can get away and read a book.

I would not claim for a moment that those years I spent at St. Thomas's Hospital gave me a complete knowledge of human nature. I do not suppose anyone can hope to have that. I have been studying it, consciously and subconsciously, for forty years and I still find men unaccountable; people I know intimately can surprise me by some action of which I never thought them capable or by the discovery of some trait exhibit a side of themselves that I never even suspected. It is possible that my training gave me a warped view, for at St. Thomas's the persons I came in contact with were for the most part sick and poor and ill-educated. I have tried to guard against this. I have tried also to guard against my own prepossessions. I have no natural trust in others. I am more inclined to expect them to do ill than to do good. This is the price one has to pay for having a sense of humour. A sense of humour leads you to take pleasure in the discrepancies of human nature; it leads you to mistrust great professions and look for the unworthy motive that they conceal; the disparity between appearance and reality diverts you and you are apt when you cannot find it to create it. You tend to close your eyes to truth, beauty and goodness because they give no scope to your sense of the ridiculous. The humorist has a quick eye for the humbug; he does not always recognize the saint. But if to see men one-sidedly is a heavy price to pay for a sense of humour there is a compensation that has a value too. You are not angry with people when you laugh at them. Humour teaches tolerance, and the humorist, with a smile and perhaps a sigh, is more likely to shrug his shoulders than to condemn. He does not moralize, he is content to understand; and it is true that to understand is to pity and forgive.

But I must admit that, with these reservations that I have tried always to remember, the experience of all the years that have followed has only confirmed the observations on human nature that I made, not deliberately, for I was too young, but unconsciously, in the out-patients' departments and in the wards of St. Thomas's Hospital. I have seen men since as I saw them then, and thus have I drawn them. It may not be a true picture and I know that many have thought it an unpleasant one. It is doubtless partial, for naturally I have seen men through my own idiosyncrasies. A buoyant, optimistic, healthy and sentimental person would have seen the same people quite differently. I can only claim to have seen them coherently. Many writers seem to me not to observe at all, but to create their characters in stock sizes from images in their own fancy. They are like draughtsmen who draw their figures from recollections of the antique and have never attempted to draw from the living model. At their best they can only give living shape to the fantasies of their own minds. If their minds are noble they can give you noble figures and perhaps it does not matter if they lack the infinite complication of common life.

I have always worked from the living model. I remember that once in the dissecting room when I was going over my "part" with the demonstrator, he asked me what some nerve was and I did not know. He told me; whereupon I remonstrated, for it was in the wrong place. Nevertheless he insisted that it was the nerve I had been in vain looking for. I complained of the abnormality and he, smiling, said that in anatomy it was the normal that was uncommon. I was only annoyed at the time, but the remark sank into my mind and since then it has been forced upon me that it was true of man as well as of anatomy. The normal is what you find but rarely. The normal is an ideal. It is a picture that one fabricates of the average characteristics of men, and to find them all in a single man is hardly to be expected. It is this false picture that the writers I have spoke of take as their model and it is because they describe what is so exceptional that they seldom achieve the effect of life. Selfishness and kindliness, idealism and sensuality, vanity, shyness, disinterestedness, courage, laziness, nervousness, obstinacy, and diffidence, they can all exist in a single person and form a plausible harmony. It has taken a long time to persuade readers of the truth of this.

I do not suppose men in past centuries were any different from the men we know, but they must surely have appeared to their contemporaries more of a piece than they do to us now, or writers would not have thus represented them. It seemed reasonable to describe every man in his humour. The miser was nothing but miserly, the fop foppish, and the glutton gluttonous. It never occurred to anyone that the miser might be foppish and gluttonous; and yet we see constantly people who are; still less, that he might be an honest and upright man with a disinterested zeal for public service and a genuine passion for art. When novelists began to disclose the diversity that they had found in themselves or seen in others they were accused of maligning the human race. So far as I know the first novelist who did this with deliberate intention was Stendhal in *Le Rouge et le Noir*. Contemporary criticism was outraged. Even Sainte-Beuve, who needed only to look into his own heart to discover what contrary qualities could exist side by side in some kind of harmony, took him to task. Julien Sorel is one of the most interesting characters that a novelist has ever created. I do not think that Stendhal has succeeded in making him entirely plausible, but that, I believe, is due to causes that I shall mention in another part of this book. For the first three quarters of the novel he is perfectly consistent. Sometimes he fills you with horror; sometimes he is entirely sympathetic; but he has an inner coherence, so that though you often shudder you accept.

But it was long before Stendhal's example bore fruit. Balzac, with all his genius, drew his characters after the old models. He gave them his own immense vitality so that you accept them as real; but in fact they are humours as definitely as are the characters of old comedy. His people are unforgettable, but they are seen from the standpoint of the ruling passion that affected those with whom they were brought in contact. I suppose it is a natural prepossession of mankind to take people as though they were homogeneous. It is evidently less trouble to make up one's mind about a man one way or the other and dismiss suspense with the phrase, he's one of the best or he's a dirty dog. It is disconcerting to find that the saviour of his country may be stingy or that the poet who has opened new horizons to our consciousness may be a snob. Our natural egoism leads us to judge people by their relations to ourselves. We want them to be certain things to us, and for us that is what they are; because the rest of them is no good to us, we ignore it.

These reasons perhaps explain why there is so great a disinclination to accept the attempts to portray man with his incongruous and diverse qualities and why people turn away with dismay when candid biographers reveal the truth about famous persons. It is distressing to think that the composer of the quintet in the *Meistersinger* was dishonest in money matters and treacherous to those who had benefited him. But it may be that he could not have had great qualities if he had not also had great failings. I do not believe they are right who say that the defects of famous men should be ignored; I think it is better that we should know them. Then, though we are conscious of having faults as glaring as theirs, we can believe that that is no hindrance to our achieving also something of their virtues.

Besides teaching me something about human nature my training in a medical school furnished me with an elementary knowledge of science and scientific method. Till then I had been concerned only with art and literature. It was a very limited knowledge, for the demands of the curriculum at that time were small, but at all events it showed me the road that led to a region of which I was completely ignorant. I grew familiar with certain principles. The scientific world of which I thus obtained a cursory glimpse was rigidly materialistic and because its conceptions coincided with my own prepossessions I embraced them with alacrity; "For men," as Pope observed, "let them say what they will, never approve any other's sense, but as it squares with their own." I was glad to learn that the mind of man (himself the product of natural causes) was a function of the brain subject like the rest of his body to the laws of cause and effect and that these laws were the same as those that governed the movements of star and atom. I exulted at the thought that the universe was no more than a vast machine in which every event was determined by a preceding event so that nothing could be other than it was. These conceptions not only appealed to my dramatic instinct; they filled me besides with a very delectable sense of liberation. With the ferocity of youth I welcomed the hypothesis of the Survival of the Fittest. It gave me much satisfaction to learn that the earth was a speck of mud whirling round a second-rate star which was gradually cooling; and that evolution, which had produced man, would by forcing him to adapt himself to his environment deprive him of all the qualities he had acquired but those that were necessary to enable him to combat the increasing cold till at last the planet, an icy cinder, would no longer support even a vestige of life. I believed that we were wretched puppets at the mercy of a ruthless fate; and that, bound by the inexorable laws of nature, we were doomed to take part in the ceaseless struggle for existence with nothing to look forward to but inevitable defeat. I learnt that men were moved by a savage egoism, that love was only the dirty trick nature played on us to achieve the continuation of the species, and I decided that, whatever aims men set themselves, they were deluded, for it was impossible for them to aim at anything but their own selfish pleasures. When once I happened to do a friend a good turn (for what reasons, since I knew that all our actions were purely selfish, I did not stop to think) and wanting to show his gratitude (which of course he had no business to feel, for my apparent kindness was rigidly determined) he asked me what I would like as a present, I answered without hesitation Herbert Spencer's *First Principles*. I read it with complacency. But I was impatient of Spencer's maudlin belief in progress: the world I knew was going from bad to worse and I was as pleased as Punch at the thought of my remote descendants, having long forgotten art and science and handicraft, cowering skin-clad in caverns as they watched the approach of the cold and eternal night. I was violently pessimistic. All the same, having abundant vitality, I was getting on the whole a lot of fun out of life. I was ambitious to make a name for myself as a writer. I exposed myself to every vicissitude that seemed to offer a chance of gaining the greater experience that I wanted and I read everything I could lay my hands on.

WILLIAM CARLOS WILLIAMS

WILLIAM CARLOS WILLIAMS (1883–1963). *American poet, essayist, and short-story writer. A practicing physician, Williams delivered more than three thousand babies in a working-class, ethnically mixed neighborhood of Rutherford, New Jersey, where he was born. He changed the face of American poetry with his emphasis on everyday life and speech and his insistence on "no ideas but in things": an exhortation to capture within poetry the physical things of this world. His most famous poem begins, "so much depends / upon / a red wheel / barrow . . ." He won the Bollingen Prize, the National Book Award, and, posthumously, the Pulitzer Prize.*

THE PRACTICE

It's the humdrum, day-in, day-out, everyday work that is the real satisfaction of the practice of medicine; the million and a half patients a man has seen on his daily visits over a forty-year period of weekdays and Sundays that make up his life. I have never had a money practice; it would have been impossible for me. But the actual calling on people, at all times and under all conditions, the coming to grips with the intimate conditions of their lives, when they were being born, when they were dying, watching them die, watching them get well when they were ill, has always absorbed me.

I lost myself in the very properties of their minds: for the moment at least I actually became *them,* whoever they should be, so that when I detached myself from them at the end of a half-hour of intense concentration over some illness which was affecting them, it was as though I were reawakening from a sleep. For the moment I myself did not exist, nothing of myself affected me. As a consequence I came back to myself, as from any other sleep, rested.

Time after time I have gone out into my office in the evening feeling as if I couldn't keep my eyes open a moment longer. I would start out on my morning calls after only a few hours' sleep, sit in front of some house waiting to get the courage to climb the steps and push the front-door bell. But once I saw the patient all that would disappear. In a flash the details of the case would begin to formulate themselves into a recognizable outline, the diagnosis would unravel itself, or would refuse to make itself plain, and the hunt was on. Along with that the patient himself would shape up into something that called for attention, his peculiarities, her reticences or candors. And though I might be attracted or repelled, the professional attitude which every physician must call on would steady me, dictate the terms on which I was to proceed. Many a time a man must watch the patient's mind as it watches him, distrusting him, ready to fly off at a tangent at the first opportunity; sees himself distrusted, sees the patient turn to someone else, rejecting him.

More than once we have all seen ourselves rejected, seen some hard-pressed mother or husband go to some other adviser when we know that the advice we have given him has been correct. That too is part of the game. But in general it is the rest, the peace of mind that comes from adopting the patient's condition as one's own to be struggled with toward a solution during those few minutes or that hour or those trying days when we are searching for causes, trying to relate this to that to build a reasonable basis for action which really gives us our peace. As I say, often after I have gone into my office harassed by personal perplexities of whatever sort, fatigued physically and mentally, after two hours of intense application to the work, I came out at the finish completely rested (and I mean rested), ready to smile and to laugh as if the day were just starting.

That is why as a writer I have never felt that medicine interfered with me but rather that it was my very food and drink, the very thing which made it possible for me to write. Was I not interested in man? There the thing was, right in front of me. I could touch it, smell it. It was myself, naked, just as it was, without a lie telling itself to me in its own terms. Oh, I knew it wasn't for the most part giving me anything very profound, but it was giving me terms, basic terms with which I could spell out matters as profound as I cared to think of.

I knew it was an elementary world that I was facing, but I have always been amazed at the authenticity with which the simple-minded often face that world when compared with the tawdriness of the public viewpoint exhibited in reports from the world at large. The public view which affects the behavior of so many is a very shabby thing when compared with what I see every day in my practice of medicine. I can almost say it is the interference of the public view of their lives with what I see which makes the difficulty, in most instances, between sham and a satisfactory basis of thought.

I don't care much about that, however. I don't care a rap what people are or believe. They come to me. I care for them and either they become my friends or they don't. That is their business. My business, aside from the mere physical diagnosis, is to make a different sort of diagnosis concerning them as individuals, quite apart from anything for which they seek my advice. That fascinates me. From the very beginning that fascinated me even more than I myself knew. For no matter where I might find myself, every sort of individual that it is possible to imagine in some phase of his development, from the highest to the lowest, at some time exhibited himself to me. I am sure I have seen them all. And all have contributed to my pie. Let the successful carry off their blue ribbons; I have known the unsuccessful, far better persons than their more lucky brothers. One can laugh at them both, whatever the costumes they adopt. And when one is able to reveal them to themselves, high or low, they are always grateful as they are surprised that one can so have revealed the inner secrets of another's private motives. To do this is what makes a writer worth heeding: that somehow or other, whatever the source may be, he has gone to the base of the matter to lay it bare before us in terms which, try as we may, we cannot in the end escape. There is no choice then but to accept him and make him a hero.

All day long the doctor carries on this work, observing, weighing, comparing values of which neither he nor his patients may know the significance. He may be insensitive. But if in addition to actually being an accurate craftsman and a man of insight he has the added quality of—some distress of mind, a restless concern with the . . . If he is not satisfied with mere cures, if he lacks ambition, if he is content to . . . If there is no content in him and likely to be none; if in other words, without wishing to force it, since that would interfere with his lifelong observation, he allows himself to be called a name! What can one think of him?

He is half-ashamed to have people suspect him of carrying on a clandestine, a sort of underhand piece of spying on the public at large. They naively ask him, "How do you do it? How can you carry on an active business like that and at the same time find time to write? You must be superhuman. You must have at the very least the energy of two men." But they do not grasp that one occupation complements the other, that they are two parts of a whole, that it is not two jobs at all, that one rests the man when the other fatigues him. The only person to feel sorry for is his wife. She practically becomes a recluse. His only fear is that the source of his interest, his daily going about among human beings of all sorts, all ages, all conditions will be terminated. That he will be found out.

As far as the writing itself is concerned it takes next to no time at all. Much too much is written every day of our lives. We are overwhelmed by it. But when at times we see through the welter of evasive or interested patter, when by chance we penetrate to some moving detail of a life, there is always time to bang out a few pages. The thing isn't to find the time for it—we waste hours every day doing absolutely nothing at all—the difficulty is to catch the evasive life of the thing, to phrase the words in such a way that stereotype will yield a moment of insight. That is where the difficulty lies. We are lucky when that underground current can be tapped and the secret spring of all our lives will send up its pure water. It seldom happens. A thousand trivialities push themselves to the front, our lying habits of everyday speech and thought are foremost, telling us that *that* is what "they" want to hear. Tell them something else. You know you want to be a successful writer. This sort of chitchat the daily practice of medicine tends drastically to cure.

Forget writing, it's a trivial matter. But day in, day out, when the inarticulate patient struggles to lay himself bare for you, or with nothing more than a boil on his back is so caught off balance that he reveals some secret twist of a whole community's pathetic way of thought, a man is suddenly seized again with a desire to speak of the underground stream which for a moment has come up just under the surface. It is just a glimpse, an intimation of all that which the daily print misses or deliberately hides, but the excitement is intense and the rush to write is on again. It is then we see, by this constant feeling for a meaning, from the unselected nature of the material, just as it comes in over the phone or at the office door, that there is no better way to get an intimation of what is going on in the world.

We catch a glimpse of something, from time to time, which shows us that a presence has just brushed past us, some rare thing—just when the smiling little Italian woman has left us. For a moment we are dazzled. What was that? We can't name it; we know it never gets into any recognizable avenue of expression; men will be long dead before they can have so much as ever approached it. Whole lives are spent in the tremendous affairs of daily events without even approaching the great sights that I see every day. My patients do not know what is about them among their very husbands and children, their wives and acquaintances. But there is no need for us to be such strangers to each other, saving alone laziness, indifference and age-old besotted ignorance.

So for me the practice of medicine has become the pursuit of a rare element which may appear at any time, at any place, at a glance. It can be most embarrassing. Mutual recognition is likely to flare up at a moment's notice. The relationship between physician and patient, if it were literally followed, would give us a world of extraordinary fertility of the imagination which we can hardly afford. There's no use trying to multiply cases, it is there, it is magnificent, it fills my thoughts, it reaches to the farthest limits of our lives.

What is the use of reading the common news of the day, the tragic deaths and abuses of daily living, when for over half a lifetime we have known that they must have occurred just as they have occurred given the conditions that cause them? There is no light in it. It is trivial fill-gap. We know the plane will crash, the train be derailed. And we know why. No one cares, no one can care. We get the news and discount it, we are quite right in doing so. It is trivial. But the hunted news I get from some obscure patients' eyes is not trivial. It is profound: whole academies of learning, whole ecclesiastical hierarchies are founded upon it and have developed what they call their dialectic upon nothing else, their lying dialectics. A dialectic is any arbitrary system, which, since all systems are mere inventions, is necessarily in each case a false premise, upon which a closed system is built shutting those who confine themselves to it from the rest of the world. All men one way or another use a dialectic of some sort into which they are shut, whether it be an Argentina or a Japan. So each group is maimed. Each is enclosed in a dialectic cloud, incommunicado, and for that reason we rush into wars and prides of the most superficial natures.

Do we not see that we are inarticulate? That is what defeats us. It is our inability to communicate to another how we are locked within ourselves, unable to say the simplest thing of importance to one another, any of us, even the most valuable, that makes our lives like those of a litter of kittens in a wood-pile. That gives the physician, and I don't mean the high-priced psychoanalyst, his opportunity; psychoanalysis amounts to no more than another dialectic into which to be locked.

The physician enjoys a wonderful opportunity actually to witness the words being born. Their actual colors and shapes are laid before him carrying their tiny burdens which he is privileged to take into his care with their unspoiled newness. He may see the difficulty with which they have been born and what they are destined to do. No one else is present but the speaker and ourselves, we have been the words' very parents. Nothing is more moving.

But after we have run the gamut of the simple meanings that come to one over the years, a change gradually occurs. We have grown used to the range of communication which is likely to reach us. The girl who comes to me breathless, staggering into my office, in her underwear a still breathing infant, asking me to lock her mother out of the room; the man whose mind is gone—all of them finally say the same thing. And then a new meaning begins to intervene. For under the language to which we have been listening all our lives a new, a more profound language underlying all the dialectics offers itself. It is what they call poetry. That is the final phase.

It is that, we realize, which beyond all they have been saying is what they have been trying to say. They laugh (For are they not laughable?); they can think of nothing more useless (What else are they but the same?); something made of words (Have they not been trying to use words all their lives?). We begin to see that the underlying meaning of all they want to tell us and have always failed to communicate is the poem, the poem which their lives are being lived to realize. No one will believe it. And it is the actual words, as we hear them spoken under all circumstances, which contain it. It is actually there, in the life before us, every minute that we are listening, a rarest element—not in our imaginations but there, there in fact. It is that essence which is hidden in the very words which are going in at our ears and from which we must recover underlying meaning as realistically as we recover metal out of ore.

The poem that each is trying actually to communicate to us lies in the words. It is at least the words that make it articulate. It has always been so. Occasionally that named person is born who catches a rumor of it, a Homer, a Villon, and his race and the world perpetuates his memory. Is it not plain why? The physician, listening from day to day, catches a hint of it in his preoccupation. By listening to the minutest variations of the speech we begin to detect that today, as always, the essence is also to be found, hidden under the verbiage, seeking to be realized.

But one of the characteristics of this rare presence is that it is jealous of exposure and that it is shy and revengeful. It is not a name that is bandied about in the market place, no more than it is something that can be captured and exploited by the academy. Its face is a particular face, it is likely to appear under the most unlikely disguises. You cannot recognize it from past appearances—in fact it is always a new face. It knows all that we are in the habit of describing. It will not use the same appearance for any new materialization. And it is our very life. It is we ourselves, at our rarest moments, but inarticulate for the most part except when in the poem one man, every five or six hundred years, escapes to formulate a few gifted sentences.

The poem springs from the half-spoken words of such patients as the physician sees from day to day. He observes it in the peculiar, actual conformations in which its life is hid. Humbly he presents himself before it and by long practice he strives as best he can to interpret the manner of its speech. In that the secret lies. This, in the end, comes perhaps to be the occupation of the physician after a lifetime of careful listening.

THE ARTIST

Mr. T.
    bareheaded
        in a soiled undershirt
his hair standing out
    on all sides
        stood on his toes
heels together
    arms gracefully
        for the moment
curled above his head.
    Then he whirled about
        bounded
into the air
    and with an *entrechat*
        perfectly achieved
completed the figure.
    My mother
        taken by surprise
where she sat
    in her invalid's chair
        was left speechless.
Bravo! she cried at last
    and clapped her hands.
        The man's wife
came from the kitchen:
    What goes on here? she said.
        But the show was over.

BETWEEN WALLS

    the back wings
    of the

    hospital where
    nothing

    will grow lie
    cinders

in which shine
the broken

pieces of a green
bottle

LE MÉDECIN MALGRÉ LUI

Oh I suppose I should
wash the walls of my office
polish the rust from
my instruments and keep them
definitely in order
build shelves in the laboratory
empty out the old stains
clean the bottles
and refill them, buy
another lens, put
my journals on edge instead of
letting them lie flat
in heaps—then begin
ten years back and
gradually
read them to date
cataloguing important
articles for ready reference.
I suppose I should
read the new books.
If to this I added
a bill at the tailor's
and at the cleaner's
grew a decent beard
and cultivated a look
of importance—
Who can tell? I might be
a credit to my Lady Happiness
and never think anything
but a white thought!

THE BIRTH

A 40 odd year old Para 10
    Navarra
        or Navatta she didn't know
uncomplaining
    in the little room
        where we had been working all night long
dozing off
    by 10 or 15 minute intervals
        her great pendulous belly
marked
    by contraction rings
        under the skin.
No progress.
It was restfully quiet
    approaching dawn on Guinea Hill
        in those days.
Wha's a ma', Doc?
    It do'n wanna come.
That finally roused me.
I got me a strong sheet
    wrapped it
        tight
around her belly.
    When the pains seized her again
        the direction
was changed
    not
        against her own backbone
but downward
    toward the exit.
        It began to move—stupid
not to have thought of that earlier.
Finally
    without a cry out of her
        more than a low animal moaning
the head emerged
    up to the neck.
It took its own time
    rotating.

I thought of a good joke
    about an infant
        at that moment of its career
and smiled to myself quietly
    behind my mask.
        I am a feminist.
After a while
    I was able
        to extract the shoulders
one at a time
    a tight fit.
        Madonna!
13½ pounds!
    Not a man among us
        can have equaled
that.

THE LAST WORDS OF MY ENGLISH GRANDMOTHER

There were some dirty plates
and a glass of milk
beside her on a small table
near the rank, disheveled bed—

Wrinkled and nearly blind
she lay and snored
rousing with anger in her tones
to cry for food,

Gimme something to eat—
They're starving me—
I'm all right I won't go
to the hospital. No, no, no

Give me something to eat
Let me take you
to the hospital, I said
and after you are well

you can do as you please.
She smiled, Yes
you do what you please first
then I can do what I please—

Oh, oh, oh! she cried
as the ambulance men lifted
her to the stretcher—
Is this what you call

making me comfortable?
By now her mind was clear—
Oh you think you're smart
you young people,

she said, but I'll tell you
you don't know anything.
Then we started.
On the way

we passed a long row
of elms. She looked at them
awhile out of
the ambulance window and said,

What are all those
fuzzy-looking things out there?
Trees? Well, I'm tired
of them and rolled her head away.

THE GIRL WITH A PIMPLY FACE

One of the local druggists sent in the call: 50 Summer St., second floor, the door to the left. It's a baby they've just brought from the hospital. Pretty bad condition I should imagine. Do you want to make it? I think they've had somebody else but don't like him, he added as an afterthought.

It was half past twelve. I was just sitting down to lunch. Can't they wait till after office hours?

Oh I guess so. But they're foreigners and you know how they are. Make it as soon as you can. I guess the baby's pretty bad.

It was two-thirty when I got to the place, over a shop in the business part of town. One of those street doors between plate glass show windows. A narrow entry with smashed mail boxes on one side and a dark stair leading straight up. I'd been to the address a number of times during the past years to see various people who had lived there.

Going up I found no bell so I rapped vigorously on the wavy-glass door-panel to the left. I knew it to be the door to the kitchen, which occupied the rear of that apartment.

Come in, said a loud childish voice.

I opened the door and saw a lank-haired girl of about fifteen standing chewing gum and eyeing me curiously from beside the kitchen table. The hair was coal black and one of her eyelids drooped a little as she spoke. Well, what do you want? she said. Boy, she was tough and no kidding but I fell for her immediately. There was that hard, straight thing about her that in itself gives an impression of excellence.

I'm the doctor, I said.

Oh, you're the doctor. The baby's inside. She looked at me. Want to see her?

Sure, that's what I came for. Where's your mother?

She's out. I don't know when she's coming back. But you can take a look at the baby if you want to.

All right. Let's see her.

She led the way into the bedroom, toward the front of the flat, one of the unlit rooms, the only windows being those in the kitchen and along the facade of the building.

There she is.

I looked on the bed and saw a small face, emaciated but quiet, unnaturally quiet, sticking out of the upper end of a tightly rolled bundle made by the rest of the baby encircled in a blue cotton blanket. The whole wasn't much larger than a good sized loaf of rye bread. Hands and everything were rolled up. Just the yellowish face showed, tightly hatted and framed around by a corner of the blanket.

What's the matter with her, I asked.

I dunno, said the girl as fresh as paint and seeming about as indifferent as though it had been no relative of hers instead of her sister. I looked at my informer very much amused and she looked back at me, chewing her gum vigorously, standing there her feet well apart. She cocked her head to one side and gave it to me straight in the eye, as much as to say, Well? I looked back at her. She had one of those small, squeezed up faces, snub nose, overhanging eyebrows, low brow and a terrible complexion, pimply and coarse.

When's your mother coming back do you *think,* I asked again.

Maybe in an hour. But maybe you'd better come some time when my father's here. He talks English. He ought to come in around five I guess.

But can't you tell me something about the baby? I hear it's been sick. Does it have a fever?

I dunno.

But has it diarrhoea, are its movements green?

Sure, she said, I guess so. It's been in the hospital but it got worse so my father brought it home today.

What are they feeding it?

A bottle. You can see that yourself. There it is.

There was a cold bottle of half finished milk lying on the coverlet the nipple end of it fallen behind the baby's head.

How old is she? It's a girl, did you say?

Yeah, it's a girl.

Your sister?

Sure. Want to examine it?

No thanks, I said. For the moment at least I had lost all interest in the baby. This young kid in charge of the house did something to me that I liked. She was just a child but nobody was putting anything over on her if she knew it, yet the real thing about her was the complete lack of the rotten smell of a liar. She wasn't in the least presumptive. Just straight.

But after all she wasn't such a child. She had breasts you knew would be like small stones to the hand, good muscular arms and fine hard legs. Her bare feet were stuck into broken down leather sandals such as you see worn by children at the beach in summer. She was heavily tanned too, wherever her skin showed. Just one of the kids you'll find loafing around the pools they have outside towns and cities everywhere these days. A tough little nut finding her own way in the world.

What's the matter with your legs? I asked. They were bare and covered with scabby sores.

Poison ivy, she answered, pulling up her skirts to show me.

Gee, but you ought to seen it two days ago. This ain't nothing. You're a doctor. What can I do for it?

Let's see, I said.

She put her leg up on a chair. It had been badly bitten by mosquitoes, as I saw the thing, but she insisted on poison ivy. She had torn at the affected places with her finger nails and that's what made it look worse.

Oh that's not so bad, I said, if you'll only leave it alone and stop scratching it.

Yeah, I know that but I can't. Scratching's the only thing makes it feel better.

What's that on your foot?

Where? looking.

That big brown spot there on the back of your foot.

Dirt I guess. Her gum chewing never stopped and her fixed defensive non-expression never changed.

Why don't you wash it?

I do. Say, what could I do for my face?

I looked at it closely. You have what they call acne, I told her. All those blackheads and pimples you see there, well, let's see, the first thing you ought to do, I suppose, is to get some good soap.

What kind of soap? Lifebuoy?

No. I'd suggest one of those cakes of Lux. Not the flakes but the cake.

Yeah, I know, she said. Three for seventeen.

Use it. Use it every morning. Bathe your face in very hot water. You know, until the skin is red from it. That's to bring the blood up to the skin. Then take a piece of ice. You have ice, haven't you?

Sure, we have ice.

Hold it in a face cloth—or whatever you have—and rub that all over your face. Do that right after you've washed it in the very hot water—before it has cooled. Rub the ice all over. And do it every day—for a month. Your skin will improve. If you like, you can take some cold cream once in a while, not much, just a little and rub that in last of all, if your face feels too dry.

Will that help me?

If you stick to it, it'll help you.

All right.

There's a lotion I could give you to use along with that. Remind me of it when I come back later. Why aren't you in school?

Agh, I'm not going any more. They can't make me. Can they?

They can try.

How can they? I know a girl thirteen that don't go and they can't make her either.

Don't you want to learn things?

I know enough already.

Going to get a job?

I got a job. Here. I been helping the Jews across the hall. They give me three fifty a week—all summer.

Good for you, I said. Think your father'll be here around five?

Guess so. He ought to be.

I'll come back then. Make it all the same call.

All right, she said, looking straight at me and chewing her gum as vigorously as ever.

Just then a little blond-haired thing of about seven came in through the kitchen and walked to me looking curiously at my satchel and then at the baby.

What are you, a doctor?

See you later, I said to the older girl and went out.

At five-thirty I once more climbed the wooden stairs after passing two women at the street entrance who looked me up and down from where they were leaning on the brick wall of the building talking.

This time a woman's voice said, Come in, when I knocked on the kitchen door.

It was the mother. She was impressive, a bulky woman, growing toward fifty, in a black dress, with lank graying hair and a long seamed face. She stood by the enameled kitchen table. A younger, plumpish woman with blond hair, well cared for and in a neat house dress—as if she had dolled herself up for the occasion—was standing beside her. The small blank child was there too and the older girl, behind the others, overshadowed by her mother, the two older women at least a head taller than she. No one spoke.

Hello, I said to the girl I had been talking to earlier. She didn't answer me.

Doctor, began the mother, save my baby. She very sick. The woman spoke with a thick, heavy voice and seemed overcome with grief and apprehension. Doctor! Doctor! she all but wept.

All right, I said to cut the woman short, let's take a look at her first.

So everybody headed toward the front of the house, the mother in the lead. As they went I lagged behind to speak to the second woman, the interpreter. What happened?

The baby was not doing so well. So they took it to the hospital to see if the doctors there could help it. But it got worse. So her husband took it out this morning. It looks bad to me.

Yes, said the mother who had overheard us. Me got seven children. One daughter married. This my baby, pointing to the child on the bed. And she wiped her face with the back of her hand. This baby no do good. Me almost crazy. Don't know who can help. What doctor, I don't know. Somebody tell me take to hospital. I think maybe do some good. Five days she there. Cost me two dollar every day. Ten dollar. I no got money. And when I see my baby, she worse. She look dead. I can't leave she there. No. No. I say to everybody, no. I take she home. Doctor, you save my baby. I pay you. I pay you everything—

Wait a minute, wait a minute, I said. Then I turned to the other woman. What happened?

The baby got like a diarrhoea in the hospital. And she was all dirty when they went to see her. They got all excited—

All sore behind, broke in the mother—

The younger woman said a few words to her in some language that sounded like Russian but it didn't stop her—

No. No. I send she to hospital. And when I see my baby like that I can't leave she there. My babies no that way. Never, she emphasized. Never! I take she home.

Take your time, I said. Take off her clothes. Everything off. This is a regular party. It's warm enough in here. Does she vomit?

She no eat. How she can vomit? said the mother.

But the other woman contradicted her. Yes, she was vomiting in the hospital, the nurse said.

It happens that this September we had been having a lot of such cases in my hospital also, an infectious diarrhoea which practically all the children got when they came in from any cause. I supposed that this was what happened to this child. No doubt it had been in a bad way before that, improper feeding, etc., etc. And then when they took it in there, for whatever had been the matter with it, the diarrhoea had developed. These things sometimes don't turn out so well. Lucky, no doubt, that they had brought it home when they did. I told them so, explaining at the same time: One nurse for ten or twenty babies, they do all they can but you can't run and change the whole ward every five minutes. But the infant looked too lifeless for that only to be the matter with it.

You want all clothes off, asked the mother again, hesitating and trying to keep the baby covered with the cotton blanket while undressing it.

Everything off, I said.

There it lay, just skin and bones with a round fleshless head at the top and the usual pot belly you find in such cases.

Look, said the mother, tilting the infant over on its right side with her big hands so that I might see the reddened buttocks. What kind of nurse that. My babies never that way.

Take your time, take your time, I told her. That's not bad. And it wasn't either. Any child with loose movements might have had the same half an hour after being cared for. Come on. Move away, I said and give me a chance. She kept hovering over the baby as if afraid I might expose it.

It had no temperature. There was no rash. The mouth was in reasonably good shape. Eyes, ears negative. The moment I put my stethoscope to the little bony chest, however, the whole thing became clear. The infant had a severe congenital heart defect, a roar when you listened over the heart that meant, to put it crudely, that she was no good, never would be.

The mother was watching me. I straightened up and looking at her told her plainly: She's got a bad heart.

That was the sign for tears. The big woman cried while she spoke. Doctor, she pleaded in blubbering anguish, save my baby.

I'll help her, I said, but she's got a bad heart. That will never be any better. But I knew perfectly well she wouldn't pay the least attention to what I was saying.

I give you anything, she went on. I pay you. I pay you twenty dollar. Doctor, you fix my baby. You good doctor. You fix.

All right, all right, I said. What are you feeding it?

They told me and it was a ridiculous formula, unboiled besides. I regulated it properly for them and told them how to proceed to make it up. Have you got enough bottles, I asked the young girl.

Sure, we got bottles, she told me.

O.K., then go ahead.

You think you cure she? The mother with her long, tearful face was at me again, so different from her tough female fifteen-year-old.

You do what I tell you for three days, I said, and I'll come back and see how you're getting on.

Tank you, doctor, so much. I pay you. I got today no money. I pay ten dollar to hospital. They cheat me. I got no more money. I pay you Friday when my husband get pay. You save my baby.

Boy! what a woman. I couldn't get away.

She my baby, doctor. I no want to lose. Me got seven children—

Yes, you told me.

But this my baby. You understand. She very sick. You good doctor—

Oh my God! To get away from her I turned again to the kid. You better get going after more bottles before the stores close. I'll come back Friday morning.

How about that stuff for my face you were gonna give me.

That's right. Wait a minute. And I sat down on the edge of the bed to write out a prescription for some lotio alba comp. such as we use in acne. The two older women looked at me in astonishment—wondering, I suppose, how I knew the girl. I finished writing the thing and handed it to her. Sop it on your face at bedtime, I said, and let it dry on. Don't get it into your eyes.

No, I won't.

I'll see you in a couple of days, I said to them all.

Doctor! the old woman was still after me. You come back. I pay you. But all a time short. Always tomorrow come milk man. Must pay rent, must pay coal. And no got money. Too much work. Too much wash. Too much cook. Nobody help. I don't know what's a matter. This door, doctor, this door. This house make sick. Make sick.

Do the best I can, I said as I was leaving.

The girl followed on the stairs. How much is this going to cost, she asked shrewdly holding the prescription.

Not much, I said, and then started to think. Tell them you only got half a dollar. Tell them I said that's all it's worth.

Is that right, she said.

Absolutely. Don't pay a cent more for it.

Say, you're all right, she looked at me appreciatively.

Have you got half a dollar?

Sure. Why not.

What's it all about, my wife asked me in the evening. She had heard about the case. Gee! I sure met a wonderful girl, I told her.

What! another?

Some tough baby. I'm crazy about her. Talk about straight stuff . . . And I recounted to her the sort of case it was and what I had done. The mother's an odd one too. I don't quite make her out.

Did they pay you?

No. I don't suppose they have any cash.

Going back?

Sure. Have to.

Well, I don't see why you have to do all this charity work. Now that's a case you should report to the Emergency Relief. You'll get at least two dollars a call from them.

But the father has a job, I understand. That counts me out.

What sort of a job?

I dunno. Forgot to ask.

What's the baby's name so I can put it in the book?

Damn it. I never thought to ask them that either. I think they must have told me but I can't remember it. Some kind of a Russian name—

You're the limit. Dumbbell, she laughed. Honestly— Who are they anyhow?

You know, I think it must be that family Kate was telling us about. Don't you remember. The time the little kid was playing there one afternoon after school, fell down the front steps and knocked herself senseless.

I don't recall.

Sure you do. That's the family. I get it now. Kate took the brat down there in a taxi and went up with her to see that everything was all right. Yop, that's it. The old woman took the older kid by the hair, because she hadn't watched her sister. And what a beating she gave her. Don't you remember Kate telling us afterward. She thought the old woman was going to murder the child she screamed and threw her around so. Some old gal. You can see they're all afraid of her. What a world. I suppose the damned brat drives her cuckoo. But boy, how she clings to that baby.

The last hope, I suppose, said my wife.

Yeah, and the worst bet in the lot. There's a break for you.

She'll love it just the same.

More, usually.

Three days later I called at the flat again. Come in. This time a resonant male voice. I entered, keenly interested.

By the same kitchen table stood a short, thickset man in baggy working pants and a heavy cotton undershirt. He seemed to have the stability of a cube placed on one of its facets, a smooth, highly colored Slavic face, long black moustaches and widely separated, perfectly candid blue eyes. His black hair, glossy and profuse, stood out carelessly all over his large round head. By his look he reminded me at once of his blond-haired daughter, absolutely unruffled. The shoulders of an ox. You the doctor, he said. Come in.

The girl and the small child were beside him, the mother was in the bedroom.

The baby no better. Won't eat, said the man in answer to my first question.

How are its bowels?

Not so bad.

Does it vomit?

No.

Then it is better, I objected. But by this time the mother had heard us talking and came in. She seemed worse than the last time. Absolutely inconsolable. Doctor! Doctor! She came up to me.

Somewhat irritated I put her aside and went in to the baby. Of course it was better, much better. So I told them. But the heart, naturally, was the same.

How she heart? the mother pressed me eagerly. Today little better?

I started to explain things to the man who was standing back giving his wife precedence but as soon as she got the drift of what I was saying she was all over me again and the tears began to pour. There was no use my talking. Doctor, you good doctor. You do something fix my baby. And before I could move she took my left hand in both hers and kissed it through her tears. As she did so I realized finally that she had been drinking.

I turned toward the man, looking a good bit like the sun at noonday and as indifferent, then back to the woman and I felt deeply sorry for her.

Then, not knowing why I said it nor of whom, precisely, I was speaking, I felt myself choking inwardly with the words: Hell! God damn it. The sons of bitches. Why do these things have to be?

The next morning as I came into the coat room at the hospital there were several of the visiting staff standing there with their cigarettes, talking. It was about a hunting dog belonging to one of the doctors. It had come down with distemper and seemed likely to die.

I called up half a dozen vets around here, one of them was saying. I even called up the one in your town, he added turning to me as I came in. And do you know how much they wanted to charge me for giving the serum to that animal?

Nobody answered.

They had the nerve to want to charge me five dollars a shot for it. Can you beat that? Five dollars a shot.

Did you give them the job, someone spoke up facetiously.

Did I? I should say I did not, the first answered. But can you beat that. Why we're nothing but a lot of slop-heels compared to those guys. We deserve to starve.

Get it out of them, someone rasped, kidding. That's the stuff.

Then the original speaker went on, buttonholing me as some of the others faded from the room. Did you ever see practice so rotten. By the way, I was called over to your town about a week ago to see a kid I delivered up here during the summer. Do you know anything about the case?

I probably got them on my list, I said. Russians?

Yeah, I thought as much. Has a job as a road worker or something. Said they couldn't pay me. Well, I took the trouble of going up to your court house and finding out what he was getting. Eighteen dollars a week. Just the type. And they had the nerve to tell me they couldn't pay me.

She told me ten.

She's a liar.

Natural maternal instinct, I guess.

Whisky appetite, if you should ask me.

Same thing.

O.K., buddy. Only I'm telling you. And did I tell *them*. They'll never call me down there again, believe me. I had that much satisfaction out of them anyway. You make 'em pay you. Don't you do anything for them unless they do. He's paid by the county. I tell you if I had taxes to pay down there I'd go and take it out of his salary.

You and how many others?

Say, they're bad actors, that crew. Do you know what they really do with their money? Whisky. Now I'm telling you. That old woman is the slickest customer you ever saw. She's drunk all the time. Didn't you notice it?

Not while I was there.

Don't you let them put any of that sympathy game over on you. Why they tell me she leaves that baby lying on the bed all day long screaming its lungs out until the neighbors complain to the police about it. I'm not lying to you.

Yeah, the old skate's got nerves, you can see that. I can imagine she's a bugger when she gets going.

But what about the young girl, I asked weakly. She seems like a pretty straight kid.

My confrere let out a wild howl. That thing! You mean that pimply-faced little bitch. Say, if I had my way I'd run her out of the town tomorrow. There's about a dozen wise guys on her trail every night in the week. Ask the cops. Just ask them. They know. Only nobody wants to bring in a complaint. They say you'll stumble over her on the roof, behind the stairs, anytime at all. Boy, they sure took you in.

Yes, I suppose they did, I said.

But the old woman's the ringleader. She's got the brains. Take my advice and make them pay.

The last time I went I heard the Come in! from the front of the house. The fifteen-year-old was in there at the window in a rocking chair with the tightly wrapped baby in her arms. She got up. Her legs were bare to the hips. A powerful little animal.

What are you doing? Going swimming? I asked.

Naw, that's my gym suit. What the kids wear for Physical Training in school.

How's the baby?

She's all right.

Do you mean it?

Sure, she eats fine now.

Tell your mother to bring it to the office some day so I can weigh it. The food'll need increasing in another week or two anyway.

I'll tell her.

How's your face?

Gettin' better.

My God, it *is,* I said. And it was much better. Going back to school now?

Yeah, I had tuh.

THE USE OF FORCE

They were new patients to me, all I had was the name, Olson. Please come down as soon as you can, my daughter is very sick.

When I arrived I was met by the mother, a big startled looking woman, very clean and apologetic who merely said, Is this the doctor? and let me in. In the back, she added. You must excuse us, doctor, we have her in the kitchen where it is warm. It is very damp here sometimes.

The child was fully dressed and sitting on her father's lap near the kitchen table. He tried to get up, but I motioned for him not to bother, took off my overcoat and started to look things over. I could see that they were all very nervous, eyeing me up and down distrustfully. As often, in such cases, they weren't telling me more than they had to, it was up to me to tell them; that's why they were spending three dollars on me.

The child was fairly eating me up with her cold, steady eyes, and no expression to her face whatever. She did not move and seemed, inwardly, quiet; an unusually attractive little thing, and as strong as a heifer in appearance. But her face was flushed, she was breathing rapidly, and I realized that she had a high fever. She had magnificent blond hair, in profusion. One of those picture children often reproduced in advertising leaflets and the photogravure sections of the Sunday papers.

She's had a fever for three days, began the father, and we don't know what it comes from. My wife has given her things, you know, like people do, but it don't do no good. And there's been a lot of sickness around. So we tho't you'd better look her over and tell us what is the matter.

As doctors often do I took a trial shot at it as a point of departure. Has she had a sore throat?

Both parents answered me together, No . . . No, she says her throat don't hurt her.

Does your throat hurt you? added the mother to the child. But the little girl's expression didn't change nor did she move her eyes from my face.

Have you looked?

I tried to, said the mother, but I couldn't see.

As it happens we had been having a number of cases of diphtheria in the school to which this child went during that month and we were all, quite apparently, thinking of that, though no one had as yet spoken of the thing.

Well, I said, suppose we take a look at the throat first. I smiled in my best professional manner and asking for the child's first name I said, come on, Mathilda, open your mouth and let's take a look at your throat.

Nothing doing.

Aw, come on, I coaxed, just open your mouth wide and let me take a look. Look, I said opening both hands wide, I haven't anything in my hands. Just open up and let me see.

Such a nice man, put in the mother. Look how kind he is to you. Come on, do what he tells you to. He won't hurt you.

At that I ground my teeth in disgust. If only they wouldn't use the word "hurt" I might be able to get somewhere. But I did not allow myself to be hurried or disturbed but speaking quietly and slowly I approached the child again.

As I moved my chair a little nearer suddenly with one cat-like movement both her hands clawed instinctively for my eyes and she almost reached them too. In fact she knocked my glasses flying and they fell, though unbroken, several feet away from me on the kitchen floor.

Both the mother and father almost turned themselves inside out in embarrassment and apology. You bad girl, said the mother, taking her and shaking her by one arm. Look what you've done. The nice man . . .

For heaven's sake, I broke in. Don't call me a nice man to her. I'm here to look at her throat on the chance that she might have diphtheria and possibly die of it. But that's nothing to her. Look here, I said to the child, we're going to look at your throat. You're old enough to under-stand what I'm saying. Will you open it now by yourself or shall we have to open it for you?

Not a move. Even her expression hadn't changed. Her breaths however were coming faster and faster. Then the battle began. I had to do it. I had to have a throat culture for her own protection. But first I told the parents that it was entirely up to them. I explained the danger but said that I would not insist on a throat examination so long as they would take the responsibility.

If you don't do what the doctor says you'll have to go to the hospital, the mother admonished her severely.

Oh yeah? I had to smile to myself. After all, I had already fallen in love with the savage brat, the parents were contemptible to me. In the ensuing struggle they grew more and more abject, crushed, exhausted while she surely rose to magnificent heights of insane fury of effort bred of her terror of me.

The father tried his best, and he was a big man but the fact that she was his daughter, his shame at her behavior and his dread of hurting her made him release her just at the critical moment several times when I had almost achieved success, till I wanted to kill him. But his dread also that she might have diphtheria made him tell me to go on, go on though he himself was almost fainting, while the mother moved back and forth behind us raising and lowering her hands in an agony of apprehension.

Put her in front of you on your lap, I ordered, and hold both her wrists.

But as soon as he did the child let out a scream. Don't, you're hurting me. Let go of my hands. Let them go I tell you. Then she shrieked terrifyingly, hysterically. Stop it! Stop it! You're killing me!

Do you think she can stand it, doctor! said the mother.

You get out, said the husband to his wife. Do you want her to die of diphtheria?

Come on now, hold her, I said.

Then I grasped the child's head with my left hand and tried to get the wooden tongue depressor between her teeth. She fought, with clenched teeth, desperately! But now I also had grown furious—at a child. I tried to hold myself down but I couldn't. I know how to expose a throat for inspection. And I did my best. When finally I got the wooden spatula behind the last teeth and just the point of it into the mouth cavity, she opened up for an instant but before I could see anything she came down again and gripping the wooden blade between her molars she reduced it to splinters before I could get it out again.

Aren't you ashamed, the mother yelled at her. Aren't you ashamed to act like that in front of the doctor?

Get me a smooth-handled spoon of some sort, I told the mother. We're going through with this. The child's mouth was already bleeding. Her tongue was cut and she was screaming in wild hysterical shrieks. Perhaps I should have desisted and come back in an hour or more. No doubt it would have been better. But I have seen at least two children lying dead in bed of neglect in such cases, and feeling that I must get a diagnosis now or never I went at it again. But the worst of it was that I too had got beyond reason. I could have torn the child apart in my own fury and enjoyed it. It was a pleasure to attack her. My face was burning with it.

The damned little brat must be protected against her own idiocy, one says to one's self at such times. Others must be protected against her. It is social necessity. And all these things are true. But a blind fury, a feeling of adult shame, bred of a longing for muscular release are the operatives. One goes on to the end.

In a final unreasoning assault I overpowered the child's neck and jaws. I forced the heavy silver spoon back of her teeth and down her throat till she gagged. And there it was—both tonsils covered with membrane. She had fought valiantly to keep me from knowing her secret. She had been hiding that sore throat for three days at least and lying to her parents in order to escape just such an outcome as this.

Now truly she *was* furious. She had been on the defensive before but now she attacked. Tried to get off her father's lap and fly at me while tears of defeat blinded her eyes.

Franz Kafka

FRANZ KAFKA (1883–1924). *Novelist and short-story writer. Born in Prague and educated in the law, Kafka supported himself with a government job at the Workers Accident Insurance Institute, a position that provided good pay and short hours. Among his works are the novels* The Trial, The Castle, *and* Amerika, *all published posthumously against his wishes, and "The Metamorphosis," a short masterpiece. He died of tuberculosis.*

A COUNTRY DOCTOR

I was in great perplexity; I had to start on an urgent journey; a seriously ill patient was waiting for me in a village ten miles off; a thick blizzard of snow filled all the wide spaces between him and me; I had a gig, a light gig with big wheels, exactly right for our country roads; muffled in furs, my bag of instruments in my hand, I was in the courtyard all ready for the journey; but there was no horse to be had, no horse. My own horse had died in the night, worn out by the fatigues of this icy winter; my servant girl was now running round the village trying to borrow a horse; but it was hopeless, I knew it, and I stood there forlornly, with the snow gathering more and more thickly upon me, more and more unable to move. In the gateway the girl appeared, alone, and waved the lantern; of course, who would lend a horse at this time for such a journey? I strode through the courtyard once more; I could see no way out; in my confused distress I kicked at the dilapidated door of the yearlong uninhabited pigsty. It flew open and flapped to and fro on its hinges. A steam and smell as of horses came out from it. A dim stable lantern was swinging inside from a rope. A man, crouching on his hams in that low space, showed an open blue-eyed face. "Shall I yoke up?" he asked, crawling out on all fours. I did not know what to say and merely stooped down to see what else was in the sty. The servant girl was standing beside me. "You never know what you're going to find in your own house," she said, and we both laughed. "Hey there, Brother, hey there, Sister!" called the groom, and two horses, enormous creatures with powerful flanks, one after the other, their legs tucked close to their bodies, each well-shaped head lowered like a camel's, by sheer strength of buttocking squeezed out through the door hole which they filled entirely. But at once they were standing up, their legs long and their bodies steaming thickly. "Give him a hand," I said, and the willing girl hurried to help the groom with the harnessing. Yet hardly was she beside him when the groom clipped hold of her and pushed his face against hers. She screamed and fled back to me; on her cheek stood out in red the marks of two rows of teeth. "You brute," I yelled in fury, "do you want a whipping?" but in the same moment reflected that the man was a stranger; that I did not know where he came from, and that of his own free will he was helping me out when everyone else had failed me. As if he knew my thoughts he took no offense at my threat but, still busied with the horses, only turned round once towards me. "Get in," he said then, and indeed: everything was ready. A magnificent pair of horses, I observed, such as I had never sat behind, and I climbed in happily. "But I'll drive, you don't know the way," I said. "Of course," said he, "I'm not coming with you anyway, I'm staying with Rose." "No," shrieked Rose, fleeing into the house with a justified presentiment that her fate was inescapable; I heard the door chain rattle as she put it up; I heard the key turn in the lock; I could see, moreover, how she put out the lights in the entrance hall and in further flight all through the rooms to keep herself from being discovered. "You're coming with me," I said to the groom, "or I won't go, urgent as my journey is. I'm not thinking of paying for it by handing the girl over to you." "Gee up!" he said; clapped his hands; the gig whirled off like a log in a freshet; I could just hear the door of my house splitting and bursting as the groom charged at it and then I was deafened and blinded by a storming rush that steadily buffeted all my senses. But this only for a moment, since, as if my patient's farmyard had opened out just before my courtyard gate, I was already there; the horses had come quietly to a standstill; the blizzard had stopped; moonlight all around; my patient's parents hurried out of the house, his sister behind them; I was almost lifted out of the gig; from their confused ejaculations I gathered not a word; in the sickroom the air was almost unbreathable; the neglected stove was smoking; I wanted to push open a window; but first I had to look at my patient. Gaunt, without any fever, not cold, not warm, with vacant eyes, without a shirt, the youngster heaved himself up from under the feather bedding, threw his arms round my neck, and whispered in my ear: "Doctor, let me die." I glanced round the room; no one had heard it; the parents were leaning forward in silence waiting for my verdict; the sister had set a chair for my handbag; I opened the bag and hunted among my instruments; the boy kept clutching at me from his bed to remind me of his entreaty; I picked up a pair of tweezers, examined them in the candlelight and laid them down again. "Yes," I thought blasphemously, "in cases like this the gods are helpful, send the missing horse, add to it a second because of the urgency, and to crown everything bestow even a groom—" And only now did I remember Rose again; what was I to do, how could I rescue her, how could I pull her away from under that groom at ten miles' distance, with a team of horses I couldn't control. These horses, now, they had somehow slipped the reins loose, pushed the windows open from outside, I did not know how; each of them had stuck a head in at a window and, quite unmoved by the startled cries of the family, stood eyeing the patient. "Better go back at once," I thought, as if the horses were summoning me to the return journey, yet I permitted the patient's sister, who fancied that I was dazed by the heat, to take my fur coat from me. A glass of rum was poured out for me, the old man clapped me on the shoulder, a familiarity justified by this offer of his treasure. I shook my head; in the narrow confines of the old man's thoughts I felt ill; that was my only reason for refusing the drink. The mother stood by the bedside and cajoled me towards it; I yielded, and, while one of the horses whinnied loudly to the ceiling, laid my head to the boy's breast, which shivered under my wet beard. I confirmed what I already knew; the boy was quite sound, something a little wrong with his circulation, saturated with coffee by his solicitous mother, but sound and best turned out of bed with one shove. I am no world reformer and so I let him lie. I was the district doctor and did my duty to the uttermost, to the point where it became almost too much. I was badly paid and yet generous and helpful to the poor. I had still to see that Rose was all right, and then the boy might have his way and I wanted to die too. What was I doing there in that endless winter! My horse was dead, and not a single person in the village would lend me another. I had to get my team out of the pigsty; if they hadn't chanced to be horses I should have had to travel with swine. That was how it was. And I nodded to the family. They knew nothing about it, and, had they known, would not have believed it. To write prescriptions is easy, but to come to an understanding with people is hard. Well, this should be the end of my visit, I had once more been called out needlessly, I was used to that, the whole district made my life a torment with my night bell, but that I should have to sacrifice Rose this time as well, the pretty girl who had lived in my house for years almost without my noticing her—that sacrifice was too much to ask, and I had somehow to get it reasoned out in my head with the help of what craft I could muster, in order not to let fly at this family, which with the best will in the world could not restore Rose to me. But as I shut my bag and put an arm out for my fur coat, the family meanwhile standing together, the father sniffing at the glass of rum in his hand, the mother, apparently disappointed in me—why, what do people expect?—biting her lips with tears in her eyes, the sister fluttering a blood-soaked towel, I was somehow ready to admit conditionally that the boy might be ill after all. I went towards him, he welcomed me smiling as if I were bringing him the most nourishing invalid broth—ah, now both horses were whinnying together, the noise, I suppose, was ordained by heaven to assist my examination of the patient—and this time I discovered that the boy was indeed ill. In his right side, near the hip, was an open wound as big as the palm of my hand. Rose-red, in many variations of shade, dark in the hollows, lighter at the edges, softly granulated, with irregular clots of blood, open as a surface mine to the daylight. That was how it looked from a distance. But on a closer inspection there was another complication. I could not help a low whistle of surprise. Worms, as thick and as long as my little finger, themselves rose-red and blood-spotted as well, were wriggling from their fastness in the interior of the wound towards the light, with small white heads and many little legs. Poor boy, you were past helping. I had discovered your great wound; this blossom in your side was destroying you. The family was pleased; they saw me busying myself; the sister told the mother, the mother the father, the father told several guests who were coming in, through the moonlight at the open door, walking on tiptoe, keeping their balance with out-stretched arms. "Will you save me?" whispered the boy with a sob, quite blinded by the life within his wound. That is what people are like in my district. Always expecting the impossible from the doctor. They have lost their ancient beliefs; the parson sits at home and unravels his vestments, one after another; but the doctor is supposed to be omnip-otent with his merciful surgeon's hand. Well, as it pleases them; I have not thrust my services on them; if they misuse me for sacred ends, I let that happen to me too; what better do I want, old country doctor that I am, bereft of my servant girl! And so they came, the family and the village elders, and stripped my clothes off me; a school choir with the teacher at the head of it stood before the house and sang these words to an utterly simple tune:

> Strip his clothes off, then he'll heal us,
> If he doesn't, kill him dead!
> Only a doctor, only a doctor.

Then my clothes were off and I looked at the people quietly, my fingers in my beard and my head cocked to one side. I was altogether composed and equal to the situation and remained so, although it was no help to me, since they now took me by the head and feet and carried me to the bed. They laid me down in it next to the wall, on the side of the wound. Then they all left the room; the door was shut; the singing stopped; clouds covered the moon; the bedding was warm around me; the horses' heads in the open windows wavered like shadows. "Do you know," said a voice in my ear, "I have very little confidence in you. Why, you were only blown in here, you didn't come on your own feet. Instead of helping me, you're cramping me on my deathbed. What I'd like best is to scratch your eyes out." "Right," I said, "it is a shame. And yet I am a doctor. What am I to do? Believe me, it is not too easy for me either." "Am I supposed to be content with this apology? Oh, I must be, I can't help it. I always have to put up with things. A fine wound is all I brought into the world; that was my sole endowment." "My young friend," said I, "your mistake is: you have not a wide enough view. I have been in all the sickrooms, far and wide, and I tell you: your wound is not so bad. Done in a tight corner with two strokes of the ax. Many a one proffers his side and can hardly hear the ax in the forest, far less that it is coming nearer to him." "Is that really so, or are you deluding me in my fever?" "It is really so, take the word of honor of an official doctor." And he took it and lay still. But now it was time for me to think of escaping. The horses were still standing faithfully in their places. My clothes, my fur coat, my bag were quickly collected; I didn't want to waste time dressing; if the horses raced home as they had come, I should only be springing, as it were, out of this bed into my own. Obediently a horse backed away from the window; I threw my bundle into the gig; the fur coat missed its mark and was caught on a hook only by the sleeve. Good enough. I swung myself onto the horse. With the reins loosely trailing, one horse barely fastened to the other, the gig swaying behind, my fur coat last of all in the snow. "Gee up" I said, but there was no galloping; slowly, like old men, we crawled through the snowy wastes; a long time echoed behind us the new but faulty song of the children:

> O be joyful, all you patients,
> The doctors laid in bed beside you!

Never shall I reach home at this rate; my flourishing practice is done for; my successor is robbing me, but in vain, for he cannot take my place; in my house the disgusting groom is raging; Rose is his victim; I do not want to think about it any more. Naked, exposed to the frost of this most unhappy of ages, with an earthly vehicle, unearthly horses, old man that I am, I wander astray. My fur coat is hanging from the back of the gig, but I cannot reach it, and none of my limber pack of patients lifts a finger. Betrayed! Betrayed! A false alarm on the night bell once answered—it cannot be made good, not ever.

TRANSLATED BY WILLA AND EDWIN MUIR

FRANCES CORNFORD

FRANCES CORNFORD (1886–1960). *English poet. The granddaughter of Charles Darwin, Frances Cornford lived most of her life in Cambridge, England, where she spent her time writing delicate poems of an intensely personal nature; she is best remembered for her sublime illumination of the emotions. Her* Collected Poems *was published in 1956.*

THE WATCH

I wakened on my hot, hard bed,
Upon the pillow lay my head;
Beneath the pillow I could hear
My little watch was ticking clear.
I thought the throbbing of it went
Like my continual discontent.
I thought it said in every tick:
I am so sick, so sick, so sick.
O death, come quick, come quick, come quick,
Come quick, come quick, come quick, come quick!

JORGE LUIS BORGES

JORGE LUIS BORGES (1899–1986). *Argentinian poet, essayist, and fiction writer. Educated in Europe, Borges returned to Buenos Aires in 1921 and became the leader of a South American literary movement known as magic realism. During the regime of Juan Perón, he was removed from his directorship of the National Library for political reasons and made a chicken inspector. He is best known for the short-story collection* Ficciones *(tr. 1962),* The Aleph and Other Stories *(tr. 1970), and* Dreamtigers *(tr. 1964), a collection of poems and short parables, of which the title piece is an account of Homer's blindness. (Borges himself was nearly blind by 1960, when the collection was first published in Spanish.) His last works were* Dr. Brodie's Report *(tr. 1972) and* The Book of Sand *(tr. 1977).*

THE IMMORTALS

And see, no longer blinded by our eyes.
—RUPERT BROOKE

Whoever could have foreseen, way back in that innocent summer of 1923, that the novelette *The Chosen One* by Camilo N. Huergo, presented to me by the author with his personal inscription on the flyleaf (which I had the decorum to tear out before offering the volume for sale to successive men of the book trade), hid under the thin varnish of fiction a prophetic truth. Huergo's photograph, in an oval frame, adorns the cover. Each time I look at it, I have the impression that the snapshot is about to cough, a victim of that lung disease which nipped in the bud a promising career. Tuberculosis, in short, denied him the happiness of acknowledging the letter I wrote him in one of my characteristic outbursts of generosity.

The epigraph prefixed to this thoughtful essay has been taken from the aforementioned novelette; I requested Dr. Montenegro, of the Academy, to render it into Spanish, but the results were negative. To give the unprepared reader the gist of the matter, I shall now sketch, in condensed form, an outline of Huergo's narrative, as follows:

The storyteller pays a visit, far to the south in Chubut, to the English rancher don Guillermo Blake, who devotes his energies not only to the breeding of sheep but also to the ramblings of the world-famous Plato and to the latest and more freakish experiments in the field of surgical medicine. On the basis of his reading, don Guillermo concludes that the five senses obstruct or deform the apprehension of reality and that, could we free ourselves of them, we would see the world as it is—endless and timeless. He comes to think that the eternal models of things lie in the depths of the soul and that the organs of perception with which the Creator has endowed us are, *grosso modo*, hindrances. They are no better than dark spectacles that blind us to what exists outside, diverting our attention at the same time from the splendor we carry within us.

Blake begets a son by one of the farm girls so that the boy may one day become acquainted with reality. To anesthetize him for life, to make him blind and deaf and dumb, to emancipate him from the senses of smell and taste, were the father's first concerns. He took, in the same way, all possible measures to make the chosen one unaware of his own body. As to the rest, this was arranged with contrivances designed to take over respiration, circulation, nourishment, digestion, and elimination. It was a pity that the boy, fully liberated, was cut off from all human contact.

Owing to the press of practical matters, the narrator goes away. After ten years, he returns. Don Guillermo has died; his son goes on living after his fashion, with natural breathing, heart regular, in a dusty shack cluttered with mechanical devices. The narrator, about to leave for good, drops a cigarette butt that sets fire to the shack and he never quite knows whether this act was done on purpose or by pure chance. So ends Huergo's story, strange enough for its time but now, of course, more than outstripped by the rockets and astronauts of our men of science.

Having dashed off this disinterested compendium of the tale of a now dead and forgotten author—from whom I have nothing to gain—I steer back to the heart of the matter. Memory restores to me a Saturday morning in 1964 when I had an appointment with the eminent gerontologist Dr. Raúl Narbondo. The sad truth is that we young bloods of yesteryear are getting on; the thick mop begins to thin, one or another ear stops up, the wrinkles collect grime, molars grow hollow, a cough takes root, the backbone hunches up, the foot trips on a pebble, and, to put it plainly, the paterfamilias falters and withers. There was no doubt about it, the moment had come to see Dr. Narbondo for a general checkup, particularly considering the fact that he specialized in the replacement of malfunctioning organs.

Sick at heart because that afternoon the Palermo Juniors and the Spanish Sports were playing a return match and maybe I could not

occupy my place in the front row to bolster my team, I betook myself to
the clinic on Corrientes Avenue near Pasteur. The clinic, as its fame
betrays, occupies the fifteenth floor of the Adamant Building. I went up
by elevator (manufactured by the Electra Company). Eye to eye with
Narbondo's brass shingle, I pressed the bell, and at long last, taking my
courage in both hands, I slipped through the partly open door and
entered into the waiting room proper. There, alone with the latest issues
of *Ladies' Companion* and *Jumbo*, I whiled away the passing hours until
a cuckoo clock struck twelve and sent me leaping from my armchair. At
once, I asked myself, What happened? Planning my every move now
like a sleuth, I took a step or two toward the next room, peeped in,
ready, admittedly, to fly the coop at the slightest sound. From the streets
far below came the noise of horns and traffic, the cry of a newspaper
hawker, the squeal of brakes sparing some pedestrian, but, all around
me, a reign of silence. I crossed a kind of laboratory, or pharmaceutical
back room, furnished with instruments and flasks of all sorts. Stimulated
by the aim of reaching the men's room, I pushed open a door at the far
end of the lab.

Inside, I saw something that my eyes did not understand. The small
enclosure was circular, painted white, with a low ceiling and neon lighting, and without a single window to relieve the sense of claustrophobia.
The room was inhabited by four personages, or pieces of furniture.
Their color was the same as the walls, their material wood, their form
cubic. On each cube was another small cube with a latticed opening and
below it a slot as in a mailbox. Carefully scrutinizing the grilled opening,
you noted with alarm that from the interior you were being watched by
something like eyes. The slots emitted, from time to time, a chorus of
sighs or whisperings that the good Lord himself could not have made
head or tail of. The placement of these cubes was such that they faced
each other in the form of a square, composing a kind of conclave. I
don't know how many minutes lapsed. At this point, the doctor came in
and said to me, "My pardon, Bustos, for having kept you waiting. I was
just out getting myself an advance ticket for today's match between the
Palermo Juniors and the Spanish Sports." He went on, indicating the
cubes, "Let me introduce you to Santiago Silberman, to retired clerk-
of-court Ludueña, to Aquiles Molinari, and to Miss Bugard."

Out of the furniture came faint rumbling sounds. I quickly reached
out a hand and, without the pleasure of shaking theirs, withdrew in
good order, a frozen smile on my lips. Reaching the vestibule as best I
could, I managed to stammer, "A drink. A stiff drink."

Narbondo came out of the lab with a graduated beaker filled with
water and dissolved some effervescent drops into it. Blessed concoc-

tion—the wretched taste brought me to my senses. Then, the door to the small room closed and locked tight, came the explanation:

"I'm glad to see, my dear Bustos, that my immortals have made quite an impact on you. Whoever would have thought that *Homo sapiens*, Darwin's barely human ape, could achieve such perfection? This, my house, I assure you, is the only one in all Indo-America where Dr. Eric Stapledon's methodology has been fully applied. You recall, no doubt, the consternation that the death of the late lamented doctor, which took place in New Zealand, occasioned in scientific circles. I flatter myself, furthermore, for having implemented his precursory labors with a few Argentinean touches. In itself, the thesis—Newton's apple all over again—is fairly simple. The death of the body is a result, always, of the failure of some organ or other, call it the kidney, lungs, heart, or what you like. With the replacement of the organism's various components, in themselves perishable, with other corresponding stainless or polyethylene parts, there is no earthly reason whatever why the soul, why you yourself—Bustos Domecq—should not be immortal. None of your philosophical niceties here; the body can be vulcanized and from time to time recaulked, and so the mind keeps going. Surgery brings immortality to mankind. Life's essential aim has been attained—the mind lives on without fear of cessation. Each of our immortals is comforted by the certainty, backed by our firm's guarantee, of being a witness *in aeternum*. The brain, refreshed night and day by a system of electrical charges, is the last organic bulwark in which ball bearings and cells collaborate. The rest is Formica, steel, plastics. Respiration, alimentation, generation, mobility—elimination itself!—belong to the past. Our immortal is real estate. One or two minor touches are still missing, it's true. Oral articulation, dialogue, may still be improved. As for the costs, you need not worry yourself. By means of a procedure that circumvents legal red tape, the candidate transfers his property to us, and the Narbondo Company, Inc.—I, my son, his descendants—guarantees your upkeep, *in statu quo*, to the end of time. And, I might add, a money-back guarantee."

It was then that he laid a friendly hand on my shoulder. I felt his will taking power over me. "Ha-ha! I see I've whetted your appetite, I've tempted you, dear Bustos. You'll need a couple of months or so to get your affairs in order and to have your stock portfolio signed over to us. As far as the operation goes, naturally, as a friend, I want to save you a little something. Instead of our usual fee of ten thousand dollars, for you, ninety-five hundred—in cash, of course. The rest is yours. It goes to pay your lodging, care, and service. The medical procedure in itself is painless. No more than a question of amputation and replacement.

Nothing to worry about. On the eve, just keep yourself calm, untroubled. Avoid heavy meals, tobacco, and alcohol, apart from your accustomed and imported, I hope, Scotch or two. Above all, refrain from impatience."

"Why two months?" I asked him. "One's enough, and then some. I come out of the anesthesia and I'm one more of your cubes. You have my address and phone number. We'll keep in touch. I'll be back next Friday at the latest."

At the escape hatch he handed me the card of Nemirovski, Nemirovski & Nemirovski, Counsellors at Law, who would put themselves at my disposal for all the details of drawing up the will. With perfect composure I walked to the subway entrance, then took the stairs at a run. I lost no time. That same night, without leaving the slightest trace behind, I moved to the New Impartial, in whose register I figure under the assumed name of Aquiles Silberman. Here, in my bedroom at the far rear of this modest hotel, wearing a false beard and dark spectacles, I am setting down this account of the facts.

TRANSLATED BY NORMAN THOMAS DI GIOVANNI

ERNEST HEMINGWAY

ERNEST HEMINGWAY (1899–1961). *American journalist and fiction writer. Son of a doctor, Hemingway went to Italy after graduating from high school to volunteer as an ambulance driver for the Red Cross. He then served in the Italian army and was seriously wounded; this experience later inspired one of his finest novels,* A Farewell to Arms *(1929). Success had already come, with* The Sun Also Rises *(1926), followed by the short-story collection* Men Without Women *(1927). Among Hemingway's most notable works was* The Old Man and the Sea, *which won the 1953 Pulitzer Prize and helped him win the Nobel Prize for literature in 1954.*

INDIAN CAMP

At the lake shore there was another rowboat drawn up. The two Indians stood waiting.

Nick and his father got in the stern of the boat and the Indians shoved it off and one of them got in to row. Uncle George sat in the stern of the camp rowboat. The young Indian shoved the camp boat off and got in to row Uncle George.

The two boats started off in the dark. Nick heard the oarlocks of the other boat quite a way ahead of them in the mist. The Indians rowed with quick choppy strokes. Nick lay back with his father's arm around him. It was cold on the water. The Indian who was rowing them was working very hard, but the other boat moved further ahead in the mist all the time.

"Where are we going, Dad?" Nick asked.

"Over to the Indian camp. There is an Indian lady very sick."

"Oh," said Nick.

Across the bay they found the other boat beached. Uncle George was smoking a cigar in the dark. The young Indian pulled the boat way up on the beach. Uncle George gave both the Indians cigars.

They walked up from the beach through a meadow that was soaking wet with dew, following the young Indian who carried a lantern. Then they went into the woods and followed a trail that led to the logging road that ran back into the hills. It was much lighter on the logging road as the timber was cut away on both sides. The young Indian stopped and blew out his lantern and they all walked on along the road.

They came around a bend and a dog came out barking. Ahead were the lights of the shanties where the Indian bark-peelers lived. More dogs rushed out at them. The two Indians sent them back to the shanties. In the shanty nearest the road there was a light in the window. An old woman stood in the doorway holding a lamp.

Inside on a wooden bunk lay a young Indian woman. She had been trying to have her baby for two days. All the old women in the camp had been helping her. The men had moved off up the road to sit in the dark and smoke out of range of the noise she made. She screamed just as Nick and the two Indians followed his father and Uncle George into the shanty. She lay in the lower bunk, very big under a quilt. Her head was turned to one side. In the upper bunk was her husband. He had cut his foot very badly with an ax three days before. He was smoking a pipe. The room smelled very bad.

Nick's father ordered some water to be put on the stove, and while it was heating he spoke to Nick.

"This lady is going to have a baby, Nick," he said.

"I know," said Nick.

"You don't know," said his father. "Listen to me. What she is going through is called being in labor. The baby wants to be born and she wants it to be born. All her muscles are trying to get the baby born. That is what is happening when she screams."

"I see," Nick said.

Just then the woman cried out.

"Oh, Daddy, can't you give her something to make her stop screaming?" asked Nick.

"No. I haven't any anæsthetic," his father said. "But her screams are not important. I don't hear them because they are not important."

The husband in the upper bunk rolled over against the wall.

The woman in the kitchen motioned to the doctor that the water was hot. Nick's father went into the kitchen and poured about half of the water out of the big kettle into a basin. Into the water left in the kettle he put several things he unwrapped from a handkerchief.

"Those must boil," he said, and began to scrub his hands in the basin of hot water with a cake of soap he had brought from the camp. Nick watched his father's hands scrubbing each other with the soap. While his father washed his hands very carefully and thoroughly, he talked.

"You see, Nick, babies are supposed to be born head first but sometimes they're not. When they're not they make a lot of trouble for everybody. Maybe I'll have to operate on this lady. We'll know in a little while."

When he was satisfied with his hands he went in and went to work.

"Pull back that quilt, will you, George?" he said. "I'd rather not touch it."

Later when he started to operate Uncle George and three Indian men held the woman still. She bit Uncle George on the arm and Uncle George said, "Damn squaw bitch!" and the young Indian who had rowed Uncle George over laughed at him. Nick held the basin for his father. It all took a long time.

His father picked the baby up and slapped it to make it breathe and handed it to the old woman.

"See, it's a boy, Nick," he said. "How do you like being an interne?"

Nick said, "All right." He was looking away so as not to see what his father was doing.

"There. That gets it," said his father and put something into the basin.

Nick didn't look at it.

"Now," his father said, "there's some stitches to put in. You can watch this or not, Nick, just as you like. I'm going to sew up the incision I made."

Nick did not watch. His curiosity had been gone for a long time.

His father finished and stood up. Uncle George and the three Indian men stood up. Nick put the basin out in the kitchen.

Uncle George looked at his arm. The young Indian smiled reminiscently.

"I'll put some peroxide on that, George," the doctor said.

He bent over the Indian woman. She was quiet now and her eyes were closed. She looked very pale. She did not know what had become of the baby or anything.

"I'll be back in the morning," the doctor said, standing up. "The nurse should be here from St. Ignace by noon and she'll bring everything we need."

He was feeling exalted and talkative as football players are in the dressing room after a game.

"That's one for the medical journal, George," he said. "Doing a Cæsarian with a jack-knife and sewing it up with nine-foot, tapered gut leaders."

Uncle George was standing against the wall, looking at his arm.

"Oh, you're a great man, all right," he said.

"Ought to have a look at the proud father. They're usually the worst sufferers in these little affairs," the doctor said. "I must say he took it all pretty quietly."

He pulled back the blanket from the Indian's head. His hand came away wet. He mounted on the edge of the lower bunk with the lamp in one hand and looked in. The Indian lay with his face toward the wall. His throat had been cut from ear to ear. The blood had flowed down into a pool where his body sagged the bunk. His head rested on his left arm. The open razor lay, edge up, in the blankets.

"Take Nick out of the shanty, George," the doctor said.

There was no need of that. Nick, standing in the door of the kitchen, had a good view of the upper bunk when his father, the lamp in one hand, tipped the Indian's head back.

It was just beginning to be daylight when they walked along the logging road back toward the lake.

"I'm terribly sorry I brought you along, Nickie," said his father, all his post-operative exhilaration gone. "It was an awful mess to put you through."

"Do ladies always have such a hard time having babies?" Nick asked.

"No, that was very, very exceptional."

"Why did he kill himself, Daddy?"

"I don't know, Nick. He couldn't stand things, I guess."

"Do many men kill themselves, Daddy?"

"Not very many, Nick."

"Do many women?"

"Hardly ever."

"Don't they ever?"

"Oh, yes. They do sometimes."

"Daddy?"

"Yes."

"Where did Uncle George go?"

"He'll turn up all right."

"Is dying hard, Daddy?"

"No, I think it's pretty easy, Nick. It all depends."

They were seated in the boat, Nick in the stern, his father rowing. The sun was coming up over the hills. A bass jumped, making a circle in the water. Nick trailed his hand in the water. It felt warm in the sharp chill of the morning.

In the early morning on the lake sitting in the stern of the boat with his father rowing, he felt quite sure that he would never die.

HILLS LIKE WHITE ELEPHANTS

The hills across the valley of the Ebro were long and white. On this side there was no shade and no trees and the station was between two lines of rails in the sun. Close against the side of the station there was the warm shadow of the building and a curtain, made of strings of bamboo beads, hung across the open door into the bar, to keep out flies. The American and the girl with him sat at a table in the shade, outside the building. It was very hot and the express from Barcelona would come in forty minutes. It stopped at this junction for two minutes and went on to Madrid.

"What should we drink?" the girl asked. She had taken off her hat and put it on the table.

"It's pretty hot," the man said.

"Let's drink beer."

"Dos cervezas," the man said into the curtain.

"Big ones?" a woman asked from the doorway.

"Yes. Two big ones."

The woman brought two glasses of beer and two felt pads. She put the felt pads and the beer glasses on the table and looked at the man and the girl. The girl was looking off at the line of hills. They were white in the sun and the country was brown and dry.

"They look like white elephants," she said.

"I've never seen one," the man drank his beer.

"No, you wouldn't have."

"I might have," the man said. "Just because you say I wouldn't have doesn't prove anything."

The girl looked at the bead curtain. "They've painted something on it," she said. "What does it say?"

"Anis del Toro. It's a drink."

"Could we try it?"

The man called "Listen" through the curtain. The woman came out from the bar.

"Four reales."

"We want two Anis del Toro."

"With water?"

"Do you want it with water?"

"I don't know," the girl said. "Is it good with water?"

"It's all right."

"You want them with water?" asked the woman.

"Yes, with water."

"It tastes like licorice," the girl said and put the glass down.

"That's the way with everything."

"Yes," said the girl. "Everything tastes of licorice. Especially all the things you've waited so long for, like absinthe."

"Oh, cut it out."

"You started it," the girl said. "I was being amused. I was having a fine time."

"Well, let's try and have a fine time."

"All right. I was trying. I said the mountains looked like white elephants. Wasn't that bright?"

"That was bright."

"I wanted to try this new drink. That's all we do, isn't it—look at things and try new drinks?"

"I guess so."

The girl looked across at the hills.

"They're lovely hills," she said. "They don't really look like white elephants. I just meant the coloring of their skin through the trees."

"Should we have another drink?"

"All right."

The warm wind blew the bead curtain against the table.

"The beer's nice and cool," the man said.

"It's lovely," the girl said.

"It's really an awfully simple operation, Jig," the man said. "It's not really an operation at all."

The girl looked at the ground the table legs rested on.

"I know you wouldn't mind it, Jig. It's really not anything. It's just to let the air in."

The girl did not say anything.

"I'll go with you and I'll stay with you all the time. They just let the air in and then it's all perfectly natural."

"Then what will we do afterward?"

"We'll be fine afterward. Just like we were before."

"What makes you think so?"

"That's the only thing that bothers us. It's the only thing that's made us unhappy."

The girl looked at the bead curtain, put her hand out and took hold of two of the strings of beads.

"And you think then we'll be all right and be happy."

"I know we will. You don't have to be afraid. I've known lots of people that have done it."

"So have I," said the girl. "And afterward they were all so happy."

"Well," the man said, "if you don't want to you don't have to. I wouldn't have you do it if you didn't want to. But I know it's perfectly simple."

"And you really want to?"

"I think it's the best thing to do. But I don't want you to do it if you don't really want to."

"And if I do it you'll be happy and things will be like they were and you'll love me?"

"I love you now. You know I love you."

"I know. But if I do it, then it will be nice again if I say things are like white elephants, and you'll like it?"

"I'll love it. I love it now but I just can't think about it. You know how I get when I worry."

"If I do it you won't ever worry?"

"I won't worry about that because it's perfectly simple."

"Then I'll do it. Because I don't care about me."

"What do you mean?"

"I don't care about me."

"Well, I care about you."

"Oh, yes. But I don't care about me. And I'll do it and then everything will be fine."

"I don't want you to do it if you feel that way."

The girl stood up and walked to the end of the station. Across, on the other side, were fields of grain and trees along the banks of the Ebro. Far away, beyond the river, were mountains. The shadow of a cloud moved across the field of grain and she saw the river through the trees.

"And we could have all this," she said. "And we could have everything and every day we make it more impossible."

"What did you say?"

"I said we could have everything."

"We can have everything."

"No, we can't."

"We can have the whole world."

"No, we can't."

"We can go everywhere."

"No, we can't. It isn't ours any more."

"It's ours."

"No, it isn't. And once they take it away, you never get it back."

"But they haven't taken it away."

"We'll wait and see."

"Come on back in the shade," he said. "You mustn't feel that way."

"I don't feel any way," the girl said. "I just know things."

"I don't want you to do anything that you don't want to do—"

"Nor that isn't good for me," she said. "I know. Could we have another beer?"

"All right. But you've got to realize—"

"I realize," the girl said. "Can't we maybe stop talking?"

They sat down at the table and the girl looked across at the hills on the dry side of the valley and the man looked at her and at the table.

"You've got to realize," he said, "that I don't want you to do it if you don't want to. I'm perfectly willing to go through with it if it means anything to you."

"Doesn't it mean anything to you? We could get along."

"Of course it does. But I don't want anybody but you. I don't want any one else. And I know it's perfectly simple."

"Yes, you know it's perfectly simple."

"It's all right for you to say that, but I do know it."

"Would you do something for me now?"

"I'd do anything for you."

"Would you please please please please please please please stop talking?"

He did not say anything but looked at the bags against the wall of the station. There were labels on them from all the hotels where they had spent nights.

"But I don't want you to," he said, "I don't care anything about it."

"I'll scream," the girl said.

The woman came out through the curtains with two glasses of beer and put them down on the damp felt pads. "The train comes in five minutes," she said.

"What did she say?" asked the girl.

"That the train is coming in five minutes."

The girl smiled brightly at the woman, to thank her.

"I'd better take the bags over to the other side of the station," the man said. She smiled at him.

"All right. Then come back and we'll finish the beer."

He picked up the two heavy bags and carried them around the station to the other tracks. He looked up the tracks but could not see the train. Coming back, he walked through the barroom, where people waiting for the train were drinking. He drank an Anis at the bar and looked at the people. They were all waiting reasonably for the train. He went out through the bead curtains. She was sitting at the table and smiled at him.

"Do you feel better?" he asked.

"I feel fine," she said. "There's nothing wrong with me. I feel fine."

ARNA BONTEMPS

ARNA BONTEMPS (1902–1974). *African-American novelist. Bontemps's work focused on the black experience in the United States and in Haiti. His novels include* God Sends Sunday *(1931; later dramatized, with Countee Cullen, as* St. Louis Woman*),* Black Thunder *(1935), and* Drums at Dusk *(1939).*

A SUMMER TRAGEDY

Old Jeff Patton, the black share farmer, fumbled with his bow tie. His fingers trembled and the high stiff collar pinched his throat. A fellow loses his hand for such vanities after thirty or forty years of simple life. Once a year, or maybe twice if there's a wedding among his kinfolks, he may spruce up; but generally fancy clothes do nothing but adorn the wall of the big room and feed the moths. That had been Jeff Patton's experience. He had not worn his stiff-bosomed shirt more than a dozen times in all his married life. His swallowtailed coat lay on the bed beside him, freshly brushed and pressed, but it was as full of holes as the overalls in which he worked on weekdays. The moths had used it badly. Jeff twisted his mouth into a hideous toothless grimace as he contended with the obstinate bow. He stamped his good foot and decided to give up the struggle.

"Jennie," he called.

"What's that, Jeff?" His wife's shrunken voice came out of the adjoining room like an echo. It was hardly bigger than a whisper.

"I reckon you'll have to help me wid this heah bow tie, baby," he said meekly. "Dog if I can hitch it up."

Her answer was not strong enough to reach him, but presently the old woman came to the door, feeling her way with a stick. She had a wasted, dead-leaf appearance. Her body, as scrawny and gnarled as a string bean, seemed less than nothing in the ocean of frayed and faded petticoats that surrounded her. These hung an inch or two above the tops of her heavy unlaced shoes and showed little grotesque piles where the stockings had fallen down from her negligible legs.

"You oughta could do a heap mo' wid a thing like that'n me— beingst as you got yo' good sight."

"Looks like I oughta could," he admitted. "But ma fingers is gone democrat on me. I get all mixed up in the looking glass and can't tell wicha way to twist the devilish thing."

Jennie sat on the side of the bed and old Jeff Patton got down on one knee while she tied the bow knot. It was a slow and painful ordeal for each of them in this position. Jeff's bones cracked, his knee ached, and it was only after a half dozen attempts that Jennie worked a semblance of a bow into the tie.

"I got to dress maself now," the old woman whispered. "These is ma old shoes and stockings, and I ain't so much as unwrapped ma dress."

"Well, don't worry 'bout me no mo', baby," Jess said. "That 'bout finishes me. All I gotta do now is slip on that old coat 'n ves' an' I'll be fixed to leave."

Jennie disappeared again through the dim passage into the shed room. Being blind was no handicap to her in that black hole. Jeff heard the cane placed against the wall beside the door and knew that his wife was on easy ground. He put on his coat, took a battered top hat from the bedpost and hobbled to the front door. He was ready to travel. As soon as Jennie could get on her Sunday shoes and her old black silk dress, they would start.

Outside the tiny log house, the day was warm and mellow with sunshine. A host of wasps were humming with busy excitement in the trunk of a dead sycamore. Gray squirrels were searching through the grass for hickory nuts and blue jays were in the trees, hopping from branch to branch. Pine woods stretched away to the left like a black sea. Among them were scattered scores of log houses like Jeff's, houses of black share farmers. Cows and pigs wandered freely among the trees. There was no danger of loss. Each farmer knew his own stock and knew his neighbor's as well as he knew his neighbor's children.

Down the slope to the right were the cultivated acres on which the colored folks worked. They extended to the river, more than two miles away, and they were today green with the unmade cotton crop. A tiny thread of a road, which passed directly in front of Jeff's place, ran through these green fields like a pencil mark.

Jeff, standing outside the door, with his absurd hat in his left hand, surveyed the wide scene tenderly. He had been forty-five years on these acres. He loved them with the unexplained affection that others have for the countries to which they belong.

The sun was hot on his head, his collar still pinched his throat, and the Sunday clothes were intolerably hot. Jeff transferred the hat to his right hand and began fanning with it. Suddenly the whisper that was Jennie's voice came out of the shed room.

"You can bring the car round front whilst you's waitin'," it said feebly. There was a tired pause; then it added, "I'll soon be fixed to go."

"A'right, baby," Jeff answered. "I'll get it in a minute."

But he didn't move. A thought struck him that made his mouth fall open. The mention of the car brought to his mind, with new intensity, the trip he and Jennie were about to take. Fear came into his eyes; excitement took his breath. Lord, Jesus!

"Jeff . . . O Jeff," the old woman's whisper called.

He awakened with a jolt. "Hunh, baby?"

"What you doin'?"

"Nuthin'. Jes studyin'. I jes been turnin' things round 'n round in ma mind."

"You could be gettin' the car," she said.

"Oh yes, right away, baby."

He started round to the shed, limping heavily on his bad leg. There were three frizzly chickens in the yard. All his other chickens had been killed or stolen recently. But the frizzly chickens had been saved somehow. That was fortunate indeed, for these curious creatures had a way of devouring "Poison" from the yard and in that way protecting against conjure and black luck and spells. But even the frizzly chickens seemed now to be in a stupor. Jeff thought they had some ailment; he expected all three of them to die shortly.

The shed in which the old T-model Ford stood was only a grass roof held up by four corner poles. It had been built by tremulous hands at a time when the little rattletrap car had been regarded as a peculiar treasure. And, miraculously, despite wind and downpour, it still stood.

Jeff adjusted the crank and put his weight upon it. The engine came to life with a sputter and bang that rattled the old car from radiator to taillight. Jeff hopped into the seat and put his foot on the accelerator. The sputtering and banging increased. The rattling became more violent. That was good. It was good banging, good sputtering and rattling, and it meant that the aged car was still in running condition. She could be depended on for this trip.

Again Jeff's thought halted as if paralyzed. The suggestion of the trip fell into the machinery of his mind like a wrench. He felt dazed and weak. He swung the car out into the yard, made a half turn and drove around to the front door. When he took his hands off the wheel, he noticed that he was trembling violently. He cut off the motor and climbed to the ground to wait for Jennie.

A few minutes later she was at the window, her voice rattling against the pane like a broken shutter.

"I'm ready, Jeff."

He did not answer, but limped into the house and took her by the arm. He led her slowly through the big room, down the step and across the yard.

"You reckon I'd oughta lock the do'?" he asked softly.

They stopped and Jennie weighed the question. Finally she shook her head.

"Ne' mind the do'," she said. "I don't see no cause to lock up things."

"You right," Jeff agreed. "No cause to lock up."

Jeff opened the door and helped his wife into the car. A quick shudder passed over him. Jesus! Again he trembled.

"How come you shaking so?" Jennie whispered.

"I don't know," he said.

"You mus' be scairt, Jeff."

"No, baby, I ain't scairt."

He slammed the door after her and went around to crank up again. The motor started easily. Jeff wished that it had not been so responsive. He would have liked a few more minutes in which to turn things around in his head. As it was, with Jennie chiding him about being afraid, he had to keep going. He swung the car into the little pencil-mark road and started off toward the river, driving very slowly, very cautiously.

Chugging across the green countryside, the small battered Ford seemed tiny indeed. Jeff felt a familiar excitement, a thrill, as they came down the first slope to the immense levels on which the cotton was growing. He could not help reflecting that the crops were good. He knew what that meant, too; he had made forty-five of them with his own hands. It was true that he had worn out nearly a dozen mules, but that was the fault of old man Stevenson, the owner of the land. Major Stevenson had the odd notion that one mule was all a share farmer needed to work a thirty-acre plot. It was an expensive notion, the way it killed mules from overwork, but the old man held to it. Jeff thought it killed a good many share farmers as well as mules, but he had no sympathy for them. He had always been strong, and he had been taught to have no patience with weakness in men. Women or children might be tolerated if they were puny, but a weak man was a curse. Of course, his own children—

Jeff's thought halted there. He and Jennie never mentioned their dead children any more. And naturally he did not wish to dwell upon them in his mind. Before he knew it, some remark would slip out of his mouth and that would make Jennie feel blue. Perhaps she would cry. A woman like Jennie could not easily throw off the grief that comes from losing five grown children within two years. Even Jeff was still staggered by the blow. His memory had not been much good recently. He frequently talked to himself. And, although he had kept it a secret, he knew that his courage had left him. He was terrified by the least unfamiliar sound at night. He was reluctant to venture far from home in the daytime. And that habit of trembling when he felt fearful was now far beyond his control. Sometimes he became afraid and trembled without knowing what had frightened him. The feeling would just come over him like a chill.

The car rattled slowly over the dusty road. Jennie sat erect and silent, with a little absurd hat pinned to her hair. Her useless eyes seemed very large, very white in their deep sockets. Suddenly Jeff heard her voice, and he inclined his head to catch the words.

"Is we passed Delia Moore's house yet?" she asked.

"Not yet," he said.

"You must be drivin' mighty slow, Jeff."

"We might just as well take our time, baby."

There was a pause. A little puff of steam was coming out of the radiator of the car. Heat wavered above the hood. Delia Moore's house was nearly half a mile away. After a moment Jennie spoke again.

"You ain't really scairt, is you, Jeff?"

"Nah, baby, I ain't scairt."

"You know how we agreed—we gotta keep on goin'."

Jewels of perspiration appeared on Jeff's forehead. His eyes rounded, blinked, becamed fixed on the road.

"I don't know," he said with a shiver. "I reckon it's the only thing to do."

"Hm."

A flock of guinea fowls, pecking in the road, were scattered by the passing car. Some of them took to their wings; others hid under bushes. A blue jay, swaying on a leafy twig, was annoying a roadside squirrel. Jeff held an even speed till he came near Delia's place. Then he slowed down noticeably.

Delia's house was really no house at all, but an abandoned store building converted into a dwelling. It sat near a crossroads, beneath a single black cedar tree. There Delia, a catish old creature of Jennie's age, lived alone. She had been there more years than anybody could remember, and long ago had won the disfavor of such women as Jennie. For in her young days Delia had been gayer, yellower and saucier than seemed proper in those parts. Her ways with menfolks had been dark and suspicious. And the fact that she had had as many husbands as children did not help her reputation.

"Yonder's old Delia," Jeff said as they passed.

"What she doin'?"

"Jes sittin' in the do'," he said.

"She see us?"

"Hm," Jeff said. "Musta did."

That relieved Jennie. It strengthened her to know that her old enemy had seen her pass in her best clothes. That would give the old she-devil something to chew her gums and fret about, Jennie thought. Wouldn't she have a fit if she didn't find out? Old evil Delia! This would be just the thing for her. It would pay her back for being so evil. It would also pay her, Jennie thought, for the way she used to grin at Jeff—long ago when her teeth were good.

The road became smooth and red, and Jeff could tell by the smell of the air that they were nearing the river. He could see the rise where the road turned and ran along parallel to the stream. The car chugged on monotonously. After a long silent spell, Jennie leaned against Jeff and spoke.

"How many bale o' cotton you think we got standin'?" she said.

Jeff wrinkled his forehead as he calculated.

" 'Bout twenty-five, I reckon."

"How many you make las' year?"

"Twenty-eight," he said. "How come you ask that?"

"I's jes thinkin'," Jennie said quietly.

"It don't make a speck o' difference though," Jeff reflected. "If we get much or if we get little, we still gonna be in debt to old man Stevenson when he gets through counting up agin us. It's took us a long time to learn that."

Jennie was not listening to these words. She had fallen into a trance-like meditation. Her lips twitched. She chewed her gums and rubbed her gnarled hands nervously. Suddenly she leaned forward, buried her face in the nervous hands and burst into tears. She cried aloud in a dry cracked voice that suggested the rattle of fodder on dead stalks. She cried aloud like a child, for she had never learned to suppress a genuine sob. Her slight old frame shook heavily and seemed hardly able to sustain such violent grief.

"What's the matter, baby?" Jeff asked awkwardly. "Why you cryin' like all that?"

"I's jes thinkin'," she said.

"So you the one what's scairt now, hunh?"

"I ain't scairt, Jeff. I's jes thinkin' 'bout leavin' eve'thing like this— eve'thing we been used to. It's right sad-like."

Jeff did not answer, and presently Jennie buried her face again and cried.

The sun was almost overhead. It beat down furiously on the dusty wagon-path road, on the parched roadside grass and the tiny battered car. Jeff's hands, gripping the wheel, became wet with perspiration; his forehead sparkled. Jeff's lips parted. His mouth shaped a hideous grimace. His face suggested the face of a man being burned. But the torture passed and his expression softened again.

"You mustn't cry, baby," he said to his wife. "We gotta be strong. We can't break down."

Jennie waited a few seconds, then said, "You reckon we oughta do it, Jeff? You reckon we oughta go 'head an' do it, really?"

Jeff's voice choked; his eyes blurred. He was terrified to hear Jennie say the thing that had been in his mind all morning. She had egged him on when he had wanted more than anything in the world to wait, to reconsider, to think things over a little longer. Now she was getting cold feet. Actually there was no need of thinking the question through again. It would only end in making the same painful decision once more. Jeff knew that. There was no need of fooling around longer.

"We jes as well to do like we planned," he said. "They ain't nothin' else for us now—it's the bes' thing."

Jeff thought of the handicaps, the near impossibility, of making another crop with his leg bothering him more and more each week. Then there was always the chance that he would have another stroke, like the one that had made him lame. Another one might kill him. The least it could do would be to leave him helpless. Jeff gasped—Lord, Jesus! He could not bear to think of being helpless, like a baby, on Jennie's hands. Frail, blind Jennie.

The little pounding motor of the car worked harder and harder. The puff of steam from the cracked radiator became larger. Jeff realized that they were climbing a little rise. A moment later the road turned abruptly and he looked down upon the face of the river.

"Jeff."

"Hunh?"

"Is that the water I hear?"

"Hm. Tha's it."

"Well, which way you goin' now?"

"Down this a way," he said. "The road runs 'longside o' the water a lil piece."

She waited a while calmly. Then she said, "Drive faster."

"A'right, baby," Jeff said.

The water roared in the bed of the river. It was fifty or sixty feet below the level of the road. Between the road and the water there was a long smooth slope, sharply inclined. The slope was dry, the clay hardened by prolonged summer heat. The water below, roaring in a narrow channel, was noisy and wild.

"Jeff."

"Hunh?"

"How far you goin'?"

"Jes a lil piece down the road."

"You ain't scairt, is you, Jeff?"

"Nah, baby," he said trembling. "I ain't scairt."

"Remember how we planned it, Jeff. We gotta do it like we said. Brave-like."

"Hm."

Jeff's brain darkened. Things suddenly seemed unreal, like figures in a dream. Thoughts swam in his mind foolishly, hysterically, like little blind fish in a pool within a dense cave. They rushed, crossed one another, jostled, collided, retreated and rushed again. Jeff soon became dizzy. He shuddered violently and turned to his wife.

"Jennie, I can't do it. I can't." His voice broke pitifully.

She did not appear to be listening. All the grief had gone from her face. She sat erect, her unseeing eyes wide open, strained and frightful. Her glossy black skin had become dull. She seemed as thin, as sharp and bony, as a starved bird. Now, having suffered and endured the sadness of tearing herself away from beloved things, she showed no anguish. She was absorbed with her own thoughts, and she didn't even hear Jeff's voice shouting in her ear.

Jeff said nothing more. For an instant there was light in his cavernous brain. The great chamber was, for less than a second, peopled by characters he knew and loved. They were simple, healthy creatures, and they behaved in a manner that he could understand. They had quality. But since he had already taken leave of them long ago, the remembrance did not break his heart again. Young Jeff Patton was among them, the Jeff Patton of fifty years ago who went down to New Orleans with a crowd of country boys to the Mardi Gras doings. The gay young crowd, boys with candy-striped shirts and rouged-brown girls in noisy silks, was like a picture in his head. Yet it did not make him sad. On that very trip Slim Burns had killed Joe Beasley—the crowd had been broken up. Since then Jeff Patton's world had been the Greenbriar Plantation. If there had been other Mardi Gras carnivals, he had not heard of them. Since then there had been no time; the years had fallen on him like waves. Now he was old, worn out. Another paralytic stroke (like the one he had already suffered) would put him on his back for keeps. In that condition, with a frail blind woman to look after him, he would be worse off than if he were dead.

Suddenly Jeff's hands became steady. He actually felt brave. He slowed down the motor of the car and carefully pulled off the road. Below, the water of the stream boomed, a soft thunder in the deep channel. Jeff ran the car onto the clay slope, pointed it directly toward the stream and put his foot heavily on the accelerator. The little car leaped furiously down the steep incline toward the water. The movement was nearly as swift and direct as a fall. The two old black folks, sitting quietly side by side, showed no excitement. In another instant the car hit the water and dropped immediately out of sight.

A little later it lodged in the mud of a shallow place. One wheel of the crushed and upturned little Ford became visible above the rushing water.

Zora Neale Hurston

ZORA NEALE HURSTON (1903–1960). *African-American anthropologist and writer. Hurston graduated from Barnard College in 1928 with a specialty in anthropological research. Very much a woman before her time, Zora Neale Hurston is now more than ever being recognized and appreciated for the multitalented genius she was. Among her novels, short stories, and anthropological studies are the recently republished* Mules and Men; Their Eyes Were Watching God; Moses, Man of the Mountain; *and* Tell My Horse. *Also reissued are her* Complete Stories.

MY MOST HUMILIATING
JIM CROW EXPERIENCE

My most humiliating Jim Crow experience came in New York instead of the South as one would have expected. It was in 1931 when Mrs. R. Osgood Mason was financing my researches in anthropology. I returned to New York from the Bahama Islands ill with some disturbances of the digestive tract.

Godmother (Mrs. Mason liked for me to call her Godmother) became concerned about my condition and suggested a certain white specialist at her expense. His office was in Brooklyn.

Mr. Paul Chapin called up and made the appointment for me. The doctor told the wealthy and prominent Paul Chapin that I would get the best of care.

So two days later I journeyed to Brooklyn to submit myself to the care of the great specialist.

His reception room was more than swanky, with a magnificent hammered copper door and other decor on the same plane as the door.

But his receptionist was obviously embarrassed when I showed up. I mentioned the appointment and got inside the door. She went into the private office and stayed a few minutes, then the doctor appeared in the door all in white, looking very important, and also very unhappy from behind his rotund stomach.

He did not approach me at all, but told one of his nurses to take me into a private examination room.

The room was private all right, but I would not rate it highly as an examination room. Under any other circumstances, I would have sworn it was a closet where the soiled towels and uniforms were tossed until called for by the laundry. But I will say this for it, there was a chair in there wedged in between the wall and the pile of soiled linen.

The nurse took me in there, closed the door quickly, and disappeared. The doctor came in immediately and began in a desultory manner to ask me about my symptoms. It was evident he meant to get me off the premises as quickly as possible. Being the sort of objective person I am, I did not get up and sweep out angrily as I was first disposed to do. I stayed to see just what would happen, and further to torture him more. He went through some motions, stuck a tube down my throat to extract some bile from my gall bladder, wrote a prescription and asked for twenty dollars as fee.

I got up, set my hat at a reckless angle and walked out, telling him that I would send him a check, which I never did. I went away feeling the pathos of Anglo-Saxon civilization.

And I still mean pathos, for I know that anything with such a false foundation cannot last. Whom the gods would destroy, they first made mad.

PABLO NERUDA

PABLO NERUDA (1904–1973). *Chilean writer of poetry and fiction, social observer, and political leader. Neruda received the Lenin and Stalin Peace Prize in 1953 and the Nobel Prize in Literature in 1971, though he has always been cherished as dearly for the earthy sensuality and eroticism of his love poetry as for his statements of political belief. His works have been translated into many languages and include* Un Canto para Bolívar *(1941),* Alturas de Macchu-Picchu *(1948),* Obras Completas *(1957), and* Cien Sonetas de Amor *(1960).*

LARYNX

Now this is it, said Death,
and as far as I could see
Death was looking at me, at me.

This all happened in hospital,
in washed out corridors,
and the doctor peered at me
with periscopic eyes.
He stuck his head in my mouth,
scratched away at my larynx—
perhaps a small seed
of death was stuck there.

At first, I turned into smoke
so that the cindery one
would pass and not recognize me.
I played the fool, I grew thin,
pretended to be simple or transparent—
I wanted to be a cyclist
to pedal out of death's range.

Then rage came over me
and I said, "Death, you bastard,
must you always keep butting in?
Haven't you enough with all those bones?
I'll tell you exactly what I think:

you have no discrimination, you're deaf
and stupid beyond belief.

"Why are you following me?
What do you want with my skeleton?
Why don't you take the miserable one,
the cataleptic, the smart one,
the bitter, the unfaithful, the ruthless,
the murderer, the adulterers,
the two-faced judge,
the deceiving journalist,
tyrants from islands,
those who set fire to mountains,
the chiefs of police,
jailers and burglars?
Why do you have to take me?
What business have I with Heaven?
Hell doesn't suit me—
I feel fine on the earth."

With such internal mutterings
I kept myself going
while the restless doctor
went tramping through my lungs,
from bronchea to bronchea
like a bird from branch to branch.
I couldn't feel my throat;
my mouth was open like the jaws of a suit
    of armor,
and the doctor ran up and down
my larynx on his bicycle,
till, serious and certain,
he looked at me through his telescope
and pried me loose from death.

It wasn't what they had thought.
It wasn't my turn.

If I tell you I suffered a lot,
and really loved the mystery,
that Our Lord and Our Lady
were waiting for me in their oasis,
if I talk of enchantment,
and being eaten up by distress

at not being close to dying,
if I say like a stupid chicken
that I die by not dying,
give me a boot in the butt,
fit punishment for a liar.

TRANSLATED BY ALASTAIR REID

SIR JOHN BETJEMAN

SIR JOHN BETJEMAN (1906–1984). *English poet, journalist, and authority on English architecture. Born in London, Betjeman was educated at Magdalen College of Oxford University. He published many books, including* Collected Poems (1958), *which became extraordinarily popular. A friend of royalty, he was knighted in 1969. He received several honorary degrees during the course of his long career, and in 1972 was named poet laureate of Great Britain.*

BEFORE THE ANAESTHETIC, OR A REAL FRIGHT

Intolerably sad, profound
St Giles's bells are ringing round,
They bring the slanting summer rain
To tap the chestnut boughs again
Whose shadowy cave of rainy leaves
The gusty belfry-song receives.
Intolerably sad and true,
Victorian red and jewel blue,
The mellow bells are ringing round
And charge the evening light with sound,
And I look motionless from bed
On heavy trees and purple red
And hear the midland bricks and tiles
Throw back the bells of stone St Giles,
Bells, ancient now as castle walls,
Now hard and new as pitchpine stalls,
Now full with help from ages past,
Now dull with death and hell at last.
Swing up! and give me hope of life,
Swing down! and plunge the surgeon's knife.
I, breathing for a moment, see
Death wing himself away from me
And think, as on this bed I lie,
Is it extinction when I die?
I move my limbs and use my sight;
Not yet, thank God, not yet the Night.
Oh better far those echoing hells
Half-threatened in the pealing bells

Than that this 'I' should cease to be—
Come quickly, Lord, come quick to me.
St Giles's bells are asking now
'And hast thou known the Lord, hast thou?'
St Giles's bells, they richly ring
'And was that Lord our Christ the King?'
St Giles's bells they hear me call
I never knew the Lord at all.
Oh not in me your Saviour dwells
You ancient, rich St Giles's bells.
Illuminated missals—spires—
Wide screens and decorated quires—
All these I loved, and on my knees
I thanked myself for knowing these
And watched the morning sunlight pass
Through richly stained Victorian glass
And in the colour-shafted air
I, kneeling, thought the Lord was there.
Now, lying in the gathering mist
I know that Lord did not exist;
Now, lest this 'I' should cease to be,
Come, real Lord, come quick to me.
With every gust the chestnut sighs,
With every breath, a mortal dies;
The man who smiled alone, alone,
And went his journey on his own
With 'Will you give my wife this letter,
In case, of course, I don't get better?'
Waits for his coffin lid to close
On waxen head and yellow toes.
Almighty Saviour, had I Faith
There'd be no fight with kindly Death.
Intolerably long and deep
St Giles's bells swing on in sleep:
'But still you go from here alone'
Say all the bells about the Throne.

W. H. AUDEN

W. H. AUDEN (1907–1973). *English poet and dramatist. As a youth, Auden specialized in biology, but by the time he was fifteen he had discovered his vocation as a poet. Earning his living as a schoolmaster, Auden published poetry widely throughout the 1930s; he became known as the leading radical, antifascist poet of that decade, as much of his writing served as social criticism in verse form without ever becoming mere propaganda. In 1939, he left England with the intention of residing permanently in the United States, but spent the latter years of his life in both Kirchstetten, Austria, and New York City. His later verse, collected in* New Year Letter *(1941),* The Age of Anxiety *(1947),* Homage to Clio *(1960), and* About the House *(1965), lost its radical political bent and became overtly Christian. Today, Auden is recognized as one of the major figures in twentieth-century Anglo-American poetry.*

MUSÉE DES BEAUX ARTS

About suffering they were never wrong,
The Old Masters: how well they understood
Its human position; how it takes place
While someone else is eating or opening a window or just walking
    dully along;
How, when the aged are reverently, passionately waiting
For the miraculous birth, there always must be
Children who did not specially want it to happen, skating
On a pond at the edge of the wood:
They never forgot
That even the dreadful martyrdom must run its course
Anyhow in a corner, some untidy spot
Where the dogs go on with their doggy life and the torturer's horse
Scratches its innocent behind on a tree.

In Brueghel's *Icarus,* for instance: how everything turns away
Quite leisurely from the disaster; the ploughman may
Have heard the splash, the forsaken cry,
But for him it was not an important failure; the sun shone
As it had to on the white legs disappearing into the green
Water; and the expensive delicate ship that must have seen
Something amazing, a boy falling out of the sky,
Had somewhere to get to and sailed calmly on.

Landscape with the Fall of Icarus by Pieter Brueghel

In mythology, Icarus and his father, Daedalus, escaped from captivity by flying on wings made of feathers held together with wax. But, ignoring his father's admonitions, the exuberant Icarus flew too near the sun; its heat melted the wax on his wings, and he fell into the ocean and drowned. In Brueghel's painting, Icarus is seen in the right foreground, his "white legs disappearing into the green water."

THE ART OF HEALING

(In Memoriam David Protetch, M.D.)

Most patients believe
dying is something they do,
        not their physician,
        that white-coated sage,
never to be imagined
        naked or married.

Begotten by one,
I should know better. 'Healing,'
        Papa would tell me,
        'is not a science,
but the intuitive art
        of wooing Nature.

Plants, beasts, may react
according to the common
        whim of their species,
        but all humans have
prejudices of their own
        which can't be foreseen.

To some, ill-health is
a way to be important,
        others are stoics,
        a few fanatics,
who won't feel happy until
        they are cut open.'

Warned by him to shun
the sadist, the nod-crafty,
        and the fee-conscious,
        I knew when we met,
I had found a consultant
        who thought as he did,

yourself a victim
of medical engineers
    and their arrogance,
    when they atom-bombed
your sick pituitary
    and over-killed it.

    'Every sickness
is a musical problem,'
    so said Novalis,
    'and every cure
a musical solution':
    You knew that also.

    Not that in my case
you heard any shattering
    discords to resolve:
    to date my organs
still seem pretty sure of their
    self-identity.

    For my small ailments
you, who were mortally sick,
    prescribed with success:
    my major vices,
my mad addictions, you left
    to my own conscience.

    Was it your very
predicament that made me
    sure I could trust you,
    if I were dying,
to say so, not insult me
    with soothing fictions?

    Must diabetics
all contend with a nisus
    to self-destruction?
    One day you told me:
'It is only bad temper
    that keeps me going.'

But neither anger
nor lust are omnipotent,
    nor should we even
    want our friends to be
superhuman. Dear David,
    dead one, rest in peace,

    having been what all
doctors should be, but few are,
    and, even when most
    difficult, condign
of our biassed affection
    and objective praise.

EUDORA WELTY

EUDORA WELTY (1909–). American fiction writer. Although her early ambition was to be a painter, Welty devoted her life to writing after the success of her first book of stories, A Curtain of Green *(1941). She is widely admired as a writer who values and records the richness of her home region (the South, especially Mississippi) and comments perceptively on the inward awareness of the individual. Her collections of stories are many, including* The Wide Net *(1943),* The Golden Apples *(1949),* The Bride of Innisfallen *(1955),* Thirteen Stories *(1965), and* Collected Stories of Eudora Welty *(1980). Welty's recent works include* A Worn Path *(1991) and* The Shoe Bird *(1993).*

A WORN PATH

It was December—a bright frozen day in the early morning. Far out in the country there was an old Negro woman with her head tied in a red rag, coming along a path through the pinewoods. Her name was Phoenix Jackson. She was very old and small and she walked slowly in the dark pine shadows, moving a little from side to side in her steps, with the balanced heaviness and lightness of a pendulum in a grandfather clock. She carried a thin, small cane made from an umbrella, and with this she kept tapping the frozen earth in front of her. This made a grave and persistent noise in the still air, that seemed meditative like the chirping of a solitary little bird.

She wore a dark striped dress reaching down to her shoe tops, and an equally long apron of bleached sugar sacks, with a full pocket: all neat and tidy, but every time she took a step she might have fallen over her shoelaces, which dragged from her unlaced shoes. She looked straight ahead. Her eyes were blue with age. Her skin had a pattern all its own of numberless branching wrinkles and as though a whole little tree stood in the middle of her forehead, but a golden color ran underneath, and the two knobs of her cheeks were illumined by a yellow burning under the dark. Under the red rag her hair came down on her neck in the frailest of ringlets, still black, and with an odor like copper.

Now and then there was a quivering in the thicket. Old Phoenix said, "Out of my way, all you foxes, owls, beetles, jack rabbits, coons and wild animals! . . . Keep out from under these feet, little bobwhites. . . . Keep the big wild hogs out of my path. Don't let none of those come running my direction. I got a long way." Under her small black-freckled hand her cane, limber as a buggy whip, would switch at the brush as if to rouse up any hiding things.

On she went. The woods were deep and still. The sun made the pine needles almost too bright to look at, up where the wind rocked. The cones dropped as light as feathers. Down in the hollow was the mourning dove—it was not too late for him.

The path ran up a hill. "Seem like there is chains about my feet, time I get this far," she said, in the voice of argument old people keep to use with themselves. "Something always take a hold of me on this hill—pleads I should stay."

After she got to the top she turned and gave a full, severe look behind her where she had come. "Up through pines," she said at length. "Now down through oaks."

Her eyes opened their widest, and she started down gently. But before she got to the bottom of the hill a bush caught her dress.

Her fingers were busy and intent, but her skirts were full and long, so that before she could pull them free in one place they were caught in another. It was not possible to allow the dress to tear. "I in the thorny bush," she said. "Thorns, you doing your appointed work. Never want to let folks pass, no sir. Old eyes thought you was a pretty little *green* bush."

Finally, trembling all over, she stood free, and after a moment dared to stoop for her cane.

"Sun so high!" she cried, leaning back and looking, while the thick tears went over her eyes. "The time getting all gone here."

At the foot of this hill was a place where a log was laid across the creek.

"Now comes the trail," said Phoenix.

Putting her right foot out, she mounted the log and shut her eyes. Lifting her skirt, leveling her cane fiercely before her, like a festival figure in some parade, she began to march across. Then she opened her eyes and she was safe on the other side.

"I wasn't as old as I thought," she said.

But she sat down to rest. She spread her skirts on the bank around her and folded her hands over her knees. Up above her was a tree in a pearly cloud of mistletoe. She did not dare to close her eyes, and when a little boy brought her a plate with a slice of marble-cake on it she spoke to him. "That would be acceptable," she said. But when she went to take it there was just her own hand in the air.

So she left that tree, and had to go through a barbed-wire fence. There she had to creep and crawl, spreading her knees and stretching her fingers like a baby trying to climb the steps. But she talked loudly to herself: she could not let her dress be torn now, so late in the day, and she could not pay for having her arm or her leg sawed off if she got caught fast where she was.

At last she was safe through the fence and risen up out in the clearing. Big dead trees, like black men with one arm, were standing in the purple stalks of the withered cotton field. There sat a buzzard.

"Who you watching?"

In the furrow she made her way along.

"Glad this not the season for bulls," she said, looking sideways, "and the good Lord made his snakes to curl up and sleep in the winter. A pleasure I don't see no two-headed snake coming around that tree, where it come once. It took a while to get by him, back in the summer."

She passed through the old cotton and went into a field of dead corn. It whispered and shook and was taller than her head. "Through the maze now," she said, for there was no path.

Then there was something tall, black, and skinny there, moving before her.

At first she took it for a man. It could have been a man dancing in the field. But she stood still and listened, and it did not make a sound. It was as silent as a ghost.

"Ghost," she said sharply, "who be you the ghost of? For I have heard of nary death close by."

But there was no answer—only the ragged dancing in the wind.

She shut her eyes, reached out her hand, and touched a sleeve. She found a coat and inside that an emptiness, cold as ice.

"You scarecrow," she said. Her face lighted. "I ought to be shut up for good," she said with laughter. "My senses is gone. I too old. I the oldest people I ever know. Dance, old scarecrow," she said, "while I dancing with you."

She kicked her foot over the furrow, and with mouth drawn down, shook her head once or twice in a little strutting way. Some husks blew down and whirled in streamers about her skirts.

Then she went on, parting her way from side to side with the cane, through the whispering field. At last she came to the end, to a wagon track where the silver grass blew between the red ruts. The quail were walking around like pullets, seeming all dainty and unseen.

"Walk pretty," she said. "This the easy place. This the easy going."

She followed the track, swaying through the quiet bare fields, through the little strings of trees silver in their dead leaves, past cabins silver from weather, with the doors and windows boarded shut, all like old women under a spell sitting there. "I walking in their sleep," she said, nodding her head vigorously.

In a ravine she went where a spring was silently flowing through a hollow log. Old Phoenix bent and drank. "Sweet-gum makes the water sweet," she said, and drank more. "Nobody know who made this well, for it was here when I was born."

The track crossed a swampy part where the moss hung as white as lace from every limb. "Sleep on, alligators, and blow your bubbles." Then the track went into the road.

Deep, deep the road went down between the high green-colored banks. Overhead the live-oaks met, and it was as dark as a cave.

A black dog with a lolling tongue came up out of the weeds by the ditch. She was meditating, and not ready, and when he came at her she only hit him a little with her cane. Over she went in the ditch, like a little puff of milkweed.

Down there, her sense drifted away. A dream visited her, and she reached her hand up, but nothing reached down and gave her a pull. So she lay there and presently went to talking. "Old woman," she said to herself, "that black dog come up out of the weeds to stall you off, and now there he sitting on his fine tail, smiling at you."

A white man finally came along and found her—a hunter, a young man, with his dog on a chain.

"Well, Granny!" he laughed. "What are you doing there?"

"Lying on my back like a June-bug waiting to be turned over, mister," she said, reaching up her hand.

He lifted her up, gave her a swing in the air, and set her down. "Anything broken, Granny?"

"No sir, them old dead weeds is springy enough," said Phoenix, when she had got her breath. "I thank you for your trouble."

"Where do you live, Granny?" he asked, while the two dogs were growling at each other.

"Away back yonder, sir, behind the ridge. You can't even see it from here."

"On your way home?"

"No sir, I going to town."

"Why, that's too far! That's as far as I walk when I come out myself, and I get something for my trouble." He patted the stuffed bag he carried, and there hung down a little closed claw. It was one of the bob-whites, with its beak hooked bitterly to show it was dead. "Now you go on home, Granny!"

"I bound to go to town, mister," said Phoenix. "The time come around."

He gave another laugh, filling the whole landscape. "I know you old colored people! Wouldn't miss going to town to see Santa Claus!"

But something held old Phoenix very still. The deep lines in her face went into a fierce and different radiation. Without warning, she had seen with her own eyes a flashing nickel fall out of the man's pocket onto the ground.

"How old are you, Granny?" he was saying.

"There is no telling, mister," she said, "no telling."

Then she gave a little cry and clapped her hands and said, "Git on away from here, dog! Look! Look at that dog!" She laughed as if in admiration. "He ain't scared of nobody. He a big black dog." She whispered, "Sic him!"

"Watch me get rid of that cur," said the man. "Sic him, Pete! Sic him!"

Phoenix heard the dogs fighting, and heard the man running and throwing sticks. She even heard a gunshot. But she was slowly bending forward by that time, further and further forward, the lids stretched down over her eyes, as if she were doing this in her sleep. Her chin was lowered almost to her knees. The yellow palm of her hand came out from the fold of her apron. Her fingers slid down and along the ground under the piece of money with the grace and care they would have in lifting an egg from under a setting hen. Then she slowly straightened up, she stood erect, and the nickel was in her apron pocket. A bird flew by. Her lips moved. "God watching me the whole time. I come to stealing."

The man came back, and his own dog panted about them. "Well, I scared him off that time," he said, and then he laughed and lifted his gun and pointed it at Phoenix.

She stood straight and faced him.

"Doesn't the gun scare you?" he said, still pointing it.

"No, sir, I seen plenty go off closer by, in my day, and for less than what I done," she said, holding utterly still.

He smiled, and shouldered the gun. "Well, Granny," he said, "you must be a hundred years old, and scared of nothing. I'd give you a dime if I had any money with me. But you take my advice and stay home, and nothing will happen to you."

"I bound to go on my way, mister," said Phoenix. She inclined her head in the red rag. Then they went in different directions, but she could hear the gun shooting again and again over the hill.

She walked on. The shadows hung from the oak trees to the road like curtains. Then she smelled wood-smoke, and smelled the river, and she saw a steeple and the cabins on their steep steps. Dozens of little black children whirled around her. There ahead was Natchez shining. Bells were ringing. She walked on.

In the paved city it was Christmas time. There were red and green electric lights strung and criss-crossed everywhere, and all turned on in the daytime. Old Phoenix would have been lost if she had not distrusted her eyesight and depended on her feet to know where to take her.

She paused quietly on the sidewalk where people were passing by. A lady came along in the crowd, carrying an armful of red-, green- and silver-wrapped presents; she gave off perfume like the red roses in hot summer, and Phoenix stopped her.

"Please, missy, will you lace up my shoe?" She held up her foot.

"What do you want, Grandma?"

"See my shoe," said Phoenix. "Do all right for out in the country, but wouldn't look right to go in a big building."

"Stand still then, Grandma," said the lady. She put her packages down on the sidewalk beside her and laced and tied both shoes tightly.

"Can't lace 'em with a cane," said Phoenix. "Thank you, missy. I doesn't mind asking a nice lady to tie up my shoe, when I gets out on the street."

Moving slowly and from side to side, she went into the big building, and into a tower of steps, where she walked up and around and around until her feet knew to stop.

She entered a door, and there she saw nailed up on the wall the document that had been stamped with the gold seal and framed in the gold frame, which matched the dream that was hung up in her head.

"Here I be," she said. There was a fixed and ceremonial stiffness over her body.

"A charity case, I suppose," said an attendant who sat at the desk before her.

But Phoenix only looked above her head. There was sweat on her face, the wrinkles in her skin shone like a bright net.

"Speak up, Grandma," the woman said. "What's your name? We must have your history, you know. Have you been here before? What seems to be the trouble with you?"

Old Phoenix only gave a twitch to her face as if a fly were bothering her.

"Are you deaf?" cried the attendant.

But then the nurse came in.

"Oh, that's just old Aunt Phoenix," she said. "She doesn't come for herself—she has a little grandson. She makes these trips just as regular as clockwork. She lives away back off the Old Natchez Trace." She bent down. "Well, Aunt Phoenix, why don't you just take a seat? We won't keep you standing after your long trip." She pointed.

The old woman sat down, bolt upright in the chair.

"Now, how is the boy?" asked the nurse.

Old Phoenix did not speak.

"I said, how is the boy?"

But Phoenix only waited and stared straight ahead, her face very solemn and withdrawn into rigidity.

"Is his throat any better?" asked the nurse. "Aunt Phoenix, don't you hear me? Is your grandson's throat any better since the last time you came for the medicine?"

With her hands on her knees, the old woman waited, silent, erect and motionless, just as if she were in armor.

"You mustn't take up our time this way, Aunt Phoenix," the nurse said. "Tell us quickly about your grandson, and get it over. He isn't dead, is he?"

At last there came a flicker and then a flame of comprehension across her face, and she spoke.

"My grandson. It was my memory had left me. There I sat and forgot why I made my long trip."

"Forgot?" The nurse frowned. "After you came so far?"

Then Phoenix was like an old woman begging a dignified forgiveness for waking up frightened in the night. "I never did go to school, I was too old at the Surrender," she said in a soft voice. "I'm an old woman without an education. It was my memory fail me. My little grandson, he is just the same, and I forgot it in the coming."

"Throat never heals, does it?" said the nurse, speaking in a loud, sure voice to old Phoenix. By now she had a card with something written on it, a little list. "Yes. Swallowed lye. When was it?—January— two–three years ago—"

Phoenix spoke unasked now. "No, missy, he not dead, he just the same. Every little while his throat begin to close up again, and he not able to swallow. He not get his breath. He not able to help himself. So the time come around, and I go on another trip for the soothing medicine."

"All right. The doctor said as long as you came to get it, you could have it," said the nurse. "But it's an obstinate case."

"My little grandson, he sit up there in the house all wrapped up, waiting by himself," Phoenix went on. "We is the only two left in the world. He suffer and it don't seem to put him back at all. He got a sweet look. He going to last. He wear a little patch quilt and peep out holding his mouth open like a little bird. I remembers so plain now. I not going to forget him again, no, the whole enduring time. I could tell him from all the others in creation."

"All right." The nurse was trying to hush her now. She brought her a bottle of medicine. "Charity," she said, making a check mark in a book.

Old Phoenix held the bottle close to her eyes, and then carefully put it into her pocket.

"I thank you," she said.

"It's Christmas time, Grandma," said the attendant. "Could I give you a few pennies out of my purse?"

"Five pennies is a nickel," said Phoenix stiffly.

"Here's a nickel," said the attendant.

Phoenix rose carefully and held out her hand. She received the nickel and then fished the other nickel out of her pocket and laid it beside the new one. She stared at her palm closely, with her head on one side.

Then she gave a tap with her cane on the floor.

"This is what come to me to do," she said. "I going to the store and buy my child a little windmill they sells, made out of paper. He going to find it hard to believe there such a thing in the world. I'll march myself back where he waiting, holding it straight up in this hand."

She lifted her free hand, gave a little nod, turned around, and walked out of the doctor's office. Then her slow step began on the stairs, going down.

JOSEPHINE MILES

JOSEPHINE MILES (1911–1985). *American poet, scholar, and teacher. Born in Chicago, Miles spent most of her professional life at the University of California, Berkeley. She published ten volumes of poetry, culminating in her* Collected Poems.

THE DOCTOR WHO SITS AT THE BEDSIDE OF A RAT

The doctor who sits at the bedside of a rat
    Obtains real answers—a paw twitch,
    An ear tremor, a gain or loss of weight,
    No problem as to which
    Is temper and which is true.
    What a rat feels, he will do.

    Concomitantly then, the doctor who sits
    At the bedside of a rat
    Asks real questions, as befits
    The place, like where did that potassium go, not what
    Do you think of Willie Mays or the weather?
    So rat and doctor may converse together.

SHEEP

Led by Johns Hopkins on a trip through the heart
To the uttermost reaches of the body,
I was disappointed by X-ray and camera
At what was to be found there.

Mostly I missed the green pastures
Which I knew lay on either side of the path,
The running streams of tears in their salty waters,
Their crystal waters, and the steadfast sheep.

Sheep of my heart, where do you nibble,
At the pump of the ventricle, course of the artery,
That you do not look up into the camera
To tell on what you feed?

BARBARA PYM

BARBARA PYM (1913–1980). *English novelist noted for her gentle satire. Quartet in Autumn (1977) is considered her best novel. Other works include* Some Tame Gazelle *(1950),* Jane and Prudence *(1953), and* A Few Green Leaves *(1980).*

Excerpt from A FEW GREEN LEAVES

Monday was always a busy day at the surgery, a rather stark new building next to the village hall. "They"—the patients—had not on the whole been to church the previous day, but they atoned for this by a devout attendance at the place where they expected not so much to worship, though this did come into it for a few, as to receive advice and consultation. You might *talk* to the rector, some would admit doubtfully, but he couldn't give you a prescription. There was nothing in churchgoing to equal that triumphant moment when you came out of the surgery clutching the ritual scrap of paper.

Martin Shrubsole hurried through the waiting-room, head bent, as if he expected to receive a blow. He did not want to recognize any of the patients waiting there, preferring to be taken by surprise, but he noticed two he didn't particularly want to see—the rector's sister, and Miss Lickerish, an elderly village eccentric. Possibly they were waiting to see Dr. Gellibrand, but Martin had not heard him arrive yet so it might be that he would have to see them both.

He went into the surgery, sat down, arranged himself in a receptive, consoling attitude and prepared to interview the patients. Miss Lickerish's file lay on top of the desk so it looked as if she was to be first. He pressed the buzzer and she came in.

"Good morning, Miss Lickerish." He addressed the small bent woman in her knitted cap and ancient smelly tweed coat.

"Good morning, *doctor. . .*" It seemed as if she could hardly allow him his right to the title, but although he was not much over thirty he was as fully qualified as Dr. G. and much more up-to-date in the treatments and drugs he prescribed.

"And how are you today?" he asked tentatively, for, after all, she must be over eighty and there was something about her that did not fit in with the neat rows of meek old people in the hospital where he had developed his interest in geriatrics. Still, everyone knew that people in villages were different. Those bright beady eyes had plenty of life in them and it was perfectly sensible to ask how she did.

"It's these fleas," she said, "and that stops me sleeping. I'd like some of those sleeping pills."

"Well now, we must do something about that," he said briskly. No point in telling her that he didn't just dish out sleeping tablets to anyone who asked for them. No good explaining that if you *would* take hedgehogs into your house you'd get fleas. It wasn't really the kind of problem he expected to have to face on a Monday morning when the patients were more apt to imagine themselves to be suffering from ailments they'd read about in the Sunday papers, but Martin was equal to the challenge. "Let's get rid of those fleas first, shall we?" he said. Health visitor, district nurse, social worker, ordinary village do-gooder, even his own wife Avice—all these could be called in to help, and a note authorizing the purchase of a suitable insect powder might do the trick. "Next, please," he said to himself, pleased at having disposed of Miss Lickerish.

The next three patients were perfectly ordinary and, as it were, satisfactory—a youth with acne, a young married woman with a contraceptive problem, an older man needing to have his blood pressure checked. The fourth person to enter the room, smiling apologetically as if she knew in advance that she was going to waste his time, was the rector's sister, Daphne.

"Good morning, Miss Dagnall," he adopted his most cheerful manner, "and how's the world treating you?" A silly thing to say, as he immediately realized, trotting out the old cliché. "Sit down and let's have a chat," he went on. The doctor needed to relax as much as the patient, even with the consciousness of a full load still slumped in the waiting-room.

Daphne was not exactly sure what, if anything, was the matter with her. She was depressed (or "in a depressed situation"), she longed to get away from the village, from the damp spring of West Oxfordshire, to live in a whitewashed cottage on the shores of the Aegean.

"Do they have cottages there, as we know them?" Martin asked, playing for time. Why on earth didn't she go to Dr. G.? he wondered. She must have been his patient long before he (Martin) came into the practice. He could not know that Daphne had deliberately chosen him because she knew only too well what Dr. G. would say to her. ("We're all getting on a bit—it's been a long winter—very natural to feel a bit under the weather—go and buy yourself a new hat, my dear"—his panacea for most feminine ills, when women hadn't worn hats for years. Such old-fashioned advice and he wouldn't even prescribe suitable tablets.) She hoped for better things from Martin Shrubsole.

"Of course I can't leave my brother," she said. "I suppose that's the trouble, in a way."

"You don't like living at the rectory?" If this were so it was ironical, for the beautiful old grey stone rectory was the one house in the village that he and his wife coveted. *"That's* the house I want," Avice had said.

"It's so big and rambling," Daphne went on hopelessly. "You've no idea how difficult it is to heat."

Avice had pointed out that they hadn't even got night-storage heaters, Martin remembered, just a few paraffin stoves and rather inefficient ones at that. Would they be eligible for some additional heating allowance? he wondered. Probably not, as they were neither of them pensioners yet. Did Miss Dagnall wear warm enough clothes? Was her blouse adequate for this chilly spring day? "Of course I could recommend woollen underwear," he said jokingly, hoping to jolly her out of her depression.

"Don't talk to me about wool," she said. "You know my brother's obsession with local history—now he's discovered that in sixteen-eighty-something people had to be buried in wool."

"You're always lived with your brother?" Martin asked.

"Oh no—only since his wife died, though that's some time ago now. I made a home for him—it seemed the only thing to do, the least I could do, people said."

"What did you do before that?"

"I had a little sort of job, nothing much, a sort of dogsbody in a travel agency. I shared a flat with a woman friend."

Perhaps she was a frustrated lesbian, Martin thought, his mind moving on somewhat conventional modern lines. Women living together in these days might suggest that, but Daphne was, of course, older. He shot a quick glance at her weatherbeaten face and untidy mane of white hair. Perhaps a new hair-do might help her—Martin was that much more up-to-date than Dr. G. and his new hat—but obviously he couldn't suggest it.

"Let's take your B.P., shall we?" he said, falling back on a more conventional treatment. Her arm was thin and dried up, either from Greek sun or approaching age. "You probably ought to put on a bit of weight," he said. "How's your appetite?"

Going out of the surgery, clutching her bit of paper, a prescription for *something*, at least, Daphne felt that Martin, the "new doctor" as he was called in the village, had done her good. He had listened, he had been sympathetic and she felt decidedly better. Much better than she would have felt if she'd gone to Dr. G.—*he* never even bothered to take your blood pressure.

The other surgery was a larger room, superior to the one where Martin Shrubsole officiated, but Dr. Gellibrand still regretted the old days when he had seen patients in the more gracious surroundings of his own home. Now he was cheerfully confirming the pregnancy of a young village woman obviously destined to be the mother of many fine children. She was short and stocky, with massive thighs fully revealed by the unfashionably short skirt she was wearing. It seemed entirely appropriate that Dr. G., now in his late sixties, should deal with the young, while Martin, with his interest in geriatrics, should be responsible for the elderly. Dr. G. did not much like the elderly but he loved the whole idea of life burgeoning and going on. It had been a relief to him to be able to off-load some of his older patients—a young cheerful face, and Martin certainly had that, would do them the world of good. For Dr. G., although well liked and respected in the village, wasn't exactly cheerful-looking—people often said that he looked more like a clergyman than the rector did, but that wasn't surprising because he was the son of a clergyman and his younger brother was the vicar of a London parish.

When the young pregnant woman had gone there was a pause and the receptionist brought in coffee. Dr. G.'s thoughts now were not as much on his patients as on the visit he had paid to his brother at the weekend. "A change is as good as a rest" was one of his favourite sayings and he could always benefit from this himself, getting away occasionally from his bossy wife Christabel. The place where his brother was vicar was seedy and run-down, "immigrants living in tenements," he had thought, somewhat inaccurately, but although the church was not a particularly flourishing one he had been impressed and a little envious of the "show" his brother Harry had put on for High Mass. It reminded him of the days, getting on for fifty years ago now, when he himself had toyed with the idea of taking Holy Orders. He had pictured himself officiating at various festivals of the church, preaching splendid sermons and leading magnificent processions, but had remembered in time all the other duties that went with being a parish priest, not forgetting the innumerable cups of sweet tea and biscuits, as his brother never tired of reminding him. Then, perhaps because he had been christened Luke, he had seen himself as a distinguished physician or surgeon, performing dramatically successful operations, the sort of thing that one now saw on medical television programmes imported from the U.S.A. In the end, of course, it had been general practice, the much-loved physician, the old family doctor, *Dr. Finlay's Casebook* rather than the more highly coloured series . . .

His receptionist was at the door. Had Dr. G. dozed off over his coffee? The next patient was waiting and he had not pressed his buzzer. Brisk and kindly she addressed him, "Are you ready for the next one, Dr. G.? It's Miss Grundy," she added, as if tempting him with some choice dish.

But he knew in advance that Miss Grundy would probably be very much like his other elderly female patients, unmarried women of uncertain age, the sort of patients he was glad to hand over to Martin Shrubsole. The rector's sister appeared to have handed herself over, he thought with satisfaction.

EDWARD LOWBURY

EDWARD LOWBURY (1913–   ). *English physician, microbiologist, and poet. Lowbury has been much honored for his work on hospital infection control and the treatment of burns. Born in London, he earned degrees in physiology and medicine at Oxford University (where he also won the Newdigate Prize for poetry and the Matthew Arnold prize for a critical essay). His poetry has appeared in more than twenty books and pamphlets, most recently* Selected and New Poems (1935–1989). *Now retired from the practice of medicine, Dr. Lowbury lives in Birmingham, England.*

GLAUCOMA

Shadows are creeping in
From a grey perimeter:
My blinkered years begin—

Not blindness, but a smear
On the landscape, where once
The outlines were clear.

I curse this whim of chance
that monkeyed with my sight
and led my steps a dance;

Then think how Milton might
Have cried for joy if his
Perpetual black night

Had given way to this
Imperfect light of mine:
Its touch would be a kiss,

Its taste a heady wine,
While field, flock, herd,
Bloom, human face divine,

Once lost, now disinterred,
Would bring back his lyric youth;
And yet, the last word,—

The dazzling epic truth,
He gleaned by *inner* light.
That memory can soothe

My nerves, as I recite
This catalogue of moans
About my blinkered sight:

I'll give up picking bones.

LEWIS THOMAS

LEWIS THOMAS (1913–1993). *American physician and essayist. Dr. Thomas was a professor, dean, and chairman of pathology departments at several medical schools. He was for many years president of Memorial Sloan-Kettering Cancer Center, and in 1992 he retired from Cornell University Medical Center in New York City, where he served as scholar-in-residence. His many books include* The Lives of a Cell *(which won the National Book Award);* The Medusa and the Snail; Late Night Thoughts on Listening to Mahler's Ninth Symphony; The Youngest Science: Notes of a Medicine Watcher; *and* Et Cetera, Et Cetera, *an exploration of the vagaries of word origins.*

HOUSE CALLS

My father took me along on house calls whenever I was around the house, all through my childhood. He liked company, and I liked watching him and listening to him. This must have started when I was five years old, for I remember riding in the front seat from one house to another, and back and forth from the hospital, when my father and many of the people on the streets were wearing gauze masks; it was the 1918 influenza epidemic.

One of the frequent calls which I found fascinating was at a big house on Sanford Avenue; he never parked the car in front of this house, but usually left it, and me, a block away around the corner. Later, he explained that the patient was a prominent Christian Scientist, a pillar of that church. He could perfectly well have parked in front if there had been a clearer understanding all around of what he was up to, for it was, in its way, faith healing.

I took the greatest interest in his doctor's bag, a miniature black suitcase, fitted inside to hold his stethoscope and various glass bottles and ampules, syringes and needles, and a small metal case for instruments. It smelled of Lysol and ether. All he had in the bag was a handful of things. Morphine was the most important, and the only really indispensable drug in the whole pharmacopoeia. Digitalis was next in value. Insulin had arrived by the time he had been practicing for twenty years, and he had it. Adrenalin was there, in small glass ampules, in case he ran into a case of anaphylactic shock; he never did. As he drove his rounds, he talked about the patients he was seeing.

I'm quite sure my father always hoped I would want to become a doctor, and that must have been part of the reason for taking me along on his visits. But the general drift of his conversation was intended to make clear to me, early on, the aspect of medicine that troubled him most all through his professional life; there were so many people needing help, and so little that he could do for any of them. It was necessary for him to be available, and to make all these calls at their homes, but I was not to have the idea that he could do anything much to change the course of their illnesses. It was important to my father that I understand this; it was a central feature of the profession, and a doctor should not only be prepared for it but be even more prepared to be honest with himself about it.

It was not always easy to be honest, he said. One of his first patients, who had come to see him in his new office when he was an unknown in town, was a man complaining of grossly bloody urine. My father examined him at length, took a sample of the flawed urine, did a few other tests, and found himself without a diagnosis. To buy time enough to read up on the matter, he gave the patient a bottle of Blaud's pills, a popular iron remedy for anemia at the time, and told him to come back to the office in four days. The patient returned on the appointed day jubilant, carrying a flask of crystal-clear urine, totally cured. In the following months my father discovered that his reputation had been made by this therapeutic triumph. The word was out, all over town, that that new doctor, Thomas, had gifts beyond his own knowledge—this last because my father's outraged protests that his Blaud's pills could have had nothing whatever to do with recovery from bloody urine. The man had probably passed a silent kidney stone and that was all there was to it, said my father. But he had already gained the reputation of a healer, and it grew through all the years of his practice, and there was nothing he could do about it.

Even now, twenty-five years after his death, I meet people from time to time who lived once in Flushing, or whose parents lived there, and I hear the same anecdotes about his abilities: children with meningitis or rheumatic fever whose lives had been saved by him, patients with pneumonia who had recovered under his care, even people with incurable endocarditis, overwhelming typhoid fever, peritonitis, what-all.

But the same stories are told about any good, hardworking general practitioner of that day. Patients do get better, some of them anyway, from even the worst diseases; there are very few illnesses, like rabies, that kill all comers. Most of them tend to kill some patients and spare others, and if you are one of the lucky ones and have also had at hand a steady, knowledgeable doctor, you become convinced that the doctor saved you. My father's early instructions to me, sitting in the front of his

Dr. Ernest Ceriani, the only doctor in Kremmling, Colorado, makes his way through an unkempt yard to call on a patient.

car on his rounds, were that I should be careful not to believe this of myself if I became a doctor.

Nevertheless, despite his skepticism, he carried his prescription pad everywhere and wrote voluminous prescriptions for all his patients. These were fantastic formulations, containing five or six different vegetable ingredients, each one requiring careful measuring and weighing by the druggist, who pounded the powder, dissolved it in alcohol, and bottled it with a label giving only the patient's name, the date, and the instructions about dosage. The contents were a deep mystery, and intended to be a mystery. The prescriptions were always written in Latin, to heighten the mystery. The purpose of this kind of therapy was essentially reassurance. A skilled, experienced physician might have dozens of different formulations in his memory, ready for writing out in flawless detail at a moment's notice, but all he could have predicted about them with any certainty were the variations in the degree of bitterness of taste, the color, the smell, and the likely effects of the concentrations of alcohol used as solvent. They were placebos, and they had been the principal mainstay of medicine, the sole technology, for so long a time—millennia—that they had the incantatory power of religious ritual. My father had little faith in the effectiveness of any of them, but he used them daily in his practice. They were expected by his patients; a doctor who did not provide such prescriptions would soon have no practice at all; they did no harm, so far as he could see; if nothing else, they gave the patient something to do while the illness, whatever, was working its way through its appointed course.

The United States Pharmacopoeia, an enormous book, big as the family Bible, stood on a bookshelf in my father's office, along with scores of textbooks and monographs on medicine and surgery. The ingredients that went into the prescriptions, and the recipes for their compounding and administration, were contained in the Pharmacopoeia. There was no mistaking the earnestness of that volume; it was a thousand pages of true belief: this set of ingredients was useful in pulmonary tuberculosis, that one in "acute indigestion" (the term then used for what later turned out to be coronary thrombosis), another in neurasthenia (weak nerves; almost all patients had weak nerves, one time or another), and so on, down through the known catalogue of human ailments. There was a different prescription for every circumstance, often three or four. The most popular and widely used ones were the "tonics," good for bucking up the spirits; these contained the headiest concentrations of alcohol. Opium had been the prime ingredient in the prescriptions of the nineteenth century, edited out when it was realized that great numbers of elderly people, especially "nervous" women, were sitting in their rocking chairs, addicted beyond recall.

The tradition still held when I was a medical student at Harvard. In the outpatient department of the Boston City Hospital, through which hundreds of patients filed each day for renewal of their medications, each doctor's desk had a drawerful of prescriptions already printed out to save time, needing only the doctor's signature. The most popular one, used for patients with chronic, obscure complaints, was *Elixir of I, Q and S,* iron, quinine, and strychnine, each ingredient present in tiny amounts, dissolved in the equivalent of bourbon.

Medicine was subject to recurrent fads in therapy throughout my father's career. Long before his time, homeopathy emerged and still had many devout practitioners during his early years; this complex theory, involving what was believed to be the therapeutic value of "like versus like," and the administration of minuscule quantities of drugs that imitated the symptoms of the illness in question, took hold in the midnineteenth century in reaction against the powerfully toxic drugs then in common use—mercury, arsenic, bismuth, strychnine, aconite, and the like. Patients given the homeopathic drugs felt better and had a better chance of surviving, about the same as they would have had without treatment, and the theory swept the field for many decades.

A new theory, attributing all human disease to the absorption of toxins from the lower intestinal tract, achieved high fashion in the first decade of this century. "Autointoxication" became the fundamental disorder to be overcome by treatment, and the strongest measures were introduced to empty the large bowel and keep it empty. Cathartics, ingenious variations of the enema, and other devices for stimulating peristalsis took over medical therapy. My father, under persuasion by a detail man from one of the medical supply houses, purchased one of these in 1912, a round lead object the size of a bowling ball, encased in leather. This was to be loaned to the patient, who was instructed to lie flat in bed several times daily and roll it clockwise around the abdomen, following the course of the colon. My father tried it for a short while on a few patients, with discouraging results, and one day placed it atop a cigar box which he had equipped with wheels and a long string, and presented it to my eldest sister, who tugged it with pleasure around the corner to a neighbor's house. That was the last he saw of the ball until twelve years later, when the local newspaper announced in banner headlines that a Revolutionary War cannon ball had been discovered in the excavated garden behind our neighbor's yard. The ball was displayed for public view on the neighbor's mantel, to the mystification of visiting historians, who were unable to figure out the trajectory from any of the known engagements of the British or American forces; several learned papers were written on the problem. My father claimed privately to his family, swearing us to secrecy, that he had, in an indirect sense anyway, made medical history.

So far as I know, he was never caught up again by medical theory. He did not believe in focal infections when this notion appeared in the 1920s, and must have lost a lucrative practice by not removing normal tonsils, appendixes, and gallbladders. When the time for psychosomatic disease arrived, he remained a skeptic. He indulged my mother by endorsing her administration of cod-liver oil to the whole family, excepting himself, and even allowed her to give us something for our nerves called Eskay's Neurophosphates, which arrived as samples from one of the pharmaceutical houses. But he never convinced himself about the value of medicine.

His long disenchantment with medical therapy was gradually replaced by an interest in surgery, for which he found himself endowed with a special talent. At last, when he was in his early fifties, he decided to give up general practice and concentrate exclusively on surgery. He was very good at it, and his innate skepticism made him uniquely successful as a surgical consultant. Years later, after his death, I was told by some of his younger colleagues that his opinion was especially valued, and widely sought throughout the county, because of his known reluctance to operate on a patient until he was entirely convinced that the operation was absolutely necessary. His income must have suffered because of this, but his reputation was solidly established.

LEECH LEECH, ET CETERA

A few years ago, I blundered into the fringes of a marvelous field of scholarship, comparative philology. I wondered—I forget the occasion—why leech was the word for the doctor and at the same time for the worm used by the doctor for so many centuries. Which came first, leech the doctor or leech the worm?

The lovely *American Heritage Dictionary* has a fifty-page appendix of Indo-European roots, based in large part on *Pokorny's Dictionary of Indo-European Languages*. My wife searched New York's bookstores and found a copy of *Pokorny* in a rare-book store for my birthday, and I have never since looked back.

The evolution of language can be compared to the biological evolution of species, depending on how far you are willing to stretch analogies. The first and deepest question is open and unanswerable in both cases: how did life start up at its very beginning? What was the first human speech like?

Fossils exist for both, making it possible to track back to somewhere near the beginning. The earliest forms of life were the prokaryotes, organisms of the same shape and size as bacteria; chains of cocci and bacilli left unmistakable imprints within rocks dating back as far as 3.5 billion years. Similar microorganisms comprised the total life of the planet for the next 2.5 billion years, living free or, more often, gathered together as immense colonies in "algal mats," which later on fossilized into the formidable geological structures known as stromatolites. It was only recently, perhaps a billion years ago, that the prokaryotic algae had pumped enough oxygen into the earth's atmosphere so that nucleated cells could be formed. The mitochondria, which provide oxidative energy for all nucleated cells, and the chloroplasts of plant cells, which engage the sun's energy for producing the planet's food and oxygen, are the lineal descendants of bacteria and blue-green algae, and have lived as symbionts with the rest of us for a billion years.

The fossils of human language are much more recent, of course, and can only be scrutinized by the indirect methods of comparative philology, but they are certainly there. The most familiar ones are the Indo-European roots, prokaryote equivalents, the ancestors of most of the Western and some of the Eastern languages: Sanskrit, Greek, Latin, all the Slavic and Germanic tongues, Hittite, Tocharian, Iranian, Indic, some others, all originating in a common speech more than 20,000 years ago at a very rough guess. The original words from which the languages evolved were probably, at the outset, expressions of simple, non-nucleated ideas, unambiguous etymons.

The two leeches are an example of biological mimicry at work in language. The root for leech the doctor goes back to the start of language: *leg* was a word meaning "to collect, with derivatives meaning to speak" and carried somehow the implication of knowledge and wisdom. It became *laece* in Old English, *lake* in Middle Dutch, with the meaning of doctor. Along the way, in early Germanic, it yielded *lekjaz,* a word meaning "an enchanter, speaking magic words," which would fit well with the duties of early physicians. The doctor was called the leech in English for many centuries, and a Danish doctor is still known as *Laege,* a Swedish one as *Lakere.*

Leg gave spawn to other progeny, different from the doctor but with related meanings. Lecture, logic, and logos are examples to flatter medicine's heart.

Leech the worm is harder to trace. The *OED* has it in tenth-century records as *lyce,* later *laece,* and then the two leeches became, for all practical purposes, the same general idea. Leech the doctor made his living by the use of leech the worm; leech the worm was believed (wrongly, I think) to have had restorative, health-giving gifts and was therefore, in its way, a sort of doctor. The technical term "assimilation" is used for this fusion of words with two different meanings into a single word carrying both. The idea of collecting has perhaps sustained the fusion, persisting inside each usage: blood for the leech, fees (and blood as well) for the doctor. Tax collectors were once called leeches, for the worm meaning, of course.

The word doctor came from *dek,* meaning something proper and acceptable, useful. It became *docere* in Latin, to teach, also *discere,* to learn, hence disciple. In Greek it was understood to mean an acceptable kind of teaching, thus dogma and orthodox. Decorum and decency are cognate words.

Medicine itself emerged from root *med,* which meant something like measuring out, or taking appropriate measures. Latin used *med* to make *mederi,* to look after, to heal. The English words moderate and modest are also descendants of *med,* carrying instructions for medicine long since forgotten; medical students ought to meditate (another cognate) from time to time about these etymological cousins.

The physician came from a wonderful word, one of the master roots in the old language, *bheu,* meaning nature itself, being, existence. *Phusis* was made from this root in Greek, on its way to the English word physic, used for medicine in general, and physics, meaning the study of nature.

Doctor, medicine, and physician, taken together with the cognate words that grew up around them, tell us a great deal about society's ancient expectations from the profession, hard to live up to. Of all the list, moderate and modest seem to me the ones most in need of remembering. The root *med* has tucked itself inside these words, living as a successful symbiont, and its similar existence all these years inside medicine should be a steady message for the teacher, the healer, the collector of science, the old leech.

Medicine was once the most respected of all the professions. Today, when it possesses an array of technologies for treating (or curing) diseases which were simply beyond comprehension a few years ago, medicine is under attack for all sorts of reasons. Doctors, the critics say, are applied scientists, concerned only with the disease at hand but never with the patient as an individual, whole person. They do not really listen. They are unwilling or incapable of explaining things to sick people or their families. They make mistakes in their risky technologies;

hence the rapidly escalating cost of malpractice insurance. They are accessible only in their offices in huge, alarming clinics or within the walls of terrifying hospitals. The word "dehumanizing" is used as an epithet for the way they are trained, and for the way they practice. The old art of medicine has been lost, forgotten.

The American medical schools are under pressure from all sides to bring back the family doctor—the sagacious, avuncular physician who used to make house calls, look after the illnesses of every member of the family, was even able to call the family dog by name. Whole new academic departments have been installed—some of them, in the state-run medical schools, actually legislated into existence—called, in the official catalogues, *Family Practice, Primary Health Care, Preventive Medicine, Primary Medicine*. The avowed intention is to turn out more general practitioners of the type that everyone remembers from childhood or from one's parents' or grandparents' childhood, or from books, movies, and television.

What is it that people have always expected from the doctor? How, indeed, has the profession of medicine survived for so much of human history? Doctors as a class have always been criticized for their deficiencies. Montaigne in his time, Molière in his, and Shaw had less regard for doctors and their medicine than today's critics. What on earth were the patients of physicians in the nineteenth century and the centuries before, all the way back to my professional ancestors, the shamans of prehistory, hoping for when they called for the doctor? In the years of the great plagues, when carts came through the town streets each night to pick up the dead and carry them off for burial, what was the function of the doctor? Bubonic plague, typhus, tuberculosis, and syphilis were representative examples of a great number of rapidly progressive and usually lethal infections, killing off most of the victims no matter what was done by the doctor. What did the man do, when called out at night to visit the sick for whom he had nothing to offer for palliation, much less cure?

Well, one thing he did, early on in history, was plainly magic. The shaman learned his profession the hardest way: he was compelled to go through something like a version of death itself, personally, and when he emerged he was considered qualified to deal with patients. He had epileptic fits, saw visions, and heard voices, lost himself in the wilderness for weeks on end, fell into long stretches of coma, and when he came back to life he was licensed to practice, dancing around the bedside, making smoke, chanting incomprehensibilities, and *touching* the patient everywhere. The touching was the real professional secret, never acknowledged as the central, essential skill, always obscured by the dancing and the chanting, but always busily there, the laying on of hands.

There, I think, is the oldest and most effective act of doctors, the touching. Some people don't like being handled by others, but not, or almost never, sick people. They *need* being touched, and part of the dismay in being very sick is the lack of close human contact. Ordinary people, even close friends, even family members, tend to stay away from the very sick, touching them as infrequently as possible for fear of interfering, or catching the illness, or just for fear of bad luck. The doctor's oldest skill in trade was to place his hands on the patient.

Over the centuries, the skill became more specialized and refined, the hands learned other things to do beyond mere contact. They probed to feel the pulse at the wrist, the tip of the spleen, or the edge of the liver, thumped to elicit resonant or dull sounds over the lungs, spread ointments over the skin, nicked veins for bleeding, but the same time touched, caressed, and at the end held on to the patient's fingers.

Most of the men who practiced this laying on of hands must have possessed, to begin with, the gift of affection. There are, certainly, some people who do not like other people much, and they would have been likely to stay away from an occupation requiring touching. If, by mistake, they found themselves apprenticed for medicine, they probably backed off or, if not, turned into unsuccessful doctors.

Touching with the naked ear was one of the great advances in the history of medicine. Once it was learned that the heart and lungs made sounds of their own, and that the sounds were sometimes useful for diagnosis, physicians placed an ear over the heart, and over areas on the front and back of the chest, and listened. It is hard to imagine a friendlier human gesture, a more intimate signal of personal concern and affection, than these close bowed heads affixed to the skin. The stethoscope was invented in the nineteenth century, vastly enhancing the acoustics of the thorax, but removing the physician a certain distance from his patient. It was the earliest device of many still to come, one new technology after another, designed to increase that distance.

Today, the doctor can perform a great many of his most essential tasks from his office in another building without ever seeing the patient. There are even computer programs for the taking of a history: a clerk can ask the questions and check the boxes on a printed form, and the computer will instantly provide a printout of the diagnostic possibilities to be considered and the laboratory procedures to be undertaken. Instead of spending forty-five minutes listening to the chest and palpating the abdomen, the doctor can sign a slip which sends the patient off to the X-ray department for a CT scan, with the expectation of seeing within the hour, in exquisite detail, all the body's internal organs which he formerly had to make guesses about with his fingers and ears. The biochemistry laboratory eliminates the need for pondering and waiting for the appearance of new signs and symptoms. Computerized devices reveal electronic intimacies of the flawed heart or malfunctioning brain with a precision far beyond the touch or reach, or even the imagining, of the physician at the bedside a few generations back.

The doctor can set himself, if he likes, at a distance, remote from the patient and the family, never touching anyone beyond a perfunctory handshake as the first and only contact. Medicine is no longer the laying on of hands, it is more like the reading of signals from machines.

The mechanization of scientific medicine is here to stay. The new medicine works. It is a vastly more complicated profession, with more things to be done on short notice on which issues of life or death depend. The physician has the same obligations that he carried, over-worked and often despairingly, fifty years ago, but now with any num-ber of technological maneuvers to be undertaken quickly and with precision. It looks to the patient like a different experience from what his parents told him about, with something important left out. The doctor seems less like the close friend and confidant, less interested in him as a person, wholly concerned with treating the disease. And there is no changing this, no going back; nor, when you think about it, is there really any reason for wanting to go back. If I develop the signs and symptoms of malignant hypertension, or cancer of the colon, or sub-acute bacterial endocarditis, I want as much comfort and friendship as I can find at hand, but mostly I want to be treated quickly and effectively so as to survive, if that is possible. If I am in bed in a modern hospital, worrying about the cost of that bed as well, I want to get out as fast as possible, whole if possible.

In my father's time, talking with the patient was the biggest part of medicine, for it was almost all there was to do. The doctor–patient relationship was, for better or worse, a long conversation in which the patient was at the epicenter of concern and knew it. When I was an intern and scientific technology was in its earliest stage, the talk was still there, but hurried, often on the run.

Today, with the advance of medicine's various and complicated new technologies, the ward rounds now at the foot of the bed, the drawing of blood samples for automated assessment of every known (or sug-gested) biochemical abnormality, the rolling of wheelchairs and litters down through the corridors to the X-ray department, there is less time for talking. The longest and most personal conversations held with hospital patients when they come to the hospital are discussions of finances and insurance, engaged in by personnel trained in accountancy, whose scientific instruments are the computers. The hospitalized patient feels, for a time, like a working part of an immense, automated apparatus. He is admitted and discharged by batteries of computers, sometimes without even learning the doctors' names. The difference can be strange and vaguely dismaying for patients. But there is another difference, worth emphasis. Many patients go home speedily, in good health, cured of their diseases. In my father's day this happened much less often, and when it did, it was a matter of good luck or a strong constitution. When it happens today, it is more frequently due to technology.

There are costs to be faced. Not just money, the real and heavy dollar costs. The close-up, reassuring, warm touch of the physician, the comfort and concern, the long, leisurely discussions in which everything including the dog can be worked into the conversation, are disappearing from the practice of medicine, and this may turn out to be too great a loss for the doctor as well as for the patient. This uniquely subtle, personal relationship has roots that go back into the beginnings of medicine's history, and needs preserving. To do it right has never been easy; it takes the best of doctors, the best of friends. Once lost, even for as short a time as one generation, it may be too difficult a task to bring it back again.

If I were a medical student or an intern, just getting ready to begin, I would be more worried about this aspect of my future than anything else. I would be apprehensive that my real job, caring for sick people, might soon be taken away, leaving me with the quite different occupation of looking after machines. I would be trying to figure out ways to keep this from happening.

DYLAN THOMAS

DYLAN THOMAS (1914–1953). *Welsh poet, short-story writer, and playwright. Thomas is acclaimed for his carefully ordered images, which focus on the recurring themes of man, nature, and the love of God. An antic spirit, Thomas was a popular reader of his own (and others') poetry, and much in demand as a lecturer during his short life.*

DO NOT GO GENTLE INTO THAT GOOD NIGHT

Do not go gentle into that good night,
Old age should burn and rave at close of day;
Rage, rage against the dying of the light.

Though wise men at their end know dark is right,
Because their words had forked no lightning they
Do not go gentle into that good night.

Good men, the last wave by, crying how bright
Their frail deeds might have danced in a green bay.
Rage, rage against the dying of the light.

Wild men who caught and sang the sun in flight,
And learn, too late, they grieved it on its way,
Do not go gentle into that good night.

Grave men, near death, who see with blinding sight
Blind eyes could blaze like meteors and be gay,
Rage, rage against the dying of the light.

And you, my father, there on the sad height,
Curse, bless, me now with your fierce tears, I pray.
Do not go gentle into that good night.
Rage, rage against the dying of the light.

RANDALL JARRELL

RANDALL JARRELL (1914–1965). *American poet, critic, and novelist. Born in Nashville, Tennessee, Jarrell served in the Air Force in the Second World War, then taught at a number of universities and was consultant in poetry at the Library of Congress from 1956 to 1958. Jarrell was considered a critic of great integrity for his incisive and lively essays, which are collected in* Poetry and the Age *(1953),* A Sad Heart at the Supermarket *(1962), and* The Third Book of Criticism *(1971). His* Complete Poems *appeared posthumously in 1969.*

NEXT DAY

Moving from Cheer to Joy, from Joy to All,
I take a box
And add it to my wild rice, my Cornish game hens.
The slacked or shorted, basketed, identical
Food-gathering flocks
Are selves I overlook. Wisdom, said William James,

Is learning what to overlook. And I am wise
If that is wisdom.
Yet somehow, as I buy All from these shelves
And the boy takes it to my station wagon,
What I've become
Troubles me even if I shut my eyes.

When I was young and miserable and pretty
And poor, I'd wish
What all girls wish: to have a husband,
A house and children. Now that I'm old, my wish
Is womanish:
That the boy putting groceries in my car

See me. It bewilders me he doesn't see me.
For so many years
I was good enough to eat: the world looked at me
And its mouth watered. How often they have undressed me,
The eyes of strangers!
And, holding their flesh within my flesh, their vile

162

Imaginings within my imagining,
I too have taken
The chance of life. Now the boy pats my dog
And we start home. Now I am good.
The last mistaken,
Ecstatic, accidental bliss, the blind

Happiness that, bursting, leaves upon the palm
Some soap and water—
It was so long ago, back in some Gay
Twenties, Nineties, I don't know . . . Today I miss
My lovely daughter
Away at school, my sons away at school,

My husband away at work—I wish for them.
The dog, the maid,
And I go through the sure unvarying days
At home in them. As I look at my life,
I am afraid
Only that it will change, as I am changing:

I am afraid, this morning, of my face.
It looks at me
From the rear-view mirror, with the eyes I hate,
The smile I hate. Its plain, lined look
Of gray discovery
Repeats to me: "You're old." That's all, I'm old.

And yet I'm afraid, as I was at the funeral
I went to yesterday,
My friend's cold made-up face, granite among its flowers,
Her undressed, operated-on, dressed body
Were my face and body.
As I think of her I hear her telling me

How young I seem; I *am* exceptional;
I think of all I have.
But really no one is exceptional,
No one has anything, I'm anybody,
I stand beside my grave
Confused with my life, that is commonplace and solitary.

JOHN CIARDI

JOHN CIARDI (1916–1986). *American poet, essayist, translator, lexicographer, teacher, and lecturer. Ciardi wrote and edited several dozen books, including splendid poetry for both adults and children* (Selected Poems *for adults;* I Met a Man *and* Fast and Slow *for children). His was the standard translation of Dante's* Divine Comedy. *For many years he was the poetry editor and a columnist and essayist for* The Saturday Review. *For nineteen years, he also served as director of the Bread Loaf Writers' Conference in Vermont, which continues as a vital center for American letters.*

WASHING YOUR FEET

Washing your feet is hard when you get fat.
* * *
In lither times the act was unstrained and pleasurable.
* * *
You spread the toes for signs of athlete's foot.
* * *
You used creams, and rubbing alcohol, and you powdered.
* * *
You bent over, all in order, and did everything.
* * *
Mary Magdalene made a prayer meeting of it.
* * *
She, of course, was washing not her feet but God's.
* * *
Degas painted ladies washing their own feet.
* * *
Somehow they also seem to be washing God's feet.
* * *
To touch any body anywhere should be ritual.
* * *
To touch one's own body anywhere should be ritual.
* * *
Fat makes the ritual wheezy and a bit ridiculous.
* * *
Ritual and its idea should breathe easy.
* * *
They are memorial, meditative, immortal.
* * *
Toenails keep growing after one is dead.
* * *
Washing my feet, I think of immortal toenails.
* * *
What are they doing on these ten crimped polyps?
* * *

I reach to wash them and begin to wheeze.
*   *   *
I wish I could paint like Degas or believe like Mary.
*   *   *
It is sad to be naked and to lack talent.
*   *   *
It is sad to be fat and to have dirty feet.

GWENDOLYN BROOKS

GWENDOLYN BROOKS (1917–   ). *African-American poet and novelist. The author of twenty books of poems, including* In the Mecca *(1964), Brooks was born in Topeka, Kansas, and grew up in Chicago, where she has lived most of her life. She was thirteen when her first poem was published, and she went on to become the first African-American woman to be awarded a Pulitzer Prize, in 1950, for her collection of poems* Annie Allen. *Since then, she has become widely recognized as one of the preeminent poets of this century. She is a writer-in-residence at Chicago State University, and has received innumerable awards; most recently, she was named the 1994 Jefferson Lecturer (this is the highest honor bestowed by the federal government for intellectual achievement in the humanities) and won the 1994 National Book Foundation medal for distinguished contribution to American letters. She holds more than seventy honorary doctorates.*

THE BEAN EATERS

They eat beans mostly, this old yellow pair.
Dinner is a casual affair.
Plain chipware on a plain and creaking wood,
Tin flatware.

Two who are Mostly Good.
Two who have lived their day,
But keep on putting on their clothes
And putting things away.

And remembering . . .
Remembering, with twinklings and twinges,
As they lean over the beans in their
   rented back room that is full of beads and
   receipts and dolls and cloths, tobacco
   crumbs, vases and fringes.

DORIS GRUMBACH

DORIS GRUMBACH (1918–   ). *American novelist and memoirist. Grumbach's novels include* The Magician's Girl *(1987),* Chamber Music *(1980),* The Ladies *(1985), and* The Missing Person *(1993). The following selection is from her memoir* Coming into the End Zone *(1991), an intensely personal account of the year following her seventieth birthday, during which she is "haunted by death in the daily reminders of her own diminishing vitality" despite a full, active existence spent writing fiction, reviewing books, and traveling. Her two most recent works—*Extra Innings *(1993) and* Fifty Days of Solitude *(1994)—pick up where* End Zone *leaves off, with a move from Washington, D.C., to a secluded farmhouse in Maine in her seventy-fourth year, and the rediscovery of her artistry during seven weeks spent alone during a harsh Maine winter.*

COMING INTO THE END ZONE

It is eccentric and inaccurate to claim that the July of my seventieth birthday is a landmark in my life. Surely there were other important Julys scattered throughout those many years. For instance, that month of my fifth year when I realized I had to go to school in September. It was a prospect I dreaded, believing in my heart that I was already sufficiently educated by Central Park, by the books I had read since I was three and a half, and by the disruptive arrival that year of a baby sister who taught me terrible lessons in displacement, resentment, hatred.

In the July of my twentieth year after I had graduated from college, I ignored the event because I was in a state of shock. During the May that preceded it, my friend and classmate John Ricksecker had jumped from the roof of the School of Commerce at New York University, ending his troubled life and my innocence about how good life was and how hopeful our future. It was May 1939, a few months before Hitler marched into Poland. Was he determined not to be made to go to war? I never knew why he chose to jump, or whether he did. For he said as he was dying that he "climbed up and fell." I have always mourned him and felt responsible for his death. As a woman not liable to be "called up," I was overwhelmed by the unfairness of the draft, making me realize the destructive power of sexual inequities and the injustice of death.

There was the July two years later after I married in May. I began to see that legal unions did not solve problems of inner turmoil and loneliness. . . . The Julys in my middle years after two of my children were born and I began to have serious doubts about my capacity for motherhood. The July I lay in bed in a tiny room in a country house, afflicted with viral pneumonia, listening to the sounds of husband and children downstairs, and wondering how to escape from everything and everyone I knew.

My sixtieth July was terrible. I remembered, as though I had been struck a blow, that my mother had died at fifty-nine. Somehow, to have exceeded her life span by a year seemed to me a terrible betrayal. It was worse than the guilt that choked me later at the thought of having lived eighteen years longer than the little sister I had once hoped would disappear from her crib during the night, stolen by an evil fairy, or dead at the hand of a careless Fräulein.

At sixty-five I must have been resigned to aging and death: I can remember no raging against the night, no anger about what Yeats described as "decrepit age that has been tied to me / As to a dog's tail."

But seventy. This is different. The month at seventy seems disastrous, so without redeeming moments that, in despair, I am taking notes, hoping to find in the recording process a positive value to living so long, some glory to survival, even vainglory if true glory is impossible.

The terrible Twelfth goes on. I invite Peggy, our host, to share May Sarton's gift of champagne with us. Friends from up the road, Ted Nowick and Bob Taylor, will come too. I suddenly think: A more suitable way to celebrate this dread event would be alone, not in society. I ought to let go of the cheerful illusions of company and surrender to the true state of old age, remembering Virginia Woolf's conviction that at bottom we are all alone and lonely.

The sun moves to the other side of the house. I go in to change to slacks and a shirt with sleeves. In the process I do an unusual thing. I look skeptically, exploringly, at my body in the floor-length mirror. In my young years I remember that I enjoyed feeling the firmness of my arms and legs, neck and fingers, chin and breasts. Once the result of such examinations was less reassuring I stopped doing it. Thereafter, I never resorted to a mirror, believing it would be better not to know the truth about change and decline. In my memory of my body nothing had changed.

Now I look, hard. I see the pull of gravity on the soft tissues of my breasts and buttocks. I see the heavy rings that encircle my neck like Ubangi jewelry. I notice bones that seem to have thinned and shrunk.

Muscles appear to be watered down. The walls of my abdomen, like Jericho, have softened and now press outward. There is nothing lovely about the sight of me. I have been taught that firm and unlined is beautiful. Shall I try to learn to love what I am left with? I wonder. It would be easier to resolve never again to look into a full-length mirror.

October 10. I put down this date, although my habit in journals is not to do so. If something is worth recording, I have always thought, it ought to be general enough to be free of dull, diurnal notation. But this day:

I take the very early Metroliner (six-fifty, an unusual hour for me to take a train) to New York for a meeting of the board of the National Book Critics Circle, a group I have belonged to for many years. A law has been passed that, I believe, makes this the last year of my term, so I am determined to attend every meeting, despite the cost of travel. We are reimbursed only for the two last meetings in the year if we do not serve an institution that pays our way. National Public Radio does not do this for me.

We talk about NBCC business and possible recommendations of books deserving of nomination for an award. It is always fun to meet with other critics and editors. We hole up on the third floor of the Algonquin Hotel, and argue, insult each other pleasantly by challenging the validity of views different from our own, eat a buffet lunch together as we work, and take notes on books of interest we have missed and ought now to read.

At four o'clock the meeting is over. I planned to meet my daughter Jane at the public library for a cocktail party a publisher is giving to celebrate the appearance of the first volume of T. S. Eliot's letters. I need coffee, as I always do between events. Caffeine acts as oil with which to shift gears, sustenance for my flagging spirits. Flagging: Why is that adjective always used for spirits? The *Oxford English Dictionary* informs me that the usage is three hundred years old and first referred to falling down through feebleness. It then was used for the heart, then the circulation. Matthew Arnold was the first to speak of "a spiritual flagging." I buy coffee in a plastic cup and carry it to the benches on Forty-fourth Street and Sixth Avenue (now called, grandly, the Avenue of the Americas, but in my youth known simply by its common number).

While I drink I watch a street lady eating a hot dog on a roll. Behind her and across Sixth Avenue is the store from which her food must have come. There is a huge sign over the door that reads: AMERICA'S 24 HOUR HOST. STEAK'N'EGGS. She converses with herself between bites in a loud, harsh voice and shakes her head at what I assume are the answers she hears in the air.

Her hair is composed of switches pinned, it seems, to a wig base, and at the top there is a great heavy bun. Her eyebrows are crusted and red, the same flush that covers her light-brown skin and culminates in an angry red ball at the end of her nose. Her body is very thin under a coat composed, like her hair, of parts that are pinned together, but her thinness disappears at her neck, which is full of thick folds of skin, like the necklaces African women wear to elongate their necks for beauty.

She finishes her hot dog, rises slowly, and walks to the trash container near the door to the office building. She moves as if her steps were painful. Her face suggests misery and resentment, as though the weight of all the bunches of cloth tacked on to her were depressing her spirits. She returns to her bench. Her profile is Flemish: the long, thin nose, the chin that falls away, a large black mole on her cheek. She wipes her mouth and her nose on her fingers and then puts them in her mouth. I shudder.

I finish my coffee, stand up to walk to the trash container, and, inexplicably, fall on my face. There is pain in my right ankle that turned and caused me to fall, and greater pain in my left shoulder, so intense that I cannot get up. I lie there, seeing two sets of feet in well-shined shoes pass me by without breaking stride. I try to think of a strategy that will get me on my feet, but without the use of my left arm and hand nothing works.

Then I see a brown hand near my face and hear the street lady's rough voice say: "Here. Hold on here."

I do as she says, doubling my arm against hers and gripping her loose flesh as she holds mine. She pulls hard. I hold tight, I am up, dizzy. She puts her arm around my shoulders and puts me down on the bench. She sits beside me.

The next hour I remember with disbelief. The street lady, Nancy, and I talked about her life while she inquired about my pain and dizziness and advised me about therapy. "Don't get up yet," she said, "or you'll conk out." I think about finding a telephone to tell my daughter, who might still be at work at the Ballet Society, to meet me here instead of in front of the library. Is there a telephone in this office building? I ask her. "Yes," she says, "but whatever you do don't use it. The AT and T puts devils on the wires and they get into your ears." I give up my idea of calling Jane for fear of offending Nancy.

She tells me that she has money to buy a winter coat but storekeepers won't let her try their coats on. Silently I determine to come back and find her, take her to a store for a coat, try it on, and then let her buy it. She tells me she went through high school, took an "industrial" course, got a good job, married, had a daughter who lives now in another part of the city. "She never comes by to see me. I don't know her address."

In the same year she lost both her husband and her job "and never could get ahead again." She shares a room in a welfare hotel on Forty-sixth Street with three other women; they sleep in one bed in shifts. In warm weather she prefers to bed down in the doorways of her street, where the mattress devils can't get at her. And the evil spirits in the pillows. "But I like to have an address. Welfare checks come to me there. So I have some little to get by on," she tells me.

"Winter is worst," she says. "Even now, in October, it's too cold." Her parents came from Haiti, she says with some pride. Her mother told her she never was warm once she got here. "But she saw I went to high school and then she died from her lungs and I married a bum, a devil."

Five-thirty. I get up with difficulty. "I'll walk with you," she says, but I say no. I can make it now. I thank her and give her a hug and tell her I hope to get back to New York soon and then I will look her up at her hotel. She says, "Oh yeah. Watch out for that devil at the front door. She's into voodoo and hexing." I say I will, and limp down Forty-second Street to find an Ace bandage for my swollen ankle.

My daughter takes me to her apartment and then, this morning, to the ballet's orthopedic fellow. He says my shoulder is broken, gives me pills and a sling and a warning to do therapeutic exercises after a week or else suffer permanent stiffness. I resolve to do as he says. But already, in all the night's pain and the next day's scurry to be relieved by a doctor and medicine, the memory of Nancy seems less distinct. Will I look her up if I come to New York at the end of the month for the ballet's trip to Paris? Probably not, knowing how such resolves usually end for me.

Yesterday I sat in the waiting room of the physician who is taking care of my slowly healing shoulder. Around me are elderly patients with casts on ankles, arms, necks, a few in wheelchairs accompanied by exasperated-looking middle-aged children. There is a look I have grown to recognize on the faces of captive offspring caring for parents they have long since ceased to love.

A white-gowned young blond woman with the high, structured hairdo called a beehive appears at the door of the waiting room and says:

"We're ready for you now, Lucy."

One of the annoyed-looking men stands up and wheels "Lucy,"

who is clearly over eighty, through the door. He is carrying the pink slips that indicate "Lucy" is a first-time patient.

I am in my customary state of fury. How dare that receptionist, surely not more than twenty years old, address the elderly woman by her first name. She has never met her before, knows nothing about her except that she is old, and sick. *Lucy!*

I sit there fuming, remembering a visit I made a few years ago to a nursing home on Wisconsin Avenue in Washington. My acquaintance, a professor emeritus of English literature, had broken her hip, and was here to recuperate. We talked for a while, about the study of Whitman by Paul Zweig she had been reading, about the new Marguerite Yourcenar I was reviewing. Then a young woman in white carrying a pail and mop came into the room, smiled brightly to the professor (whose doctoral work had been done, as I recall, at Oxford), and said:

"Hiya, Eda Lou. Don't mind me. I'll be out in a minute."

Professor Morton shut her eyes.

"That's a good girl. Don't need to watch while I clean."

I said: "She is Dr. Morton, not Eda Lou."

But the young woman, engrossed in her task, which took her through the middle of the professor's room but under nothing, seemed not to hear me. She finished quickly while I sat stonily and the professor lay with her eyes closed as if waiting for the final assault. It came as the young woman went out the door, calling behind her:

"Be good, Eda Lou. See ya tomorra."

Let neither the peculiar quality of anything nor its value escape you. The peculiar quality of this encounter has stayed with me, sensitizing me to the indignity, in hospitals and nursing homes and waiting rooms, of reducing the elderly sick to children, ignoring the respect due their years and accomplishments, and the dignity of their adult titles or married names.

My turn comes for the orthopedic surgeon's attention.

"Ready for you now, Doris," the woman with the beehive head says, the same bright smile on her face as the cleaning woman had in the nursing home, displaying her affected charm and familiarity with the patient.

This time I am ready. I do not move.

"Doris?" the young woman says, somewhat louder, suggesting by her tone that I, the only woman left in the room, must be deaf.

Aha, I think, I have her. She comes toward me, by now convinced I must be both deaf and, as we used to say, dumb.

"DORIS?" she shouts almost in my ear.

I stand up, forcing her to step back.

"Miss," I say, "I am Mrs. Grumbach. A stranger to you. About fifty years older than you, I would guess. Don't call me by my first name. What is *your* name, by the way?"

"Susan, er, I mean, Miss Lewis."

To her credit, she blushes furiously, apologizes, and follows me into the doctor's office. "Please be seated, Mrs. Grumbach," she says. "Dr. Moore will be with you in a moment."

"Thank you, Miss Lewis," I say. The war, of course, is still to be waged, but I have won this small skirmish. As it turns out, my shoulder appears to be better. Probably because the weight of my indignation has been lifted from it.

I need new batteries for my hearing aids. They are tiny things, little curls the size of infant snails. Last year I was made to face my loss of hearing, which had clearly begun to annoy Sybil, my dear friend and housemate of many years, and others to whom I turned an almost deaf ear—indeed, ears. But the compelling force to acquire two disturbing, overmagnifying instruments was my realization that the music I heard so clearly in my head (and could remember well although I could not sing it) was not what I was actually hearing, hard as I tried to listen more intently to records and tapes, the radio and television.

When I was young I made sure I heard everything, listened in on every conversation, as though widening my sphere of sound would permit me entry into the larger world. "I have heard that . . ." was a customary start to my sentences, and "Have you heard that . . . ?" another. I relied heavily on what I heard in order to fill my conversation and the page.

Losing a good part of my hearing reduced my avidity. Now I am grateful for hearing less, being left alone with my own silences, away from the raucous world of unnecessary talk, loud machines, the shrill chatter of cicadas in our American elm tree, the unending peeps of baby sparrows that nest under the air conditioner outside the bedroom window, the terrified nightmare screams of the neighbor's child through our wall at three o'clock in the morning.

I acquired hearing aids for use in public places—speeches in large auditoriums, classes, workshops, restaurants, theaters, concerts, and other such places. But I find I wear them less and less, preferring not to listen to the conclusions of most speeches, the sounds of dishes at a distant waiter's station, and the confidences exchanged at a nearby table. At some plays it is a comfortable kind of literary criticism to turn the little buttons off so I hear less of the inane dialogue being exchanged by unbelievable characters in a dull and unconvincing situation.

*   *   *

July 12, 1989: No longer am I burdened by the weight of my years. My new age today, a year later, does not worry me. Alone for most of the day, until the promise of dinner with friends tonight, I went for a swim in the cove (outside our house in Sargentville, Maine), conquering its temperature (sixty degrees) by thinking it was not as cold as I expected it to be.

Nor is this day as painful as I thought it might be. I seem not to have grown older in the year, but more content with whatever age it is I am. I accept the addition, hardly noticing it. There may well be the enduring challenge of the 365 steps up the face of the Temple of the Dwarf at Chichén Itzá, but the certainty that I shall never again climb them no longer disturbs me.

O'Henry's last words are said to have been: "Turn up the lights—I don't want to go home in the dark." I've begun to try to turn up the lights on what remains of my life.

Waiting on the deck for Ted, Bob, and Peggy to take me to a birthday dinner, I watch my unknown neighbor bring his sailboat to anchor in the cove, furl and wrap his sails, and stand for a moment in the prow looking out to the reach. The light is dimming, the water flattens out from gray to dark-blue calm, the sun sets, coloring the sky like an obscured klieg light, out of my sight.

Now I shall sail by the ash breeze, standing still on the deck.

Living in this beautiful place, I look forward to the solitude it affords me, and to friends to break it with. At the end of the day I shall welcome them to share my board and my luck. Who knows, I may be entertaining angels.

Unlike Anna Pavlova, I have no immediate use for a swan costume. I am ready to begin the end.

ANATOLE BROYARD

ANATOLE BROYARD (1920–1990). *American editor, literary critic, and essayist. Anatole Broyard grew up in Brooklyn and attended the New School for Social Research. After serving in World War II, he taught fiction writing at Columbia and New York University and began his forty-year career writing reviews for* The New York Times. *Broyard is celebrated for his brilliant, penetrating observations on life, art, and culture in New York City in such works as* Kafka Was the Rage: A Greenwich Village Memoir *(republished in 1993), but he is most famous for* Intoxicated by My Illness: And Other Writings of Life and Mortality *(1992), a courageous autobiographical collection of essays on the subject of his illness (prostate cancer).*

DOCTOR, TALK TO ME

When, in the summer of 1989, I moved from Connecticut to Cambridge, Massachusetts, I found that I had difficulty urinating. I was like Portnoy, in *Portnoy's Complaint,* who couldn't fornicate in Israel. I had always wanted to live in Cambridge, and the thought passed through my mind that I couldn't urinate because—like Israel for Portnoy—Cambridge was a transcendent place for me.

When my inhibition persisted, I began to think about a doctor, and I set about finding one in the superstitious manner most of us fall back on: I asked a couple I knew for a recommendation. To be recommended, for whatever unreasonable reasons, gives a doctor an aura, a history, a shred of magic. Though I thought of my disorder as a simple matter—prostatitis is common in men of my age—I still wanted a potent doctor.

I applied to this particular couple for a recommendation because they are the two most critical people I know: critics of philosophy, politics, history, literature, drama, music. They are the sort of people for whom information is a religion, and the rigor of their conversation is legendary. To talk with them is an ordeal, a fatigue of fine distinctions, and I wanted a doctor who had survived such a scrutiny.

They could only give me the name of their internist, who referred me to a urologist. The recommendation was diluted, but it was better than none, so I made an appointment to see the urologist in a local hospital. The visit began well. The secretary was attractive, efficient, and alert. She remembered my name. I was shown into a pleasant office and told that the doctor would be with me in a few minutes.

While I waited, I subjected the doctor to a preliminary semiotic scrutiny. Sitting in his office, I read his signs. The diplomas I took for granted; what interested me was the fact that the room was furnished with taste. There were well-made, well-filled bookcases, an antique desk and chairs, a reasonable Oriental rug on the floor. A large window opened one wall of the office to the panorama of Boston, and this suggested status, an earned respect. I imagined the doctor taking the long view out of his window.

On the walls and desk were pictures of three healthy-looking, conspicuously happy children, photographed in a prosperous outdoor setting of lawn, flowers and trees. As I remember, one of the photographs showed a sailboat. From the evidence, their father knew how to live—and by extension, how to look after the lives of others.

Soon the doctor came in and introduced himself. "Let's go into my office," he said, and I realized that I had been waiting among someone else's effects. I felt that I had been tricked. Having already warmed myself to the first doctor, I was obliged to follow this second man, this impostor, into another office, which turned out to be modern and anonymous. There were no antiques, no Oriental rug, and no pictures that I could see.

From the beginning, I had a negative feeling about this doctor. He didn't seem intense enough or determined enough to prevail over something powerful and demonic like illness. He had a pink, soft face and blue eyes, and his manner was hearty and vague at the same time, polite where politeness was irrelevant. He reminded me of a salesman with nothing to sell but his inoffensiveness.

I didn't like the way he spoke: it struck me as deliberately deliberate, a man fixed in a pose, playing doctor. There was no sign of a tragic sense of life in him that I could see, no furious desire to oppose himself to fate. I realized, of course, that what I was looking for was extravagant, that I was demanding nothing less than an ideal doctor, yet isn't that what we all want?

In the end, it didn't matter whether my reading of this particular man was just or unjust—I simply couldn't warm up to him. Choosing a doctor is difficult because it is our first explicit confrontation of our illness. "How good is this man?" is simply the reverse of "How bad am I?" To be sick brings out all our prejudices and primitive feelings. Like fear, or love, it makes us a little crazy. Yet the craziness of the patient is part of his condition.

I was also aware of a certain predisposition in myself in favor of Jewish doctors. I thought of them as the trouble-shooters—the physicians, lawyers, brokers, arbiters, and artists—of contemporary life. History had convinced them that life was a disease. My father, who was an old-fashioned Southern anti-Semite, insisted on a Jewish doctor when he developed cancer of the bladder. A Jewish doctor, he argued, had been bred to medicine. In my father's biblical conception, a Jew's life was a story of study, repair, and reform. A Jewish doctor knew what survival was worth, because he had had to fight for his. Obliged to treat life as a business as well as a pleasure, Jews drove hard bargains. To lose a patient was bad business. In his heart, I think my father believed that a Jewish doctor was closer to God and could use that connection to "Jew down" death.

This other, all-too-human doctor took me into an examining room and felt my prostate. It appeared to me that he had not yet overcome his self-consciousness about this procedure. Back in his office, he summed up his findings. There were hard lumps in my prostate, he said, which suggested tumors, and these "mandated" further investigation. He used the word "mandate" twice in his summary, as well as the word "significantly."

But he was the only urologist I knew in Cambridge, and so, a few days later, I allowed him to perform a cystoscopy, a procedure in which a small scope was inserted through my urethra up to my prostate and bladder. During surgical procedures, doctors wear a tight-fitting white cap, a sort of skullcap like the one Alan Alda wears in *M*A*S*H*. To this, my doctor had added what looked like a clear plastic shower cap, and the moment I saw him in these two caps, I turned irrevocably against him. He wore them absolutely without inflection or style, with none of the jauntiness that usually comes with long practice. He wore them like an American in France who affects a beret without understanding how to shape or cock it. To my eyes, this doctor simply didn't have the charisma to overcome or assimilate those caps, and that finished him off for me.

I want to point out that this man is in all likelihood an able, even a talented doctor. Certainly, I'm no judge of his medical competence, nor do I mean to criticize it. What turned me against him was what I saw as a lack of style. I realized that I wanted my doctor to have style—which I think of as a dash of magic—as well as medical ability. It was like having a *lucky* doctor. I've described all this—a patient's madness—to show how irrational such transactions are, how far removed from any notion of dispassionate objectivity. To be sick is already to be disordered in your mind as well. Still, this does not necessarily mean that I was wrong to want to change doctors: I was simply listening to my unconscious telling me what I needed.

*   *   *

Now that I know I have cancer of the prostate, the lymph nodes, and part of my skeleton, what *do* I want in a doctor? I would say that I want one who is a close reader of illness and a good critic of medicine. I secretly believe that criticism can wither cancer. Also, I would like a doctor who is not only a talented physician but a bit of a metaphysician too, someone who can treat body and soul. I used to get restless when people talked about soul, but now I know better. Soul is the part of you that you summon up in emergencies. You don't need to be religious to believe in the soul or to have one.

My ideal doctor would be my Virgil, leading me through my purgatory or inferno, pointing out the sights as we go. He would resemble Oliver Sacks, the neurologist who wrote *Awakenings* and *The Man Who Mistook His Wife for a Hat*. I can imagine Dr. Sacks *entering* my condition, looking around at it from the inside like a benevolent landlord with a tenant, trying to see how he could make the premises more livable for me. He would see the genius of my illness. He would mingle his daemon with mine; we would wrestle with my fate together. Inside every patient, there's a poet trying to get out. My ideal doctor would "read" my poetry, my literature. He would see that my sickness has purified me, weakening my worst parts and strengthening the best.

To most physicians, my illness is a routine incident in their rounds, while for me it's the crisis of my life. I would feel better if I had a doctor who at least perceived this incongruity. I don't ask him to love me—in fact, I think the role of love is greatly exaggerated by many writers on illness. Of course you want your family and close friends to love you, but the situation shouldn't become a hunting season for love, or a competition, a desperate kiss before dying. To a critically ill person, love may begin to resemble an anesthetic. In a novel by Joy Williams called *State of Grace,* a character asks: "What can be beyond love? I want to get there." The sick man has got there: he's at a point where what he wants from most people is not love but a spacious, flaring grasp of his situation, what is known now in the literature of illness as "empathetic witnessing." The patient is always on the brink of revelation, and he needs someone who can recognize it when it comes.

Just as I see no reason for my physician to love me, I would not expect him to suffer with me either. On the contrary, what would please me most would be a doctor who *enjoyed* me. I want to be a good story for him, to give him some of my art in exchange for his. If a patient expects a doctor to be interested in him, he ought to try to *be* interesting. When he shows nothing but a greediness for care, nothing but the coarser forms of anxiety, it's only natural for the physician to feel an aversion. There is an etiquette to being sick.

I wouldn't demand a lot of my doctor's time; I just wish he would *brood* on my situation for perhaps five minutes, that he would give me his whole mind just once. I would like to think of him as going through my character, as he goes through my flesh, to get at my illness, for each man is ill in his own way. Proust complained that his physician did not allow for his having read Shakespeare. I have a wistful desire for my relation to my doctor to be beautiful—but I don't know how this can be brought about. Though I see us framed in an epiphany, I can't make out the content.

Just as he orders blood tests and bone scans of my body, I'd like my doctor to scan *me,* to grope for my spirit as well as my prostate. While he inevitably feels superior to me because he is the doctor and I am the patient, I'd like him to know that I feel superior to him too, that he is my patient also and I have my diagnosis of him. There should be a place where our respective superiorities could meet and frolic together.

Since technology deprives me of the intimacy of my illness, makes it not mine but something that belongs to science, I wish my doctor could somehow restore it to me and make it personal again. When my father's father died in the French Quarter of New Orleans sixty years ago, the popularly accepted story was that on a humid night in mid-August, he had eaten a dozen bananas and then taken a cold bath. He was a man of eighty-seven whose life had been a strenuous assertion of his appetites, and this explanation suited him, just as it suited his friends in the French Quarter. It would be more satisfying to me, it would allow me to feel that I *owned* my illness, if my urologist were to say: "You know, you've beat the hell out of this prostate of yours. It looks like a worn-out baseball." Nobody wants an anonymous illness. I'd much rather think that I brought it on myself than that it was a mere accident of nature.

It is only natural for a patient to feel some dismay at the changes brought about in his body by illness, and I wonder whether an innovative doctor—again, like Oliver Sacks—couldn't find a way to reconceptualize this situation. If only the patient could be allowed to see his illness as not so much a *failure* of his body as a natural consumption of it. Any reconciling idea would do. The doctor could say, "You've spent your self unselfishly, like a philanthropist who gives all his money away." If the patient could feel that he has *earned* his illness, that his sickness represents the decadence that follows a great flowering, he might look upon the ruin of his body as tourists look upon the ruins of antiquity. (Of course I'm offering these suggestions playfully, as experiments in thinking about medicine.)

Physicians have been taught in medical school that they must keep the patient at a distance because there isn't time to accommodate his personality, or because if the doctor becomes "involved" in the patient's predicament, the emotional burden will be too great. As I've suggested, it doesn't take much time to make good contact, but beyond that, the emotional burden of *avoiding* the patient may be much harder on the doctor than he imagines. It may be this that sometimes makes him complain of feeling harassed. The patient's unanswered questions will always thunder in his stethoscope. A doctor's job would be so much more interesting and satisfying if he would occasionally let himself plunge into the patient, if he could lose his own fear of falling.

Applying to other friends, following new recommendations, I found another urologist. He's highly regarded in his field, and he inspired such confidence in me that my cancer immediately went into remission. My only regret is that he doesn't talk very much—and when he does, he sounds like everybody else. His brilliance has no voice—at least not when he's with me. There's a paradox here at the heart of medicine, because a doctor, like a writer, must have a voice of his own, something that conveys the timbre, the rhythm, the diction, and the music of his humanity, that compensates us for all the speechless machines. When a doctor makes a difficult diagnosis, it is not his medical knowledge only that determines it, but a voice in his head. Such a diagnosis depends as much on inspiration as art does. Whether he wants to be or not, the doctor is a storyteller, and he can turn our lives into good or bad stories, regardless of the diagnosis. If my doctor would allow me, I would be glad to help him here, to take him on as *my* patient. Perhaps later, when he is older, he'll have learned how to converse. Astute as he is, he doesn't yet understand that all cures are partly "talking cures." Every patient needs mouth-to-mouth resuscitation, for talk is the kiss of life.

Yet it's too easy to accuse the doctor, to blame the absence of natural talk on him. It's also true that some of what the patient asks is ineffable. Even a doctor like Chekhov would be hard put to answer him. For example, I would like to discuss my prostate with my urologist not as a diseased organ but as a philosopher's stone. Every patient invites the doctor to combine the role of the priest, the philosopher, the poet, the scholar. He expects the doctor to evaluate his entire life, like a biographer.

Of course, a physician may reasonably ask: "But what am I supposed to say? All I can tell the patient is the facts, if there are any facts." But this is not quite true. The doctor's answer to his patient is yet to be born. It will come naturally—or at first unnaturally—from the intersecting of the patient's needs with the physician's as yet untried imagination. Just as a mother ushers her child into the world, so the doctor must usher the patient out of the ordinary world into whatever place awaits him. The physician is the patient's only familiar in a foreign country.

To help the doctor reach the patient, and the patient reach the doctor, the mood of the hospital might have to be modified. It might be less like a laboratory and more like a theater, which would be only fitting, since no place contains more drama. The laboratory atmosphere can probably be traced back to the idea of asepsis, to the avoidance of contagion. Originally, the patient was protected by the sterility of the hospital. Only the sterility went too far: It sterilized the doctor's thinking. It sterilized the patient's entire experience in the hospital. It sterilized the very notion of illness to the point where we can't bring our soiled thoughts to bear on it. But the sick man needs the contagion of life.

Not every patient can be saved, but his illness may be eased by the way the doctor responds to him—and in responding to him, the doctor may save himself. But first he must become a student again; he has to dissect the cadaver of his professional persona; he must see that his silence and neutrality are *unnatural*. It may be necessary to give up some of his authority in exchange for his humanity, but as the old family doctors knew, this is not a bad bargain. In learning to talk to his patients, the doctor may talk himself back into loving his work. He has little to lose and much to gain by letting the sick man into his heart. If he does, they can share, as few others can, the wonder, terror, and exaltation of being on the edge of being, between the natural and the supernatural.

PHILIP LARKIN

PHILIP LARKIN (1922–1985). *English poet and critic. A retiring man (except in his writing), Larkin worked for many years as a librarian. His first collection of poetry,* The North Ship *(1945), attracted little attention, but after the publication of* The Less Deceived *(1955), Larkin was considered the most distinguished voice of a new generation. He possessed a keen sensibility and the rare ability to subtly transform ordinary experience into revelation.*

FAITH HEALING

Slowly the women file to where he stands
Upright in rimless glasses, silver hair,
Dark suit, white collar. Stewards tirelessly
Persuade them onwards to his voice and hands,
Within whose warm spring rain of loving care
Each dwells some twenty seconds. *Now, dear child,
What's wrong,* the deep American voice demands,
And, scarcely pausing, goes into a prayer
Directing God about this eye, that knee.
Their heads are clasped abruptly; then, exiled

Like losing thoughts, they go in silence; some
Sheepishly stray, not back into their lives
Just yet; but some stay stiff, twitching and loud
With deep hoarse tears, as if a kind of dumb
And idiot child within them still survives
To re-awake at kindness, thinking a voice
At last calls them alone, that hands have come
To lift and lighten; and such joy arrives
Their thick tongues blort, their eyes squeeze grief, a crowd
Of huge unheard answers jam and rejoice—

What's wrong! Moustached in flowered frocks they shake:
By now, all's wrong. In everyone there sleeps
A sense of life lived according to love.
To some it means the difference they could make
By loving others, but across most it sweeps

As all they might have done had they been loved.
That nothing cures. An immense slackening ache,
As when, thawing, the rigid landscape weeps,
Spreads slowly through them—that, and the voice above
Saying *Dear child,* and all time has disproved.

FERROL SAMS

FERROL SAMS (1922–   ). *American physician, writer, and lecturer. Dr. Sams was educated at Mercer University and Emory University School of Medicine. A popular speaker and master storyteller, he has written a number of books, including* Run with the Horsemen, Whisper of the River *(both novels),* The Widow's Mite *(short stories),* The Passing: Perspectives on the Rural South, When All the World Was Young, *and* Christmas Gift! *His most recent book is* Epiphany: Stories by Ferrol Sams.

SABA
(An Affirmation)

Dear Natalie and Matthew,

For four years I have loved your father. It has been more than the love one feels for a friend new-found in late life, although that is beautiful enough in its own right, an event to be cherished for the rarity and purity of it. It has been, rather, the feeling I could have only for another son, were it possible to have a son borne by a woman I never met and nurtured in a land I never knew, one to spring into my awareness all grown and fully formed, fierce and proud and beautifully intelligent, polished into grace in his profession, a son to watch with pride no matter from what distance. No ties of blood have I with him but rather a deep current of awareness that transcends such ties.

That current is fed by something for which and on which blood has been spilled since there have been humans who walked erect and knew the thick, hot fluid of life coursing through resilient flesh and exulted that there was something in the world worthy of that blood and that flesh. A man of worth, having nothing to which he can sacrifice himself, will soon or late find something worthy of sacrifice or he loses his worth. Even the basest of beasts will defend its lair.

Your father and I are bound by love of the land. My land, of course, is Georgia, here in the United States of America, beginning now its third century of the greatest exercise the world has ever known in brotherhood. Your father's land is Lebanon, millennia older than Georgia. I know little of Lebanon. I know that the cedars for King Solomon's temple came from there, for all Georgia boys are familiar with the Jewish history recorded in the Old Testament. I remember that much was made of those trees, and they must have been beautiful indeed because they are lauded in the Song of Songs itself. I know that Lebanon, because of its location, must have known Nebuchadnezzar and Cyrus and Darius and Alexander and Caesar and Mohammed and Ataturk. Lebanon was aware, I am sure, of Saul and Samuel and David and Daniel and also Saul of Tarsus, who changed his name to Paul and traveled extensively. Somewhere along the way Lebanon heard of Jesus of Nazareth and many believed. Of course, many also did not believe, a statement that applies equally to Georgia.

Regrettably I know little of the autonomy of your father's land or of the physical characteristics of it. I know that in the mid-twentieth century its capital of Beirut was the financial center of the Mediterranean and the Near East and it was regarded as one of the most civilized capitals of the world, an example of political harmony for all to emulate. There was a prestige about the American University in Beirut that spread even to Georgia and had something of the same ring to it as the Capital City Club in Atlanta. I know that in the last ten years Lebanon has gone to hell in a bucket and that the city of Beirut has been trashed into a wasteland and that no one in America fully understands the politics there or the age-old reasons that neighbors are killing each other, that Moslems and Christians are at each other's throats, that even those two religions are divided into sects that war with one another.

In America, in Georgia, we read the papers and we watch television. We listen to commentators with different analyses, and we get the impression that these men are pretending to a learning about Lebanon that they do not possess. In Georgia we shake our heads, as men do when their minds cannot fathom something, and say, "Those people are crazy." There is much human blood soaking the soil of Lebanon today, and the land is littered with chunks of flesh and random, unidentified bits of bone, for the weapons of terrorists are messy, explosive, and often indiscriminate. We do not understand.

Into this atmosphere your father chose to carry you two children and his blond, Carolina-born wife in August of 1986. I understood why he did it, but I was fearful.

In 1982 a novel I had written was published. In this book I had set down as well as I could not only the description of farm life in the Georgia of my childhood but also the feelings that a child experienced growing up in that era in that place. At that time I had not personally known your father. I had referred patients to him, as a general practitioner does to specialists, for I had been told by professors at Emory Medical School that Joseph Saba was a most excellent neurologist. I had been delighted with his care, his diagnoses, his compassion, but I am a busy man and so is Joseph Saba, and our relationship had been limited to an exchange of letters about patients, objective, clearly-typed missives crammed with cold facts and nothing more. His were always signed with a scrawl that was not only indecipherable but resembled a cipher or an exotic monogram, threatening at any moment to open out into an incomprehensible Arabic phrase.

If I failed to send a letter along with a new referral, which I more often did than not, this man would call me before he saw the patient and bluntly ask, "Dr. Sams, what do you want me to do for this patient?" The first time this happened I was taken aback, for specialists are not usually that open or that direct, and I am afraid I stammered a little with confusion and surprise. Then I learned just as bluntly to reply, "Prove to me he does not have a brain tumor," or, "Tell me she is having migraines," or, "I am worried about multiple sclerosis and need you to confirm or deny it," or even, "She is a crock and forgive me for dumping on you."

We were two busy men, both of us busier than we should be and both of us determined to look after sick folks and to do it as thoroughly and economically as possible. It was professional teamwork that was as mutually satisfying to us as intricate plays, when they work, must be to those athletes whom we in America reward with millions of dollars to cavort in sweat and physical perfection across our playing fields and television screens. I never said a personal thing to Joseph Saba, nor he to me, but I wondered occasionally what he looked like and from which country he had acquired his accent. Our relationship was good, and there was no need to tamper with it.

One day I received a different sort of letter from him. It was fat with many pages and it was written in perfectly legible cursive script. "Dear Dr. Sams," it began, "I have stayed up all night and have begun this letter many times. Your oldest son had told me about your book and that it was very good, and I had passed this off indulgently to family boasting. Then I was walking through the mall and saw the book and on impulse bought it. Last night I finished reading it. Dr. Sams, I have never been so homesick in my life. I travel to market with my grandfather again, except the mules are carrying loads of olives instead of cotton. You have transported me from Georgia to the hills of Lebanon, to the land of my childhood, and I have been flooded with memories that make me laugh and make me weep. My grandfather is a very strong man and I have never felt so secure as when he took me by the hand down a row in the field or a street in the village and said, 'Look you here; this is thus and so,' or, 'This we do and this we never do, in this family. You are a Saba.'

"The book made me remember the body being the temple of the soul, Dr. Sams, and how I defiled it daily. And on Saturday I would repent and walk in glorious righteousness all day on Sunday only to begin my sin anew each Monday. I remember the Baptist missionary coming to our village and arguing with our priest. My grandfather's brother-in-law was converted from the ancient faith, and I can remember my grandfather snorting when he came to our house and saying to my grandmother, 'Here comes the holy one. He has been saved,' but later he accepted the change and would visit in the village with him in harmony."

There was much more, and then the letter ended, "Oh, Dr. Sams, your book has made me want to return to Lebanon and my grandfather, and I dream that in this crazy world some day I might lie in peace in my native village in the common grave of our family under the watchful eye of the statue of the Virgin Mary. Thank you, Dr. Sams, for taking this Lebanese boy home once again."

I tell you children this so that by the time you read these words you will have some idea of the bond between your father and me; that you may understand the love of land; that you may know the importance of person and place. Your father is forever in my heart.

The following summer I developed a monstrous weakness in my right hand. I could write only if I held the hand with my left for added strength and control; I could not cut a slice of tomato with my fork. I could not grasp a piece of paper with any firmness between my fingers. I noted that the muscles in my calves were so beset with little involuntary fibrillary twitchings that they seemed to harbor beneath the skin a multitude of spastic worms. When I fancied that my left hand was also becoming weak, I made an appointment with your father and drove myself to his office.

I felt uncomfortably pretentious when he said, "You honor me, Dr. Sams, with your presence and your trust," but he was so busy with his hammer and his needles and his machine that delivers electric shocks that I was caught up in admiration of his absorption, his thoroughness. He moved in his long white coat as lithe and lean as a swimming eel, the muscles and tendons of his fingers under absolute control of directive intelligence. When all was done, he invited me to dress and wait in his office. Closing the door on me, he said he would return as soon as he saw his next patient. I had not heard nor seen another patient but thought little of it. "You can sit in this chair behind my desk and make yourself at home, Dr. Sams."

It is almost embarrassing to be closeted alone in the private office of another. One feels sneaky about indulging idle curiosity and looking with more than casual interest at anything other than photographs or framed documents hanging on the wall. One averts one's eyes from opened correspondence lest one be accused of prying into personal things not of one's concern. I looked at your father's diplomas, his record of residencies in prestigious hospitals, the certification that he had achieved Diplomate status in his subspecialty. I roamed the small room restlessly, resistant to the idea of sitting in his chair. This was his domain. I had no desire to usurp his throne, even if on invitation and only for a while. The silence grew until I was aware of the singing of cicadas in my ears, herald of incipient deafness announcing the approach of age. I moved to Joseph's chair and sat. The desk top was clear of litter and I thought of his horror could he see mine.

There was one book on the desk, its linen covers frayed with use, its pages softened by frequent thumbing. It was a textbook of neurology and it was small as such tomes go. I fancied that it might snug itself into one of the larger pockets on Joseph's coat. It lay open and there were focusing lines of red underscoring some of the sentences. Obviously this was an old companion from Joseph's student days. I drew it to me.

"Amyotrophic Lateral Sclerosis"

The heading startled me and gained my total attention. Lou Gehrig's disease. Yes. The terrible, inexorable, progressive affliction that creeps over a man until he drowns in his own juices, unable to swallow any of them and too paralyzed to expel them. I read of demyelinating the lateral horn cells of the central nervous system, a process I could describe to you children as similar to stripping the insulation from multiple electric wires until the current in an entire circuit is shorted out. It cannot be repaired. It is a permanent loss. The lights supplied by those particular wires will never shine again. I read that the disease usually begins on one side and rapidly spreads to the other. Underscored in red was the statement: "It is always associated with muscular fasciculation, primarily in the legs." Then another statement emphasized by heavy red lines: "Unfortunately death always ensues, never more than three years after diagnosis."

I was caught by the word *unfortunately*. It is rare to find a hint of compassion in so clinically explicit a textbook of diagnosis.

I had attended a patient once with ALS, a vibrant tower of manhood brought low and humiliated by the slow extinction of all his lights. He was the spinoff of specialists and hospitals, set loose to die in his own home at the pace of his marching conqueror, but not of his own will. The hands were the first to go and he could no longer use the releasing pistol, and rapidly he could not even spoon food into his mouth. I made calls and observed a saint of a neighbor bathing him like a child, turning him constantly, freeing his airway of secretions, listening to his words, pressing his hand. He adored her and rapidly refused to have his daughter in the room. He only tolerated his wife. He clung to the neighbor. She was his death partner, and only she made him comfortable with his shame. When his speech failed him, she could understand him long after others looked mystified at his guttural explosions. When the current to his larynx finally sputtered out, she helped him to communicate by going through the alphabet and letting him blink his eyelids to spell out a word of direction. Soon that failed. The last light to go out was the rage within his eyes. I remembered him as being a tyrant, a despot who had fought and flailed and ranted and would have drowned in hate had he not had an angel for a neighbor.

I moved from Joseph's chair to the window. My head was as clear as sunup in January, my emotions just as frozen. I wondered how the specialist would handle this one, how much range of feeling would be exhibited from doctor to doctor, how he would handle the onerous burden of announcement and how I would bear the weight of listening.

He walked rapidly across the room (a redundancy, since I never saw him walk any way but rapidly) straight to his desk, his legs scissoring so vigorously they threatened to leave his long white coat. He reached over, closed the textbook and then turned to me. He neither invited me to sit nor gave any indication of seating himself. Not three feet apart we faced each other, shoulders squared, heads erect, as formal as soldiers in dress review.

"Dr. Sams, you have either a spinal cord tumor or amyotrophic lateral sclerosis. You need a spinal tap and a myelogram to rule out the former. I would rather a neurosurgeon do the myelogram, since, in the unlikely event it is a cord tumor, it is quite high." His voice was rigidly calm.

Rising to the challenge, following his lead, I was also calm. "I am grateful for your candor."

"Dr. Sams, is there anything else I can do for you? Do you have any questions?"

"Yes, Joseph. I have some questions. Have you heard from your grandfather? How is he faring through this mess in Lebanon? Are you worried about him?"

His smile cut through in flashing white beneath his glistening brows and through the blueness of his close-shaven face. "He is well, Dr. Sams. I heard from him two weeks ago. He is in no danger, really, for our village is high in the mountains and very isolated. He says that I should not worry. He says there is nothing to do but let the crazies all kill themselves. When that is over, he says, there will still be the land and he will be on it and then we can rebuild Lebanon. My grandfather is a very strong man, Dr. Sams."

I held out my hand. "Thank you for everything you have done, Joseph. You are making this easier for me. I shall try to be like your grandfather."

He moved rapidly to escort me to the door. As I stepped over the portal he said, "You are already like my grandfather, Dr. Sams. Very like."

"Now it is you who honors me, Joseph."

"No, Dr. Sams. Not in one hundred years could I repay the trust you have shown in me today. Are you all right?"

"Joseph, I am fine. Thanks to you. And thanks to your grandfather. I will let you hear."

Well, there I was—full of Anglo-Saxon and Celtic genes, all of them programmed for caterwauling histrionics. I remembered my father being so grandly mysterious about his Peyronie's disease that the family went into frantic speculation every time he sighed and distantly proclaimed that he had "an incurable disease." I thought back to my aunts and uncles and my grandparents and how they dramatized physical complaints; how even a head cold could become the axis around which the attention of the clan revolved. Here I was driving home alone, praying that I had a spinal cord tumor because at least there was a chance, however slim, of curing that, and my behavior was being totally manipulated by a Lebanese immigrant who was less than half my age. I resolved that I would be as matter-of-fact and controlled with my wife and family as your father had been with me. Suddenly I laughed. To pray for a spinal cord tumor is the ultimate in the unexpected and the height of optimism. A line of verse flashed through my head.

"The Assyrian came down like a wolf on a fold,
And his cohorts were gleaming in purple and gold. . . ."

I wondered why this had come up to remind me of your father. Then there came to me the concluding line of another poem and I said aloud,

"For there is neither East nor West,
Border nor breed nor birth,
When two strong men stand face to face,
Though they come from the ends of the earth."

The resolve to be like your great-grandfather carried me through the next two weeks with an absolute minimum of self-pity, fear, or dramatization. My wife was quickly on the telephone with her nephew, The Neurosurgeon, to ask who he thought was the best man in the United States on spinal cords. "Or England, for that matter," she told me. "You know, he did have that fellowship over there." My wife puts slightly different values and use on shared genes than I. The upshot of all this was that I wound up at Ochsner Clinic in New Orleans with a specialist who was a giant of a man with the gentlest hands on earth. The lumbar puncture and the subsequent myelogram were entirely normal except for a few more cells than usual in the spinal fluid. I did not have a spinal cord tumor.

I lay for twenty-four hours with head perfectly flat to avoid any post-manipulative headache, succored in that foreign city by the presence of my oldest son and The Neurosurgeon and comforted by the nursing skills of an angel of a daughter-in-law. As I considered Lou Gehrig's disease and my possible interaction with such an entity, I realized that my weakness had disappeared. The grip in my hand was strong. I could grasp objects once more with surety and use my hands with precision. Those marvelous appendages adorned with opposing thumbs, which have elevated us above all our viviparous suckling brothers, were restored to the marvel of their complex and wonderful perfection.

Cautiously I asked the specialist about amyotrophic lateral sclerosis. Plateau, yes. Remission, occasionally. Improvement never. ALS was ruled out. Consensus impugned a low-grade virus, something like Guillain-Barré, and the giant in New Orleans predicted complete recovery.

I asked my oldest son to telephone your father. Back came his answer: "Never in my life, Dr. Sams, have I been so happy to be wrong."

I tell you all this only to show how strong the bonds are between me and your father. I did progress to complete recovery. I was busy, your father was busy, we had interchange primarily about patients and saw each other only on rare occasions. In August I went to your house to meet a neurologist your father was thinking of inviting into his practice. We were around the swimming pool when I said, "Joseph, what's this I hear about you? Are you really going back to Lebanon?"

"Yes, Dr. Sams, all the arrangements are made and we leave next week."

"We? Who?"

"My wife and children and I, Dr. Sams."

"Joseph, you are crazy. You cannot take these babies into Lebanon! They look like you and maybe you could get by with them, but what are you going to do with a blond American wife? She'll be a hostage in five minutes."

"Dr. Sams, we will be perfectly safe, I promise you. We are going into Syria and my family is going to join us there. The village is quite near the Syrian border and it is no problem. All arrangements have been made and there is no danger."

I looked around his teasing grin and into his eyes. He wears that grin all the time except when talking about amyotrophic lateral sclerosis and spinal tumors. "Joseph, I don't know why you are going and it's none of my business, but you cannot take those two children with you. Helen and I will keep them until you get back."

The grin faded. The eyes deepened. "Dr. Sams, the reason we are going is because of the children. My grandfather is eighty-five years old and has never seen them. I could not bear it if something happened to him and he had never seen my children. Natalie is three and Matthew a year and a half, and my grandfather has never beheld them. I promise you they will be safe, and I promise you the person would never be safe again anywhere in the world who harmed one hair of their heads. Do not worry, Dr. Sams. I promise you."

Someone else came up and I went to the kitchen and served my plate and made small talk with the young neurologist. Your father is about to kill himself working and desperately needs help, and I thought perhaps we might, between us, teach this young doctor about medicine in the real world.

I don't for the life of me know why the older generation worries about the younger generation killing itself working, since all of us with any perspicacity should look around and realize that we have seen many more people die from playing, or its complications, than from working, and that our longer-lived peers are more frequently those who have worked hard than those who have frolicked with excess leisure. A person who has disciplined himself to hard work more easily disciplines himself to good health habits; ergo it boils down to a matter of discipline. Nonetheless, your father does work too hard and has little time with you children, and he needs help.

Joseph escorted me in departure with hospitality that would shame a Southern Colonel. At the door he assured me again that his family and he would be absolutely safe during the upcoming sortie to the Middle East. I assured him in turn that I would worry until I heard of their return.

"What do you want me to bring you from Lebanon, Dr. Sams?" His mocking smile was stilled, his voice had the timbre of sincerity in it. "I mean it. What would you like to have more than anything else from Lebanon? What can I bring you from my country?"

I searched his eyes and thought about it. "Joseph," I said, and I also was very sincere, "bring me the blessing of your grandfather."

I looked back as my wife and I drove away. Your father was waving to us, but abstractedly, as though in deep thought.

Over the next three weeks I thought often of you all. I prayed frequently, but I did not worry, since there is absolutely no logic whatever in a Christian doing both. It was with relief that I heard you had returned. Since neither of you was old enough to have any detailed or permanent memory of this trip, let me tell you what I have heard of it. Much of my account comes round about from my son talking with your father in the hospital, for neither I nor Joseph has yet had the time to sit down leisurely and visit with each other, dropping those little inconsequential details into our conversation that are the delight of both a good friendship and a good story. I am hoping that visit will come, but I want this letter written to you in case it does not.

The four of you flew into Damascus. I've had no details of that trip except that you two, at ages three and eighteen months, took over the airplane until your foresighted father finally sedated you. You children right now are beautiful, loving, and bright, but you are also possessed of an energy level the suppression of which I fancy caused a gaggle of flight attendants to rise up and call your father blessed. Unanimously.

In Syria you went to the designated rendezvous, but there was no word waiting from the contact with Joseph's grandfather's village. Apparently there was no way to telephone. After a day and a half, Joseph piled you two dark-haired, olive-skinned babies and your blonde, blue-eyed mother into an automobile and simply drove across the border into Lebanon. I am glad I learned of this only post facto or else my prayers would certainly have degenerated into worry, for your mother's skin is as white as milk. She had no visa for visiting Lebanon and she must have shone in that land like a barrel of spilled flour. At any rate, you traveled without incident to your native village, to your ancestral hearth, and found nothing amiss. No one in the family had received your father's last message about where to meet. Your father's grandfather was well and in good spirits. It was a joyous reunion; the old man adored you children and you, in turn, were in your happiest and most winning form for him. Joseph felt fulfilled.

On the second or third day of your visit, things had calmed down enough for Joseph to idle some time with his grandfather in relaxed conversation, a time I fancy that was synchronous in more than pure coincidence with the first afternoon nap that you two had been induced to take in Lebanon. He told his grandfather of his friend in America, the Georgia man who loved the land, the country doctor who enjoyed reciprocal love with his people, the author of books that had spoken to a Lebanese man and made him feel homesick for his childhood. I have no idea how much detail he recounted, but he ended with, "I asked Dr. Sams what he wanted me to bring him from Lebanon, and he said, 'Bring me the blessing of your grandfather.' "

With this, I am told, your great-grandfather jumped up and went into the important room of his house, what we Southerners call the parlor, the supreme repository of both memorabilia and relics, the emotion of acquisition leaving only posterity to distinguish indifferently between trash and heirloom. He returned to Joseph and said, "Give these to Dr. Sams."

Joseph looked down at the objects. He had seen them all his life, ensconced high above the reach of children, admired and revered.

"Grandfather! I cannot possibly take those to Dr. Sams. How do you propose that I get them out of the country?"

"Joseph. I am placing these in your hands and I am telling you to place them in the hands of Dr. Sams. How you manage to do that is your concern. Do not bother me with it. Tell him that he has the blessing of your grandfather."

The family had another feast and celebration that evening, for everyone in the village was glad that you and your parents had come. Lebanese blood is warmed by kin, and the heart of a friend beats with steady devotion. The following afternoon your father and his grandfather were once again having a quiet visit. Of a sudden, the grandfather stood up.

"Joseph, my heart is hurting fiercely. I am dying."

And so he did, children. That moment. In your father's arms. Your father attempted resuscitation, but he told me later he knew in the beginning it was futile. He was glad he was there to make arrangements, to summon his uncle from Paris, to arrange the funeral, to be the leader of the family in the last rites for the man who had meant so much to him. He was glad that you children were there.

There were many anxious times on the way back to America. First off, you were apprehended by the border patrol in Lebanon. Your father had a visa, your mother did not, a fact which produced both concern and agitation among the patrol. After several hours of interrogation and lectures, you were permitted to depart. It turned finally on your mother's giving a solemn pledge that she would never again visit Lebanon without a visa, a demand she met with such alacrity and enthusiasm that a more insecure man than your father might have felt his very background being disapproved.

You were barely out of this predicament when you crossed the Syrian border and were detained by the patrol there. Your father said that he used all the personality and persuasion he possessed and still the guards became ever more obstinate and obstructive.

"Why do you want to live in America," one asked, "where crime rules the streets and you are liable to be beaten or killed if you set foot out of your house?"

When the man discovered that your father is a physician, and an American-trained one at that, he insisted on describing some symptoms he was having and asking your father's advice. Another guard heard and wanted a consultation about his brother who was gravely ill. Then another. Joseph said that soon he had gathered a roadside medical clinic there on the border between Syria and Lebanon and that he was pushing himself to his limits of graciousness and geniality. He dared do nothing else. Among other concerns, I am sure that he was conscious of his grandfather's blessing to Dr. Sams, concealed God knows where. When he told me of it, I thought of Rachel smuggling away the household gods of Laban for Jacob, spiritual insult added to the economic injury of the dappled herds, but I refrained from query. There is a slight distance of dignity between your father and me and we both respect it.

The cars lined up behind you, and still your father dispensed professional concern and consult on the Syrian road bank. An impulsive driver several cars back had the temerity to blow his horn in impatience, and a guard went rushing back to him, snatched open the door, threw the driver to the ground and began kicking him in the head.

"Control yourself," he shouted, "you donkey dung, you roadside scum! Can't you see that we are very busy with important matters the likes of you could not be expected to understand? We do not look with favor on anyone who interferes with our duties or interrupts our routine. Get back in your car and behave yourself or it will not go well with you. Do you hear me, disobedient dog of a driver? Do as I tell you!" He delivered a final kick and rejoined the group around your father. "Tell me, doctor, about back pain in old women. Just here, and here. I know an examination would be better, but my mother-in-law would never forgive me if I missed the opportunity to ask an American doctor who understands Arabic so well."

When all of you were finally permitted to leave, this same guard leaned through the window with a final admonition. "Guard yourself and your loved ones well on the violent streets of the United States, doctor." Your mother was not required at this point to make a pledge about return visits, but I am sure she would have been willing. I understand, however, that she fell in love with Damascus. She liked the Grand Mosque and the shops, and your father gave her an extra day or so to compensate for the Lebanese and Syrian patrols. You children have the genes of courage from the Celtic side also.

Back in the United States, Joseph called me and came over. As usual, he was in a hurry. He told me about his grandfather and about the blessing he sent to me. Then he placed in my hands the two most unlikely objects I could imagine to have come forth from Lebanon. They were tusks of ivory. Each was about two feet long and most gorgeously carved. At the base was the head of a crocodile, jaws gaping wide, pulling on the trunk of the first in a string of six progressively smaller elephants. I was reminded instantly of Rudyard Kipling's tale of the great gray-green, greasy Limpopo River all set about with fever trees, and I must find the occasion to read that story to you children.

The tusks were beautiful, but in addition there was an aura about them, a command of one's attention that emanates only from true art. Of course, being primitive, there was also something phallic about them.

"Joseph! These are lovely!"

"I am glad you like them, Dr. Sams."

"But, Joseph, these are not Lebanese. These are African. I am certainly no expert, but this is primitive African art of a superb quality. These pieces should be in a museum. This is a treasure, and I cannot possibly accept it."

"You have no choice, Dr. Sams. I am only a delivery boy, and I have performed my function."

"But, Joseph, these pieces are family heirlooms and should stay in your family. Truly, I feel most uncomfortable accepting these from you."

"You are not accepting them from me, Dr. Sams. They are from my grandfather. You are accepting them from him. You can someday discuss your discomfort with him, but for the present you have no choice." His smile brightened my tears.

"Joseph, I am overwhelmed. I shall guard these for my lifetime and I shall specify in my will that they go to one of your children at my death."

"Not so, Dr. Sams. They are now in your family. I must go now. I am pleased that you like them, and my grandfather would be pleased. He thought I needed an American grandfather."

Half an hour after his departure I had a thousand questions to ask. Some are still unanswered, and I await the leisurely afternoon or evening, the slow comfort of a good bottle of wine, the languid coursing of friendship so frequently dreamt and so rarely attained. To the pressing question of how Joseph's grandfather acquired these carvings, however, I have learned the answer. It amazes me, and I must share it with you.

The grandfather was one of two sons in his family. They were very close in years although not so close in other ways. His older brother was what we in the South euphemistically label "slow"; he was good with his hands and had a strong back but he required a great deal of direction and was noticeably lacking in imagination. He was equally loved and nurtured in the family as the grandfather and had the same emotional and educational opportunities, such as they were. Lebanon was very poor.

When your great-grandfather was twelve years old, his father sat him down for a talk. He delineated the boundaries of the family land that he owned, which had been handed down to him from his father and in turn his father's father and so on back beyond the memory of the family. In America we are so accustomed to vast acreage and the history of homesteading that we have to gear down our concepts to comprehend the situation in older, more densely settled countries. Land was the life source, the raison d'être, when the grandfather's father ushered him into manhood.

He told him that the family holdings would support one son but not two. They considered this for a while and then the grandfather's father said to him with the gruffness that insulates love too intense to manifest itself without burning the speaker, "You have the brains. You leave. He gets the land."

When I heard this, I remembered Reading Gaol.

> "Yet each man kills the things he loves;
> By each let this be heard.
> Some do it with a bitter look,
> Some with a flattering word.
> The coward does it with a kiss,
> The brave man with a sword."

The grandfather emigrated. He had no choice. He could read and write but the only means of livelihood in his village lay in the land, in farming, and he no longer had any prospects of sustenance at home.

He made his way to Marseilles and hired on board a ship that went up and down the coast of Africa. He soon settled in a country called the Ivory Coast and became a peddler. Carrying trinkets and notions in a pack on his back, he walked into the countryside and jungles, selling for a profit and living off the land. He learned the language and saved his money. Before long he bought a horse. Then from the chieftain of one of the tribes out in the brush he began buying cows.

In a scenario reminiscent of the American West, he herded the cows across the lower reaches of the Sahara Desert and sold them, fighting rustlers and bandits along the way. He prospered and hired others to help him. Always he traded and always for profit; there was suspicion that he had Phoenician blood in his veins. Carefully he saved his money, never carousing or wenching as he saw other white men doing in this alien land. The chieftain also prospered.

The young Levantine sat with dignity in the councils of the men, and when he departed Africa he left behind no wife or black babies. He left a reputation for fierceness, fairness, and honesty, and he departed as a wealthy man. He was nineteen years old.

At his farewell meeting with his friend and business partner, the old African chief presented him with the carved ivories, family relics that had been given to the chieftain's grandfather when he assumed leadership of the tribe. The young man was reluctant to accept them but there comes a time when a strong person must face the ceremonies of honor simply and with poise. It was from his African experience that he developed the pronouncement he later gave Joseph. "A Saba will always be first, even if on the road to Hell."

When he returned to his Lebanese village, there was great rejoicing. He bought land. He bought ancestral land and looked after his older brother for the rest of his life. His father said to him, "I do not know what happened to you in Africa, nor do I want to know, but you have returned as a person of great substance. You are nineteen years old and you should have a wife. She must be chosen carefully. I have in another village a distant cousin who is known far and wide as a virtuous woman. You journey to that village with gifts for the mother and ask for her oldest daughter in marriage." (This, little children, is the Lebanese version of the old Georgia saying, "Salt the cow to catch the calf.")

The grandfather did his father's bidding and was welcomed most graciously. When he asked about the older daughter, he was told that she was absent on a visit to some cousins. The virtuous woman assured him that if he would wait a week, her daughter would return and be most happy to marry such a fine man. Your great-grandfather said, "A week? I cannot spare a week. I have things to do. Don't you have somebody else?" The lady thereupon presented her younger daughter and he carried her back to his village as his wife. She became your "Grandma Linda." From what we Americans would regard as a most unlikely beginning there evolved a very long and happy marriage and a marvelous family.

The grandfather never quit trading and never quit being fierce and honest and fair. He was obsessed with the importance of education. At one time there were one hundred and twenty children from his apartment complexes in school and one hundred eighteen of them were on the honor roll. He saw to it. He demanded to see report cards. For B's and C's he administered spankings, for straight A's he awarded five dollars. The children were not kin of his; they were his responsibility because they belonged to his tenants.

He paid well for educating his own children. One he sent for seven years to the Sorbonne in Paris. The other son was Joseph's father and he sent him to Rio de Janeiro forever because he did not approve of his behavior. Joseph and his mother and sisters remained in the village under the eye and beneath the wing of the grandfather. He was indeed a very strong man. He understood Reading Gaol very well.

The elephant tusks, most magically and artfully carved, had been carried from the jungles and savannahs of Africa to the hills of rural Lebanon. The grandfather placed them in a hallowed spot in his house and there they rested for the duration of his life, an ever-present reminder that trust does indeed attain fulfillment between men of honor, that virtues are not relative but absolute, that good on occasion triumphs beautifully in replacing evil, that a good name is more to be sought than great riches. They were even testimonial that the sword, be it one of truth and justice, does not always kill, but sometimes prunes and invigorates.

Now the ivories are similarly enshrined in my house, their beauty magnified a hundred-fold by what I feel about them. I am in awe of two men I have never met, an African lord and a Lebanese patriarch. I marvel at events the skeptic would label coincidence and the believer would call choreography. The carvings are symbols to me of the ascendancy of innate ability over material inheritance, but they are more. They have a luster about them of the love of one's land; the story of Antaeus no longer seems a myth.

I hear a voice that never reached my ear saying, "Leave them alone. When the crazies all kill themselves the land will still be here and we will rebuild."

And another: "You have the brains. You leave."

And the voice of Joseph: "You either have ALS or a spinal cord tumor."

And my own: "Bring me the blessing of your grandfather."

The ivories tell a story. A story of brave men face to face. A story of courage and a sword. A story of continuity, of love, of the importance of the land.

I, being of sound mind and disposing nature and in acknowledg-
ment of a flow of events that has to be divine, do will and bequeath the
elephant tusks I hold in trust from the mountains of Lebanon and the
plains of the Ivory Coast to the children of Joseph Saba, my adopted
grandson.

Go always with God, little children.

FERROL SAMS

KURT VONNEGUT

KURT VONNEGUT (1922–   ). *American writer. Vonnegut was born in Indianapolis, Indiana, and educated at Cornell, the University of Chicago, and the Carnegie Institute. His black humor, satiric voice, and incomparable imagination first captured America's attention in* The Sirens of Titan *(1959). In the 1960s, he emerged as one of America's most influential, potent, and provocative writers, a ribald commentator on the horrors of this century. The publication of* Cat's Cradle *in 1963 is said to have established him as "a true artist." Vonnegut is the author of dozens of short stories and essays and eighteen highly acclaimed books, including* Slaughterhouse-Five *(1969),* Mother Night *(1972) and* Deadeye Dick *(1982).*

FORTITUDE

DR. ELBERT LITTLE   a kindly, attractive young general practitioner, is being shown around by the creator and boss of the operation, DR. NORBERT FRANKENSTEIN

FRANKENSTEIN   FRANKENSTEIN is 65, a crass medical genius.
DR. TOM SWIFT   Seated at the console, wearing headphones and watching meters and flashing lights, is FRANKEN-STEIN'S enthusiastic first assistant.

THE TIME   The present.
THE PLACE   Upstate New York, a large room filled with pulsing, writhing, panting machines that perform the functions of various organs of the human body—heart, lungs, liver, and so on. Color-coded pipes and wires swoop upward from the machines to converge and pass through a hole in the ceiling. To one side is a fantastically complicated master control console.

LITTLE   Oh, my God—oh, my God—

FRANKENSTEIN   Yeah. Those are her kidneys over there. That's her liver, of course. There you got her pancreas.

LITTLE   Amazing. Dr. Frankenstein, after seeing this, I wonder if I've even been *practicing* medicine, if I've ever even *been* to medical school. (*Pointing*) That's her *heart?*

FRANKENSTEIN   That's a Westinghouse heart. They make a damn good

201

heart, if you ever need one. They make a kidney I wouldn't touch with a ten-foot pole.

LITTLE   That heart is probably worth more than the whole township where I practice.

FRANKENSTEIN   That pancreas is worth your whole state. *Vermont?*

LITTLE   Vermont.

FRANKENSTEIN   What we paid for the pancreas—yeah, we could have bought Vermont for that. Nobody'd ever made a pancreas before, and we had to have one in ten days or lose the patient. So we told all the big organ manufacturers, "OK, you guys got to have a crash program for a pancreas. Put every man you got on the job. We don't care what it costs, as long as we get a pancreas by next Tuesday."

LITTLE   And they succeeded.

FRANKENSTEIN   The patient's still alive, isn't she? Believe me, those are some expensive sweetbreads.

LITTLE   But the patient could afford them.

FRANKENSTEIN   You don't live like this on Blue Cross.

LITTLE   And how many operations has she had? In how many years?

FRANKENSTEIN   I gave her her first major operation thirty-six years ago. She's had seventy-eight operations since then.

LITTLE   And how old is she?

FRANKENSTEIN   One hundred.

LITTLE   What *guts* that woman must have!

FRANKENSTEIN   You're looking at 'em.

LITTLE   I mean—what *courage!* What *fortitude!*

FRANKENSTEIN   We knock her out, you know. We don't operate without anesthetics.

LITTLE   Even so . . .

FRANKENSTEIN *taps* SWIFT *on the shoulder,* SWIFT *frees an ear from the headphones, divides his attention between the visitors and the console.*

FRANKENSTEIN   Dr. Tom Swift, this is Dr. Elbert Little. Tom here is my first assistant.

SWIFT   Howdy-doody.

FRANKENSTEIN   Dr. Little has a practice up in Vermont. He happened to be in the neighborhood. He asked for a tour.

LITTLE   What do you hear in the headphones?

SWIFT   Anything that's going on in the patient's room. (*He offers the headphones*) Be my guest.

LITTLE   (*Listening to headphones:*) Nothing.

SWIFT   She's having her hair brushed now. The beautician's up there. She's always quiet when her hair's being brushed. (*He takes the headphones back.*)

FRANKENSTEIN   (To SWIFT:) We should *congratulate* our young visitor here.

SWIFT   What for?

LITTLE   Good question. What for?

FRANKENSTEIN   Oh, I know about the great honor that has come your way.

LITTLE   I'm not sure *I* do.

FRANKENSTEIN   You are *the* Dr. Little, aren't you, who was named the Family Doctor of the Year by the *Ladies' Home Journal* last month?

LITTLE   Yes—that's right. I don't know how in the hell they decided. And I'm even more flabbergasted that a man of *your* caliber would know about it.

FRANKENSTEIN   I read the *Ladies' Home Journal* from cover to cover every month.

LITTLE   You *do?*

FRANKENSTEIN   I only got one patient, Mrs. Lovejoy. And Mrs. Lovejoy reads the *Ladies' Home Journal,* so I read it, too. That's what we talk about—what's in the *Ladies' Home Journal.* We read all about you last month. Mrs. Lovejoy kept saying, "Oh, what a nice young man he must be. *So understanding.*"

LITTLE   Um.

FRANKENSTEIN   Now here you are in the flesh. I bet she wrote you a letter.

LITTLE   Yes—she did.

FRANKENSTEIN   She writes thousands of letters a year, gets thousands of letters back. Some pen pal she is.

LITTLE   Is she—uh—generally *cheerful* most of the time?

FRANKENSTEIN   If she isn't, that's our fault down here. If she gets unhappy, that means something down *here* isn't working right. She was blue about a month ago. Turned out it was a bum transistor in the console. (*He reaches over* SWIFT'S *shoulder, changes a setting on the console. The machinery subtly adjusts to the new setting.*) There— she'll be all depressed for a couple of minutes now. (*He changes the setting again.*) *There.* Now, pretty quick, she'll be happier than she was before. She'll sing like a bird.

LITTLE *conceals his horror imperfectly.* CUT TO *patient's room, which is full of flowers and candy boxes and books. The patient is* SYLVIA LOVEJOY, *a billionaire's widow.* SYLVIA *is no longer anything but a head connected to pipes and wires coming up through the floor, but this is not immediately apparent. The first shot of her is a* CLOSE-UP, *with* GLORIA, *a gorgeous beautician, standing behind her.* SYLVIA *is a heartbreakingly good-looking old lady, once a famous beauty. She is crying now.*

SYLVIA Gloria—

GLORIA Ma'am?

SYLVIA Wipe these tears away before somebody comes in and sees them.

GLORIA (*Wanting to cry herself:*) Yes, ma'am. (*She wipes the tears away with Kleenex, studies the results.*) There. There.

SYLVIA I don't know what came over me. Suddenly I was so sad I couldn't stand it.

GLORIA Everybody has to cry *sometimes.*

SYLVIA It's passing now. Can you tell I've been crying?

GLORIA *No. No.*

She is unable to control her own tears anymore. She goes to a window so SYLVIA *can't see her cry.* CAMERA BACKS AWAY *to reveal the tidy, clinical abomination of the head and wires and pipes. The head is on a tripod. There is a black box with winking colored lights hanging under the head, where the chest would normally be. Mechanical arms come out of the box where arms would normally be. There is a table within easy reach of the arms. On it are a pen and paper, a partially solved jigsaw puzzle, and a bulky knitting bag. Sticking out of the bag are needles and a sweater in progress. Hanging over* SYLVIA's *head is a microphone on a boom.*

SYLVIA (*sighing:*) Oh, what a *foolish* old woman you must think I am. (GLORIA *shakes her head in denial, is unable to reply.*) Gloria? Are you still there?

GLORIA Yes.

SYLVIA Is anything the matter?

GLORIA No.

SYLVIA You're *such* a good friend, Gloria. I want you to know I feel that with all my heart.

GLORIA I like you, too.

SYLVIA If you ever have any problems I can help you with, I hope you'll ask me.

GLORIA I will, I *will.*

HOWARD DERBY, *the hospital mail clerk, dances in with an arm-load of letters. He is a merry old fool.*

DERBY   Mailman! Mailman!
SYLVIA   (*Brightening:*) Mailman! God *bless* the mailman!
DERBY   How's the patient today?
SYLVIA   Very sad a moment ago. But now that I see you, I want to sing like a bird.
DERBY   Fifty-three letters today. There's even one from Leningrad.
SYLVIA   There's a blind woman in Leningrad. Poor soul, *poor* soul.
DERBY   (*Making a fan of the mail, reading postmarks:*) West Virginia, Honolulu, Brisbane, Australia—

SYLVIA *selects an envelope at random.*

SYLVIA   Wheeling, West Virginia. Now, who do I know in Wheeling? (*She opens the envelope expertly with her mechanical hands, reads.*) "Dear Mrs. Lovejoy: You don't know me, but I just read about you in the *Reader's Digest,* and I'm sitting here with tears streaming down my cheeks." *Reader's Digest?* My goodness that article was printed fourteen years ago! And she just *read* it?
DERBY   Old *Reader's Digest*s go on and on. I've got one at home I'll bet is ten years old. I still read it every time I need a little inspiration.
SYLVIA   (*Reading on:*) "I am never going to complain about anything that ever happens to me ever again. I thought I was as unfortunate as a person can get when my husband shot his girlfriend six months ago and then blew his own brains out. He left me with seven children and with eight payments still to go on a Buick Roadmaster with three flat tires and a busted transmission. After reading about you, though, I sit here and count my blessings." Isn't that a nice letter?
DERBY   Sure is.
SYLVIA   There's a P.S.: "Get well real soon, you *hear?*" (*She puts the letter on the table.*) There isn't a letter from Vermont, is there?
DERBY   Vermont?
SYLVIA   Last month, when I had that low spell, I wrote what I'm afraid was a very stupid, self-centered, self-pitying letter to a young doctor I read about in the *Ladies' Home Journal.* I'm so ashamed. I live in fear and trembling of what he's going to say back to me—if he answers at all.
GLORIA   What could he say? What could he *possibly* say?
SYLVIA   He could tell me about the *real* suffering going on out there in the world, about people who don't know where the next meal is

coming from, about people so poor they've never *been* to a doctor in their whole *lives*. And to think of all the help I've had—all the tender, loving care, all the latest wonders science has to offer.

CUT TO *corridor outside* SYLVIA's *room. There is a sign on the door saying,* ALWAYS ENTER SMILING! FRANKENSTEIN *and* LITTLE *are about to enter.*

LITTLE   She's in *there?*
FRANKENSTEIN   Every part of her that isn't downstairs.
LITTLE   And everybody obeys this sign, I'm sure.
FRANKENSTEIN   Part of the therapy. We treat the *whole* patient here.

GLORIA *comes from the room, closes the door tightly, then bursts into noisy tears.*

FRANKENSTEIN   (*To* GLORIA, *disgusted:*) Oh, for crying out loud. And what is this?
GLORIA   Let her *die,* Dr. Frankenstein. For the love of God, let her *die!*
LITTLE   This is her *nurse?*
FRANKENSTEIN   She hasn't got the brains enough to be a nurse. She is a lousy beautician. A hundred bucks a week she makes—just to take care of one woman's face and hair. (*To* GLORIA:) You blew it, honeybunch. You're through.
GLORIA   What?
FRANKENSTEIN   Pick up your check and scram.
GLORIA   I'm her closest friend.
FRANKENSTEIN   Some friend! You just asked me to knock her off.
GLORIA   In the name of mercy, yes, I did.
FRANKENSTEIN   You're that sure there's a heaven, eh? You want to send her right up there so she can get her wings and harp.
GLORIA   I know there's a hell. I've seen it. It's in there, and you're its great inventor.
FRANKENSTEIN   (*Stung, letting a moment pass before replying:*) Christ— the things people say sometimes.
GLORIA   It's time somebody who loves her spoke up.
FRANKENSTEIN   Love.
GLORIA   You wouldn't know what that is.
FRANKENSTEIN   Love. (*More to himself than to her:*) Do I have a wife? No. Do I have a mistress? No, I have loved only two women in my life—my mother and that women in there. I wasn't able to save my

mother from death. I had just graduated from medical school and my mother was dying of cancer of the everything. "OK, wise guy," I said to myself, "you're such a hot-shot doctor from Heidelberg, now, let's see you save your mother from death." And everybody told me there wasn't anything I could do for her, and I said, "I don't give a damn. I'm gonna do something anyway." And they finally decided I was nuts and they put me in a crazyhouse for a little while. When I got out, she was dead—the way all the wise men said she had to be. What those wise men didn't know was all the wonderful things machinery could do—and neither did I, but I was gonna find out. So I went to the Massachusetts Institute of Technology and I studied mechanical engineering and electrical engineering and chemical engineering for six long years. I lived in an attic. I ate two-day-old bread and the kind of cheese they put in mousetraps. When I got out of MIT, I said to myself, "OK, boy—it's just barely possible now that you're the only guy on earth with the proper education to practice twentieth-century medicine." I went to work for the Curley Clinic in Boston. They brought in this woman who was beautiful on the outside and a mess on the inside. She was the image of my mother. She was the widow of a man who had left her five hundred million dollars. She didn't have any relatives. The wise men said again, "This lady's gotta die." And I said to them, "Shut up and listen. I'm gonna tell you what we're gonna do."

(*Silence.*)

LITTLE   That's—that's quite a story.

FRANKENSTEIN   It's a story about *love*. (*To* GLORIA:) That love story started years and years before you were born, you great lover, you. And it's still going on.

GLORIA   Last month, she asked me to bring her a pistol so she could shoot herself.

FRANKENSTEIN   You think I don't know that? (*Jerking a thumb at* LITTLE:) Last month, she wrote him a letter and said, "Bring me some cyanide, doctor, if you're a doctor with any heart at all."

LITTLE   (*Startled:*) You *knew* that. You—you read her mail?

FRANKENSTEIN   So we'll know what she's *really* feeling. She might try to fool us sometime—just *pretend* to be happy. I told you about that bum transistor last month. We maybe wouldn't have known anything was wrong if we hadn't read her mail and listened to what she was saying to lame-brains like this one here. (*Feeling challenged:*) Look—you go in there all by yourself. Stay as long as you want, ask her anything. Then you come back out and tell me the truth: Is that a happy woman in there, or is that a woman in hell?

LITTLE   (*Hesitating:*) I—

FRANKENSTEIN   Go on in! I got some more things to say to this young lady—to Miss Mercy Killing of the Year. I'd like to show her a body that's been in a casket for a couple of years sometime—let her see how pretty death is, this thing she wants for her friend.

LITTLE *gropes for something to say, finally mimes his wish to be fair to everyone. He enters the patient's room.* CUT TO *room.* SYLVIA *is alone, faced away from the door.*

SYLVIA   Who's that?

LITTLE   A friend—somebody you wrote a letter to.

SYLVIA   That could be anybody. Can I see you, please? (LITTLE *obliges. She looks him over with growing affection.*) Dr. Little—family doctor from Vermont.

LITTLE   (*Bowing slightly:*) Mrs. Lovejoy—how are you today?

SYLVIA   Did you bring me cyanide?

LITTLE   No.

SYLVIA   I wouldn't take it today. It's such a lovely day. I wouldn't want to miss it, or tomorrow, either. Did you come on a snow-white horse?

LITTLE   In a blue Oldsmobile.

SYLVIA   What about your patients, who love and need you so?

LITTLE   Another doctor is covering for me. I'm taking a week off.

SYLVIA   Not on my account.

LITTLE   No.

SYLVIA   Because I'm fine. You can see what wonderful hands I'm in.

LITTLE   Yes.

SYLVIA   One thing I don't need is another doctor.

LITTLE   Right.

Pause.

SYLVIA   I do wish I had somebody to talk to about death, though. You've seen a lot of it, I suppose.

LITTLE   Some.

SYLVIA   And it was a blessing for some of them—when they died?

LITTLE   I've heard that said.

SYLVIA   But you don't say so yourself.

LITTLE   It's not a professional thing for a doctor to say, Mrs. Lovejoy.

SYLVIA   Why have other people said that certain deaths have been a blessing?

LITTLE   Because of the pain the patient was in, because he couldn't be cured at any price—at any price within his means. Or because the patient was a vegetable, had lost his mind and couldn't get it back.

SYLVIA   At any price.

LITTLE   As far as I know, it is not now possible to beg, borrow, and steal an artificial mind for someone who's lost one. If I asked Dr. Frankenstein about it, he might tell me that it's the coming thing.

(*Pause*)

SYLVIA   It *is* the coming thing.

LITTLE   He's told you so?

SYLVIA   I asked him yesterday what would happen if my brain started to go. He was serene. He said I wasn't to worry my pretty little head about that. "We'll cross that bridge when we come to it," he told me. (*Pause.*) Oh, God, the bridges I've crossed!

CUT TO *room full of organs, as before.* SWIFT *is at the console.* FRANKENSTEIN *and* LITTLE *enter.*

FRANKENSTEIN   You've made the grand tour and now here you are back at the beginning.

LITTLE   And I still have to say what I said at the beginning: "My God—oh, my God."

FRANKENSTEIN   It's gonna be a little tough going back to the aspirin-and-laxative trade after this, eh?

LITTLE   Yes. (*Pause.*) What's the cheapest thing here?

FRANKENSTEIN   The simplest thing. It's the goddamn pump.

LITTLE   What does a heart go for these days?

FRANKENSTEIN   Sixty thousand dollars. There are cheaper ones and more expensive ones. The cheap ones are junk. The expensive ones are jewelry.

LITTLE   And how many are sold a year now?

FRANKENSTEIN   Six hundred, give or take a few.

LITTLE   Give one, that's life. Take one, that's death.

FRANKENSTEIN   If the trouble is the heart. It's lucky if you have trouble that cheap. (*To* SWIFT:) Hey, Tom—put her to sleep so he can see how the day ends around here.

SWIFT   It's twenty minutes ahead of time.

FRANKENSTEIN   What's the difference? We put her to sleep for twenty minutes extra, she still wakes up tomorrow feeling like a million bucks, unless we got another bum transistor.

LITTLE   Why don't you have a television camera aimed at her, so you can watch her on a screen?

FRANKENSTEIN   She didn't want one.

LITTLE   She gets what she wants?

FRANKENSTEIN   She got *that.* What the hell do we have to watch her face for? We can look at the meters down here and find out more about her than she can know about herself. (*To* SWIFT:) Put her to sleep, Tom.

SWIFT   (*To* LITTLE:) It's just like slowing down a car or banking a furnace.

LITTLE   Um.

FRANKENSTEIN   Tom, too, has degrees in both engineering and medicine.

LITTLE   Are you tired at the end of a day, Tom?

SWIFT   It's a good kind of tiredness—as though I'd flown a big jet from New York to Honolulu, or something like that. (*Taking hold of a lever:*) And now we'll bring Mrs. Lovejoy in for a happy landing. (*He pulls the lever gradually and the machinery slows down.*) There.

FRANKENSTEIN   Beautiful.

LITTLE   She's asleep?

FRANKENSTEIN   Like a baby.

SWIFT   All I have to do now is wait for the night man to come on.

LITTLE   Has anybody ever brought her a suicide weapon?

FRANKENSTEIN   No. We wouldn't worry about it if they did. The arms are designed so she can't possibly point a gun at herself or get poison to her lips, no matter how she tries. That was Tom's stroke of genius.

LITTLE   Congratulations.

Alarm bell rings. Light flashes.

FRANKENSTEIN   Who could that be? (*To* LITTLE:) Somebody just went into her room. We better check! (*To* SWIFT:) Lock the door up there, Tom—so whoever it is, we got 'em. (SWIFT *pushes a button that locks door upstairs. To* LITTLE:) You come with me.

CUT TO *patient's room.* SYLVIA *is asleep, snoring gently.* GLORIA *has just sneaked in. She looks around furtively, takes a revolver from her purse, makes sure it's loaded, then hides it in* SYLVIA's *knitting bag. She is barely finished when* FRANKEN-

STEIN *and* LITTLE *enter breathlessly,* FRANKENSTEIN *opening the door with a key.*

FRANKENSTEIN   What's this?

GLORIA   I left my watch up here. (*Pointing to watch:*) I've got it now.

FRANKENSTEIN   Thought I told you never to come into this building again.

GLORIA   I won't.

FRANKENSTEIN   (*To* LITTLE:) You keep her right there. I'm gonna check things over. Maybe there's been a little huggery buggery. (*To* GLORIA:) How would you like to be in court for attempted murder, eh? (*Into microphone:*) Tom? Can you hear me?

SWIFT   (*Voice from squawk box on wall:*) I hear you.

FRANKENSTEIN   Wake her up again. I gotta give her a check.

SWIFT   Cock-a-doodle-doo.

Machinery can be heard speeding up below. SYLVIA *opens her eyes, sweetly dazed.*

SYLVIA   (*To* FRANKENSTEIN:) Good morning, Norbert.

FRANKENSTEIN   How do you feel?

SYLVIA   The way I always feel when I wake up—fine—vaguely at sea. Gloria! Good morning!

GLORIA   Good morning.

SYLVIA   Dr. Little! You're staying another day?

FRANKENSTEIN   It isn't morning. We'll put you back to sleep in a minute.

SYLVIA   I'm sick again?

FRANKENSTEIN   I don't think so.

SYLVIA   I'm going to have to have another operation?

FRANKENSTEIN   Calm down, calm down. (*He takes an ophthalmoscope from his pocket.*)

SYLVIA   How can I be calm when I think about another operation?

FRANKENSTEIN   (*Into microphone:*) Tom—give her some tranquilizers.

SWIFT   (*Squawk box:*) Coming up.

SYLVIA   What else do I have to lose? My ears? My hair?

FRANKENSTEIN   You'll be calm in a minute.

SYLVIA   My eyes? My eyes. Norbert—are they going next?

FRANKENSTEIN   (*To* GLORIA:) Oh, boy, baby doll—will you look what you've done? (*Into microphone:*) Where the hell are those tranquilizers?

SWIFT   Should be taking effect just about now.

SYLVIA Oh, well. It doesn't matter. (*As* FRANKENSTEIN *examines her eyes:*) It *is* my eyes, isn't it?

FRANKENSTEIN It isn't your anything.

SYLVIA Easy come, easy go.

FRANKENSTEIN You're healthy as a horse.

SYLVIA I'm sure somebody manufactures excellent eyes.

FRANKENSTEIN RCA makes a damn good eye, but we aren't gonna buy one for a while yet. (*He backs away, satisfied.*) Everything's all right up here. (*To* GLORIA:) Lucky for you.

SYLVIA I love it when friends of mine are lucky.

SWIFT Put her to sleep again?

FRANKENSTEIN Not yet. I want to check a couple of things down there.

SWIFT Roger and out.

CUT TO LITTLE, GLORIA *and* FRANKENSTEIN *entering the machinery room minutes later.* SWIFT *is at the console.*

SWIFT Night man's late.

FRANKENSTEIN He's got troubles at home. You want a good piece of advice, boy? Don't ever get married. (*He scrutinizes meter after meter.*)

GLORIA (*Appalled by her surroundings:*) My God—oh, my God—

LITTLE You've never seen this before?

GLORIA No.

FRANKENSTEIN She was the great hair specialist. We took care of everything else—everything but the hair. (*The reading on a meter puzzles him.*) What's this? (*He socks the meter, which then gives him the proper reading.*) That's more like it.

GLORIA (*Emptily:*) Science.

FRANKENSTEIN What did you think it was like down here?

GLORIA I was afraid to think. Now I can see why.

FRANKENSTEIN You got any scientific background at all—any way of appreciating even slightly what you're seeing here?

GLORIA I flunked earth science twice in high school.

FRANKENSTEIN What do they teach in beauty college?

GLORIA Dumb things for dumb people. How to paint a face. How to curl and uncurl hair. How to cut hair. How to dye hair. Fingernails. Toenails in the summertime.

FRANKENSTEIN I suppose you're gonna crack off about this place after you get out of here—gonna tell people all the crazy stuff that goes on.

GLORIA Maybe.

FRANKENSTEIN   Just remember this: You haven't got the brains or the education to talk about any aspect of our operation. Right?

GLORIA   Maybe.

FRANKENSTEIN   What *will* you say to the outside world?

GLORIA   Nothing very complicated—just that . . .

FRANKENSTEIN   Yes?

GLORIA   That you have the head of a dead woman connected to a lot of machinery, and you play with it all day long, and you aren't married or anything, and that's all you do.

FREEZE SCENE *as a still photograph.* FADE TO *black.* FADE IN *same still. Figures begin to move.*

FRANKENSTEIN   (*Aghast:*) How can you call her dead? She reads the *Ladies' Home Journal!* She talks! She knits! She writes letters to pen pals all over the world!

GLORIA   She's like some horrible fortunetelling machine in a penny arcade.

FRANKENSTEIN   I thought you loved her.

GLORIA   Every so often, I see a tiny little spark of what she used to be. I love that spark. Most people say they love her for her courage. What's that courage worth, when it comes from down here? You could turn a few faucets and switches down here and she'd be volunteering to fly a rocket ship to the moon. But no matter what you do down here, that little spark goes on thinking, "For the love of God—somebody get me out of here!"

FRANKENSTEIN   (*Glancing at the console:*) Dr. Swift—is that microphone open?

SWIFT   Yeah. (*Snapping his fingers:*) I'm sorry.

FRANKENSTEIN   Leave it open. (*To* GLORIA:) She's heard every word you've said. How does that make you feel?

GLORIA   She can hear me now?

FRANKENSTEIN   Run off at the mouth some more. You're saving me a lot of trouble. Now I won't have to explain to her what sort of friend you really were and why I gave you the old heave-ho.

GLORIA   (*Drawing nearer to the microphone:*) Mrs. Lovejoy?

SWIFT   (*Reporting what he has heard on the headphones:*) She says, "What is it, dear?"

GLORIA   There's a loaded revolver in your knitting bag, Mrs. Lovejoy—in case you don't want to live anymore.

FRANKENSTEIN   (*Not in the least worried about the pistol but filled with contempt and disgust for* GLORIA:) You total imbecile. Where did you get a pistol?

GLORIA From a mail-order house in Chicago. They had an ad in *True Romances.*

FRANKENSTEIN They sell guns to crazy broads.

GLORIA I could have had a bazooka if I'd wanted one. Fourteen-ninety-eight.

FRANKENSTEIN I am going to get that pistol now and it is going to be exhibit A at your trial. (*He leaves.*)

LITTLE (*To* SWIFT:) Shouldn't you put the patient to sleep?

SWIFT There's no way she can hurt herself.

GLORIA (*To* LITTLE:) What does he mean?

LITTLE Her arms are fixed so she can't point a gun at herself.

GLORIA (*sickened:*) They even thought of that.

CUT TO SYLVIA's *room.* FRANKENSTEIN *is entering.* SYLVIA *is holding the pistol thoughtfully.*

FRANKENSTEIN Nice playthings you have.

SYLVIA You mustn't get mad at Gloria, Norbert. I asked her for this. I begged her for this.

FRANKENSTEIN Last month.

SYLVIA Yes.

FRANKENSTEIN But everything is better now.

SYLVIA Everything but the spark.

FRANKENSTEIN Spark?

SYLVIA The spark that Gloria says she loves—the tiny spark of what I used to be. As happy as I am right now, that spark is begging me to take this gun and put it out.

FRANKENSTEIN And what is your reply?

SYLVIA I am going to do it, Norbert. This is good-bye. (*She tries every which way to aim the gun at herself, fails and fails, while* FRANKEN-STEIN *stands calmly by.*) That's no accident, is it?

FRANKENSTEIN We very much don't want you to hurt yourself. We love you, too.

SYLVIA And how much longer must I live like this? I've never dared ask before.

FRANKENSTEIN I would have to pull a figure out of a hat.

SYLVIA Maybe you'd better not. (*Pause.*) Did you pull one out of a hat?

FRANKENSTEIN At least five hundred years.

Silence.

SYLVIA So I will still be alive—long after you are gone?

FRANKENSTEIN Now is the time, my dear Sylvia, to tell you something I have wanted to tell you for years. Every organ downstairs has the capacity to take care of two human beings instead of one. And the plumbing and wiring have been designed so that a second human being can be hooked up in two shakes of a lamb's tail. (*Silence.*) Do you understand what I am saying to you, Sylvia? (*Silence. Passionately:*) Sylvia! I will be that second human being! Talk about marriage! Talk about great love stories from the past! Your kidney will be my kidney! Your liver will be my liver! Your heart will be my heart! Your ups will be my ups and your downs will be my downs! We will live in such perfect harmony, Sylvia, that the gods themselves will tear out their hair in envy!

SYLVIA This is what you want!

FRANKENSTEIN More than anything in this world.

SYLVIA Well, then—here it is, Norbert. (*She empties the revolver into him.*)

CUT TO *same room almost a half hour later. A second tripod has been set up, with* FRANKENSTEIN's *head on top.* FRANKENSTEIN *is asleep and so is* SYLVIA. SWIFT, *with* LITTLE *standing by, is feverishly making a final connection to the machinery below. There are pipe wrenches and a blowtorch and other plumber's and electrician's tools lying around.*

SWIFT That's gotta be it. (*He straightens up, looks around.*) That's gotta be it.

LITTLE (*Consulting watch:*) Twenty-eight minutes since the first shot was fired.

SWIFT Thank God you were around.

LITTLE What you really needed was a plumber.

SWIFT (*Into microphone:*) Charley—we're all set up here. You all set down there?

CHARLEY (*Squawk box:*) All set.

SWIFT Give 'em plenty of martinis.

GLORIA *appears numbly in doorway.*

CHARLEY They've got 'em. They'll be higher than kites.

SWIFT Better give 'em a touch of LSD, too.

CHARLEY Coming up.

SWIFT Hold it! I forgot the phonograph. (*To* LITTLE:) Dr. Frankenstein said that if this ever happened, he wanted a certain record playing when he came to. He said it was in with the other records—in a plain white jacket. (*To* GLORIA:) See if you can find it.

GLORIA *goes to phonograph, finds the record.*

GLORIA   This it?
SWIFT   Put it on.
GLORIA   Which side?
SWIFT   I don't know.
GLORIA   There's tape over one side.
SWIFT   The side *without* tape. (GLORIA *puts record on. Into microphone:*) Stand by to wake up the patients.
CHARLEY   Standing by.

Record begins to play. It is a Jeanette MacDonald–Nelson Eddy duet, "Ah, Sweet Mystery of Life."

SWIFT   (*Into microphone:*) Wake 'em up!

FRANKENSTEIN *and* SYLVIA *wake up, filled with formless pleasure. They dreamily appreciate the music, eventually catch sight of each other, perceive each other as old and beloved friends.*

SYLVIA   Hi, there.
FRANKENSTEIN   Hello.
SYLVIA   How do you feel?
FRANKENSTEIN   Fine. Just fine.

GRACE PALEY

GRACE PALEY (1922–   ). *American fiction writer and poet. A
storyteller for thirty-five years, Grace Paley is the author of the
short-story collections* Enormous Changes at the Last Minute *(1974)*,
The Little Disturbances of Man *(1985), and* Later the Same Day
*(1985), as well as two books of poetry and a book of poems and
prose pieces. A frequent lecturer at universities and writing workshops,
Paley counts among her many awards and honors the 1994 Jewish
Cultural Achievement Award, the 1992 Rea Award for Short Stories,
and the 1989 Edith Wharton Award. Her most recent work,* The
Collected Stories, *was a finalist for the 1994 National Book Award in
fiction.*

A MAN TOLD ME THE STORY OF HIS LIFE

Vicente said: I wanted to be a doctor. I wanted to be a doctor with my
whole heart.

I learned every bone, every organ in the body. What is it for? Why
does it work?

The school said to me: Vicente, be an engineer. That would be
good. You understand mathematics.

I said to the school: I want to be a doctor. I already know how the
organs connect. When something goes wrong, I'll understand how to
make repairs.

The school said: Vicente, you will really be an excellent engineer.
You show on all the tests what a good engineer you will be. It doesn't
show whether you'll be a good doctor.

I said: Oh, I long to be a doctor. I nearly cried. I was seventeen. I
said: But perhaps you're right. You're the teacher. You're the principal.
I know I'm young.

The school said: And besides, you're going into the army.

And then I was made a cook. I prepared food for two thousand
men.

Now you see me. I have a good job. I have three children. This is my
wife, Consuela. Did you know I saved her life?

Look, she suffered pain. The doctor said: What is this? Are you
tired? Have you had too much company? How many children? Rest
overnight, then tomorrow we'll make tests.

The next morning I called the doctor. I said: She must be operated

217

immediately. I have looked in the book. I see where her pain is. I understand what the pressure is, where it comes from. I see clearly the organ that is making trouble.

The doctor made a test. He said: She must be operated at once. He said to me: Vicente, how did you know?

JAMES KIRKUP

JAMES KIRKUP (1923–). *English poet and writer. Kirkup was born in South Shields, Durham, and vividly describes an unusually happy childhood in his autobiography* The Only Child *(1957). A prolific author, he has written several plays and many books of poetry; his most famous poem, "A Correct Compassion," follows. He has worked both as a teacher and a reviewer, at times living abroad in the United States and Japan. Among his latest books are* Queens Have Died Young and Fair *and* Me All Over: Memoirs of a Misfit *(1994).*

A CORRECT COMPASSION

To Mr. Philip Allison, after watching him perform a Mitral Stenosis Valvulotomy in the General Infirmary at Leeds.

Cleanly, sir, you went to the core of the matter.
Using the purest kind of wit, a balance of belief and art,
You with a curious nervous elegance laid bare
The root of life, and put your finger on its beating heart.

The glistening theatre swarms with eyes, and hands, and eyes.
On green-clothed tables, ranks of instruments transmit a sterile
    gleam.
The masks are on, and no unnecessary smile betrays
A certain tension, true concomitant of calm.

Here we communicate by looks, though words,
Too, are used, as in continuous historic present
You describe our observations and your deeds.
All gesture is reduced to its result, an instrument.

She who does not know she is a patient lies
Within a tent of green, and sleeps without a sound
Beneath the lamps, and the reflectors that devise
Illuminations probing the profoundest wound.

A calligraphic master, improvising, you invent
The first incision, and no poet's hesitation
Before his snow-blank page mars your intent:
The flowing stroke is drawn like an uncalculated inspiration.

A garland of flowers unfurls across the painted flesh.
With quick precision the arterial forceps click.
Yellow threads are knotted with a simple flourish.
Transfused, the blood preserves its rose, though it is sick.

Meters record the blood, measure heart-beats, control the breath.
Hieratic gesture: scalpel bares a creamy rib; with pincer knives
The bone quietly is clipped, and lifted out. Beneath,
The pink, black-mottled lung like a revolted creature heaves,

Collapses; as if by extra fingers is neatly held aside
By two ordinary egg-beaters, kitchen tools that curve
Like extraordinary hands. Heart, laid bare, silently beats. It can hide
No longer yet is not revealed.—'A local anaesthetic in the cardiac
    nerve.'

Now, in firm hands that quiver with a careful strength,
Your knife feels through the heart's transparent skin; at first,
Inside the pericardium, slit down half its length,
The heart, black-veined, swells like a fruit about to burst,

But goes on beating, love's poignant image bleeding at the dart
Of a more grievous passion, as a bird, dreaming of flight, sleeps on
Within its leafy cage.—'It generally upsets the heart
A bit, though not unduly when I make the first injection.'

Still, still the patient sleeps, and still the speaking heart is dumb.
The watchers breathe as air far sweeter, rarer than the room's.
The cold walls listen. Each in his own blood hears the drum
She hears, tented in green, unfathomable calms.

'I make a purse-strong suture here, with a reserve
Suture, which I must make first, and deeper,
As a safeguard, should the other burst. In the cardiac nerve
I inject again a local anaesthetic. Could we have fresh towels to cover

All these adventitious ones. Now can you all see.
When I put my finger inside the valve, there may be a lot
Of blood, and it may come with quite a bang. But I let it flow,
In case there are any clots, to give the heart a good clean-out.

Now can you give me every bit of light you've got.'
We stand on the benches, peering over his shoulder.
The lamp's intensest rays are concentrated on an inmost heart.
Someone coughs. 'If you have to cough, you will do it outside this
    theatre.'—'Yes, sir.'

'How's she breathing, Doug? Do you feel quite happy?'—'Yes, fairly
Happy.'—'Now. I am putting my finger in the opening of the valve.
I can only get the tip of my finger in.—It's gradually
Giving way.—I'm inside.—No clots.—I can feel the valve

Breathing freely now around my finger, and the heart working.
Not too much blood. It opened very nicely.
I should say that anatomically speaking
This is a perfect case.—Anatomically.

For of course, anatomy is not physiology.'
We find we breathe again, and hear the surgeon hum.
Outside, in the street, a car starts up. The heart regularly
Thunders.—'I do not stitch up the pericardium.

It is not necessary.'—For this is imagination's other place,
Where only necessary things are done, with the supreme and grave
Dexterity that ignores technique; with proper grace
Informing a correct compassion, that performs its love, and makes it
    live.

DANNIE ABSE

DANNIE ABSE (1923–). *British physician, poet, and playwright. Born in Cardiff, Wales, Abse was educated at the University of Wales, at Kings College in London, and at Westminster Hospital. A prolific writer, he has written award-winning plays, novels such as* Ash on a Young Man's Sleeve *and a compelling autobiography,* A Poet in the Family. *He is perhaps best known for his poetry, including* White Coat, Purple Coat. *His* Intermittent Journals *was published in 1994;* Selected Poems *appeared recently from Penguin.*

X-RAY

Some prowl sea-beds, some hurtle to a star
and, mother, some obsessed turn over every stone
or open graves to let that starlight in.
There are men who would open anything.

Harvey, the circulation of the blood,
and Freud, the circulation of our dreams,
pried honourably and honoured are
like all explorers. Men who'd open men.

And those others, mother, with diseases
like great streets named after them: Addison,
Parkinson, Hodgkin—physicians who'd arrive
fast and first on any sour death-bed scene.

I am their slowcoach colleague—half afraid,
incurious. As a boy it was so: you know how
my small hand never teased to pieces
an alarm clock or flensed a perished mouse.

And this larger hand's the same. It stretches now
out from a white sleeve to hold up, mother,
your X-ray to the glowing screen. My eyes look
but don't want to, I still don't want to know.

CASE HISTORY

"Most Welshmen are worthless,
an inferior breed, doctor."

He did not know I was Welsh.
Then he praised the architects
of the German death-camps—
did not know I was a Jew.
He called liberals, "White blacks,"
and continued to invent curses.

When I palpated his liver
I felt the soft liver of Goering;
when I lifted my stethoscope
I heard the heartbeats of Himmler;
when I read his encephalograph
I thought, *"Sieg heil, mein Führer."*

In the clinic's dispensary
red berry of black bryony,
cowbane, deadly nightshade, deathcap.
Yet I prescribed for him
as if he were my brother.

Later that night I must have slept
on my arm: momentarily
my right hand lost its cunning.

CARNAL KNOWLEDGE

I

You, student, whistling those elusive bits
of Schubert when phut, phut, phut, throbbed the sky
of London. Listen: the servo-engine cut
and the silence was not the desired silence
between two movements of music. Then
Finale, the Aldwych echo of crunch
and the urgent ambulances loaded
with the fresh dead. You, young, whistled again,
entered King's, climbed the stone-murky steps
to the high and brilliant Dissecting Room
where nameless others, naked on the slabs,
reclined in disgraceful silences—twenty
amazing sculptures waiting to be vandalized.

2

You, corpse, I pried into your bloodless meat
without the morbid curiosity of Vesalius,
did not care that the great Galen was wrong,
Avicenna mistaken, that they had described
the approximate structure of pigs and monkeys
rather than the human body. With scalpel
I dug deep into your stale formaldehyde
unaware of Pope Boniface's decree
but, as instructed, violated you—
the reek of you in my eyes, my nostrils,
clothes, in the kisses of my girlfriends.
You, anonymous. Who were you, mister?
Your thin mouth could not reply, "Absent, sir,"
or utter with inquisitionary rage.

Your neck exposed, muscles, nerves, vessels,
a mere coloured plate in some anatomy book;
your right hand, too, dissected, never belonged,
it seemed, to somebody once shockingly alive,
never held, surely, another hand in greeting
or tenderness, never clenched a fist in anger,
never took up a pen to sign an authentic name.

You, dead man, Thing, each day, each week,
each month, you, slowly decreasing Thing,
visibly losing Divine proportions,
you, residue, mere trunk of a man's body,
you, X, legless, armless, headless Thing
that I dissected so casually.

Then went downstairs to drink wartime coffee.

3

When the hospital priest, Father Jerome,
remarked, "The Devil made the lower parts
of a man's body, God the upper,"
I said, "Father, it's the other way round."
So, the anatomy course over, Jerome,
thanatologist, did not invite me
to the Special Service for the Twenty Dead,
did not say to me, "Come for the relatives' sake."
(Surprise, surprise, that they had relatives,
those lifeless-size, innominate creatures.)

Other students accepted, joined in the fake chanting,
organ solemnity, cobwebbed theatre.
And that's all it would have been,
a ceremony propitious and routine,
an obligation forgotten soon enough
had not the strict priest with premeditated rage
called out the Register of the Twenty Dead—
each non-cephalic carcass gloatingly identified
with a local habitation and a name
till one by one, made culpable, the students cried.

4

I did not learn the name of my intimate,
the twentieth sculpture, the one next to the door.
No matter. Now all these years later
I know those twenty sculptures were but one,
the same one duplicated. You.
I hear not Father Jerome but St. Jerome cry,
"No, John will be John, Mary will be Mary,"
as if the dead would have ears to hear
the Register on Judgement Day.
    Look, on gravestones many names.
There should be one only. Yours.
No, not even one since you have no name.
In the newspapers' memorial columns
many names. A joke.
On the canvases of masterpieces
the same figure always in disguise. Yours.
Even in the portraits of the old anchorite
fingering a dry skull you are half concealed
lest onlookers should turn away blinded.
In certain music, too, with its sound of loss,
in that Schubert Quintet, for instance,
you are there in the Adagio,
playing the third cello that cannot be heard.
    You are there and there and there, nameless,
and here I am, older by far and nearer,
perplexed, trying to recall what you looked like
before I dissected your face—you, threat,
molesting presence, and I in a white coat
your enemy, in a purple one, your nuncio,

writing this while a winter twig, not you,
scrapes, scrapes the windowpane.
    Soon I shall climb the stairs. Gratefully,
I shall wind up the usual clock at bedtime
(the steam vanishing from the bathroom mirror)
with my hand, my living hand.

JAMES DICKEY

JAMES DICKEY (1923–   ). *American poet, novelist, and critic. Dickey was born in Atlanta and attended Clemson and Vanderbilt universities. As a pilot in the Air Force, he flew a hundred missions on the Pacific front, and later saw military duty in Korea. He worked briefly in advertising, but after receiving a Guggenheim Fellowship left the world of business to focus exclusively on his writing. He won the National Book Award for poetry in 1966, and served as poetry consultant to the Library of Congress from 1966 to 1968. In addition to being a widely published poet, Dickey is the author of the novel* Deliverance *(1970); his most recent book is* To the White Sea *(1993). He has also published literary criticism and children's poetry. Dickey is currently a professor at the University of South Carolina.*

DIABETES

I
Sugar

One night I thirsted like a prince
Then like a king
Then like an empire   like a world
On fire. I rose and flowed away and fell
Once more to sleep. In an hour I was back
In the kingdom   staggering, my belly going round with self-
Made night-water, wondering what
The hell. Months of having a tongue
Of flame convinced me: I had better not go
On this way. The doctor was young

And nice. He said, I must tell you,
My friend, that it is needles moderation
And exercise. You don't want to look forward
To gangrene and kidney

Failure   boils blindness infection skin trouble falling
Teeth coma and death.
O.K.
In sleep my mouth went dry
With my answer   and in it burned the sands

Of time with new fury. Sleep could give me no water
But my own. Gangrene in white
Was in my wife's hand at breakfast
Heaped like a mountain. Moderation, moderation,
My friend, and exercise. Each time the barbell
Rose   each time a foot fell
Jogging, it counted itself
One death   two death   three death and resurrection
For a little while. Not bad! I always knew it would have to be
                                        somewhere around
The house: the real
Symbol of Time I could eat
And live with, coming true when I opened my mouth:
True in the coffee and the child's birthday
Cake   helping sickness be fire-
tongued, sleepless and water-
logged   but not bad, sweet sand
Of time, my friend, an everyday—
A livable death at last.

II
Under Buzzards

(for Robert Penn Warren)

Heavy summer. Heavy. Companion, if we climb our mortal bodies
High with great effort, we shall find ourselves
Flying with the life
Of the birds of death. We have come up
Under buzzards   they face us

Slowly   slowly circling   and as we watch them they turn us
Around, and you and I spin
Slowly, slowly rounding
Out the hill. We are level
Exactly on this moment: exactly on the same bird-

plane with those deaths. They are the salvation of our sense
Of glorious movement. Brother, it is right for us to face
Them every which way, and come to ourselves and come
From every direction
There is. Whirl and stand fast!
Whence cometh death, O Lord?
On the downwind, riding fire,

Of Hogback Ridge.
But listen: what is dead here?
They are not falling but waiting   but waiting
Riding, and they may know
The rotten, nervous sweetness of my blood.
Somewhere riding the updraft
Of a far forest fire, they sensed the city sugar
The doctors found in time.
My eyes are green as lettuce with my diet,
My weight is down,
One pocket nailed with needles and injections, the other dragging
With sugar cubes to balance me in life
And hold my blood
Level, level. Tell me, black riders, does this do any good?
Tell me what I need to know about my time
In the world. O out of the fiery

Furnace of pine-woods, in the sap-smoke and crownfire of needles,
Say when I'll die. When will the sugar rise boiling
Against me, and my brain be sweetened
to death?
In heavy summer, like this day.
All right! Physicians, witness! I will shoot my veins
Full of insulin. Let the needle burn
In. From your terrible heads
The flight-blood drains   and you are falling back
Back to the body-raising
Fire.
Heavy summer. Heavy. My blood is clear
For a time. Is it too clear? Heat waves are rising
Without birds. But something is gone from me,
Friend. This is too sensible. Really it is better
To know when to die   better for my blood
To stream with the death-wish of birds.
You know, I had just as soon crush
This doomed syringe
Between two mountain rocks, and bury this needle in needles

Of trees. Companion, open that beer.
How the body works   how hard it works
For its medical books is not
Everything: everything is how
Much glory is in it: heavy summer is right

229

For a long drink of beer. Red sugar of my eyeballs
Feels them turn blindly
In the fire   rising   turning   turning
Back to Hogback Ridge, and it is all
Delicious, brother: my body is turning   is flashing unbalanced
Sweetness everywhere, and I am calling my birds.

THE CANCER MATCH

Lord, you've sent both
And may have come yourself. I will sit down, bearing up under
The death of light very well, and we will all
Have a drink. Two or three, maybe.
I see now the delights

Of being let "come home"
From the hospital.
Night!
I don't have all the time
In the world, but I have all night.
I have space for me and my house,
And I have cancer and whiskey

In a lovely relation.
They are squared off, here on my ground. They are fighting,
Or are they dancing? I have been told   and told
That medicine has no hope, or anything
More to give,

But they have no idea
What hope is, or how it comes. You take these two things:
This bourbon and this thing growing. Why,
They are like boys! They bow
To each other

Like judo masters,
One of them jumping for joy, and I watch them struggle
All around the room, inside and out
Of the house, as they battle
Near the mailbox

And superbly
For the street-lights! Internally, I rise like my old self
To watch: and remember, ladies and gentlemen,
We are looking at this match
From the standpoint

Of tonight
Alone, swarm over him, my joy, my laughter, my Basic Life
Force! Let your bright sword-arm stream
Into that turgid hulk, the worst
Of me, growing:

Get 'im, O Self
Like a beloved son! One more time! Tonight we are going
Good   better and better   we are going
To win, and not only win but win
Big, win big.

DENISE LEVERTOV

DENISE LEVERTOV (1923–   ). *English-born poet who remained in the United States after her marriage to an American in 1948. Her writings, influenced by William Carlos Williams and other contemporary poets, span more than three decades, from the publication of* Five Poems *(1958) and* The Jacob's Ladder *(1961) to* A Door in the Hive *(1989) and* Evening Train *(1993), with more than a dozen other volumes in between.*

TALKING TO GRIEF

Ah, grief, I should not treat you
like a homeless dog
who comes to the back door
for a crust, for a meatless bone.
I should trust you.

I should coax you
into the house and give you
your own corner,
a worn mat to lie on,
your own water dish.

You think I don't know you've been living
under my porch.
You long for your real place to be readied
before winter comes. You need
your name,
your collar and tag. You need
the right to warn off intruders,
to consider
my house your own
and me your person
and yourself
my own dog.

DEATH PSALM: O LORD OF MYSTERIES

She grew old.
She made ready to die.
She gave counsel to women and men, to young girls and
                                                  young boys.

She remembered her griefs.
She remembered her happinesses.
She watered the garden.
She accused herself.
She forgave herself.
She learned new fragments of wisdom.
She forgot old fragments of wisdom.
She abandoned certain angers.
She gave away gold and precious stones.
She counted-over her handkerchiefs of fine lawn.
She continued to laugh on some days, to cry on others,
                        unfolding the design of her identity.
She practiced the songs she knew, her voice
                                gone out of tune
                but the breathing-pattern perfected.
She told her sons and daughters she was ready.
She maintained her readiness.
She grew very old.
She watched the generations increase.
She watched the passing of seasons and years.
She did not die.

She did not die, but lies half-speechless, incontinent,
                aching in body, wandering in mind
                in a hospital room.
A plastic tube, taped to her nose,
        disappears into one nostril.
Plastic tubes are attached to veins in her arms.
Her urine runs through a tube into a bottle under the bed.
On her back and ankles are black sores.

The black sores are parts of her that have died.
The beat of her heart is steady.
She is not whole.

She made ready to die, she prayed, she made her peace,
        she read daily from the lectionary.

She tended the green garden she had made,
    she fought off the destroying ants,
    she watered the plants daily
    and took note of their blossoming.
She gave sustenance to the needy.
She prepared her life for the hour of death.
But the hour has passed and she has not died.

O Lord of mysteries, how beautiful is sudden death
    when the spirit vanishes
    boldly and without casting
    a single shadowy feather of hesitation
    onto the felled body.

O Lord of mysteries, how baffling, how clueless
    is laggard death, disregarding
    all that is set before it
        in the dignity of welcome—
    laggard death, that steals
        insignificant patches of flesh—
    laggard death, that shuffles
    past the open gate,
    past the open hand,
    past the open,
        ancient,
        courteously waiting life.

FLANNERY O'CONNOR

FLANNERY O'CONNOR (1925–1964). *American fiction writer. A Southern writer whose early serious illness (lupus erythematosus) forced her to spend most of her life on a farm in Georgia, O'Connor's fiction abounds in comic-grotesque characters set loose in an unfathomable world. She was awarded three O. Henry awards during her lifetime, and a National Book Award posthumously. Her books include* Wise Blood *(1952),* a Good Man Is Hard to Find *(1955),* The Violent Bear It Away *(1960), and* Everything That Rises Must Converge *(1965).*

EVERYTHING THAT RISES MUST CONVERGE

Her doctor had told Julian's mother that she must lose twenty pounds on account of her blood pressure, so on Wednesday nights Julian had to take her downtown on the bus for a reducing class at the Y. The reducing class was designed for working girls over fifty, who weighed from 165 to 200 pounds. His mother was one of the slimmer ones, but she said ladies did not tell their age or weight. She would not ride the buses by herself at night since they had been integrated, and because the reducing class was one of her few pleasures, necessary for her health, and *free,* she said Julian could at least put himself out to take her, considering all she did for him. Julian did not like to consider all she did for him, but every Wednesday night he braced himself and took her.

She was almost ready to go, standing before the hall mirror, putting on her hat, while he, his hands behind him, appeared pinned to the door frame, waiting like Saint Sebastian for the arrows to begin piercing him. The hat was new and had cost her seven dollars and a half. She kept saying, "Maybe I shouldn't have paid that for it. No, I shouldn't have. I'll take it off and return it tomorrow. I shouldn't have bought it."

Julian raised his eyes to heaven. "Yes, you should have bought it," he said. "Put it on and let's go." It was a hideous hat. A purple velvet flap came down on one side of it and stood up on the other; the rest of it was green and looked like a cushion with the stuffing out. He decided it was less comical than jaunty and pathetic. Everything that gave her pleasure was small and depressed him.

She lifted the hat one more time and set it down slowly on top of her head. Two wings of gray hair protruded on either side of her florid face, but her eyes, sky-blue, were as innocent and untouched by experience as they must have been when she was ten. Were it not that she was a widow who had struggled fiercely to feed and clothe and put him through school and who was supporting him still, "until he got on his feet," she might have been a little girl that he had to take to town.

"It's all right, it's all right," he said. "Let's go." He opened the door himself and started down the walk to get her going. The sky was a dying violet and the houses stood out darkly against it, bulbous liver-colored monstrosities of a uniform ugliness though no two were alike. Since this had been a fashionable neighborhood forty years ago, his mother persisted in thinking they did well to have an apartment in it. Each house had a narrow collar of dirt around it in which sat, usually, a grubby child. Julian walked with his hands in his pockets, his head down and thrust forward and his eyes glazed with the determination to make himself completely numb during the time he would be sacrificed to her pleasure.

The door closed and he turned to find the dumpy figure, surmounted by the atrocious hat, coming toward him. "Well," she said, "you only live once and paying a little more for it, I at least won't meet myself coming and going."

"Some day I'll start making money," Julian said gloomily—he knew he never would—"and you can have one of those jokes whenever you take the fit." But first they would move. He visualized a place where the nearest neighbors would be three miles away on either side.

"I think you're doing fine," she said, drawing on her gloves. "You've only been out of school a year. Rome wasn't built in a day."

She was one of the few members of the Y reducing class who arrived in hat and gloves and who had a son who had been to college. "It takes time," she said, "and the world is in such a mess. This hat looked better on me than any of the others, though when she brought it out I said, 'Take that thing back. I wouldn't have it on my head,' and she said, 'Now wait till you see it on,' and when she put it on me, I said, 'We-ull,' and she said, 'If you ask me, that hat does something for you and you do something for the hat, and besides,' she said, 'with that hat, you won't meet yourself coming and going.'"

Julian thought he could have stood his lot better if she had been selfish, if she had been an old hag who drank and screamed at him. He walked along, saturated in depression, as if in the midst of his martyrdom he had lost his faith. Catching sight of his long, hopeless, irritated face, she stopped suddenly with a grief-stricken look, and pulled back on his arm. "Wait on me," she said. "I'm going back to the house and take this thing off and tomorrow I'm going to return it. I was out of my head. I can pay the gas bill with the seven-fifty."

He caught her arm in a vicious grip. "You are not going to take it back," he said. "I like it."

"Well," she said, "I don't think I ought . . ."

"Shut up and enjoy it," he muttered, more depressed than ever.

"With the world in the mess it's in," she said, "it's a wonder we can enjoy anything. I tell you, the bottom rail is on the top."

Julian sighed.

"Of course," she said, "if you know who you are, you can go anywhere." She said this every time he took her to the reducing class. "Most of them in it are not our kind of people," she said, "but I can be gracious to anybody. I know who I am."

"They don't give a damn for your graciousness," Julian said savagely. "Knowing who you are is good for one generation only. You haven't the foggiest idea where you stand now or who you are."

She stopped and allowed her eyes to flash at him. "I most certainly do know who I am," she said, "and if you don't know who you are, I'm ashamed of you."

"Oh hell," Julian said.

"Your great-grandfather was a former governor of this state," she said. "Your grandfather was a prosperous landowner. Your grandmother was a Godhigh."

"Will you look around you," he said tensely, "and see where you are now?" and he swept his arm jerkily out to indicate the neighborhood, which the growing darkness at least made less dingy.

"You remain what you are," she said. "Your great-grandfather had a plantation and two hundred slaves."

"There are no more slaves," he said irritably.

"They were better off when they were," she said. He groaned to see that she was off on that topic. She rolled onto it every few days like a train on an open track. He knew every stop, every junction, every swamp along the way, and knew the exact point at which her conclusion would roll majestically into the station: "It's ridiculous. It's simply not realistic. They should rise, yes, but on their own side of the fence."

"Let's skip it," Julian said.

"The ones I feel sorry for," she said, "are the ones that are half white. They're tragic."

"Will you skip it?"

"Suppose we were half white. We would certainly have mixed feelings."

"I have mixed feelings now," he groaned.

"Well let's talk about something pleasant," she said. "I remember going to Grandpa's when I was a little girl. Then the house had double stairways that went up to what was really the second floor—all the cooking was done on the first. I used to like to stay down in the kitchen on account of the way the walls smelled. I would sit with my nose pressed against the plaster and take deep breaths. Actually the place belonged to the Godhighs but your grandfather Chestny paid the mortgage and saved it for them. They were in reduced circumstances," she said, "but reduced or not, they never forgot who they were."

"Doubtless that decayed mansion reminded them," Julian muttered. He never spoke of it without contempt or thought of it without longing. He had seen it once when he was a child before it had been sold. The double stairways had rotted and been torn down. Negroes were living in it. But it remained in his mind as his mother had known it. It appeared in his dreams regularly. He would stand on the wide porch, listening to the rustle of oak leaves, then wander through the high-ceilinged hall into the parlor that opened onto it and gaze at the worn rugs and faded draperies. It occurred to him that it was he, not she, who could have appreciated it. He preferred its threadbare elegance to anything he could name and it was because of it that all the neighborhoods they had lived in had been a torment to him—whereas she had hardly known the difference. She called her insensitivity "being adjustable."

"And I remember the old darky who was my nurse, Caroline. There was no better person in the world. I've always had a great respect for my colored friends," she said. "I'd do anything in the world for them and they'd . . ."

"Will you for God's sake get off that subject?" Julian said. When he got on a bus by himself, he made it a point to sit down beside a Negro, in reparation as it were for his mother's sins.

"You're mighty touchy tonight," she said. "Do you feel all right?"

"Yes I feel all right," he said. "Now lay off."

She pursed her lips. "Well, you certainly are in a vile humor," she observed. "I just won't speak to you at all."

They had reached the bus stop. There was no bus in sight and Julian, his hands still jammed in his pockets and his head thrust forward, scowled down the empty street. The frustration of having to wait on the bus as well as ride on it began to creep up his neck like a hot hand. The presence of his mother was borne in upon him as she gave a pained sigh. He looked at her bleakly. She was holding herself very erect under the preposterous hat, wearing it like a banner of her imaginary dignity. There was in him an evil urge to break her spirit. He suddenly unloosened his tie and pulled it off and put it in his pocket.

She stiffened. "Why must you look like *that* when you take me to town?" she said. "Why must you deliberately embarrass me?"

"If you'll never learn where you are," he said, "you can at least learn where I am."

"You look like a—thug," she said.

"Then I must be one," he murmured.

"I'll just go home," she said. "I will not bother you. If you can't do a little thing like that for me . . ."

Rolling his eyes upward, he put his tie back on. "Restored to my class," he muttered. He thrust his face toward her and hissed, "True culture is in the mind, the *mind*," he said, and tapped his head, "the mind."

"It's in the heart," she said, "and in how you do things and how you do things is because of who you *are*."

"Nobody in the damn bus cares who you are."

"I care who I am," she said icily.

The lighted bus appeared on top of the next hill and as it approached, they moved out into the street to meet it. He put his hand under her elbow and hoisted her up on the creaking step. She entered with a little smile, as if she were going into a drawing room where everyone had been waiting for her. While he put in the tokens, she sat down on one of the broad front seats for three which faced the aisle. A thin woman with protruding teeth and long yellow hair was sitting on the end of it. His mother moved up beside her and left room for Julian beside herself. He sat down and looked at the floor across the aisle where a pair of thin feet in red and white canvas sandals were planted.

His mother immediately began a general conversation meant to attract anyone who felt like talking. "Can it get any hotter?" she said and removed from her purse a folding fan, black with a Japanese scene on it, which she began to flutter before her.

"I reckon it might could," the woman with the protruding teeth said, "but I know for a fact my apartment couldn't get no hotter."

"It must get the afternoon sun," his mother said. She sat forward and looked up and down the bus. It was half filled. Everybody was white. "I see we have the bus to ourselves," she said. Julian cringed.

"For a change," said the woman across the aisle, the owner of the red and white canvas sandals. "I come on one the other day and they were thick as fleas—up front and all through."

"The world is in a mess everywhere," his mother said. "I don't know how we've let it get in this fix."

"What gets my goat is all those boys from good families stealing automobile tires," the woman with the protruding teeth said. "I told my boy, I said you may not be rich but you been raised right and if I ever catch you in any such mess, they can send you on to the reformatory. Be exactly where you belong."

"Training tells," his mother said. "Is your boy in high school?"

"Ninth grade," the woman said.

"My son just finished college last year. He wants to write but he's selling typewriters until he gets started," his mother said.

The woman leaned forward and peered at Julian. He threw her such a malevolent look that she subsided against the seat. On the floor across the aisle there was an abandoned newspaper. He got up and got it and opened it out in front of him. His mother discreetly continued the conversation in a lower tone but the woman across the aisle said in a loud voice, "Well that's nice. Selling typewriters is close to writing. He can go right from one to the other."

"I tell him," his mother said, "that Rome wasn't built in a day."

Behind the newspaper Julian was withdrawing into the inner compartment of his mind where he spent most of his time. This was a kind of mental bubble in which he established himself when he could not bear to be a part of what was going on around him. From it he could see out and judge but in it he was safe from any kind of penetration from without. It was the only place where he felt free of the general idiocy of his fellows. His mother had never entered it but from it he could see her with absolute clarity.

The old lady was clever enough and he thought that if she had started from any of the right premises, more might have been expected of her. She lived according to the laws of her own fantasy world, outside of which he had never seen her set foot. The law of it was to sacrifice herself for him after she had first created the necessity to do so by making a mess of things. If he had permitted her sacrifices, it was only because her lack of foresight had made them necessary. All of her life had been a struggle to act like a Chestny without the Chestny goods, and to give him everything she thought a Chestny ought to have; but since, said she, it was fun to struggle, why complain? And when you had won, as she had won, what fun to look back on the hard times! He could not forgive her that she had enjoyed the struggle and that she thought *she* had won.

What she meant when she said she had won was that she had brought him up successfully and had sent him to college and that he had turned out so well—good looking (her teeth had gone unfilled so that his could be straightened), intelligent (he realized he was too intelligent to be a success), and with a future ahead of him (there was of course no future ahead of him). She excused his gloominess on the grounds that he was still growing up and his radical ideas on his lack of practical experience. She said he didn't yet know a thing about "life," that he hadn't even entered the real world—when already he was as disenchanted with it as a man of fifty.

The further irony of all this was that in spite of her, he had turned out so well. In spite of going to only a third-rate college, he had, on his own initiative, come out with a first-rate education; in spite of growing up dominated by a small mind, he had ended up with a large one; in spite of all her foolish views, he was free of prejudice and unafraid to face facts. Most miraculous of all, instead of being blinded by love for her as she was for him, he had cut himself emotionally free of her and could see her with complete objectivity. He was not dominated by his mother.

The bus stopped with a sudden jerk and shook him from his meditation. A woman from the back lurched forward with little steps and barely escaped falling in his newspaper as she righted herself. She got off and a large Negro got on. Julian kept his paper lowered to watch. It gave him a certain satisfaction to see injustice in daily operation. It confirmed his view that with a few exceptions there was no one worth knowing within a radius of three hundred miles. The Negro was well dressed and carried a briefcase. He looked around and then sat down on the other end of the seat where the woman with the red and white canvas sandals was sitting. He immediately unfolded a newspaper and obscured himself behind it. Julian's mother's elbow at once prodded insistently into his ribs. "Now you see why I won't ride on these buses by myself," she whispered.

The woman with the red and white canvas sandals had risen at the same time the Negro sat down and had gone further back in the bus and taken the seat of the woman who had got off. His mother leaned forward and cast her an approving look.

Julian rose, crossed the aisle, and sat down in the place of the woman with the canvas sandals. From this position, he looked serenely across at his mother. Her face had turned an angry red. He stared at her, making his eyes the eyes of a stranger. He felt his tension suddenly lift as if he had openly declared war on her.

He would have liked to get in conversation with the Negro and to talk with him about art or politics or any subject that would be above the comprehension of those around him, but the man remained entrenched behind his paper. He was either ignoring the change of seating or had never noticed it. There was no way for Julian to convey his sympathy.

His mother kept her eyes fixed reproachfully on his face. The woman with the protruding teeth was looking at him avidly as if he were a type of monster new to her.

"Do you have a light?" he asked the Negro.

Without looking away from his paper, the man reached in his pocket and handed him a packet of matches.

"Thanks," Julian said. For a moment he held the matches foolishly. A NO SMOKING sign looked down upon him from over the door. This alone would not have deterred him; he had no cigarettes. He had quit smoking some months before because he could not afford it. "Sorry," he muttered and handed back the matches. The Negro lowered the paper and gave him an annoyed look. He took the matches and raised the paper again.

His mother continued to gaze at him but she did not take advantage of his momentary discomfort. Her eyes retained their battered look. Her face seemed to be unnaturally red, as if her blood pressure had risen. Julian allowed no glimmer of sympathy to show on his face. Having got the advantage, he wanted desperately to keep it and carry it through. He would have liked to teach her a lesson that would last her a while, but there seemed no way to continue the point. The Negro refused to come out from behind his paper.

Julian folded his arms and looked stolidly before him, facing her but as if he did not see her, as if he had ceased to recognize her existence. He visualized a scene in which, the bus having reached their stop, he would remain in his seat and when she said, "Aren't you going to get off?" he would look at her as at a stranger who had rashly addressed him. The corner they got off on was usually deserted, but it was well lighted and it would not hurt her to walk by herself the four blocks to the Y. He decided to wait until the time came and then decide whether or not he would let her get off by herself. He would have to be at the Y at ten to bring her back, but he could leave her wondering if he was going to show up. There was no reason for her to think she could always depend on him.

He retired again into the high-ceilinged room sparsely settled with large pieces of antique furniture. His soul expanded momentarily but then he became aware of his mother across from him and the vision shriveled. He studied her coldly. Her feet in little pumps dangled like a child's and did not quite reach the floor. She was training on him an exaggerated look of reproach. He felt completely detached from her. At that moment he could with pleasure have slapped her as he would have slapped a particularly obnoxious child in his charge.

He began to imagine various unlikely ways by which he could teach her a lesson. He might make friends with some distinguished Negro professor or lawyer and bring him home to spend the evening. He would be entirely justified but her blood pressure would rise to 300. He could not push her to the extent of making her have a stroke, and moreover, he had never been successful at making any Negro friends. He had tried to strike up an acquaintance on the bus with some of the better types, with ones that looked like professors or ministers or lawyers. One morning he had sat down next to a distinguished-looking dark brown man who had answered his questions with a sonorous solemnity but who had turned out to be an undertaker. Another day he had sat down beside a cigar-smoking Negro with a diamond ring on his finger, but after a few stilted pleasantries, the Negro had rung the buzzer and risen, slipping two lottery tickets into Julian's hand as he climbed over him to leave.

He imagined his mother lying desperately ill and his being able to secure only a Negro doctor for her. He toyed with that idea for a few minutes and then dropped it for a momentary vision of himself participating as a sympathizer in a sit-in demonstration. This was possible but he did not linger with it. Instead, he approached the ultimate horror. He brought home a beautiful suspiciously Negroid woman. Prepare yourself, he said. There is nothing you can do about it. This is the woman I've chosen. She's intelligent, dignified, even good, and she's suffered and she hasn't thought it *fun*. Now persecute us, go ahead and persecute us. Drive her out of here, but remember, you're driving me too. His eyes were narrowed and through the indignation he had generated, he saw his mother across the aisle, purple-faced, shrunken to the dwarf-like proportions of her moral nature, sitting like a mummy beneath the ridiculous banner of her hat.

He was tilted out of his fantasy again as the bus stopped. The door opened with a sucking hiss and out of the dark a large, gaily dressed, sullen-looking colored woman got on with a little boy. The child, who might have been four, had on a short plaid suit and a Tyrolean hat with a blue feather in it. Julian hoped that he would sit down beside him and that the woman would push in beside his mother. He could think of no better arrangement.

As she waited for her tokens, the woman was surveying the seating possibilities—he hoped with the idea of sitting where she was least wanted. There was something familiar-looking about her but Julian could not place what it was. She was a giant of a woman. Her face was set not only to meet opposition but to seek it out. The downward tilt of her large lower lip was like a warning sign: DON'T TAMPER WITH ME. Her bulging figure was encased in a green crepe dress and her feet overflowed in red shoes. She had on a hideous hat. A purple velvet flap came down on one side of it and stood up on the other; the rest of it was green and looked like a cushion with the stuffing out. She carried a mammoth red pocketbook that bulged throughout as if it were stuffed with rocks.

To Julian's disappointment, the little boy climbed up on the empty seat beside his mother. His mother lumped all children, black and white, into the common category, "cute," and she thought little Negroes were on the whole cuter than little white children. She smiled at the little boy as he climbed on the seat.

Meanwhile the woman was bearing down upon the empty seat beside Julian. To his annoyance, she squeezed herself into it. He saw his mother's face change as the woman settled herself next to him and he realized with satisfaction that this was more objectionable to her than it was to him. Her face seemed almost gray and there was a look of dull recognition in her eyes, as if suddenly she had sickened at some awful confrontation. Julian saw that it was because she and the woman had, in a sense, swapped sons. Though his mother would not realize the symbolic significance of this, she would feel it. His amusement showed plainly on his face.

The woman next to him muttered something unintelligible to herself. He was conscious of a kind of bristling next to him, muted growling like that of an angry cat. He could not see anything but the red pocketbook upright on the bulging green thighs. He visualized the woman as she had stood waiting for her tokens—the ponderous figure, rising from the red shoes upward over the solid hips, the mammoth bosom, the haughty face, to the green and purple hat.

His eyes widened.

The vision of the two hats, identical, broke upon him with the radiance of a brilliant sunrise. His face was suddenly lit with joy. He could not believe that Fate had thrust upon his mother such a lesson. He gave a loud chuckle so that she would look at him and see that he saw. She turned her eyes on him slowly. The blue in them seemed to have turned a bruised purple. For a moment he had an uncomfortable sense of her innocence, but it lasted only a second before principle rescued him. Justice entitled him to laugh. His grin hardened until it said to her as plainly as if he were saying aloud: Your punishment exactly fits your pettiness. This should teach you a permanent lesson.

Her eyes shifted to the woman. She seemed unable to bear looking at him and to find the woman preferable. He became conscious again of the bristling presence at his side. The woman was rumbling like a volcano about to become active. His mother's mouth began to twitch slightly at one corner. With a sinking heart, he saw incipient signs of recovery on her face and realized that this was going to strike her suddenly as funny and was going to be no lesson at all. She kept her eyes on the woman and an amused smile came over her face as if the woman were a monkey that had stolen her hat. The little Negro was looking up at her with large fascinated eyes. He had been trying to attract her attention for some time.

"Carver!" the woman said suddenly. "Come heah!"

When he saw that the spotlight was on him at last, Carver drew his feet up and turned himself toward Julian's mother and giggled.

"Carver!" the woman said. "You heah me? Come heah!"

Carver slid down from the seat but remained squatting with his back against the base of it, his head turned slyly around toward Julian's mother, who was smiling at him. The woman reached a hand across the aisle and snatched him to her. He righted himself and hung backwards on her knees, grinning at Julian's mother. "Isn't he cute?" Julian's mother said to the woman with the protruding teeth.

"I reckon he is," the woman said without conviction.

The Negress yanked him upright but he eased out of her grip and shot across the aisle and scrambled, giggling wildly, onto the seat beside his love.

"I think he likes me," Julian's mother said, and smiled at the woman. It was the smile she used when she was being particularly gracious to an inferior. Julian saw everything lost. The lesson had rolled off her like rain on a roof.

The woman stood up and yanked the little boy off the seat as if she were snatching him from contagion. Julian could feel the rage in her at having no weapon like his mother's smile. She gave the child a sharp slap across his leg. He howled once and then thrust his head into her stomach and kicked his feet against her shins. "Behave," she said vehemently.

The bus stopped and the Negro who had been reading the newspaper got off. The woman moved over and set the little boy down with a thump between herself and Julian. She held him firmly by the knee. In a moment he put his hands in front of his face and peeped at Julian's mother through his fingers.

"I see yoooooooo!" she said and put her hand in front of her face and peeped at him.

The woman slapped his hand down. "Quit yo' foolishness," she said, "before I knock the living Jesus out of you!"

Julian was thankful that the next stop was theirs. He reached up and pulled the cord. The woman reached up and pulled it at the same time. Oh my God, he thought. He had the terrible intuition that when they got off the bus together, his mother would open her purse and give the little boy a nickel. The gesture would be as natural to her as breathing. The bus stopped and the woman got up and lunged to the front, dragging the child, who wished to stay on, after her. Julian and his mother got up and followed. As they neared the door, Julian tried to relieve her of her pocketbook.

"No," she murmured, "I want to give the little boy a nickel."

"No!" Julian hissed. "No!"

She smiled down at the child and opened her bag. The bus door opened and the woman picked him up by the arm and descended with him, hanging at her hip. Once in the street she set him down and shook him.

Julian's mother had to close her purse while she got down the bus step but as soon as her feet were on the ground, she opened it again and began to rummage inside. "I can't find but a penny," she whispered, "but it looks like a new one."

"Don't do it!" Julian said fiercely between his teeth. There was a streetlight on the corner and she hurried to get under it so that she could better see into her pocketbook. The woman was heading off rapidly down the street with the child still hanging backwards on her hand.

"Oh little boy!" Julian's mother called and took a few quick steps and caught up with them just beyond the lamppost. "Here's a bright new penny for you," and she held out the coin, which shone bronze in the dim light.

The huge woman turned and for a moment stood, her shoulders lifted and her face frozen with frustrated rage, and stared at Julian's mother. Then all at once she seemed to explode like a piece of machinery that had been given one ounce of pressure too much. Julian saw the black fist swing out with the red pocketbook. He shut his eyes and cringed as he heard the woman shout, "He don't take nobody's pennies!" When he opened his eyes, the woman was disappearing down the street with the little boy staring wide-eyed over her shoulder. Julian's mother was sitting on the sidewalk.

"I told you not to do that," Julian said angrily. "I told you not to do that!"

He stood over her for a minute, gritting his teeth. Her legs were stretched out in front of her and her hat was on her lap. He squatted down and looked her in the face. It was totally expressionless. "You got exactly what you deserved," he said. "Now get up."

He picked up her pocketbook and put what had fallen out back in it. He picked the hat up off her lap. The penny caught his eye on the sidewalk and he picked that up and let it drop before her eyes into the purse. Then he stood up and leaned over and held his hands out to pull her up. She remained immobile. He sighed. Rising above them on either side were black apartment buildings, marked with irregular rectangles of light. At the end of the block a man came out of a door and walked off in the opposite direction. "All right," he said, "suppose somebody happens by and wants to know why you're sitting on the sidewalk?"

She took the hand and, breathing hard, pulled heavily up on it and then stood for a moment, swaying slightly as if the spots of light in the darkness were circling around her. Her eyes, shadowed and confused, finally settled on his face. He did not try to conceal his irritation. "I hope this teaches you a lesson," he said. She leaned forward and her eyes raked his face. She seemed trying to determine his identity. Then, as if she found nothing familiar about him, she started off with a head-long movement in the wrong direction.

"Aren't you going on to the Y?" he asked.

"Home," she muttered.

"Well, are we walking?"

For answer she kept going. Julian followed along, his hands behind him. He saw no reason to let the lesson she had had go without backing it up with an explanation of its meaning. She might as well be made to understand what had happened to her. "Don't think that was just an uppity Negro woman," he said. "That was the whole colored race which will no longer take your condescending pennies. That was your black double. She can wear the same hat as you, and to be sure," he added gratuitously (because he thought it was funny), "it looked better on her than it did on you. What all this means," he said, "is that the old world is gone. The old manners are obsolete and your graciousness is not worth a damn." He thought bitterly of the house that had been lost for him. "You aren't who you think you are," he said.

She continued to plow ahead, paying no attention to him. Her hair had come undone on one side. She dropped her pocketbook and took no notice. He stooped and picked it up and handed it to her but she did not take it.

"You needn't act as if the world had come to an end," he said, "because it hasn't. From now on you've got to live in a new world and face a few realities for a change. Buck up," he said, "it won't kill you."

She was breathing fast.

"Let's wait on the bus," he said.

"Home," she said thickly.

"I hate to see you behave like this," he said. "Just like a child. I should be able to expect more of you." He decided to stop where he was and make her stop and wait for a bus. "I'm not going any farther," he said, stopping. "We're going on the bus."

She continued to go on as if she had not heard him. He took a few steps and caught her arm and stopped her. He looked into her face and caught his breath. He was looking into a face he had never seen before. "Tell Grandpa to come get me," she said.

He stared, stricken.

"Tell Caroline to come get me," she said.

Stunned, he let her go and she lurched forward again, walking as if one leg were shorter than the other. A tide of darkness seemed to be sweeping her from him. "Mother!" he cried. "Darling, sweetheart, wait!" Crumpling, she fell to the pavement. He dashed forward and fell at her side, crying, "Mamma, Mamma!" He turned her over. Her face was fiercely distorted. One eye, large and staring, moved slightly to the left as if it had become unmoored. The other remained fixed on him, raked his face again, found nothing and closed.

"Wait here, wait here!" he cried and jumped up and began to run for help toward a cluster of lights he saw in the distance ahead of him. "Help, help!" he shouted, but his voice was thin, scarcely a thread of sound. The lights drifted farther away the faster he ran and his feet moved numbly as if they carried him nowhere. The tide of darkness seemed to sweep him back to her, postponing from moment to moment his entry into the world of guilt and sorrow.

L. E. SISSMAN

L. E. SISSMAN (1928–1976). *American poet. Sissman, an advertising executive, suffered from Hodgkin's disease, and some of his poetry was influenced by this chronic, debilitating illness. Poems such as "A Deathplace" describe poignant, even breathtaking thoughts about death within a hospital setting. Other works include* Dying: An Introduction *(1968),* Scattered Returns *(1969), and* Hello Darkness: The Collected Poems of L. E. Sissman *(1978). Sissman received several writing awards, including a Guggenheim Fellowship (1968) and a grant from the National Institute of Arts and Letters (1969).*

A DEATHPLACE

Very few people know where they will die,
But I do: in a brick-faced hospital,
Divided not unlike Caesarean Gaul,
Into three parts: the Dean Memorial
Wing, in the classic cast of 1910,
Green-grated in unglazed, Aeolian
Embrasures; the Maud Wiggin Building, which
Commemorates a dog-jawed Boston bitch
Who fought the brass down to their whipcord knees
In World War I, and won enlisted men
Some decent hospitals, and, being rich,
Donated her own granite monument;
The Mandeville Pavilion, pink-brick tent
With marble piping, flying snapping flags
Above the entry where our bloody rags
Are rolled in to be sponged and sewn again.
Today is fair; tomorrow, scourging rain
(If only my own tears) will see me in
Those jaundiced and distempered corridors
Off which the five-foot-wide doors slowly close.
White as my skimpy chiton, I will cringe
Before the pinpoint of the least syringe;
Before the buttered catheter goes in;
Before the I.V.'s lisp and drip begins
Inside my skin; before the rubber hand
Upon the lancet takes aim and descends

To lay me open, and upon its thumb
Retracts the trouble, a malignant plum;
And finally, I'll quail before the hour
When the authorities shut off the power
In that vast hospital, and in my bed
I'll feel my blood go thin, go white, the red,
The rose all leached away, and I'll go dead.
Then will the business of life resume:
The muffled trolley wheeled into my room,
The off-white blanket blanking off my face,
The stealing, secret, private, *largo* race
Down halls and elevators to the place
I'll be consigned to for transshipment, cased
In artificial air and light: the ward
That's underground; the terminal; the morgue.
Then one fine day when all the smart flags flap,
A booted man in black with a peaked cap
Will call for me and troll me down the hall
And slot me into his black car. That's all.

RICHARD SELZER

RICHARD SELZER (1928–   ). *American surgeon, writer, and educator. Born and raised in Troy, New York, Dr. Selzer was on the faculty of the Yale School of Medicine until 1990. He is both a popular, engaging lecturer and a widely published author; among his books are* Mortal Lessons: Notes on the Art of Surgery; Confessions of a Knife; *and* Taking the World in for Repairs. *His recent works—*Down from Troy: A Doctor Comes of Age *(1993) and* Raising the Dead: A Doctor's Encounter with His Own Mortality *(1994)—are wholly autobiographical. In* Down from Troy, *Selzer artistically chronicles the arc of his life from his childhood through his medical training, surgical career, and retirement, while in* Raising the Dead, *he captures the peculiarity of the doctor-turned-patient phenomenon by reflecting on his own excruciating experience with Legionnaires' disease.*

MERCY

It is October at the Villa Serbelloni, where I have come for a month to write. On the window ledges the cluster flies are dying. The climate is full of uncertainty. Should it cool down? Or warm up? Each day it overshoots the mark, veering from frost to steam. The flies have no uncertainty. They understand that their time has come.

What a lot of energy it takes to die! The frenzy of it. Long after they have collapsed and stayed motionless, the flies are capable of suddenly spinning so rapidly that they cannot be seen. Or seen only as a blurred glitter. They are like dervishes who whirl, then stop, and lay as quiet as before, only now and then waving a leg or two feebly, in a stuporous reenactment of locomotion. Until the very moment of death, the awful buzzing as though to swarm again.

Every morning I scoop up three dozen or so corpses with a dustpan and brush. Into the wastebasket they go, and I sit to begin the day's writing. All at once, from the wastebasket, the frantic knocking of resurrection. Here, death has not yet secured the premises. No matter the numbers slaughtered, no matter that the windows be kept shut all day, each evening the flies gather on the ledges to die, as they have lived, *ensemble.* It must be companionable to die so, matching spin for spin, knock for knock, and buzz for buzz with one's fellows. We humans have no such fraternity, but each of us must buzz and spin and knock alone.

I think of a man in New Haven! He has been my patient for seven years, ever since the day I explored his abdomen in the operating room and found the surprise lurking there—a cancer of the pancreas. He was forty-two years old then. For this man, these have been seven years of famine. For his wife and his mother as well. Until three days ago his suffering was marked by slowly increasing pain, vomiting and fatigue. Still, it was endurable. With morphine. Three days ago the pain rollicked out of control, and he entered that elect band whose suffering cannot be relieved by any means short of death. In his bed at home he seemed an eighty-pound concentrate of pain from which all other pain must be made by serial dilution. He twisted under the lash of it. An ambulance arrived. At the hospital nothing was to be done to prolong his life. Only the administration of large doses of narcotics.

"Please," he begs me. In his open mouth, upon his teeth, a brown paste of saliva. All night long he has thrashed, as though to hollow out a grave in the bed.

"I won't let you suffer," I tell him. In his struggle the sheet is thrust aside. I see the old abandoned incision, the belly stuffed with tumor. His penis, even, is skinny. One foot with five blue toes is exposed. In my cupped hand, they are cold. I think of the twenty bones of that foot laced together with tendon, each ray accompanied by its own nerve and artery. Now, this foot seems a beautiful dead animal that had once been trained to transmit the command of a man's brain to the earth.

"I'll get rid of the pain," I tell his wife.

But there is no way to kill the pain without killing the man who owns it. Morphine to the lethal dose . . . and still he miaows and bays and makes other sounds like a boat breaking up in a heavy sea. I think his pain will live on long after he dies.

"Please," begs his wife, "we cannot go on like this."

"Do it," says the old woman, his mother. "Do it now."

"To give him any more would kill him," I tell her.

"Then do it," she says. The face of the old woman is hoof-beaten with intersecting curves of loose skin. Her hair is donkey brown, donkey gray.

They wait with him while I go to the nurses' station to prepare the syringes. It is a thing that I cannot ask anyone to do for me. When I return to the room, there are three loaded syringes in my hand, a rubber tourniquet and an alcohol sponge. Alcohol sponge! To prevent infection? The old woman is standing on a small stool and leaning over the side rail of the bed. Her bosom is just above his upturned face, as though she were weaning him with sorrow and gentleness from her still-full breasts. All at once she says severely, the way she must have said it to him years ago:

"Go home, son. Go home now."

I wait just inside the doorway. The only sound is a flapping, a rustling, as in a room to which a small animal, a bat perhaps, has retreated to die. The women turn to leave. There is neither gratitude nor reproach in their gaze. I should be hooded.

At last we are alone. I stand at the bedside.

"Listen," I say, "I can get rid of the pain." The man's eyes regain their focus. His gaze is like a wound that radiates its pain outward so that all upon whom it fell would know the need of relief.

"With these." I hold up the syringes.

"Yes," he gasps. "Yes." And while the rest of his body stirs in answer to the pain, he holds his left, his acquiescent arm still for the tourniquet. An even dew of sweat covers his body. I wipe the skin with the alcohol sponge, and tap the arm smartly to bring out the veins. There is one that is still patent; the others have long since clotted and broken down. I go to insert the needle, but the tourniquet has come unknotted; the vein has collapsed. Damn! Again I tie the tourniquet. Slowly the vein fills with blood. This time it stays distended.

He reacts not at all to the puncture. In a wild sea what is one tiny wave? I press the barrel and deposit the load, detach the syringe from the needle and replace it with the second syringe. I send this home, and go on to the third. When they are all given, I pull out the needle. A drop of blood blooms on his forearm. I blot it with the alcohol sponge. It is done. In less than a minute, it is done.

"Go home," I say, repeating the words of the old woman. I turn off the light. In the darkness the contents of the bed are theoretical. No! I must watch. I turn the light back on. How reduced he is, a folded parcel, something chipped away until only its shape and a little breath are left. His impatient bones gleam as though to burst through the papery skin. I am impatient, too. I want to get it over with, then step out into the corridor where the women are waiting. His death is like a jewel to them.

My fingers at his pulse. The same rhythm as mine! As though there were one pulse that beat throughout all of nature, and every creature's heart throbbed precisely.

"You can go home now," I say. The familiar emaciated body un-tenses. The respirations slow down. Eight per minute . . . six . . . It won't be long. The pulse wavers in and out of touch. It won't be long.

"Is that better?" I ask him. His gaze is distant, opaque, preoccupied. Minutes go by. Outside, in the corridor, the murmuring of women's voices.

But this man will not die! The skeleton rouses from its stupor. The snout twitches as if to fend off a fly. What is it that shakes him like a gourd full of beans? The pulse returns, melts away, comes back again, and stays. The respirations are twelve, then fourteen. I have not done it. I did not murder him. I am innocent!

I shall walk out of the room into the corridor. They will look at me, holding their breath, expectant. I lift the sheet to cover him. All at once, there is a sharp sting in my thumb. The same needle with which I meant to kill him has pricked *me*. A drop of blood appears. I press it with the alcohol sponge. My fresh blood deepens the stain of his on the gauze. Never mind. The man in the bed swallows. His Adam's apple bobs slowly. It would be so easy to do it. Three minutes of pressure on the larynx. He is still not conscious, wouldn't feel it, wouldn't know. My thumb and fingertips hover, land on his windpipe. My pulse beating in his neck, his in mine. I look back over my shoulder. No one. Two bare IV poles in a corner, their looped metal eyes witnessing. Do it! Fingers press. Again he swallows. Look back again. How closed the door is. And . . . my hand wilts. I cannot. It is not in me to do it. Not that way. The man's head swivels like an upturned fish. The squadron of ribs battles on.

I back away from the bed, turn and flee toward the doorway. In the mirror, a glimpse of my face. It is the face of someone who has been resuscitated after a long period of cardiac arrest. There is no spot of color in the cheeks, as though this person were in shock at what he had just seen on the yonder side of the grave.

In the corridor the women lean against the wall, against each other. They are like a band of angels dispatched here to take possession of his body. It is the only thing that will satisfy them.

"He didn't die," I say. "He won't . . . or can't." They are silent.

"He isn't ready yet," I say.

"He *is* ready," the old woman says. "*You* ain't."

IMELDA

I heard the other day that Hugh Franciscus had died. I knew him once. He was the Chief of Plastic Surgery when I was a medical student at Albany Medical College. Dr. Franciscus was the archetype of the professor of surgery—tall, vigorous, muscular, as precise in his technique as he was impeccable in his dress. Each day a clean lab coat monkishly starched, that sort of thing. I doubt that he ever read books. One book only, that of the human body, took the place of all others. He never raised his eyes from it. He read it like a printed page as though he knew that in the calligraphy there just beneath the skin were all the secrets of the world. Long before it became visible to anyone else, he could detect the first sign of granulation at the base of a wound, the first blue line of new epithelium at the periphery that would tell him that a wound would heal, or the barest hint of necrosis that presaged failure. This gave him the appearance of a prophet. "This skin graft will take," he would say, and you must believe beyond all cyanosis, exudation and inflammation that it would.

He had enemies, of course, who said he was arrogant, that he exalted activity for its own sake. Perhaps. But perhaps it was no more than the honesty of one who knows his own worth. Just look at a scalpel, after all. What a feeling of sovereignty, megalomania even, when you know that it is you and you alone who will make certain use of it. It was said, too, that he was a ladies' man. I don't know about that. It was all rumor. Besides, I think he had other things in mind than mere living. Hugh Franciscus was a zealous hunter. Every fall during the season he drove upstate to hunt deer. There was a glass-front case in his office where he showed his guns. How could he shoot a deer? we asked. But he knew better. To us medical students he was someone heroic, someone made up of several gods, beheld at a distance, and always from a lesser height. If he had grown accustomed to his miracles, we had not. He had no close friends on the staff. There was something a little sad in that. As though once long ago he had been flayed by friendship and now the slightest breeze would hurt. Confidences resulted in dishonor. Perhaps the person in whom one confided would scorn him, betray. Even though he spent his days among those less fortunate, weaker than he— the sick, after all—Franciscus seemed aware of an air of personal harshness in his environment to which he reacted by keeping his own counsel, by a certain remoteness. It was what gave him the appearance of being haughty. With the patients he was forthright. All the facts laid out, every question anticipated and answered with specific information. He delivered good news and bad with the same dispassion.

I was a third-year student, just turned onto the wards for the first time, and clerking on Surgery. Everything—the operating room, the morgue, the emergency room, the patients, professors, even the nurses—was terrifying. One picked one's way among the mines and booby traps of the hospital, hoping only to avoid the hemorrhage and perforation of disgrace. The opportunity for humiliation was everywhere.

It all began on Ward Rounds. Dr. Franciscus was demonstrating a cross-leg flap graft he had constructed to cover a large fleshy defect in the leg of a merchant seaman who had injured himself in a fall. The man was from Spain and spoke no English. There had been a comminuted fracture of the femur, much soft tissue damage, necrosis. After weeks of débridement and dressings, the wound had been made ready for grafting. Now the patient was in his fifth postoperative day. What he saw was a thick web of pale blue flesh arising from the man's left thigh, and which had been sutured to the open wound on the right thigh. When the surgeon pressed the pedicle with his finger, it blanched; when he let up, there was a slow return of the violaceous color.

"The circulation is good," Franciscus announced. "It will get better." In several weeks, we were told, he would divide the tube of flesh at its site of origin, and tailor it to fit the defect to which, by then, it would have grown more solidly. All at once, the webbed man in the bed reached out, and gripping Franciscus by the arm, began to speak rapidly, pointing to his groin and hip. Franciscus stepped back at once to disengage his arm from the patient's grasp.

"Anyone here know Spanish? I didn't get a word of that."

"The cast is digging into him up above," I said. "The edges of the plaster are rough. When he moves, they hurt."

Without acknowledging my assistance, Dr. Franciscus took a plaster shears from the dressing cast and with several large snips cut away the rough edges of the cast.

"*Gracias, gracias.*" The man in the bed smiled. But Franciscus had already moved on to the next bed. He seemed to me a man of immense strength and ability, yet without affection for the patients. He did not want to be touched by them. It was less kindness that he showed them than a reassurance that he would never give up, that he would bend every effort. If anyone could, he would solve the problems of their flesh.

Ward Rounds had disbanded and I was halfway down the corridor when I heard Dr. Franciscus' voice behind me.

"You speak Spanish." It seemed a command.

"I lived in Spain for two years," I told him.

"I'm taking a surgical team to Honduras next week to operate on the natives down there. I do it every year for three weeks, somewhere.

This year, Honduras. I can arrange the time away from your duties here if you'd like to come along. You will act as interpreter. I'll show you how to use the clinical camera. What you'd see would make it worthwhile."

So it was that, a week later, the envy of my classmates, I joined the mobile surgical unit—surgeons, anesthetists, nurses and equipment—aboard a Military Air Transport plane to spend three weeks performing plastic surgery on people who had been previously selected by an advance team. Honduras. I don't suppose I shall ever see it again. Nor do I especially want to. From the plane it seemed a country made of clay—burnt umber, raw sienna, dry. It had a deadweight quality, as though the ground had no buoyancy, no air sacs through which a breeze might wander. Our destination was Comayagua, a town in the Central Highlands. The town itself was situated on the edge of one of the flatlands that were linked in a network between the granite mountains. Above, all was brown, with only an occasional Spanish cedar tree; below, patches of luxuriant tropical growth. It was a day's bus ride from the airport. For hours, the town kept appearing and disappearing with the convolutions of the road. At last, there it lay before us, panting and exhausted at the bottom of the mountain.

That was all I was to see of the countryside. From then on, there was only the derelict hospital of Comayagua, with the smell of spoiling bananas and the accumulated odors of everyone who had been sick there for the last hundred years. Of the two, I much preferred the frank smell of the sick. The heat of the place was incendiary. So hot that, as we stepped from the bus, our own words did not carry through the air, but hung limply at our lips and chins. Just in front of the hospital was a thirsty courtyard where mobs of waiting people squatted or lay in the meager shade, and where, on dry days, a fine dust rose through which untethered goats shouldered. Against the walls of this courtyard, gaunt, dejected men stood, their faces, like their country, preternaturally solemn, leaden. Here no one looked up at the sky. Every head was bent beneath a wide-brimmed straw hat. In the days that followed, from the doorway of the dispensary, I would watch the brown mountains sliding about, drinking the hospital into their shadow as the afternoon grew later and later, flattening us by their very altitude.

The people were mestizos, of mixed Spanish and Indian blood. They had flat, broad, dumb museum feet. At first they seemed to me indistinguishable the one from the other, without animation. All the vitality, the hidden sexuality, was in their black hair. Soon I was to know them by the fissures with which each face was graven. But, even so, compared to us, they were masked, shut away. My job was to follow Dr.

Franciscus around, photograph the patients before and after surgery, interpret and generally act as aide-de-camp. It was exhilarating. Within days I had decided that I was not just useful, but essential. Despite that we spent all day in each other's company, there were no overtures of friendship from Dr. Franciscus. He knew my place, and I knew it, too. In the afternoon he examined the patients scheduled for the next day's surgery. I would call out a name from the doorway to the examining room. In the courtyard someone would rise. I would usher the patient in, and nudge him to the examining table where Franciscus stood, always, I thought, on the verge of irritability. I would read aloud the case history, then wait while he carried out his examination. While I took the "before" photographs, Dr. Franciscus would dictate into a tape recorder:

"Ulcerating basal cell carcinoma of the right orbit—six by eight centimeters—involving the right eye and extending into the floor of the orbit. Operative plan: wide excision with enucleation of the eye. Later, bone and skin grafting." The next morning we would be in the operating room where the procedure would be carried out.

We were more than two weeks into our tour of duty—a few days to go—when it happened. Earlier in the day I had caught sight of her through the window of the dispensary. A thin, dark Indian girl about fourteen years old. A figurine, orange-brown, terra-cotta, and still attached to the unshaped clay from which she had been carved. An older, sun-weathered woman stood behind and somewhat to the left of the girl. The mother was short and dumpy. She wore a broad-brimmed hat with a high crown, and a shapeless dress like a cassock. The girl had long, loose black hair. There were tiny gold hoops in her ears. The dress she wore could have been her mother's. Far too big, it hung from her thin shoulders at some risk of slipping down her arms. Even with her in it, the dress was empty, something hanging on the back of a door. Her breasts made only the smallest imprint in the cloth, her hips none at all. All the while, she pressed to her mouth a filthy, pink, balled-up rag as though to stanch a flow or buttress against pain. I knew that what she had come to show us, what we were there to see, was hidden beneath that pink cloth. As I watched, the woman handed down to her a gourd from which the girl drank, lapping like a dog. She was the last patient of the day. They had been waiting in the courtyard for hours.

"Imelda Valdez," I called out. Slowly she rose to her feet, the cloth never leaving her mouth, and followed her mother to the examining-room door. I shooed them in.

"You sit up there on the table," I told her. "Mother, you stand over there, please." I read from the chart:

"This is a fourteen-year-old girl with a complete, unilateral, left-sided cleft lip and cleft palate. No other diseases or congenital defects. Laboratory tests, chest X ray—negative."

"Tell her to take the rag away," said Dr. Franciscus. I did, and the girl shrank back, pressing the cloth all the more firmly.

"Listen, this is silly," said Franciscus. "Tell her I've got to see it. Either she behaves, or send her away."

"Please give me the cloth," I said to the girl as gently as possible. She did not. She could not. Just then, Franciscus reached up and, taking the hand that held the rag, pulled it away with a hard jerk. For an instant the girl's head followed the cloth as it left her face, one arm still upflung against showing. Against all hope, she would hide herself. A moment later, she relaxed and sat still. She seemed to me then like an animal that looks outward at the infinite, at death, without fear, with recognition only.

Set as it was in the center of the girl's face, the defect was utterly hideous—a nude rubbery insect that had fastened there. The upper lip was widely split all the way to the nose. One white tooth perched upon the protruding upper jaw projected through the hole. Some of the bone seemed to have been gnawed away as well. Above the thing, clear almond eyes and long black hair reflected the light. Below, a slender neck where the pulse trilled visibly. Under our gaze the girl's eyes fell to her lap where her hands lay palms upward, half open. She was a beautiful bird with a crushed beak. And tense with the expectation of more shame.

"Open your mouth," said the surgeon. I translated. She did so, and the surgeon tipped back her head to see inside.

"The palate, too. Complete," he said. There was a long silence. At last he spoke.

"What is your name?" The margins of the wound melted until she herself was being sucked into it.

"Imelda." The syllables leaked through the hole with a slosh and a whistle.

"Tomorrow," said the surgeon, "I will fix your lip. *Mañana.*"

It seemed to me that Hugh Franciscus, in spite of his years of experience, in spite of all the dreadful things he had seen, must have been awed by the sight of this girl. I could see it flit across his face for an instant. Perhaps it was her small act of concealment, that he had had to demand that she show him the lip, that he had had to force her to show it to him. Perhaps it was her resistance that intensified the disfigurement. Had she brought her mouth to him willingly, without shame, she would have been for him neither more nor less than any other patient.

He measured the defect with calipers, studied it from different angles, turning her head with a finger at her chin.

"How can it ever be put back together?" I asked.

"Take her picture," he said. And to her, "Look straight ahead." Through the eye of the camera she seemed more pitiful than ever, her humiliation more complete.

"Wait!" The surgeon stopped me. I lowered the camera. A strand of her hair had fallen across her face and found its way to her mouth, becoming stuck there by saliva. He removed the hair and secured it behind her ear.

"Go ahead," he ordered. There was the click of the camera. The girl winced.

"Take three more, just in case."

When the girl and her mother had left, he took paper and pen and with a few lines drew a remarkable likeness of the girl's face.

"Look," he said. "If this dot is A, and this one B, this, C and this, D, the incisions are made A to B, then C to D. CD must equal AB. It is all equilateral triangles." All well and good, but then came X and Y and rotation flaps and the rest.

"Do you see?" he asked.

"It is confusing," I told him.

"It is simply a matter of dropping the upper lip into a normal position, then crossing the gap with two triangular flaps. It is geometry," he said.

"Yes," I said. "Geometry." And relinquished all hope of becoming a plastic surgeon.

In the operating room the next morning the anesthesia had already been administered when we arrived from Ward Rounds. The tube emerging from the girl's mouth was pressed against her lower lip to be kept out of the field of surgery. Already, a nurse was scrubbing the face which swam in a reddish-brown lather. The tiny gold earrings were included in the scrub. Now and then, one of them gave a brave flash. The face was washed for the last time, and dried. Green towels were placed over the face to hide everything but the mouth and nose. The drapes were applied.

"Calipers!" The surgeon measured, locating the peak of the distorted Cupid's bow.

"Marking pen!" He placed the first blue dot at the apex of the bow. The nasal sills were dotted; next, the inferior philtral dimple, the vermilion line. The A flap and the B flap were outlined. On he worked, peppering the lip and nose, making sense out of chaos, realizing the lip that lay waiting in that deep essential pink, that only he could see. The last dot and line were placed. He was ready.

"Scalpel!" He held the knife above the girl's mouth.

"O.K. to go ahead?" he asked the anesthetist.

"Yes."

He lowered the knife.

"No! Wait!" The anesthetist's voice was tense, staccato. "Hold it!"

The surgeon's hand was motionless.

"What's the matter?"

"Something's wrong. I'm not sure. God, she's hot as a pistol. Blood pressure is way up. Pulse one eighty. Get a rectal temperature." A nurse fumbled beneath the drapes. We waited. The nurse retrieved the thermometer.

"One hundred seven . . . no . . . eight." There was disbelief in her voice.

"Malignant hyperthermia," said the anesthetist. "Ice! Ice! Get lots of ice!" I raced out the door, accosted the first nurse I saw.

"Ice!" I shouted. *"Hielo!* Quickly! *Hielo!"* The woman's expression was blank. I ran to another. *"Hielo! Hielo!* For the love of God, ice."

"Hielo?" She shrugged. *"Nada."* I ran back to the operating room.

"There isn't any ice," I reported. Dr. Franciscus had ripped off his rubber gloves and was feeling the skin of the girl's abdomen. Above the mask his eyes were the eyes of a horse in battle.

"The EKG is wild . . ."

"I can't get a pulse . . ."

"What the hell . . ."

The surgeon reached for the girl's groin. No femoral pulse.

"EKG flat. My God! She's dead!"

"She can't be."

"She is."

The surgeon's fingers pressed the groin where there was no pulse to be felt, only his own pulse hammering at the girl's flesh to be let in.

It was noon, four hours later, when we left the operating room. It was a day so hot and humid I felt steamed open like an envelope. The woman was sitting on a bench in the courtyard in her dress like a cassock. In one hand she held the piece of cloth the girl had used to conceal her mouth. As we watched, she folded it once neatly, and then again, smoothing it, cleaning the cloth which might have been the head of the girl in her lap that she stroked and consoled.

"I'll do the talking here," he said. He would tell her himself, in whatever Spanish he could find. Only if she did not understand was I to speak for him. I watched him brace himself, set his shoulders. How could he tell her? I wondered. What? But I knew he would tell her everything, exactly as it had happened. As much for himself as for her, he needed to explain. But suppose she screamed, fell to the ground, attacked him, even? All that hope of love . . . gone. Even in his discomfort I knew that he was teaching me. The way to do it was professionally. Now he was standing above her. When the woman saw that he did not speak, she lifted her eyes and saw what he held crammed in his mouth to tell her. She knew, and rose to her feet.

"*Señora*," he began, "I am sorry." All at once he seemed to me shorter than he was, scarcely taller than she. There was a place at the crown of his head where the hair had grown thin. His lips were stones. He could hardly move them. The voice dry, dusty.

"No one could have known. Some bad reaction to the medicine for sleeping. It poisoned her. High fever. She did not wake up." The last, a whisper. The woman studied his lips as though she were deaf. He tried, but could not control a twitching at the corner of his mouth. He raised a thumb and forefinger to press something back into his eyes.

"*Muerte*," the woman announced to herself. Her eyes were human, deadly.

"*Sí, muerte*." At that moment he was like someone cast, still alive, as an effigy for his own tomb. He closed his eyes. Nor did he open them until he felt the touch of the woman's hand on his arm, a touch from which he did not withdraw. Then he looked and saw the grief corroding her face, breaking it down, melting the features so that eyes, nose, mouth ran together in a distortion, like the girl's. For a long time they stood in silence. It seemed to me that minutes passed. At last her face cleared, the features rearranged themselves. She spoke, the words coming slowly to make certain that he understood her. She would go home now. The next day her sons would come for the girl, to take her home for burial. The doctor must not be sad. God has decided. And she was happy now that the harelip had been fixed so that her daughter might go to Heaven without it. Her bare feet retreating were the felted pads of a great bereft animal.

The next morning I did not go to the wards, but stood at the gate leading from the courtyard to the road outside. Two young men in striped ponchos lifted the girl's body wrapped in a straw mat onto the back of a wooden cart. A donkey waited. I had been drawn to this place as one is drawn, inexplicably, to certain scenes of desolation— executions, battlefields. All at once, the woman looked up and saw me.

She had taken off her hat. The heavy-hanging coil of her hair made her head seem larger, darker, noble. I pressed some money into her hand.

"For flowers," I said. "A priest." Her cheeks shook as though minutes ago a stone had been dropped into her navel and the ripples were just now reaching her head. I regretted having come to that place.

"*Sí, sí,*" the woman said. Her own face was stitched with flies. "The doctor is one of the angels. He has finished the work of God. My daughter is beautiful."

What could she mean! The lip had not been fixed. The girl had died before he would have done it.

"Only a fine line that God will erase in time," she said.

I reached into the cart and lifted a corner of the mat in which the girl had been rolled. Where the cleft had been there was now a fresh line of tiny sutures. The Cupid's bow was delicately shaped, the vermilion border aligned. The flattened nostril had now the same rounded shape as the other one. I let the mat fall over the face of the dead girl, but not before I had seen the touching place where the finest black hairs sprang from the temple.

"*Adiós, adiós . . .*" And the cart creaked away to the sound of hooves, a tinkling bell.

There are events in a doctor's life that seem to mark the boundary between youth and age, seeing and perceiving. Like certain dreams, they illuminate a whole lifetime of past behavior. After such an event, a doctor is not the same as he was before. It had seemed to me then to have been the act of someone demented, or at least insanely arrogant. An attempt to reorder events. Her death had come to him out of order. It should have come after the lip had been repaired, not before. He could have told the mother that, no, the lip had not been fixed. But he did not. He said nothing. It had been an act of omission, one of those strange lapses to which all of us are subject and which we live to regret. It must have been then, at that moment, that the knowledge of what he would do appeared to him. The words of the mother had not consoled him; they had hunted him down. He had not done it for her. The dire necessity was his. He would not accept that Imelda had died before he could repair her lip. People who do such things break free from society. They follow their own lonely path. They have a secret which they can never reveal. I must never let on that I knew.

How often I have imagined it. Ten o'clock at night. The hospital of Comayagua is all but dark. Here and there lanterns tilt and skitter up and down the corridors. One of these lamps breaks free from the others and descends the stone steps to the underground room that is the morgue of the hospital. This room wears the expression as if it had waited all night for someone to come. No silence so deep as this place with its cargo of newly dead. Only the slow drip of water over stone. The door closes gassily and clicks shut. The lock is turned. There are four tables, each with a body encased in a paper shroud. There is no mistaking her. She is the smallest. The surgeon takes a knife from his pocket and slits open the paper shroud, that part in which the girl's head is enclosed. The wound seems to be living on long after she has died. Waves of heat emanate from it, blurring his vision. All at once, he turns to peer over his shoulder. He sees nothing, only a wooden crucifix on the wall.

He removes a package of instruments from a satchel and arranges them on a tray. Scalpel, scissors, forceps, needle holder. Sutures and gauze sponges are produced. Stealthy, hunched, engaged, he begins. The dots of blue dye are still there upon her mouth. He raises the scalpel, pauses. A second glance into the darkness. From the wall a small lizard watches and accepts. The first cut is made. A sluggish flow of dark blood appears. He wipes it away with a sponge. No new blood comes to take its place. Again and again he cuts, connecting each of the blue dots until the whole of the zigzag slice is made, first on one side of the cleft, then on the other. Now the edges of the cleft are lined with fresh tissue. He sets down the scalpel and takes up scissors and forceps, undermining the little flaps until each triangle is attached only at one side. He rotates each flap into its new position. He must be certain that they can be swung without tension. They can. He is ready to suture. He fits the tiny curved needle into the jaws of the needle holder. Each suture is placed precisely the same number of millimeters from the cut edge, and the same distance apart. He ties each knot down until the edges are apposed. Not too tightly. These are the most meticulous sutures of his life. He cuts each thread close to the knot. It goes well. The vermilion border with its white skin roll is exactly aligned. One more stitch and the Cupid's bow appears as if by magic. The man's face shines with moisture. Now the nostril is incised around the margin, released, and sutured into a round shape to match its mate. He wipes the blood from the face of the girl with gauze that he has dipped in water. Crumbs of light are scattered on the girl's face. The shroud is folded once more about her. The instruments are handed into the satchel. In a moment the morgue is dark and a lone lantern ascends the stairs and is extinguished.

*   *   *

Six weeks later I was in the darkened amphitheater of the Medical School. Tiers of seats rose in a semicircle above the small stage where Hugh Franciscus stood presenting the case material he had encountered in Honduras. It was the highlight of the year. The hall was filled. The night before he had arranged the slides in the order in which they were to be shown. I was at the controls of the slide projector.

"Next slide!" he would order from time to time in that military voice which had called forth blind obedience from generations of medical students, interns, residents and patients.

"This is a fifty-seven-year-old man with a severe burn contracture of the neck. You will notice the rigid webbing that has fused the chin to the presternal tissues. No motion of the head on the torso is possible. . . . Next slide!"

"Click," went the projector.

"Here he is after the excision of the scar tissue and with the head in full extension for the first time. The defect was then covered. . . . Next slide!"

"Click."

". . . with full-thickness drums of skin taken from the abdomen with the Padgett dermatome. Next slide!"

"Click."

And suddenly there she was, extracted from the shadows, suspended above and beyond all of us like a resurrection. There was the oval face, the long black hair unbraided, the tiny gold hoops in her ears. And that luminous gnawed mouth. The whole of her life seemed to have been summed up in this photograph. A long silence followed that was the surgeon's alone to break. Almost at once, like the anesthetist in the operating room in Comayagua, I knew that something was wrong. It was not that the man would not speak as that he could not. The audience of doctors, nurses and students seemed to have been infected by the black, limitless silence. My own pulse doubled. It was hard to breathe. Why did he not call out for the next slide? Why did he not save himself? Why had he not removed this slide from the ones to be shown? All at once I knew that he had used his camera on her again. I could see the long black shadows of her hair flowing into the darker shadows of the morgue. The sudden blinding flash . . . The next slide would be the one taken in the morgue. He would be exposed.

In the dim light reflected from the slide, I saw him gazing up at her, seeing not the colored photograph, I thought, but the negative of it where the ghost of the girl was. For me, the amphitheater had become Honduras. I saw again that courtyard littered with patients. I could see the dust in the beam of light from the projector. It was then that I knew that she was his measure of perfection and pain—the one lost, the other gained. He, too, had heard the click of the camera, had seen her wince and felt his mercy enlarge. At last he spoke.

"Imelda." It was the one word he had heard her say. At the sound of his voice I removed the next slide from the projector. "Click" . . . and she was gone. "Click" again, and in her place the man with the orbital cancer. For a long moment Franciscus looked up in my direction, on his face an expression that I have given up trying to interpret. Gratitude? Sorrow? It made me think of the gaze of the girl when at last she understood that she must hand over to him the evidence of her body.

"This is a sixty-two-year-old man with a basal cell carcinoma of the temple eroding into the bony orbit . . ." he began as though nothing had happened.

At the end of the hour, even before the lights went on, there was loud applause. I hurried to find him among the departing crowd. I could not. Some weeks went by before I caught sight of him. He seemed vaguely convalescent, as though a fever had taken its toll before burning out.

Hugh Franciscus continued to teach for fifteen years, although he operated a good deal less, then gave it up entirely. It was as though he had grown tired of blood, of always having to be involved with blood, of having to draw it, spill it, wipe it away, stanch it. He was a quieter, softer man, I heard, the ferocity diminished. There were no more expeditions to Honduras or anywhere else.

I, too, have not been entirely free of her. Now and then, in the years that have passed, I see that donkey-cart cortège, or his face bent over hers in the morgue. I would like to have told him what I now know, that his unrealistic act was one of goodness, one of those small, persevering acts done, perhaps, to ward off madness. Like lighting a lamp, boiling water for tea, washing a shirt. But, of course, it's too late now.

MAYA ANGELOU

MAYA ANGELOU (1928–). *African-American poet, fiction writer, and storyteller. Angelou's best-known work is the autobiographical* I Know Why the Caged Bird Sings *(1970), a critical and popular success imbued with optimism, humor, and homespun philosophy. Other writings include* Wouldn't Take Nothing for My Journey Now *(1994), a collection of personal reflections, and numerous collections of poetry, among them* Just Give Me a Cool Drink of Water 'Fore I Die *(1971);* Oh Pray My Wings Are Gonna Fit Me Well *(1975); And* Still I Rise *(1978);* Shaker, Why Don't You Sing? *(1981); and* I Shall Not Be Moved *(1990), read by her at the inauguration of President William Jefferson Clinton on January 20, 1993. Angelou is currently Reynolds Professor of American Studies at Wake Forest University in Winston-Salem, North Carolina.*

THE LAST DECISION

The print is too small, distressing me.
Wavering black things on the page.
Wriggling polliwogs all about.
I know it's my age.
I'll have to give up reading.

The food is too rich, revolting me.
I swallow it hot or force it down cold,
and wait all day as it sits in my throat.
Tired as I am, I know I've grown old.
I'll have to give up eating.

My children's concerns are tiring me.
They stand at my bed and move their lips,
and I cannot hear one single word.
I'd rather give up listening.

Life is too busy, wearying me.
Questions and answers and heavy thought.
I've subtracted and added and multiplied,
and all my figuring has come to naught.
Today I'll give up living.

RICHARD C. REYNOLDS

RICHARD C. REYNOLDS (1929–   ). *American physician, educator, and writer. For a number of years, Dr. Reynolds was in the private practice of internal medicine in Frederick, Maryland. His academic career has included appointments at Johns Hopkins University School of Medicine and the University of Florida. A former dean of the University of Medicine and Dentistry of New Jersey, he is currently executive vice president of the Robert Wood Johnson Foundation in Princeton.*

A DAY IN THE LIFE OF AN INTERNIST

Author's Foreword: Over the past two years there have been a number of articles describing what internists do. These have appeared in the Annals of Internal Medicine *and* The New England Journal of Medicine *and usually represent summaries of data collected from a large group of internists. Having practiced internal medicine in a community of 22,000 for nine years before returning to a full-time academic life, I found difficulty in relating what I did in everyday practice to what was being described in these articles. About this time, I came across one of my appointment books from my eighth year of practice. I thumbed through this book and was amazed by how vividly I could recall many of the patients who were identified, albeit ten years later. This prompted me to try to write this article. I suspect the passing years have made me take some liberties with the details, but I am convinced that the day I describe is representative of many such days.*

The alarm rings. Reflexly, I turn it off within seconds. It is 6:30 A.M., but I have already been awake for fifteen minutes. My sleep has been restless since the phone rang at 2:30 A.M. and the nurse from the ICU told me about the increasing number of PVCs in the forty-six-year-old man with a coronary whom I had admitted yesterday afternoon. I ordered some Lidocaine and told the nurse to be sure to call back if the patient did not improve. She did not call, but I found it difficult to fall asleep.

Contrary to common belief, most phone calls in the middle of the night, whether from the hospital or from home, indicate a major patient difficulty. I am never sure when I respond to the patient over the phone that I have not missed a situation that requires a more personal review. I suspect that the post-phone-call restlessness that I experience is caused by the uneasiness that my response may have been too cursory. I never cease to be amazed after a few years in practice how quickly and easily one can triage phone calls. That tone of panic in the voice of a spouse when the husband or wife is experiencing a major mishap or a call for help from a family that has never before asked for assistance out of regular office hours is unmistakably recognizable.

Today is Thursday. I go from the bedroom to the family room and turn on the television. While looking at "Sunrise Semester," I do my daily ritual of the Royal Canadian Air Force Exercises. These exercises coupled with some weekend tennis represent my compromise with the present exercise mania.

It is nearly seven. After quick morning ablutions and a sparse break-fast, I drive to the hospital. The nurses on One North have finished their morning report. They greet me and smile at my punctuality. If I did not start making rounds on my patients on One North at exactly 7:30 A.M., I would disappoint them. I understand that members of the nursing staff occasionally put money into a pool, with each participant choosing the minutes on either side of 7:30 A.M. that I will appear.

I have twelve patients in the hospital. My first office appointment is at 9:00 A.M. Mentally, I begin to pace my morning rounds. The first patient is completing the second week of hospitalization for his coronary thrombosis. Fifty-two years old, previously healthy and vigorous, he is in good spirits and beginning to ask about going home. This morning he has already walked the length of the corridor. I take his blood pressure and listen to his heart and lungs. Nothing is wrong. (Interesting how we always think in negatives in medical history taking and physical exam-ination. No this, no that; never good this or good that. No wonder the World Health Organization defines health as the absence of disease.) I banter with the patient. He had never previously been under my care until the day he had chest pain and was admitted. His wife had been a regular patient for years, always following the admonitions and exhor-tations of the women's magazines to have regular checkups. I make a mental note that I need to have a conversation with the patient and his wife this weekend to go over a plan for his physical activity and return to work after discharge.

In the next room is a seventy-seven-year-old lady who has been admitted with a cerebral thrombosis resulting in mild aphasia and weak-ness of her right arm. She is improving rapidly from her stroke and is sitting in a chair as I walk into the room. Two questions need answers. How aggressive a workup shall I do on this patient, who in all likelihood has a simple cerebral thrombosis, and what arrangements shall we work out for her after she leaves the hospital. She lives by herself and has always been independent. Since this stroke she has become aware of her vulnerability. I suspect in a few days she may introduce the subject of a temporary residence at a nursing home after discharge. I shall have the head nurse begin to explore the subject with her.

I walk upstairs to Two North. I see a patient I admitted a week ago when I was on call for the emergency room. This sixty-eight-year-old man had a severe urinary tract infection with sepsis that has responded to antibiotics and catheterization. He was seen by the urologist yesterday. I glance at the consultation note on the chart. He confirms my suspicion of obstructive prostate disease and recommends surgery. I need to talk to the patient about this. I begin to quicken the pace of rounds. There are still nine more patients to see before I am due at the office.

My office is only two blocks from the hospital. At five minutes to nine I walk in. My office staff has been there since 8:30. The first two patients are already there. The first one is in the examining room. I glance at the appointment book. The day is full. I see that Mrs. D is scheduled at 10:30 for fifteen minutes. There is no way that I can see that woman in fifteen minutes. It takes her longer than that to recite her neatly written list of complaints.

My office hours are 9:00 to 12:00 and 1:30 to 3:30. I keep the half hour 3:30 to 4:00 open to see sick people in need of attention that day. I schedule patients every fifteen minutes, except for annual physicals that require thirty minutes for old patients and forty-five minutes for a first time visit. Consultations are scheduled for forty-five to sixty minutes.

The first few patients today are straightforward. Mrs. G is a forty-six-year-old lady with uncomplicated hypertension, easily controlled with Diuril and Aldomet. Today her blood pressure is 135/90. Her weight has increased five pounds since her last visit three months ago. We talk about diet and exercise and her son who is a sophomore at Duke. The second patient is a thirty-four-year-old school teacher with tension headaches, who one year ago went through a miserable depressive episode. She prefers to see me every four to six weeks just to be reassured. It is not exactly clear what the reassurance is for. Both she and I know that the headaches are tension in character, and evil things such as brain tumors have long ago been eliminated from diagnostic consideration. Today we chat. I congratulate her on being selected one of the county's outstanding high school teachers. (My receptionist has placed a note in the front of her chart reminding me of this accolade.) She appears composed, more relaxed than usual. I schedule the next appointment for eight weeks hence and begin to anticipate weaning her away from her dependence on me.

I try to arrange my schedule to do one complete examination in the morning and one in the afternoon. Today the third patient, Mrs. S, is a healthy, slightly obese thirty-eight-year-old housewife who comes in for her annual evaluation. An interval history reveals no mishaps since she was here one year ago. The physical exam is ritualistic. After performing thousands of physical examinations I have noticed a tendency to lose focus of concentration during this procedure. To combat this, I have devised a scheme. The first week of each month I select one part of the examination for unusual scrutiny. This week my special attention is on the thyroid. Last month it was the ear. During the preceding week I reviewed the anatomy and examination of the thyroid. As I examine the patient I carefully observe and palpitate the thyroid, mentally identifying the poles and isthmus. Somehow, I hope this technique prevents the ritualistic examination from becoming an ineffective, cursory effort. Mrs. S's thyroid is normal. While she dresses, I enter the second examining room to see Mr. L. Mr. L is a sixty-eight-year-old retired merchant, who was in the hospital four months ago. His unexplained persistent abdominal pain led to an exploratory laparotomy, which revealed carcinoma of the pancreas. The tumor had already invaded the liver. The patient's course subsequent to surgery has been surprisingly uneventful. Mr. L is lying on the examining table. His heart and lungs are normal. I think that since he was here one month ago his liver has enlarged. I glance at his sclera and note he is slightly jaundiced. He responds to my query about abdominal discomfort by stating that it remains unchanged. I muse that neither one of us uses the word pain. I tell Mr. L to dress, and I return to my office, where my nurse has placed Mrs. S after she has dressed.

Doctors need to give every patient a chance to talk with their clothes on after the examination is over. Before the examination patients are sometimes frightened or intimidated and often forgetful or hesitant to bring up an unpleasant subject. After the examination, and if they have had a few minutes to sit in the doctor's office, they will be more composed and confident. I reassure Mrs. S that she remains in good health. I chide her good-naturedly about her eighteen extra pounds of weight. I deflect her questions of diet pills in such a way that she does not ask for any and get turned down. I do not give her a diet. I presume that no event has happened to catalyse her weight loss and that she is content being buxom. (I wonder if her husband prefers her that way.) Today, Mrs. S tells me that her only child is entering college this fall and she herself would like to enter the local community college and become a nurse. She wants to know what I think about the idea. Inwardly, I smile. Patients at times do expect their doctors to be omniscient. I ask her what her husband thinks of this career change from housewife to student to nurse. She replies that he has been encouraging. I tell Mrs. S that I believe her idea is excellent. I recall the name of another patient who made a similar career decision three years ago and who is now working in a doctor's office. I suggest she call this individual, and I also make a mental note to mention Mrs. S's aspirations to my other patient.

Mrs. S leaves and Mr. L comes in. His clothes indicate recent weight loss, and I glance at his chart and note that he has lost twelve pounds since his discharge from the hospital. Mr. L sits down. We look at one another. Neither of us says anything for a few moments. He breaks the silence. "Well, how are things?" I indicate I want to do a few tests. Actually, I want to do a bilirubin to determine the extent of his jaundice. "They are not too good," he says. I comment that the course of an individual with his malady is unpredictable, but so far he has done remarkably well. That is true; he has. I recall our conversation in the hospital. Several days after surgery when I was certain he was alert, I sat down by his bedside and shared with him his diagnosis. He asked me in his laconic way, "How long?" I said it was difficult to tell, but the course was usually somewhere between six and twelve months. He asked a few other questions about the pancreatic cancer. I assured him that I would work with him and his wife so that he would be as comfortable as possible, and I urged him to be active as long as he felt good. By mutual consent we then directed our conversation to comfortable, ordinary subjects such as sports and hospital food. Today, for the first time since our hospital conversation, he uses the word *cancer*. "The cancer is spreading." He states it as both a question and a fact. I nod confirmation. I give him a return appointment for two weeks.

The morning progresses with a steady procession of patients. Most patients have straightforward problems—a recurrent sinus infection, a streptococcal sore throat, an insurance physical examination. A few questions identify the problem, the examination confirms, and advice and/or a drug prescription are given. The medical record is reviewed to make sure that chronic problems are not overlooked or that the drug prescribed is not likely to interact with any present medication.

By 12:15 P.M. I have seen the last patient scheduled for the morning. At noon, I have scheduled an executive committee meeting of the community hospital. I have been elected chief of medicine of the community hospital and serve on this committee. Today we plan to review two audits, one on childbirth and another on urinary tract infection. Our professional care audit committees are struggling with the task of defining the character of the audit and interpreting the data resulting from the audit. The executive committee ponders what recommendations to make to the staff. The major deficiency revealed by these audits is incomplete records and inconsistent behavior on the part of attending physicians in recording data. We wonder whether the new transcribing system will improve the medical records. Another problem is introduced by the chief of surgery. One of the most respected older surgeons in the community is generating complaints by his patients of not making rounds on weekends and not returning the calls of the involved families. This is a sensitive subject that makes us all uneasy. There is a shaded reference to family problems and, hesitantly, a comment that the surgeon is imbibing too much alcohol. What to do? We agree that the chief of staff will approach one of the surgeon's close and long-standing colleagues and ask him to initiate a conversation and report back to the chief of staff.

Most doctors use lunch hours as an integral part of their professional workday. Continuing education meetings, hospital committee work, or a trip back to the hospital to check a sick patient are common events during the lunch break. If the doctor eats lunch at the hospital it is often a time of informal consultation with other doctors about patients not always requiring a formal review by another physician. I occasionally use the lunch hour to make a house call and frequently use this time to return phone calls.

I return to the office at 1:30 P.M. The afternoon proceeds much like the morning. Instead of an annual physical examination, I am seeing in consultation this afternoon a thirty-eight-year-old man with chest pain. The chest pain probably does not represent angina, but I proceed with a stress ECG. It is normal. I assure the patient that his chest pain is not cardiac in origin but represents a muscular-skeletal disorder that confused the diagnosis because of its location on the left anterior chest wall. His relief is obvious.

There has been a spate of phone calls from relatively young men asking for appointments for physical exams. Recently, a locally eminent businessman, president of the Chamber of Commerce, died suddenly from a coronary thrombosis at the age of forty-four. Whenever such an unfortunate mishap occurs to a citizen popular enough to have it recorded on the front page of the local paper, it precipitates an increased number of patient visits to many doctors' offices.

The afternoon continues. Two patients are seen for review of their drug-controlled hypertension. In moving about the office I glance at my patients in the waiting room. One of my patients sits there next to her high-school-aged daughter. Both appear tense; the daughter has been crying. My receptionist confirms my suspicion. The mother has brought the daughter in to determine—no, confirm—that she is pregnant. As they sit together in the waiting room they form a tableau that is itself almost diagnostic. When their turn comes, I ask the mother to remain in the waiting room while I examine the daughter. She is probably ten weeks pregnant. I discuss the issues and options with the daughter, who is composed. I bring the mother in with us and tell her what she already knows. There will be a family meeting tonight. I try to keep them from recriminations. I direct the attention to the daughter's pregnancy and recommend an obstetrician for care. Before they leave, I have my receptionist give the mother an appointment to see me next week. She will need some extra support at this time.

As the afternoon office hours begin to draw to an end, the secretary places on my desk six charts with phone messages attached. I am able to make a few of these calls between patients. Today, two of the phone calls concern prescription refills, which I call in directly to the drugstore. Both are for continuing medications for patients I see regularly for management of high blood pressure and osteoarthritis. Two other patients have requested information concerning their acute respiratory infections, presumably viral in origin, which necessitate only reassurance from me that the illness will probably last only three to five days. They are instructed to call again in a few days if they have not improved.

After I have seen the last patient of the day, I still have two outstanding phone calls. A twenty-seven-year-old anxious woman patient has read another article delineating the morbidity from birth control pills. Her uneasiness resulting from reading this article precipitates the phone call. Not too successfully, I allay her apprehensions. I make a note on the chart to discuss this problem at her next visit and to consider other forms of birth control. The last phone call is from a middle-aged woman who describes the symptoms of an acute urinary tract infection with sudden onset of dysuria, frequency, and urgency. I decide to treat her by prescribing a ten-day course of Gantrisin. I have the secretary schedule her for an appointment in two weeks for follow-up urinalysis and culture.

The office day is completed. The nurse and receptionist are tidying up the office and have placed my diagnostic instruments into a small black bag I carry on hospital rounds. I sit at my desk and finish some notes in the charts of patients seen during the day. I glance at my mail, which is mostly advertisements. It does include one report from a doctor in Florida who cares for one of my patients for six months each year.

I sign the letters I have dictated the night before. There are two journals in today's mail, and I carry them with me to the car and plan to scan them tonight.

Before I return to the hospital, I make a house call on an eighty-seven-year-old lady whom I have cared for for eight years. Two years ago she had a cerebral thrombosis, which resulted in some left-sided weakness. Despite mild congestive heart failure and the residua of the stroke she remains alert and engaged in the community and world, albeit from the confines of her apartment. My call is social and medical. The housekeeper reassures me that her charge has not had any problems since my last visit three months ago. I enjoy a few minutes' conversation with the patient. Her numerous contacts with people by phone and through visits to her apartment make her a social barometer for the community. At times she seems to know the well-being of some of my patients better than I. I take her blood pressure, listen to her heart and lungs, note that her ankles are not swollen. I tell her and her house-keeper to stay on the same medicines and that I will check back in three months.

I drive back to the hospital and begin my late afternoon rounds. I check on the acutely ill patients first. I make brief personal contacts with the remaining patients to see if they have any new problems and to report to them the results of any laboratory or X-ray examinations that have been done today.

I have arranged to see the wife of the sixty-eight-year-old man who was admitted with a urinary tract infection and will need prostatic surgery to relieve his urinary obstruction. She is waiting for me in her husband's room. She has many questions about the surgery and partic-ularly about its risk for her husband. I answer the questions in front of her husband and try to have her appreciate the commonplace nature of the problem and surgery. Without her asking, I mention the excellent qualifications of the urologist who will do the surgery. I get up to leave and the wife follows me to the door and out of the room. In the hallway she asks the one important question. "Doctor, is there any chance this is cancer?" Though not entirely eliminating this possibility, I share my belief that the difficulty is most commonly caused by benign enlarge-ment of the prostate gland. She seems reassured.

The early evening hours are ideal times for evaluating new patients or doing consultations for other physicians. Laboratory and X-ray stud-ies have been completed and the reports are in the charts. The hospital is usually quiet, as afternoon visitors have gone home and the evening visitors have not arrived.

I have not had any new admissions today, but an orthopedic surgeon has asked me to evaluate a seventy-two-year-old lady with a broken left hip. I review her chart and find her laboratory studies, chest X ray and ECG are normal. The patient is in pain but tries to cooperate during my examination. She has had good health and denies any cardiovascular symptoms. Physical examination confirms her good health, which is now compromised by her broken hip. I write a note on her chart indicating she should tolerate the hip surgery and that I will follow her postoperatively.

I page my colleague, Dr. C, who is taking call for our three-member group. I quickly review by phone conversation the status of my acutely ill patients in the hospital. I ask him if he returns to the hospital tonight to look in on my one patient in the intensive care unit, a forty-five-year-old man who three days ago had an acute coronary thrombosis.

It is now seven o'clock. I drive home. The day of work is finished. I know that I shall not have any more calls as I sign my phone out to the telephone answering service. I sit down to dinner with my wife and three school-age children. I listen to the children recount the activities of the day. It is March, and my wife and I begin to talk about possible vacation sites for this summer. After dinner I go to my study and take a journal from a pile of unread periodicals. I thumb through it, unable to concentrate enough to get interested in any one article. I turn on the television and begin to watch an NBA game. Later, my wife wakens me.

ROBERT COLES

ROBERT COLES (1929–   ). *American physician and essayist. A professor of psychiatry and medical humanities at Harvard, Coles is the author of over forty books, including the* Children of Crisis *series, for which he won the Pulitzer Prize. His recent books include* The Call of Service *(1994),* The Ongoing Journey *(1994), and* Anna Freud: The Dream of Psychoanalysis *(1992).*

Excerpt from THE CALL OF STORIES

At that point we were interrupted by a phone call. One of Dr. Williams' patients had suffered a relapse: a young woman of fifteen, on the road to recovery from severe pneumonia, had spiked a high fever yet again. She had a past history of rheumatic heart disease, with a congestive heart murmur and the long-term prospect of congestive heart disease. All of that and more Dr. Williams explained to me as he hurriedly drove to her home, a tenement building in Paterson, where poor families struggled hard to get by—make enough money to pay the rent, buy food, stay warm, and, yes, give their doctor, who made house calls, an occasional payment for his services. As we climbed those dark stairs to a fourth-floor apartment, the doctor suddenly whirled around and looked right at me, his eyes meeting mine. A moment's silence, and then he said: "I don't like this mother you'll see. She drives me crazy with her questions. I want to take the girl and save her. I want to take her younger brother and save him. I don't like the father, either. What a pair! The miracle is that wonderful daughter of theirs. She puts up with them, and she sees everything, all their bad habits."

A second later, he was rapping his right hand's knuckles on a door whose brown paint was peeling and whose splinters were noticeable—he had to be careful about where to make contact with the wood. Three knocks, then a shuffling of his feet to register impatience. Noise arose on the other side of the door, and I could see his face suddenly concentrating, the ears perking up, the head unselfconsciously tilting toward the door, as if he was interested but didn't want to admit to himself, never mind anyone else, that he was *that* interested—and so, abruptly, he moved away a step from the door just as it opened. (I later realized he'd probably heard, among other things, the sound of approaching steps.)

The mother opened the door and, without saying a word, stepped aside for us. I can still remember her eyes meeting those of Dr. Williams. My heart went out to her; she seemed retiring, frightened, and eager to please. She motioned to her daughter, asking her to get ready for the doctor by sitting up, and then moved away to make room for him. But the girl, febrile, seemed uninterested in what the mother wished. Meanwhile, Dr. Williams put his black bag down beside the patient's bed, glanced around the room, caught sight of a chair, pulled it toward the bed, sat down, and took the girl's left wrist into his right hand and held it firmly. At that point she picked herself up and sat half upright against the pillow, staring at her wrist and Dr. Williams' hand. He asked her how she was doing. She was doing OK, she said. He wouldn't accept her answer: "Tell me the truth." She immediately changed her reply: "Not so OK." He nodded, let go of her wrist, told her he was sure, from her pulse, that she had a fever, and announced he would soon examine her. He explained that I was a medical student and asked if she minded my being there as he listened to her chest and heart. She shook her head and smiled. It was then, as he reached for his stethoscope, that the mother entered the scene, so to speak. She drew nearer, frowning, and addressed the doctor: "Why no temperature?" Suddenly I realized I hadn't heard her voice before, and realized, a second later, that her English was imperfect. She wanted the doctor to take her daughter's temperature, to learn whether she had a fever. He barked back at her: "Leave her alone!"

I was stunned. He spoke with obvious annoyance. I knew he could be cranky; he had told me so, and I'd seen him moody and irascible at times, especially when we talked about certain literary matters. But this situation was puzzling, and for a moment I wondered whether he wasn't going beyond the ethical bounds, being rude to a patient's mother for no justifiable reason. Then came her retort: "You not do right. You always do wrong thing. She hot. Give her the thermom." While my ears concentrated on that abbreviated last word, the doctor pointedly turned his back and started doing his examination with the stethoscope. It was left for my unobstructed and idle ears to hear a tirade from the mother, uttered in a mix of broken English and fluent Italian. She had come close, very close; by the time he had finished his examination, she was nearer the doctor than I. As he looked up, her eyes were ready for him, for his eyes. Again they locked into a mutual gaze. It was then that the patient looked at her mother and said her own imploring word: "Please!" The mother backed off, and the doctor began telling the girl what he believed was happening—the pneumonia was returning. He urged fluids as well as aspirin. He asked whether she'd been taking the medicine he'd prescribed earlier. No, she had stopped. Why? The answer: "Because my fever went down, and she [the mother] told me I must stop taking the pills, since I'm cool."

Now the doctor understood all—and became enraged. He turned to the mother and opened his mouth, ready (I thought) to give her the lecture of her life. I could see the color on his face. I could also see his right hand tighten its grip on the stethoscope. No words came out of his mouth. He simply stood there, bearing down with those formidable eyes on the woman of forty or so; she didn't budge, however, nor did she stop looking right at him. I wondered who would flinch first. Neither did. He suddenly flung up his right arm, stethoscope in hand. All eyes in the room, the patient's and mine as well as the mother's, followed the course of that ancient medical instrument, that symbol of a profession's authority. With that gesture the mother retreated, and then the patient slumped back onto her pillow. Dr. Williams started getting ready to leave. He folded his stethoscope carefully and put it into his black bag. Only at that moment did I began to relax a bit—the weapon was being laid down. He turned his back on the mother yet again and began a quiet appeal to the patient—she ought to take those pills every day, as he had instructed, and not stop taking them under any circumstances whatever. He emphasized the importance of that last remark with his voice, and after he'd finished speaking, he looked directly at the girl and asked her if she understood what he had said. Yes, she did. Then he asked her why she hadn't followed his instructions and kept taking the pills. Silence. He lowered his head. But he wasn't feeling shy or humble; he was fuming. Finally the head was raised, the mouth opened, the body turned toward the older woman: "I want every one of these pills taken by her. Every one." He was pointing at the patient. His eyes once more engaged with those of the mother. Neither retreated until the daughter addressed the mother: "Please pay the doctor." It was then that the mother left the room; she came back with a tightly folded bill, which she gave to her daughter, not the doctor. The daughter immediately handed it to the doctor, who quickly put it in his pocket without so much as looking at it. I remember being curious as to the amount. In a few seconds we were out of that apartment, and shortly thereafter on our way back to Williams' Rutherford home.

He didn't speak, and I was afraid to say anything, ask anything. Usually he was a willing, animated talker; now all his energy seemed given to the act of driving his car. He held the wheel with both hands (he often used only one hand to drive), and he fussed with the windshield wipers, putting them on and then turning them off as some rain fell, then stopped falling. Suddenly came his first words: "Hell, make up your mind"—addressed, I realized, to the nameless, faceless weather.

Then he laughed, turned to me, relaxed a bit—his back slouched against the back of the seat—and began to talk: "Well, there's a lesson for you in medical psychology, in what a doctor has to put up with." He wasn't satisfied with what he had said, so he went into a long explanation while the windshield wiper worked away at nothing, the rain having stopped. I was told all about the family, the patient's medical history, the mother's psychiatric history, the neighborhood's (immigrant, impoverished) social and cultural history. I was also told about previous encounters of the kind I had just witnessed. The narrator was sometimes wry or even humorous, at other times sardonic and angry. During one of those latter spells, he pulled out the crumpled bill he'd been given, telling me as he did so that it was "only one dollar." He laughed, with a mixture of embarrassment and annoyance, at what he'd heard himself say, and he added: "I'm lucky to get anything at all! Be grateful, I guess. Don't envy your colleagues what *they* make!"

MEDICAL ETHICS AND LIVING A LIFE

A black woman in Mississippi's Delta told me in 1969, as I went from home to home with other doctors trying to understand how it went for extremely poor and hard-pressed people:

> We don't have it good here. It's no good at all. I turn and ask the Lord, a lot of times, why it's so—the unfairness in this world. But I'll never get an answer. My daddy told me: "Don't expect answers to the really big questions—not from anyone. We're put here, and we don't know why, and we try to figure out why while we're here, and we fight to stay around as long as we can, and the next thing we know, it's slipping away from us, and we're wondering where we're going, if we're going any place." If I was a doctor, I guess I'd wonder every day what it's all about, this life. A lot of times my children ask me these questions, ask me why people behave so bad toward other people, and why there's so much greed in the world, and when will God get angry and stop all the people who don't care about anything but themselves. I have to say I don't have the answers. Does anyone? If you go to college, my oldest girl said, you learn the answers. She's twelve. She thinks that the more education you get, the more you know about how to be good and live a good life. But I'll tell you, I'm not so sure. I think you can have a lot of diplomas to your credit, and not be the best person in

the world. You can be a fool, actually, and have a lot of people calling you professor, lawyer, even doctor.

That "even"—a measure of hesitation, of lingering awe, of qualified respect. She had experienced her "rough times" with doctors—not only segregated facilities, but poor care and more insults than she cared to remember. A self-described "uppity nigger," she had finally spoken up to a doctor, had an argument with him. She remembered the critical essence of their confrontation this way:

I heard him saying bad, bad words about my people on the phone, and then he came into the waiting room and he gave me the nod. He never is polite to us, the way he can be with his white patients, and the more money they have, the bigger the smile they get out of him, and he's as eager to please as he can be. But with us, it's different; we get one sour look after the other. That day he told me to "shake a leg." I guess I wasn't walking into his office fast enough. Then he started talking about all "the welfare people," and saying, "Why didn't they go get themselves work?" Then, as he poked my belly, he gave me a lecture on eating and my diabetes—how I should "shape up and eat better."

That's when I forgot myself. I told him he should look to himself sometimes and stop making cracks at others. I told him he wasn't being much of a credit to his people and his profession, the way he was making these wisecracks about us poor folks. I told him he should know better, that there wasn't the jobs, and only now are we getting the right to vote, and the schools we've had weren't like the ones he could go to. I told him I expected more of him. Isn't he a doctor? If he can lord it over people, being a doctor, then he ought to remember how our Lord, Jesus Christ behaved. He was the Son of God, but did He go around showing how big and important He was, and calling people bad names, and making wisecracks, and sidling up to the rich and looking down His nose at the poor? Jesus was a doctor; He healed the sick, and He tended after the lame, the halt and the blind, like our minister says. I told our doctor he ought to read the Bible more. I told him that instead of saying bad things about the poor people and us colored people, he should take a hard look at himself and see if he's living the best life he can—the kind of life a doctor should live—if he's going to preach to the rest of us, and be looked up to as if he's the best of the best.

She didn't get very far with such words, although, to his credit, the doctor not only heard her out but smiled and thanked her for the obvious courage (in the year 1967) that she had displayed. And it may be all too easy now, as it has surely been in past years, to call upon such an incident, the South being once again a convenient scapegoat for the rest of us. In fact, there aren't too many places in America, one suspects, where such a candid encounter could take place. How many of us in medicine have been asked by anyone—patient, friend, relative, student, colleague—to connect our professional position with the kind of life we live, the way we get on with those we attend in an office, clinic, ward? That woman, who today would be categorized as "culturally deprived" or "culturally disadvantaged" (the dreary banality of such language!), had managed to put her finger on an important issue, indeed—one that philosophers, theologians and novelists have struggled for a long time to comprehend: How does one live a decent and honorable life, and is it right to separate, in that regard, a person's "private life" from his or her working life?

In a sense, too, that woman was struggling with the issue of medical ethics: How broad and deep ought such a subject cut—to the bone of the doctor's life? Without question, we need to examine the ethical matters that press on us every day in the course of our work. Recently, such matters have gained increasing attention and have been worked into the curricula of our medical schools. The traditions and resources of analytic philosophy have been extremely helpful, as we wonder when life ends or contemplate priorities so far as scarce (or experimental) technology and medicine go. It is utterly necessary for us to confront our values (or lack of them) as, for example, we work with patients too young or too old or too sick to be able to speak for themselves. And the dying patient has, of course, by and large benefited from the recent attention given that final stretch of earthly time, though one hastens to wonder whether a certain kind of psychological self-consciousness has not had its own dangers: all those "stages" and the prescriptive arrogance that can accompany "reform." Aren't there some people who have a "right" to "denial," not to mention a belief in the Good News? When does psychological analysis become a kind of normative judgment, if not smug self-righteousness? Sometimes, as I read the "literature" on "death and dying," I get the feeling that agnostic psychological moralists have the complete run of the field, with all too many ministers worrying all too much about something called "pastoral counseling," when a few old-fashioned prayers might be in order for the sake of the patient, the attending clergyman, and the rest of us as well.

Be that as it may, the woman just quoted from the outer precincts of Clarksdale, Mississippi, was aware in her own way that there have been, all along, two philosophical traditions—the analytic and the existential. The former allows us to ponder a host of variables and to make a specific (for the doctor, medical) decision. But the latter tradition urges us to go along with Kierkegaard, who surveyed Hegel's analytic abstractions with a certain awe but managed to remind himself and his readers that a man who had scrutinized all history and come up with a comprehensive theoretical explanation of anything and everything that had happened or would take place nevertheless had not much to tell us about how we ought to live our lives—we, who ask such a question and know that we have only so much time to find an answer. The existentialists (I don't like the glib, trendy use of the word, but what can one do these days with any word?) have stressed the particulars of everyday life—hence their interest (Buber, Marcel, Camus, Sartre and the father of them all, that at once high-spirited and gloomy Dane, Kierkegaard) in short stories, novels, plays and essays concerned with specific, concrete matters, as opposed to large-scale theoretical formulations meant to explain whatever comes in sight and then some.

It is the everyday life that clinicians also contend with—the unique nature of each human being. Since no patient is quite like any other, the doctor has to step from well learned abstractions to the individual person at hand—an important move, indeed. Novelists as well are wedded to the specific, the everyday; their job is to conjure up details for us, examples for us—the magic of art. And, as our black woman friend pointed out, everyday life has its own ethical conflicts. No wonder novelists do so well examining the trials and temptations that intervene, say, in a doctor's life. The point of a medical humanities course devoted to literature is ethical reflection, not a bit of culture polish here, a touch of story enjoyment there. There is an utter methodologic precision to the aim taken by George Eliot in *Middlemarch,* F. Scott Fitzgerald in *Tender Is the Night,* Sinclair Lewis in *Arrowsmith,* Walker Percy in *Love in the Ruins.* They are interested in exploring a kind of medical ethics that has to do with the quality of a lived life.

In *Middlemarch* Dr. Lydgate, a young doctor with high ideals, gradually must contend with a world of money and power. His marriage, his friendships, his everyday attitudes and commitments are revealed to weigh heavily, in the end, on the nature of his work. When he leaves Middlemarch for his excellent practice "between London and a Continental bathing place," he is not only abandoning a promising research career; he has changed so imperceptibly that he has no notion of real change. The ethical implications of his change of career are rendered with great subtlety. This greatest of English novelists knew better than to indulge in melodrama—the high-minded doctor come to naught through bad luck or a bad marriage or the bad faith of a particular banker. She makes it clear that to the outer world Lydgate is never a failure; he becomes, rather, more and more successful, as judged by the (corrupt and ignorant, we now know) standards of his time and place. The measure of his failure is his own early and well muscled ethical resolve. He had wanted to combat typhus and cholera—aware of the social as well as personal devastation those diseases wrought. He had wanted to take issue with the "principalities and powers" in his own profession. He ends up writing a treatise on gout. No doubt, gout, too, imposes suffering on people. And who is to decide what each of us ought to do—in any profession? But Lydgate had, indeed, made a series of decisions for himself and had hoped to see certain hopes and ambitions realized. *Middlemarch* provides a chronicle of disenchantment. A steady series of minor accommodations, rationalizations, mistakes of judgment contribute to a change of purpose, if not of heart. A doctor's character is proved wanting, and the result is his professional success by the standards of the time. Such a devastating irony leaves the reader in hopes, no doubt, that a bit of contemplation will take place: a person's work is part of a person's life, and the two combined as lifework must be seen as constantly responsive to the moral decisions that we never stop making, day in and day out. What George Eliot probed was character, a quality of mind and heart sadly ignored in today's all-too-numerous psychological analyses.

Similarly in *Arrowsmith,* a novel that many of us, arguably, read and take seriously at the wrong time in our lives—as high-schoolers, rather than during medical school and the years of hospital training. Sinclair Lewis was no George Eliot; he had a ruder, more polemical nature as a writer. And he lacked her gifts of narration. But he knew how professional lives become threatened, cheapened, betrayed. And he knew that such developments take place gradually, almost innocently—the small moments in the long haul, or the seemingly irrelevant big moments, such as a decision to live with one or another person and in this or that setting. His novel offered a powerful indictment of the larger society (always Lewis' intent) that exerts its sway on medicine, even research medicine, which is supposedly insulated from the vulgar world of cash and politics. But, of course, nothing is completely removed from that world—not doctors and not writers and not church people either. *Arrowsmith* is a novel that confronts the reader with a doctor's repeated ethical choices, a novel that makes it clear that such choices not only have to do with procedures (to do or not to do) or plugs (to pull or not to pull) but with the fateful decisions of everyday life that we are constantly making.

Such decisions are the stuff of each person's life. Once made, such decisions shadow us to the last breath. That is why Dick Diver haunts us in *Tender Is the Night,* and that is why Thomas More of Walker Percy's sad, funny and compelling novel, *Love in the Ruins,* makes us so uneasy with his shrewd, satirical observations about himself and his fellow human beings. Those two physicians, the reader knows, have asked important questions about life—how to live it honorably, decently. They have also stumbled badly, and their "fall" troubles us. We want to know why. But the reasons, the explanations, are not the categorical ones of modern psychology—some emotional hang-up. Those two principal characters speak for novelists who know how seamless a web life is, how significantly each physician's career connects with his or her moral values. It is a truism that one takes a risk by isolating the various moments of one's time on earth; yet we commonly strain to do so, and we are even allowed, if not taught, to do so, in our colleges and graduate schools and post-graduate training.

Every day, for instance, I see undergraduates not only working fiercely in courses such as organic chemistry but showing evidence of malevolent, destructive competitiveness. I have talked with some of those who teach such courses—heard the horror stories, the accounts of spite and meanness and outright dishonesty. Yet, again and again one listens to it asked: What can we do? And the students tell themselves, and we tell ourselves—we, who have gone through the maze ourselves—that it is something "inevitable" and, once over, forgotten. But these bothersome novelists tell us that we don't forget, and Lord knows Freud managed to make that point rather tellingly during his lifetime. We may appear to forget; we may convince ourselves that we do, but the small compromises, evasions, surrenderings of principle have their place in the unconscious, an element of geography yet to be done justice to by psychological theorists—the way we "repress" our moral sensibility, accommodate to various situations and die in the way George Eliot indicates.

Each year I receive respectful letters from ministers, bishops and church officials of one kind or another; I am asked to pass judgment psychologically on candidates for the ministry. Once my wife, in a moment of mischief and perhaps common sense, wondered what would have happened to all of us, historically, had Rorschach tests, Thematic Apperception Tests, or, yes, psychiatric interviews, been given to St. Francis of Assisi, St. Teresa of Avila, Martin Luther or Gandhi, not to mention the Old Testament prophets or Jesus Christ. Would they have "passed" those psychiatric interviews—they with their anger at the injustices of this world and their extraordinary willingness to suffer on behalf of all of us? One shudders at the psychiatric words that might have been sent their way. For that matter, she also wondered: Would Freud be given a grant from the National Institute of Mental Health today and would he even be willing to fill out those idiotic forms, one after the other? But setting that detour of my wife's aside, one is still left with the "spectacle" (to use a word that St. Paul favored as a critical moment in the affirmation of his faith) of religious authorities relying rather eagerly on the judgment of my ilk regarding the selection of candidates—as if psychiatrists were especially successful in finding for themselves, never mind others, how it is possible to live a principled life.

In psychiatry and medicine, as in other walks of life, we might ask for a few letters ourselves—not only appraisals of "mental function" but judgments about the ethical qualities of our various candidates. Do we often enough ask for such judgments? Do we ask ourselves and our students the kind of questions that George Eliot had in mind when she gave us, forever, one hopes, Dr. Lydgate, who would soon enough realize that there are prices to be paid for not asking certain questions? Dr. Lydgate forgot to inquire about what it would mean to him to become financially dependent on the philanthropist Bulstrode. Dr. Arrowsmith saw again and again the way doctors, like others, fall in line, knuckle under to various authorities who curb and confine independent thinking, never mind research. What those novelists move us to pursue is moral inquiry of a wide-ranging kind, in the tradition of Socrates or the Augustinian *Confessions* or Pascal's *Pensées,* or again, the best of our novelists: intense scrutiny of one's assumptions, one's expectations, one's values, one's life as it is being lived or as one hopes to live it. The pivotal questions are, of course, obvious. How much money is too much money? Who commands one's time, and who does not? What balance is there to one's commitment of energy? And, from another standpoint, when do reformers start succumbing to the very arrogance or cruelty that they claim to fight? How ought we to resist various intrusions on our freedom, on our privacy as persons and as doctors—the bureaucratic statism that no one, however anxious for various governmental programs, should dismiss as being of little consequence, not after this century's testimony? And so on. Is there room to teach that kind of medical ethics, that kind of program of medical humanities in our medical schools? Is there any better way to do so than through the important stories and character portrayals of novelists who have moved close to the heart of the matter—the continuing tension between idealism and so-called "practicality" in all our lives?

X. J. KENNEDY

X. J. KENNEDY (1929–   ). *American poet. Kennedy is the author of numerous collections of poetry, and the highly regarded editor of such anthologies as* Messages: A Thematic Anthology of Poetry, Tygers of Wrath: Poems of Hate, Anger, and Invective, *and, in 1987,* Literature: An Introduction to Fiction, Poetry, and Drama. *Recent collections of poetry include* Talking Like the Rain *(1992), a book of first poems for children;* The Kite That Braved Old Orchard Beach *(1991); and* Fresh Brats *(1990), also for children.*

LITTLE ELEGY

For a Child Who Skipped Rope

Here lies resting, out of breath,
Out of turns, Elizabeth
Whose quicksilver toes not quite
Cleared the whirring edge of night.

Earth whose circles round us skim
Till they catch the lightest limb,
Shelter now Elizabeth
And for her sake trip up Death.

GERALD WEISSMANN

GERALD WEISSMANN (1930–   ). *American physician, writer, researcher, and educator. After earning his M.D. degree, Dr. Weissmann did postgraduate work in both biochemistry and cell biology. He is now professor of medicine and director of the rheumatology division at New York University Medical Center. His research on inflammation and anti-inflammatory drugs has won several awards. A frequent contributor to* Hospital Practice *and* The New York Times, *Weissmann has written three books of essays:* The Woods Hole Cantata *(1985),* They All Laughed at Christopher Columbus *(1987), and* The Doctor with Two Heads *(1990).*

AUDEN AND THE LIPOSOME

Visitors to my office at Bellevue Hospital occasionally identify, with surprise, a photograph of W. H. Auden hung amidst the usual diplomas, family pictures, and group shots of house-staff days. The poet is shown next to Erika Mann; their pairing is a minor document of the troubled thirties. The marriage, in 1935, of Thomas Mann's daughter to Auden, a British subject, conferred a happier nationality upon the stateless refugee from Hitler's Germany. In the picture, Auden wears a rumpled lounge suit; his wide lapels and gaping jacket sleeves are signals of the period. His left hand dangles the perpetual cigarette, the right hand drapes an open jacket to display the braces and skirted trousers of a time when:

> *National Services had not been suggested*
> *O-Level and A were called Certs*
> *Our waistcoats were cut double-breasted*
> *Our flannel trousers like skirts.*

> —from "A Toast"

The poet's hair is neatly trimmed, the face is unlined—no hint appears of those Icelandic crags and furrows that in later years were to transform his features into a relief map of the anxious age. His wife-in-name-only appears to be generating a conventional smile for the photographer. She is dressed in a fashionable windowpane frock, topped by a gay, polka-dotted coat. Her scarf is knotted in chic display, the hat is soft and rakishly tilted. The overall effect is of upper acadame. Indeed, the young English master and his wife have been snapped by a photographer from the school newspaper of a progressive private school.

There are two reasons why this picture hangs above my desk: the subject and the photographer. Auden's photo reminds me that what I do for a living—medical research— may begin as fun but has a social bite. And since the snapshot was taken by my sometime collaborator, Alec Bangham, I am reminded of a long Cambridge summer in the sixties when he first taught me to form liposomes and which I remember chiefly as an interlude of pure joy.

Auden himself was persuaded that science, like poetry, is a "gratuitous, not a utile, act, something one does not because one must, but because it is fun." However, it is not this aesthetic approach to the doing of science—the approach of a skirt-trousered amateur—that has engaged me in Auden's poetry and prose. I think, rather, that I respond to that mixture of appreciation and fear of modern science which informs so many of his fabrications. He is at once a lyric enthusiast of our profession—a flatterer of the enterprise—and a necessary critic of our social mischief. His oldest friends—Christopher Isherwood, Cyril Connolly—have called him a schoolboy scientist at heart; Stephen Spender acclaimed him as the diagnostician of our fears. Son of a physician, familiar with the winners of glittering prizes (his phrase) from the laboratories of Oxbridge and the New World, he paid even the least distinguished of scientists an extravagant compliment that is difficult to forget:

> The true men of action in our time, those who transform the world, are not the politicians and the statesmen, but the scientists. When I find myself in the company of scientists, I feel like a shabby curate who has strayed by mistake into a drawing room full of dukes.

Given the political convictions of his youth, so different from his predecessors'—Yeats, Eliot, Pound—this generous appraisal should come as no surprise. Auden and his fellow anti-Fascists of the thirties were convinced that the journals of science contained clues to the fellowship of man. Auden believed that the laws of physics govern servant and master alike, and that it was the job of the poet to instruct both in the language of their common history.

> As biological organisms made of matter, we are subject to the laws of physics and biology: as conscious persons who create our own history we are free to decide what that history shall be.

Without science, we should have no notion of equality: without art no notion of liberty.

With these attitudes in tow, Auden devoted much of his energy to warning of the wretched use to which both poetry and science had been put in our time, in decades during which

> *The night was full of wrong,*
> *Earthquakes and executions,*
> *And still all over Europe stood the horrible nurses*
> *Itching to boil the children*

—from "Voltaire at Ferney"

Auden was ashamed by the extent to which the children of art and science enlisted in the service of brutality, in justice, and moral squalor. Commissioned as a major at the close of the Second World War, he visited in the course of his work the concentration camps where the methods of science were mocked. He spent long evenings in Bavaria recapitulating

> *The grand apocalyptic dream*
> *In which the persecutors scream*
> *As on the evil Aryan lives*
> *Descends the night of the long knives . . .*

—from "New Year's Letter 1939"

In the suburbs of Munich—in Dachau—Professors Pfannenstiel of Marburg, Jarisch of Innsbruck, and Linger of Munich had frozen scores of inmates to death and reported carefully detailed autopsies to "proper" scientific congresses. Here too, Professor Beiglbock of Berlin forced Poles and Jews to drink an excess of seawater: descriptions of the victims' hallucinations and heart failures were exactly recorded in what passed for scientific manuscripts. At the Natzweiler camp, Professor Dr. Eugen Haagen—formerly of the Rockefeller Institute—worked to transmit viral hepatitis from prisoner to prisoner and managed successfully to kill several hundreds with experimental typhus. These examples of scientific disgrace were paralleled in the realm of the arts by the complicities of Heidegger, the gangs of Bayreuth and Oberammergau, by the films of Leni Riefenstahl. After such excess, Auden became persuaded that our best hope lay in the establishment of limits, limits to the collaboration between intellect and the tyrant, best expressed in his "Ode to Terminus," the Roman God of Limits:

In this world our colossal immodesty
has plundered and poisoned, it is possible
  You still might save us, who by now have
  learned this: that scientists, to be truthful,
must remind us to take all they say as a
tall story, that abhorred in the Heav'ns are all
  self-proclaimed poets who, to wow an
audience, utter some resonant lie.

This plea for limits seems appropriate to our new era of biological engineering and belletristic extravagance. But I sense, perhaps, another strain here: a restatement of "Without science, no equality." For Auden is speaking to us from the experience of a generation which had used the discoveries of physiology and biochemistry as a kind of shield against the biological determinism of the old Fascists. He correctly discerned in the ongoing genetic arguments based upon insect behavior (first ethology, now sociobiology) a nasty trend toward the spinning of tall tales of inequality:

Bestiaries are out, now
Research has demonstrated how
They actually behave, they strike us
As being horribly unlike us.

Though some believe (some even plan
To do it) that from Urban Man
By advertising, plus the aid
Of drugs, an insect might be made.

No, Who can learn to love his neighbor
From neuters whose one love is labor
To rid his government of knaves
From commonwealths controlled by slaves?
                              —from "Bestiaries Are Out"

These versus anticipate my own misgivings about recent attempts to offer the stunning success of modern biology—our ability to decipher the social code of bees and the genetic code of man—as excuses for undoing the notion of equality. We have detailed the biochemical errors which cause blacks to suffer from sickle cell anemia, Italians and Greeks from thalassemia, Jews from Tay-Sachs disease, and Nordics from pernicious anemia; such heritable flaws speak of biological inequality. Since the popular geneticists of race and behavior have become persuaded that social characteristics also reside in the genes, is it any wonder that neo-Fascists, such as Alan de Benoist of France, have seized upon the recent hypotheses of sociobiology and "selfish genes" to legitimize their political fantasies? Auden's worries *matter:* the tall stories of our most recent science are beginning to have a dirty fallout. Private discoveries have public consequences. That homily brings me to the second reason for the picture on my wall, which evokes not only a summer of fun but yet another worry that Auden did not live to articulate.

As I've said, Auden and Erika were photographed by A. D. Bangham, F.R.S., of Cambridge. In 1935, Alec Bangham was photographer for his school newspaper at the Downs School and had been assigned to photograph the English master and his new bride. The photo remained imprinted upon a glass negative, stored among the juvenilia of this gifted amateur photographer, until Alec produced it at a scientific conference in the English countryside held fifteen years after the discovery of liposomes. It was at this conference that half a dozen investigators agreed that the use of liposomes in the treatment of human disease was not only desirable, but imminent. Liposomes are small fatty vesicles, made in the laboratory from off-the-shelf chemicals, which Alec and his collaborators originally proposed as models of cell membranes. They were soon found to duplicate many of the properties of the natural bilayers of lipid which enclose the ferments and nucleic acids of living cells. Since liposomes are biodegradable and not at all toxic, it has been suggested that they might function as the long-searched-for vectors by means of which entrapped substances might be safely delivered to organs deep in the body. It took no great effort of the imagination on the part of the conferees at this liposome meeting to tell each other tall stories of the use of liposomes for the manipulation not only of disease, but of the genes. While such experiments are only on the drawing board right now, it may not be premature to put a second concern on the agenda of angst.

I am afraid that in the decade and a half since liposomes were first constructed, developments in biological engineering have come so far, and so fast, that we are on our way not only to explaining, but to perturbing, the fundamental properties of living things. In this decade, when schoolboys and stockbrockers know how to assemble genes in the lab, we have learned to worry not only about the political consequences of our theories, but about the biological *sequelae* of our experiments. We have launched on an endeavor which may eventually realize the prophecy of Diderot:

If anyone wants to describe . . . the steps in the production
of man or animal, he will need to make use of nothing but
physical agencies . . . eat, digest, distill in a closed vessel, and
you have the whole art of making a man.

Indeed, the distilling of lipids in a closed vessel is a fair description
of how liposomes are fashioned. We begin by dissolving lipids, fatty
materials identical to those which our own cells use to fabricate their
membranes, in chloroform, and then dropping this solution into a closed
vessel. The chloroform is evaporated off and the fats remain as a turbid,
dry film at the bottom of the vessel. Next comes an operation which
approaches magic, and which, each time I perform it, carries with it
faint intimations of the Book of Genesis. We add a watery solution
which contains any one, or several, of the purified large molecules of
life: enzymes, hormones, genes. Then, in obedience to the laws of physics and chemistry, the fats spontaneously enclose these molecules in
membranes of predictable geometric array. The suspension assumes an
opalescent sheen as the membranes—part liquid, part crystal—swell
with their cargo. By simple separative procedures we can then isolate
liposome-entrapped materials from those which have escaped capture.
Eventually we can hold in our hand—or at least in the collection flask—
lipid-entrapped enzymes or nucleic acids: things arranged very much as
they would be in a jumbled, rudimentary cell or organelle.

I've described the formation of these little vectors of enzyme or gene
in detail because they constitute one example of how the playthings of
the lab have suddenly become capable of arousing not only aesthetic joy,
but moral qualms as well. Indeed, our colleagues of molecular biology,
who can now stitch genes in the dish and harness bacterial energies for
the production of human proteins, are now engaged in efforts at intro-
ducing their genetic artifacts into the cells of mouse and man. Some of
them are probably already toying with the use of liposomes as vectors
for bioengineering. I suppose that when I express moral qualms at this
possible application of our discovery, I'm only saying that neither Alec
nor his collaborators signed up for this sort of activity when liposomes
were first made—when one first enthused about the prospect of actually
replicating a fundamental unit of life, a membrane capable of entrap-
ping the stuff of cells. Now, there is every reason to believe that in the
decades to come, when second- or third-generation liposomes can be
appropriately designed to pass safely through body fluids and deliver
their contents to vital organs or tumors, their use will prove of benefit
in the treatment of disease. But every increment in our capacity for

fiddling with the nature of things should, I believe, make us pause for moments of serious self-doubt, should make us worry that we are not engaged only in mischievous tinkering.

The current mistrust of scientific research stems, in my view, from four major insults to our moral sensibilities. I've already alluded to two of these: the unfounded confusion of modern genetics with social Darwinism, and the not unrelated abuse by German doctors of human experimentation. To these may be added two others: the consequences to our offspring of the "poisonings and plunder" of the earth (radio-isotopes and chemical pollutants), and now, fears as to the restructuring of man by the well-intentioned splicing of his genes. The accusations are not unfounded, and as a community, we in the sciences should be prepared to acknowledge our share of the guilt, without being hobbled by the admission.

It may be scientific hubris to worry about the small contribution of liposomes to the game of genetic roulette—this will probably be played whether or not our stake is critical to the transport of inheritance. The current prospects for changing our natural load of disease and aging still seem somewhat dim—and we cannot be certain that strategies based on gene splicing or liposomal delivery are even headed in the proper direction. The enterprise is only *about* to be launched. But although the enterprise itself merits concern, I do not believe that we should back off. When I was first in Cambridge, I was present at a fastidious discussion between E. M. Forster and some young transatlantic visitors on his essay entitled "Two Cheers for Democracy." (The mostly radical visitors seem to have been concerned that Forster was giving one cheer too many.) Well, at this point, I'd like to sound two cheers for biology!

It is certainly *possible* that errors and disaster will accompany our attempts to alter the biology of man: but that biology includes diabetes, childhood leukemia, crippling arthritis, and inexorable senescence. Our technical triumphs may change the matter of the natural world, but that world maintains pandemic influenza, endemic parasites of gut and liver, and the natural carcinogens of plant and virus. In the days before the early bioengineers of microbiology (Pasteur, Ehrlich, Koch, and Metchnikoff) began to manipulate the fundamental nature of an ecosystem composed of man and microbes, the natural world contained smallpox, diphtheria, poliomyelitis, tuberculosis, and cholera.

A socially prescient humanist of 1880 might well have worried about the future of man in a world freed of microbes by the microbe hunters. He would have warned us of overpopulation, of an aging populace, of consequent famine, inflation, and social unrest. While acknowledging, in partial guilt, that some of these consequences flowed from the discovery of antibiotics, would we have been wiser *not* to conquer infectious diseases? My answer, since I am now alive thanks to antibiotics, has to be negative. Like it or not, on an actuarial basis, you, dear reader, and I are alive thanks to a society that permits the risk of error and invention, that encourages private inquiry to be expressed as public gain: the whole shooting match of Western invention and activism. Those lucky enough to be supported on the playing fields of science should worry hard—before, during, and after the game—but the rules of our sport, of science, are not written in the language of our guilt. The language which we need to remind us of that guilt remains the language of the artist, the poet, the philosopher, and—ultimately—the citizen. Auden has suggested that the language of science and that of poetry are at opposite poles: we neglect the latter at our own peril, because:

> Scientific knowledge is not reciprocal like artistic knowledge: what the scientist knows cannot know him.

So I suppose that I am reassured by that picture on my wall, as I see Auden and Erika Mann looking at the photographer, the young Bangham, and through him at me. As Auden's image in the photograph overlooks my laboratory impedimenta: the many journals, monographs, and reprints, I am persuaded that he knew what scientists are up to, that he knew the extent to which we are guilty, expressing this in language as clear as the genetic code:

> *This passion of our kind*
> *For the process of finding out*
> *Is a fact one can hardly doubt*
> *But I would rejoice in it more*
> *If I knew more clearly what*
> *We wanted the knowledge for,*
> *Felt certain still that the mind*
> *Is free to know or not.*
> —from "After Reading A Child's
> Guide to Modern Physics"

MILLER WILLIAMS

MILLER WILLIAMS (1930–   ). *American poet, translator, educator, and publisher. Williams's degrees in science (biology and physiology) have influenced his prolific literary output. Among his published works are* The Boys on Their Bony Mules *(1983);* Imperfect Love *(1986); and, most recently,* Living on the Surface: New and Selected Poems *(1989), a sharp, sobering, at times witty collection representing thirty years of observations on everyday contemporary life. Formerly director of the Creative Writing and Translation Program at the University of Arkansas, Williams is now director of the University of Arkansas Press. Among his awards are the Prix de Rome of the American Academy of Arts and Letters and, in 1990, the prestigious Poets' Prize.*

GOING

The afternoon in my brother's backyard
when my mother in awful age and failing
in body not at all and twice the pity
thought I was my dead father home for dinner
I didn't know what to tell her. What could I say?
Here I am home Darling give me your hand?
Let us walk together a little while?
Here it is 1915, we are married,
the first of our children is not yet born or buried,
the war in Europe is not yet out of hand
and the one you will not forget who wanted you first
is just as we are, neither old nor dead.
He still frets about us being together.

Good woman wife with five good children to mourn for,
and children arriving with children, what can I say?

See we have come because we wanted to come.
Because of love. Because of bad dreams.
This is my wife. We live in another state.

A DAY IN THE DEATH

He is amazed how hard it is to die.
He lies in his hospital bed, his shallow breaths
audible in the hall. He wonders why—
and tries to laugh because he knows—the deaths
of heroes always seem to be so quick.
Because, he knows, heroes have to fight,
and die fighting; also they rarely get sick.
A nurse looks into the room to say good night.
They don't tell each other what they know,
that both hope these words are the last he'll hear,
but guess they aren't. He thinks of the undertow
all swimmers swimming in strange waters fear,
that grabs you from below. He tries to sink
deep enough beneath the surface of sleep
to be found there and lost. There is a stink
thickening in the room. He knows the cheap
perfume Death wears. Why does she stand around?
Why doesn't the bitch take him? He tries to laugh
and this time does, and jerks at the new sound.
Well, half is already gone; the other half
could be a survivor of Buchenwald. Today
a counselor held his hand and told him again
to let go, to let it slip away.
He turned back to see how long it had been
since he had held on. He almost said,
"I'm trying. Something's stuck. Give me a shove."
He almost did. He squeezed the hand instead,
once for reasons forgotten and once for love.
But now he tries to sleep, pretends he is led
down through a wandering tunnel, sweetly gray,
to join the deep society of the dead,
afraid when the sun comes they'll send him away,
back to that room, back to that shrinking bed,
to lie there, being a lie, another day,
his eyes, his enormous eyes, eating his head.

PATRICIA GOEDICKE

PATRICIA GOEDICKE (1931–   ). *American poet. Born in Boston, Goedicke received her B.A. at Middlebury College and her M.A. at Ohio University. She has taught at Sarah Lawrence and Hunter College, among others, and now teaches creative writing at the University of Montana at Missoula. Her poetry has been published widely (in, among other periodicals,* The New Yorker, The Kenyon Review, *and* The Hudson Review*) and she has been awarded a number of prizes, including a fellowship from the National Endowment for the Arts. Her ten books of poetry include* Crossing the Same River *(1980),* The King of Childhood *(1984),* The Wind of Our Going *(1985),* Listen, Love *(1987),* The Tongues We Speak *(1989), and, most recently,* Paul Bunyan's Bearskin *(1992), in which she brilliantly melds emotion and analysis, poetry and politics, and daily, mundane commonalities with issues of national concern.*

ONE MORE TIME

And next morning, at the medical center
Though the X-Ray Room swallows me whole,

Though cold crackles in the corridors
I brace myself against it and then relax.

Lying there on the polished steel table
Though I step right out of my body,

Suspended in icy silence
I look at myself from far off
Calmly, I feel free.

Even though I'm not, now
Or ever:

The metal teeth of death bite
But spit me out

One more time:

When the technician says breathe
I breathe.

L. J. SCHNEIDERMAN

*L. J. SCHNEIDERMAN (1932–   ). American physician, novelist, and
playwright. Born in New York, Dr. Schneiderman received his B.A.
from Yale and his M.D. from Harvard. He did postgraduate training at
the University of Rochester's Strong Memorial Hospital and several
other institutions, including Stanford and the National Institutes of
Health. He is now professor of community and family medicine at the
University of California at San Diego. Dr. Schneiderman is the author
of the novel* Sea Nymphs by the Hour; *his numerous (and
prize-winning) short stories and plays have appeared widely.*

THE APPOINTMENT

Look, I'll show you the card. Jorge Gonzales. YOU HAVE AN APPOINT-
MENT, it says. All these months I keep it for him in the drawer with my
kerchiefs, the rosary, the other clinic cards, and every day I take it out
and look at the calendar. Never, not once, do I miss an appointment for
my children. You see how it's smeared with rouge. Smell the perfume.

   "Está loca," Serafina grunts when I show it to her. Like this she
turns it over in her old, clumsy fingers, then pushes it back at me.

   "Speak English," I say.

   Serafina looks at me like she tastes something sour.

   "I'm not crazy," I say. "It's an appointment. I have to go." What
else can I tell her? I *keep* my appointments. That's what I can tell her.
Not like you, and all the rest of you. I speak English. That's how I know
what they say about us at the clinic.

   So what does she do? In her slippers she goes and sits in front of the
television. But I can tell she is watching me out of the corner of her eye.

   I make my bundle of Jorge's shoes, a pair of socks, a shirt, shorts.
Everything washed and ironed. His dress-up clothes. These same clothes
he wears in our big family picture over the sewing machine. In the
picture, Francisco, my husband, stands next to me. Serafina, she is his
aunt, she sits in front. Jorge is sitting with Graciela and Julieta on the
donkey. The poor little animal is painted to look like a zebra. Francisco
makes a deal with the man.

   It was cold that day. Sometimes it rains. The man has no business.
Francisco has money for putting new seat covers on an Anglo sailor's
car. They make the deal in a bar. Francisco rushes home. Quick, he says,
put on your best clothes. I pick some flowers for the girls—real flowers,

not those paper things they sell in the streets. We all march behind him like we're going to see the Pope. Then we squeeze around the painted donkey and the man takes our picture. The whole family, for the same price as he charges one Anglo tourist.

In the picture, Francisco looks nervous. I don't know why. Maybe he is afraid the man will change his mind and charge him a whole lot of money. But his face, it reminds me when Jorge was born. When he stands in the door of my hospital room, he acts strange. Like a stranger. Why, I thought. Is it because of me? In the mirror I see my face. *¡Mi madre!* How worn out I look. Francisco and another man from the shop. They are standing in the doorway. Afraid to come in. Francisco smiling, but so nervous. Like he brings his friend along to help him.

Eight children, I want to tell him, and you're still shy about women's things, Francisco. I want to tell him how much the labor hurt. Jorge was not easy. He takes a long time. The doctors examine me. After they finish the nurse snaps the curtains back and shouts, "Not yet. Little more. Understand? *¡Un poco más!*"

"I understand," I tell them in English.

But, at last it's over. How happy I am. "You like him?" I ask.

But Francisco just stands there in the doorway. The doctors say something is wrong with Jorge. *What?* Something with his heart, but they can fix it. *¡Gracias a Dios!* What miracles the Anglo doctors can do.

An operation. It makes Francisco nervous. The doctors say Jorge might die. Serafina is angry. That's what I get for going to *la clínica*. She hates the place. Once, a specialist does not see her. As for the other doctors, they squeeze her breasts and belly with their silky hands, and then do they give her the shot she needs? No, they tell her to lose weight. She keeps telling me to take Jorge to the *curandero,* but I tell her no. One morning I find a bowl of water with egg and pieces of palm under Jorge's bed. From then on I watch very closely.

I must protect Jorge from her and her old fashioned ways. "Can the *curandero* fix the holes in Jorge's heart?" I cry. But the old woman tries to make him drink herb teas. When I'm not looking she tries to sneak on suction cups.

If it is time for an appointment, if I dress Jorge up to take him to the clinic, she glares at me and spits on the floor.

"Stop spitting," I shout at her, and Jorge starts to cry.

"Está loca," she tells everyone. It is *mal de ojo,* the Evil Eye. If I want Jorge to live, if I want miracles, I must let her take him to the *curandero.*

Meanwhile, the doctors say Jorge is not ready for the miracle. He doesn't like to eat. He learns to walk, but he is small, smaller even than

Graciela. The doctors say he must grow a little more before they try to fix his heart. "Just a little more," they say. *"Un poco más."*

Francisco says do not to listen to Serafina. Anglo doctors, they are the best in the world. Every day you read such amazing things. Every day on television a new miracle. Francisco says be careful. Don't let his old aunt do anything to upset the Anglo doctors. But don't upset her either, he says. It is not a good thing to upset Serafina.

Years ago she was married to an Anglo. So she has a Social Security card. Now, anyone on welfare, they use her number, and if money comes Serafina is very honest. She finds the person and gives it to him. Everyone trusts Serafina. It makes her very powerful. She can make a lot of trouble.

So today, I say to her, "Serafina, I have to get dressed." Just Serafina and me in the bedroom. If Francisco was home, she would get up, grumbling and sighing, and leave the room. She knows I want to be alone. But what does she do? She pretends not to hear me and keeps her ear cupped like this to the television. The children are all outside playing. The women from next door are in the kitchen talking to Dolores, my oldest daughter.

Always the old woman likes to hear gossip. But you think this time? Well, it's getting late. So I must get dressed while Serafina watches me. For her, everything I put on tells her something. This old woman, she always forgets things, she always asks us where are her slippers, but she remembers perfectly all my clothes. She knows exactly where I get my slips, my bras, my stockings, my panties, my dresses. And remembers every time I wear them. One by one, as I put on my clothes, she is checking on me.

"Está loca." That's what she always tells Francisco. Crazy. Serafina. She doesn't care about craziness in relatives, in her friends, in total strangers who spend the night with us before crossing the border, this old woman calls me crazy.

For what? Because I insist on practicing my English? So I can get a good job someday? Citizenship even? Like my children! All my babies I am very careful to have across the border. And isn't that a smart thing to do? When Jorge was born? Can any Mexican doctor do such miracles?

And especially I keep my appointments. For checkups. For shots and examinations. So all my children when they start looking for jobs will be as strong and healthy as the Anglo children.

So what do I do? I turn my back on Serafina and pick out my best bra, the yellow lace one from my wedding. Then I worry the bra is too fancy. Serafina will tell Francisco I am carrying on with one of the Anglo doctors. So next I put on old cotton panties I share with Dolores and Alissandre. And the plainest slip. I pull a few loose strings before slipping it on. And then I get real mad at myself. Look how I'm dressing! To suit Serafina's big nose. Right away I pull down this, my lavender dress with the cherry-colored string around the collar and matching belt. It shows my knees. Right away I regret it. Who wears such a silly dress to the clinic? The doctors and nurses will look at me and their eyes will say, "Another one." The woman at the desk will ask to see my card and I must wait while they check the machine to see if I have any unpaid bills.

But too late. Serafina will tell Francisco . . . *Francisco?* . . . the whole barrio, if I try on dresses just to go to *la clínica.* Her detested *clínica.* She will hiss to everyone, Modesta is carrying on with one of the doctors.

Then I look at my watch. I have to hurry. Then I remember to check my purse before I leave to make sure I have enough money. Sometimes the children sneak into my purse and steal from me. If I'm already on a bus or in a store when I discover this I want to shout out loud, so everyone will hear what my children do to me. But instead I cry. Why should my children have to steal? But when I come home already I'm thinking something else. Isn't it better for them to steal from me than from a stranger who will put them in jail?

On my way out of the bedroom I look at Serafina. Serafina shakes her head. *"El doctor no está allá."*

"The doctor is there," I say. "See. I have an appointment."

But she shakes her head again and doesn't look.

It's true, though, what she says. Sometimes, many times, the doctor is not there. Once, Serafina got all dressed up to go to the clinic. She is supposed to see an important specialist. She even borrows money to take a taxi across the border. But when she shows up in the waiting room she is told the doctor is not there. He is in another city giving a speech. The woman at the desk can't understand why this old woman is so upset. The doctor will be happy to see her another day, she says. But Serafina is angry. The woman at the desk makes it sound like one day is as good as another. After all what does this old woman do all day, but sit around anyway. The woman at the desk is Mexican, she tells her all this in perfect Spanish. You think that makes Serafina feel better? Right there, in front of the whole waiting room she shouts and spits on the floor. Never, she says, *never* is she coming back to *la clínica.*

Now, who do you think is *loca?*

Still, I think, maybe she's right. Not me, yet, but plenty of women have the same experience. All the way to the clinic they go and are told to go home and come back another time. Even though they have an appointment. Imagine. You wait for such a long time in front of the customs station—you know what they say: what do they care? The guard with his dark glasses looks through your purse. Looks at your clothes. You show him the clinic card. One of your children has an appointment for shots and a checkup. And then you wait for the bus. And then when you get there they tell you it's a mistake. The doctor you are supposed to see is not there. Perhaps someone writes the wrong date on the card. Or the wrong time, so you arrive too late.

Or, to tell the truth, sometimes the women lose their cards. (I am so careful where I keep mine.) They go on a day they think is the right one, only it isn't. Other specialists are there. And the woman at the desk smiles and looks down her nose. Their diseases are not so big as the diseases they see that day.

Well, today, the bus is crowded. Some of the people I recognize. Mothers with children, old people with canes, young people with casts and crutches. Everyone grunting, limping, but laughing and joking with each other. Going to the clinic? they say. A hot day for it. Sí. A hot day for it. Children run up and down the aisles. A few sit quietly next to their mothers. They stare at the other children and I stare at them, until they catch my eye and I turn away.

So many children, I think. What will they do when they all grow up and bring their own children to the clinic? They'll need bigger buses. Every year they'll need bigger and bigger buses.

Myself, I have eight. Eight children. Would you believe it? Now I know it's too many. My mother, you know she had thirteen. Five are still living, or at least I think so. Two of my brothers, who knows? They got in trouble in Guadalajara and have to hide, not from the police, but from some men who say they owe them money. My mother, she cries for weeks. There is talk of shooting. Every day my poor mother is sad or scared. Some people say misfortune comes like rain, so protect yourself with many children. But I ask you, is thirteen children enough? And how does it protect you? Now I know the truth. The more children, the more sorrows.

I think about this a lot when I am carrying Jorge. I tell Francisco we must stop having more children. At first he cannot understand what I mean. Stop . . . being man and woman in bed? He cannot say the word. No, I say to him. We must do what the Anglo does, have our nights in bed, but stop making children. Francisco told me he hears of this, too. But how does one do such things? He is too embarrassed to ask any-body. He says I should ask the priest, which I do. Not a Mexican priest, but an Anglo. This priest says I must ask the doctor for something. At first Francisco does not believe me. The priest says this? Ask him yourself, I tell him.

Francisco goes. He comes back shaking. Men can have an operation on their private parts. It will keep them from having children. The way the priest says it, it will take only a few minutes. Another miracle. But I see Francisco doesn't like the idea. He shakes as he tells me this. What else does he say? The priest also says the doctor can do something to me.

Francisco is afraid, but not me. And so, Jorge is our last child. When he is born I have the operation. You can see why I am worried when Francisco looks at me strangely. Am I no longer a woman to him, I think.

But later, when I learn about Jorge, and I remember how much pain he gave me, I think something else. Is God punishing me? Is the priest the devil in disguise? *Un brujo?*

But how can that be? Isn't Jorge a beautiful baby? And don't the doctors say they can fix him? Can the devil make such miracles? And as for Francisco, he loves me just as much as ever in the bed. He is a good husband, even if he does not try so hard to learn English. He always brings us clothes and gives me money for food. And he does not drink any more than the other men, maybe a little bit less, because he always comes home at night and comes into bed to sleep with me.

I remember when I first get married, the smell of his sweat, the smell of a man's sweat so close to me. And the smell of beer coming out of his mouth and nose at night, all this is difficult for me. When I was a girl, the house I live in is in the country. It has more rooms than now I have. I sleep only with my sisters, never with my father or my older brothers. I tell you this, because I know the kind of things people say about us who come from the country.

And Jorge. Well, even if he is not sick, even if he is healthy, he must be special. My last child. To think I will never have another. It is like knowing that someone is about to die. You think about that person very hard, you want to feel the person next to you all the time. You know, sometime I am cooking in the kitchen and all the children are laughing and shouting, but I only hear Jorge. I stop and just listen.

But because of that you think I do not love my other children just as much? You're wrong. Carlos, Dolores, Alissandre, Ernesto, Graciela, Humberto, Julieta. Do I not talk about them as much? Well, I love them just as much. It is just that . . . what is it? It is like a band of musicians, you know what I mean, people singing, all of them making beautiful music. But now it is Jorge's time to sing out. It is his voice I hear most.

You think it is any different for the others? All my children, all of them, dig in the dirt and play with the hose. All of them get covered with mud. But it is only Jorge's face I see right now, covered with mud, his clothes, his shoes, a mess. And now I cry when I think how angry I get at him for getting dirty. For what? For dirt? They say Anglos throw away their clothes when they get dirty. Throw away their cars. Even their children, they say. Should I be like them? Is this why I want to learn English, so I can be like them? Then as I look out the bus window I think to myself, You sound old, Modesta. Like Serafina. You are getting old.

When the bus stops at the hospital and everyone gets out, I follow the green line to the clinic. I show the woman at the desk the appointment card and she looks in the book.

"Jorge Gonzales," she says, putting a little check next to the name in her appointment book.

I sit down with a great feeling of relief. So, there is no mistake. The appointment is for Jorge. Today, now, and the doctor is here. What a good feeling to be in the clinic, in this place of miracles. In the hall I see the doctors and nurses working. So clean, so healthy. See what miracles have done for them. And I remember how Francisco stood so nervously in this place. How shy he is to talk about personal things.

Here, I can talk about anything. Personal things, anything. You can show the doctors any part of your body, show them ugly things I am afraid to look at myself, and they never make faces.

True, they are cold, the doctors and nurses, they are cold. But that coldness is something very comforting to me. What do I care if the world of miracles is a cold place.

But, while I am sitting, I feel the sadness deep inside me, like water at the bottom of a well. Such a long time that sadness is inside me.

Suddenly I hear the nurse with a chart calling: "Gonzales!" I follow her to the examining room and wait. She does not look at me any special way as she closes the door, but I think why does she look at me that way?

It is a long wait. Outside the door I think I hear whispering. Then, at last, the door opens and in come two doctors. A woman doctor and you. The woman doctor wears a white coat and nametag. But who is this man? I think. He also wears a nametag on his shirt, but no white coat. He does not look me over like the other doctors. Instead, he looks only into my eyes.

"Mrs. Gonzales?" the woman doctor says.

"Yes."

"Aquí está el doctor . . ."

"I speak English," I say to her.

"Oh. This is Dr. Hernandez. He's a psychiatrist."

"Yes?"

"He's here to help you."

Then I see that you are both looking at Jorge's clothes which I am holding tightly in my hands. I see how tightly I am clutching them.

"He's here to help you," says the woman doctor again. "He will make you better."

"I see," I say to her. And I think to myself—maybe that will be the miracle.

LINDA PASTAN

LINDA PASTAN (1932–   ). *American poet. Pastan is the recipient of, among other honors, the Dylan Thomas Poetry Award, the di Castagnola Award, and several fellowships from the National Endowment for the Arts. Among her collections of poetry are* AM/PM: New and Selected Poems *(1982),* The Imperfect Paradise *(1988), and* Heroes in Disguise *(1991), a clear-sighted, graceful composition on the cyclical nature of life and how we as human beings fit into it. An* Early Afterlife *(1995) is Pastan's latest work.*

THE FIVE STAGES OF GRIEF

The night I lost you
someone pointed me towards
the Five Stages of Grief.
Go that way, they said,
it's easy, like learning to climb
stairs after the amputation.
And so I climbed.
Denial was first.
I sat down at breakfast
carefully setting the table
for two. I passed you the toast—
you sat there. I passed
you the paper—you hid
behind it.
Anger seemed more familiar.
I burned the toast, snatched
the paper and read the headlines myself.
But they mentioned your departure,
and so I moved on to
Bargaining. What can I exchange
for you? The silence
after storms? My typing fingers?
Before I could decide, *Depression*
came puffing up, a poor relation
its suitcase tied together
with string. In the suitcase
were bandages for the eyes

and bottles of sleep. I slid
all the way down the stairs
feeling nothing.
And all the time Hope
flashed on and off
in defective neon.
Hope was a signpost pointing
straight in the air.
Hope was my uncle's middle name,
he died of it.
After a year I am still climbing,
though my feet slip
on your stone face.
The treeline
has long since disappeared;
green is a color
I have forgotten.
But now I see what I am climbing
towards: *Acceptance*
written in capital letters,
a special headline:
Acceptance,
its name is in lights.
I struggle on,
waving and shouting.
Below, my whole life spreads its surf,
all the landscapes I've ever known
or dreamed of. Below
a fish jumps: the pulse
in your neck.
Acceptance. I finally
reach it.
But something is wrong.
Grief is a circular staircase.
I have lost you.

NOTES FROM THE DELIVERY ROOM

Strapped down,
victim in an old comic book,
I have been here before,
this place where pain winces
off the walls
like too bright light.
Bear down a doctor says,
foreman to sweating laborer,
but this work, this forcing
of one life from another
is something that I signed for
at a moment when I would have signed anything.
Babies should grow in fields;
common as beets or turnips
they should be picked and held
root end up, soil spilling
from between their toes—
and how much easier it would be later,
returning them to earth.
Bear up . . . bear down . . . the audience
grows restive, and I'm a new magician
who can't produce the rabbit
from my swollen hat.
She's crowning, someone says,
but there is no one royal here,
just me, quite barefoot,
greeting my barefoot child.

REMISSION

It seems you must grow
into your death slowly,
as if it were a pair of new shoes
waiting on the closet floor,
smelling of the animal
it came from, but still too big
too stiff for you to wear.
Meanwhile you dance barefoot
your shaky dance of pretence,
and we dance with you,
the pulses in our own wrists
ticking away.
In this small truce
the body waits,
having waged war on itself
for years. You say
the water tastes of flowers.
You steal on tiptoe
past the closet door.

JOSEPH HARDISON

JOSEPH HARDISON (1935–   ). *American physician, educator, and writer. Dr. Hardison attended Emory College and Emory University School of Medicine, where he is now a professor of medicine and associate chief of staff for extended care. His essays, by turns provocative, poignant, and humorous, have appeared widely—in* The New England Journal of Medicine, The Annals of Internal Medicine, Archives of Internal Medicine, Journal of the American Medical Association, *and* The American Journal of Medicine.

THE HOUSE OFFICER'S CHANGING WORLD

We middle-aged and older physicians are smug about our house-staff days—the days when medical giants roamed the hospital halls day and night. We prepared and stained our own blood smears, performed white-cell counts and differentials, actually looked through a microscope at our patients' urine, gram-stained sputum smears, determined circulation times, and measured venous pressures. Invasive procedures consisted of lumbar punctures, paracenteses, thoracenteses, liver biopsies, pleural biopsies, sigmoidoscopies, and bone marrow aspirations. We worked in private hospitals and in gloomy non-air-conditioned city and Veterans Administration hospitals. Patients were crowded together on large, open wards, where the nurses could see and hear everyone and where blacks were often segregated from whites.

The fund of medical knowledge was manageable. We revered and feared our teachers. Occasional intimidation and embarrassment were accepted as effective methods of teaching. Professors had time to spend with us, to teach us and get to know us. Departments of medicine were smaller, and everyone knew everyone else. Conferences were well attended, well prepared, and in most instances, given by the faculty in residence. The drug-company lecture circuit had not yet begun. Conferences were rarely interrupted. Messages were briefly flashed on the screen, or interns and residents were summoned by a display of their call numbers. Beepers were a scourge for the future. It was possible, if we worked hard, listened well, learned from our mistakes, and read about our patients' conditions, to become, in three years, confident and competent to diagnose and treat most of the diseases we would encounter in internal medicine without ever having photocopied a single article.

We worked every other night or every third night. There were frequently three or four of us in one on-call room with one telephone. Our pay averaged about 25 cents an hour. Moonlighting, though prohibited, went on and consisted almost entirely of physical examinations of clients of insurance salesmen. In most instances, the client did not come to the doctor. I performed examinations in a liquor store and a bowling alley, and I once examined a movie projectionist in his booth while John Wayne was on the screen. Most of our wives worked (there were very few women in medicine), and most of us borrowed money at low interest rates. We didn't have large debts incurred in medical school. Entertainment was infrequent and simple and usually enjoyed in the company of other house officers. We were all able to go to the annual Christmas party because the faculty covered for us.

Many of the patients whom we (and private physicians) took care of could not afford to pay and were not expected to do so. There were charity wards in most private hospitals, and the big city hospitals were primarily for the indigent. There was no Medicare, Medicaid, or diagnosis-related groups (DRGs). Most patients were uninformed about medicine. They trusted and respected their physicians and did not question the diagnosis, prognosis, or treatment. They did not accept responsibility for their health. They went to the doctor when they got sick and expected the doctor to make them well. Physicians and their patients smoked.

Medicolegal and ethical matters were relatively uncomplicated. Malpractice premiums were low, and malpractice suits were uncommon; doctors usually won and, if they lost, the awards were reasonable. The courts, by and large, saw fit to leave medical decisions to physicians. There was no need for living wills or for distinguishing brain death from death. "No code" or "do not resuscitate" orders did not exist because there was no effective cardiopulmonary resuscitation. Often patients were not told that they had cancer or leukemia; they were given the opportunity to prolong the denial of their imminent death. After all, we thought, if they really wanted to know what the score was, they could tell from our actions and what we left unsaid. There was no patient's bill of rights.

Technology consisted of stethoscopes, ophthalmoscopes, tuning forks, reflex hammers, electrocardiographs, rigid sigmoidoscopes, bronchoscopes, and various and sundry biopsy needles. There were no medical intensive care units, no coronary care units, no respiratory care units, and no arterial lines, subclavian lines, Swan-Ganz catheters, pacemakers, Holter monitors, bedside monitors, or cardioverters. Imaging consisted of roentgenography and fluoroscopy. Ultrasound, echocardiography, computerized axial tomographic scanning, and nuclear magnetic-resonance imaging were yet to come. There were no third-, or second-, or even first-generation cephalosporins, and nitrogen mustard was the only effective chemotherapy. We sterilized our needles in an autoclave and reused them; blood came in bottles. "End-stage" disease meant the end was near. There was no renal dialysis, and organs were not transplanted. We did very little to patients, and it was easier for them to die with dignity.

When we finished our training and were ready for practice or a career in academia, opportunities abounded. There weren't enough physicians to go around. There were no "docs in boxes" or preferred provider organizations, and there were very few prepaid health plans. Physicians did not advertise. We could be assured of working hard, earning a comfortable living, and being members of the most respected of professions.

Modern-day house officers find themselves in circumstances vastly different from those we experienced when we were house officers. Many of them have substantial debts from financing their medical school education. Although the salaries of the house staff are better now, many take outside ("moonlight") jobs because of their debts and a desire for a higher standard of living. Most work in emergency rooms, and few, if any, do physical examinations for life-insurance companies. Moonlighting is not the forbidden subject it used to be, and most program directors give tacit approval or simply turn the other way.

The days of working every other night are gone. Most house officers work every third or fourth night while they are on ward services. Because they work fewer nights, however, more patients are assigned to them when they do work. They become very adept at triage and at caring for many sick patients, but they have little time to read and even less to sleep. They are under enormous pressure to discharge patients, both because of pressures to contain costs from third-party payers and the DRG system, and because they have no control over the admission process.

Teaching hospitals are also moneymaking hospitals. The faculty has little time and often little inclination to teach. Attending rounds are made to ensure third-party payments. There are no monetary rewards for teaching, and teaching won't get faculty members promoted. Many big city hospitals, the former bastions of house-staff training, either have closed or are in difficult financial straits. Academic and clinical faculty members don't have time to give to these foundering behemoths. The house-staff members are given, and assume, more and more responsibility. As a result of this increased responsibility and of the decrease in the faculty's time for and interest in teaching, the house staff has become more and more independent. The faculty and the house staff have become estranged. Everyone is busy taking care of patients or doing research. House officers have role models but few heroes.

There is now much more to do for and to patients. We expect house officers to learn all the procedures we learned and many more. We expect them to be equally competent in caring for ambulatory patients and critically ill patients in intensive care units. We keep stressing the history and physical examination as the source of the most important data we gather, but everyone, faculty and house staff alike, is relying more and more on tests and procedures. You need a gimmick to make it in private practice. Because of the pressure to get their work done, the house-staff members seldom, or only reluctantly, attend conferences. When they do attend, they bring their lunches, and the speaker strives to be heard over crackling cellophane, the crunch of potato chips, the rattle of ice cubes, and a cacophony of beepers. An hour spent in conference is an hour taken from time off. House officers today have many interests other than medicine. They want to enjoy these while they are still young.

It is impossible to keep up with medicine today. Knowledge is accumulating and changing so fast that you can't be sure that what is fact today will be true tomorrow. House officers, with little time to read, instead photocopy or tear out enormous numbers of articles from journals and, like squirrels hiding acorns, bury them in ingenious filing systems in the hope that the articles will still be pertinent when they finally get around to reading them some day.

House officers and practicing physicians are under attack from the public, the legal profession, and the government. Subspecialty programs are reducing the numbers of fellowship positions, and future funding is in question. Many will lose autonomy because, by choice or necessity, they accept salaried positions. Competition for patients will create tension among colleagues. Moral, ethical, and medicolegal issues that arise because of technology, greed, and public awareness consume enormous amounts of time, resources, and energy. There is evidence that emotional impairment is increasing in today's house staff. Sleep deprivation, the responsibilities of being a new physician, and rigorous training are cited as causes of the increased strain. These stresses, however, have been present for as long as there have been training programs. Another factor may be that the medicine that today's house officers dreamed about, which they went to college and medical school and deep into debt for, no longer exists. Our young physicains are bemused and beleaguered, and they feel they have been betrayed.

I suppose it is natural for those of us who are nearer the end of a career than the beginning to extol the virtues of our house-staff training over the training of today. Each generation seems to believe it suffered more hardships and did things better than the next. House officers today have enough to worry about without hearing about how hard we worked and how dedicated we were. We accuse them of being the "me generation," of being incapable of delaying gratification. It is difficult, however, to enjoy life today when you are $30,000 in debt and haven't yet begun to earn a living. Medicine has changed drastically since we were house officers. Comparing medicine then and now is like comparing horse-and-buggy days with interplanetary travel. It is impossible to know who worked harder and learned more, and it doesn't matter. There is, however, no question about who has more to learn and more to do. House officers are not responsible for what has happened to medicine, but we are responsible for what happens to our house officers. They are intelligent, diligent, responsible, and compassionate people, and they usually end up being well trained. They deserve our support, appreciation, and affection.

FRANK GONZALES-CRUSSI

FRANK GONZALES-CRUSSI (1936–   ). *American physician and writer. A faculty member at Northwestern College of Medicine, Dr. Gonzales-Crussi is the author of several books, including* Notes of an Anatomist; Three Forms of Sudden Death and Other Reflections on the Grandeur and Misery of the Body; On the Nature of Things Erotic; *and, most recently,* The Day of the Dead and Other Mortal Reflections.

ON EMBALMING

Ceremony and ritual spring from our heart of hearts: those who govern us know it well, for they would sooner deny us bread than dare alter the observance of tradition. And yet funeral ceremonies can change. The Dayak people of Borneo used to preserve the body of a dead chief in the communal house of the living, a practice they had to abandon under the pressure of Dutch officials who did not take kindly to this form of mixed company. With equally commendable sanitary zeal, authorities in India have been known to oppose the ancient customs of the Parsis of Bombay, Zoroastrian votaries, who place the bodies of their dead atop circular constructions, where, in a matter of hours, vultures dispose neatly of all the fleshy parts. Europeans generally perceived a lurid aura about this ritual and showed little sympathy for what they saw as a "secret cult of death." Yet the Parsi custom dates its origins at least six centuries before the birth of Christ and was inspired by the currently much-vaunted goal of decreasing ecologic contamination: the Zoroastrian believes the dead body so unclean that it would contaminate the "pure elements" of the universe—earth, fire, and water.

In Europe and the United States embalming was practically unknown before the latter part of the eighteenth century. The modern technic of this procedure is generally attributed to the Scottish anatomist William Hunter. Before his day, and in the United States up to the years of the Civil War, cadavers that had to be transported or kept unburied for days were simply packed in ice. There were "cooling boards," concave devices filled with ice in which the body could fit snugly, but, beyond this rudimentary inventiveness, it may be said that corpse technology had not really been put at the service of the common people.

Consider this telling difference between East and West: among the ancient Egyptians, embalming was but one aspect of a life oversaturated with things spiritual and preoccupied with the possible fate of the soul after the body had perished. In the industrial West, there has been an equally universal and all-encompassing preoccupation. It is called desire for profit, and, as will become apparent here, it has done much for the spread of the practice of embalming.

In the West, embalming and greed seem to have been wedded from the beginning. John Hunter, younger brother of the Scottish anatomist, came across an exceptional opportunity to apply his brother's methods. A wealthy woman, Mrs. Martin Van Butchell, under motives obscure and indecipherable, wrote a peculiar will. It was her intention, duly legalized by seals and signatures, that her surviving husband should have control of her fortune only for as long as she would remain above ground. Upon her demise, her husband acted with a determination all the more admirable for being mixed with grief. John Hunter was summoned to the homestead. Mrs. Van Butchell's remains were injected intra-arterially with fluids of recent invention, and the lady ended up, fashionably clad in her best finery, inside a glass-lidded container, before which she received friends and relatives.

After these auspicious beginnings, the career of the embalming practice made impressive gains, but nowhere as sound as in the United States, where the government threw its full weight behind it. Here, embalming became mandatory by law whenever the interval between death and burial exceeds forty-eight hours (twenty-four in some states) or when the body must be transported a certain distance. To say that embalming is big business in America would be, as everyone knows, a great understatement. According to recent statistics, less than 8 percent of the lifeless population of this country is disposed of by cremation, and since alternative methods of disposal, such as cannibalism or Zoroastrian exposure, must be very infrequently practiced in America, it follows that embalming continues to be an economically important activity. This is true from the standpoint of the total economy of the nation as well as from the more restricted viewpoint of individual enterprise.

However spurious or suspect the origins of Western embalming, the pathologist ought to acknowledge his gratitude to the practitioners of this trade. Theirs is an activity that cannot be dismissed as menial, in spite of its frequent unpleasantness. At its most perfected and professional, it is no exaggeration to say that it should be called an art. Without the skillful intervention of dieners, funeral house directors, and morgue attendants, the pathologist's task would be much more onerous and frequently impossible, for it is part of his job to secure bodily parts for conscientious study—in some cases entire mandibles, eyes, femurs, or vertebral columns.

On a rare occasion, the pathologist, at the completion of his task, has looked back on the remains lying on the table and felt a chill upon realizing that professional zeal has caused him to alter the human form in a manner apt to be called a defilement. The dead possess an identity, granted by the living through the agency of intact form; so long as form remains, a cadaver remains "the same one" for associates and relatives, for friend and foe. But without spine or limbs or eyes (which virtually never are removed during an autopsy study), the form is altered and diminished; without ribs, the dead person is a frail manikin; without jaw, the human face is a grotesque mask. For the body to be viewed at this time by the most generous purveyors of identity, his loved ones, could mean disaster.

Such catastrophic events are, happily, almost unheard of. In the exceptional case of removal of a large bodily part, the adroit ministrations of the mortician will avert a sad outcome. In place of absent bones he places rigid rods or sticks; he restores and reconstructs, closes off incisions, and fills up gaps. In the end, like a proud craftsman, he sits back and contemplates his finished production awaiting the final verdict: the "viewing" ceremony. And since the dead are often the worn-out, shattered rejects of life, he can aspire, like a true artist, to improve the work of nature. Cotton pledgets under the eyelids will counteract the effects of dehydration; placed inside the cheeks, they will make the hollowed-out appearance of consumption yield to a more robust semblance of life. The eyes, fixed in a dilated state of horror, are carefully closed according to the *Manual of the Embalmer* "so that the upper eyelid covers exactly two-thirds of the globe"; then they are smeared with Vaseline to prevent drying. And even the pallor of extreme anemia (the color of shrouds) or advanced jaundice (yellow as gamboge) will disappear under the influence of dyes and bleaching agents mixed in the embalming fluid, distributed under brand names like Blossom and Spring and promoted with catchy slogans in morticians' magazines that read: "As if he were sleeping" or "Bring back the colors of spring." Yes; as long as the somewhat macabre custom of deathwatch endures, the pathologist will need beside him those dexterous assistants whose calling means protection from charges that range between minor fluke and hideous sacrilege.

When younger, I cherished the romantic notion that in the age of the New Kingdom of Egypt secrets of embalming were discovered that surpassed in effectiveness the most advanced technics of our day. The image of priests and mortician-priests uttering magical incantations inside pharaonic tombs and preserving dead bodies from decomposition for two thousand years is sure to fire the romantic fantasy of any youth. It was with some disappointment that I learned that, in terms of sheer technical efficacy, the ancient Egyptians achieved only mediocre results and that their methods are neither mysterious nor unexplainable to us. Apparently, the Egyptians covered the dead with blocks of natre, or natron, a natural salt found in the Nile Valley. Instead of being an esoteric formula, natron turns out to be a mixture of rather common-place chemicals, namely, sodium carbonate and sodium bicarbonate, with a varying amount of impurities, chiefly sodium sulfate and common salt. Thus the Egyptians merely "salted" their corpses, slowly extracting water, which is indispensable for the enzymatic actions that account for decomposition; at the same time, the salts produced a weak fixation.

The desired effects were more easily achieved by removal of the viscera, which were placed in canopic jars, but the process was slow; a job was not completed in less than a month or two. And at the end of this lengthy preparation, the task was not over for these forebears of the modern embalmer. Followed the laborious swathing with bandages soaked in resins and gum resins and the sprinkling with scents, all of which are now known to possess antibacterial agents. All according to elaborate ritual: the bandage of Nekheb on the well-oiled forehead; the bandage of Hathor on the face; and there was also the gilding of the nails, and the crystal to lighten the face, and carnelian to strengthen the steps of the deceased in the underworld. There followed a strange ceremony that stands in curious opposition to ours. This was called "the opening of the mouth." Mouth and eyes of the recently embalmed cadaver, or its effigy, were pried open by means of specially designed instruments held by a priest, in contrast to our "pious" gesture of closing the same natural orifices in the recently departed. The very concrete ideas of the Egyptians about the voyage awaiting the dead might explain this singular gesture: the deceased had to be in fit condition to pronounce the sacred incantations that were passwords to the beyond. Think of the responsibility of these ancestors of the profession: careless facial bandaging meant considerably more than a pardonable fluke; it meant precluding an immortal soul from gaining salvation, by gagging!

Though divested of their mystery, the ministrations of these predecessors of present-day morticians remain admirable. How many craftsmen, or even renowned artists, today can feel confident that their work will be admired two thousand years hence, as we admire the excellent state of preservation of Seti I? This is not to say that all Egyptian embalmers were equally competent. Archeologists must be uniquely aware that there were bunglers, especially at those times when the suspense attending the undoing of bandages turns to dismay upon discovering, instead of the majestic presence of a ruler come down the ages in gold and lapis lazuli, a heap of crumbling filth swarming with insects. Still, the Egyptian technic was compatible with a respectful and solemn attitude toward the dead. On the authority of a distinguished pathologist, Guido Majno, we know that they neither immersed them in brine, as they did—and we do—with fish, nor roasted them over slow fires, as some South American Indians have been known to do—and as we are wont to do with chickens, producing comparable results. Their procedure was, in the graphic saying of Majno, "mothballing, and with weak mothballs at that."

What is apparent to the modern embalmer, in stark contrast with the ancient calling, is that all these carryings-on are strictly for the benefit of the living. The questions are seriously raised among the practitioners of the trade whether the remains should be "laid out" with glasses on, whether cosmetics should be applied, and whether the placement of dentures is indispensable. Not for a minute is it assumed that the decedent will need to have his vision corrected or his denture fit for biting an apple; nor is he in need of any of the three shades of pink cosmetic distributed by B. and G. Products, guaranteed to reproduce "nature's own skin texture . . . the velvety appearance of living tissue." Among the highest spheres of power in the National Funeral Directors Association, the statement that embalming is a procedure designed with the living in mind would not be received without controversy. It is difficult, however, to agree on just how embalming benefits the living. For reasons not hard to guess, officialdom within the NFDA proclaims that an open-coffin ceremony serves laudable purposes, to wit, aiding in the direct expression of grief, providing a suitable atmosphere for mourning, and helping the bereaved to face the finality of death. The problem is one that has been much pondered, without a single answer yet in sight. It is counterargued that the display of the body may be traumatic to certain individuals, especially to children, even when forewarned and instructed on what to expect; that "viewing" is hardly an aid to contemplate death when the "viewee" has been meticulously restored to impart to its external appearance a close semblance of life; that a person's ability to grasp the concept of death is the product of his total life experience, quite independent of "viewing"; and that, in any case, a memorial service is sufficient reminder of the ineluctability of death, thus rendering immaterial the open or closed state of the coffin's lid.

I believe there is at the core of the embalmer's officiousness a desire to remove the harrowing aspects of death, to expunge its painful appearance, and to erase all hurtful experiences for the survivors. I also believe that this is not altogether contemptible. Perhaps this desire to beautify the unavoidable miseries of an essentially finite, hence decaying, existence is a conspicuous feature of the American way of life. At least, such a thesis was proposed and developed by the French philosopher Jacques Maritain, who illustrated it with the following autobiographical anecdote.

Maritain, newly arrived in the United States, was entirely taken by the general civility and democratic warmth which he, like most foreigners, noticed immediately upon arrival. In academic circles, he observed, the students are not treated arrogantly by their professors but consort amicably with them; and the latter, regardless of their rank, see it as their duty to ease the way of learning for the students. This contrasts with the rigid scholastic mores and the unbridgeable chasm that often separates, in other countries, the humble student from the haughty pinnacles of professional arrogance. In public offices, transactions are closed expeditiously and, allowing for the inherently frustrating nature of red tape, with considerably less humiliation than attend dealings with the bureaucracy in other lands. This polite efficiency he found also in his visits to the dentist. Immaculately attired nurses and dental assistants, working in a spotless environment among gleaming equipment, directed him, positioned him, inquired of his needs, and prepared him for the reparative dental work. All was done with the utmost efficiency and with no other interruptions than required by brief, polite questions: "Are you comfortable?" "Is everything all right?"

Suddenly, while sitting in the dentist's chair, the thought came to him that if he were to suffer a fatal heart attack right then, all these professionals, technicians, assistants, and attendants would continue to perform their most attentive, purposeful, and determined services. A cold sweat covered his forehead as he imagined the smiling nurses, professional composure undaunted, laying him out on a bier. Everything would be as orderly, methodical, and efficient as before: his arms would be brought together so that his hands would touch each other in a pious and collected gesture; his body would be smoothly transferred into a well-designed coffin with chromed edges; and all expert finishing touches would be put on his remains by attendants whose unruffled expressions would be the same as when, minutes before, they inquired of him: "Are you comfortable?" and "Is everything all right?" This vision so shockingly conflicted with Maritain's conception of a Catholic passing away to await the Day of Resurrection that he became the first patient ever to change dentists for entirely theological reasons.

Maritain was highly partial to the whitewashing instinct of white Anglo-Saxon America. In this he saw neither insensitivity nor hypocrisy. He believed in an inherent "goodness" of the American people that leads them to attempt to efface all the potentially hurtful aspects of life. Misery and suffering seem, upon but slight reflection, the inescapable lot of life; even more so: part and parcel of life, like breathing. Through a kind of heroic contumaciousness, Americans are impelled to disbelieve this appalling truth. On the positive side, this monumentally wistful attitude forms the basis of their superior technological ingenuity. If life appears to many as a fatal stupefying bondage of sweat and toil, Americans will counter by inventing machines and gadgets to shake the yoke—the same gadgets that, incidentally, will be avidly taken up by those very critics who thunder against the "dehumanizing" perils of American technology. When the funeral customs of Americans are examined by this light, it is not easy to be overly critical of the ceremony of "viewing" an embalmed dead person. Death, like the sun, cannot be viewed directly; it is like an unfathomable void that gives us a sort of metaphysical vertigo if we so much as go near the edge of the cliff. Yet if there is an element of the ridiculous in a custom that substitutes a "restored" corpse, made up to look like a living doll, for the uncontemplable spectacle of death, we must confess that the same is true for most symbolic ritual. And then all harsh criticism recedes in front of the discovery that this is yet another attempt, however naive, of a people bent on removing all unpleasantness from life; a further manifestation of the American "goodness" that wills universal politeness and whose motto might well be "Cleanliness and contentment for all!"

The ridiculous, however, is the least of dangers in such an attitude. Behind the illusion that life can be a succession of smiling scenes, with neither pain nor passion, lurks the delusion that death without anguish can be bought for money in an over-the-counter transaction. Cash, check, or credit card. And behind this counter hides the ugly mien of philistinism, for which it is impossible to feel much sympathy. In the *Consumers Report on Conventional Funerals and Burial* there is an account of alarming excesses of commercialism that plague these services. In one case, mourners were introduced into a richly furnished antechamber in which each piece of decor represented, one may reasonably suppose, an extra charge on the bill: flowers at so many dollars; background organ music for such a price; and so on. After a while an usher announced that Mrs. X was ready to receive the visitors, and the mourners went, treading on thick carpets between floral arrangements and parting dark draperies, into another room of still more luxurious decor that seemed right out of *faux* Versailles. There, as if she were a duchess, or at least a countess in a second-rate Hollywood motion picture, sat Mrs. X, or rather the remains of Mrs. X, on a canopied bed abundant in lace and ribbons, dressed in a silk robe and propped up by cushions. Mark what private enterprise can do: the death ceremony transformed into a social visit, with a touch of vulgarity proportionate to the size of the payer's pocket! In another case, a Louisiana entrepreneur hit upon the felicitous idea of organizing the "viewing" ceremony around the "drive-in" concept. Mourners could look from the reassuring security of their automobiles into a display room where the decedent was aptly shown in a most collected and well-kept attitude behind a glass window, reposing on a bier whose end was surmounted by a cross framed with blue neon-gas light tubes. While under interrogation by the congressional committee on irregular funeral practices, the businessman defended well his unorthodox services: families could mourn and pay their visit at all hours, without leaving the soothing enclosure of their own automobiles; they did not have to pay any attention to details of their dress or worry about being the targets of gossip, thus being free to express their grief in a wholesome way; and, once their visit was over, they could simply lower the window of their car, sign a thick register book within arm's reach, and "drive on."

Whereas such practices seem to step on the toes of our sense of righteousness, we might do well, before voicing our indignant execration, to probe the public sentiment on the matter. In letters to the syndicated columnist Ann Landers, complaints were expressed on the charging methods of funeral directors. In particular, severe reproof went to those who sell expensive garments with which to dress the cadaver. It was thought that luxurious raiment, difficult to justify for the living, is assuredly a wanton waste on the dead. The expensive clothes are often sold because some undertakers prepare photographs (and oil paintings!) of the decedent, which are later sold to the relatives who, grief stricken, are often vulnerable to these swindles. With her proverbial impartiality, the columnist also published letters of persons who took a different view of the subject. Among these, there was a widow who wrote, "I wouldn't take a million dollars for the pictures I made of my husband laid out in his new blue suit. He looked better in that box than he had any time in the last ten years."

As a pathologist who has seen no rise in his life insurance policy premiums despite customary corpse handling, I am naturally skeptical of reports that extoll embalming as a public health blessing. Lack of embalming of cadavers does not seem a cause of devastating epidemics in most countries, and most countries fail to routinely practice this procedure. For the fact that epidemics are uncommon we ought to acknowledge a greater debt to sanitation engineers or public health officials than to embalmers. Bacteria do proliferate in a cadaver, as anyone can confirm who is of sound nose and comes within fifty paces of the autopsy room. Highly pathogenic organisms proliferate too, but elementary precautions of antisepsis, like the wearing of surgical mask and gloves, seem to adequately protect all exposed personnel. Morgue-acquired infections are part of the romance and lore of the autopsy suite, but one hears of the macabre saga mostly secondhand. I have not been impressed by either the frequency or the nefarious quality of infections therein contracted by persons who live there day by day, although the specialized literature mentions individual instances of dire diseases acquired in this environment.

The practice of embalming dead American citizens is so massively successful that, as is well known, a person living in the United States is statistically likelier to live closer to a funeral home than to a police station or a fire department building. This comes from profit conscious-ness, not from enlightened legislation. The funeral industry is so well organized and so expertly directed that its revenues are unlikely to decrease, even if funeral customs were to change. Should cremation become the most popular form of disposal of remains, private enterprise will prove equal to the challenge and will be ready to diversify, as they say in financial circles, and to control. However, as a pathologist, too, I am not ready to condemn the practice of embalming as a shameless farce or to pass it up as nothing but a sordid hoax played by the greedy on the gullible. Rather, I see in it an impulse, not without nobility, to prevent, or at least decelerate, the ruin of the human body. Commer-cialism and dishonesty aside, the embalmer obeys that obscure dictate that would have us stave off, or at least retard, the decay of this marvel. It is our primeval vigor, our deepest creative prepotency, our basic fund of antideath energy, that infuses us with the wish, however irrational, to make the corruptible undecaying and the impermanent eternal. The ancients fancied that the soul did not abandon the body on a sudden but even after death it lingered on for forty-two days, departing gradually and as if by stages. Da Vinci reflected on this theme and thought that it was quite fitting that the soul should dally, for the body is so wondrous a habitation that the soul could not find it easy to part with it, and finding it so painful to quit its mortal domicile, it hesitates. Later, that delicately spiritual writer Paul Valéry, on reading the autobiographical passage of Leonardo that contains these reflections, was greatly in-trigued. This was for Valéry a metaphysical system of most peculiar originality: that the farewell scene between body and soul should be imagined as capable of "bringing tears to the eyes . . . of the soul"! Leonardo, it is very important to remember, had personally dissected scores of cadavers; his metaphysical construct may strike many as odd, but pathologists and embalmers should find it perfectly natural.

JOHN STONE

JOHN STONE (1936–   ). *American physician, poet, essayist, lecturer, and educator. Born in Jackson, Mississippi, Dr. Stone was educated at Millsaps College and Washington University. He did his postgraduate training in internal medicine and cardiology at Strong Memorial Hospital/University of Rochester School of Medicine and at Emory University School of Medicine. In addition to numerous medical papers, Stone was coeditor of* Principles and Practice of Emergency Medicine, *the first comprehensive textbook of that burgeoning discipline. His writing includes three books of poetry:* The Smell of Matches, In All This Rain, *and* Renaming the Streets. *His latest book is* In the Country of Hearts: Journeys in the Art of Medicine, *essays about both the literal and the metaphorical heart.*

GAUDEAMUS IGITUR

Gaudeamus Igitur *was delivered as the Valediction Address at Emory University School of Medicine, Atlanta, in July 1982. The Latin title is the first line of a medieval song that became, over the centuries, a drinking song, a song of celebration, in the universities of Europe. The Latin words of the first verse are these:*

> Gaudeamus igitur,
> Iuvenes dum sumus;
> Gaudeamus igitur,
> Iuvenes dum sumus;
> Post iucundam iuventutem,
> Post molestam senectutem,
> Nos habebit humus,
> Nos habebit humus.

The verse translates, roughly: "Therefore let us rejoice / While we are young; / After a delightful youth, / After an irksome old age, / The grave will contain us." The words and the tune to which they were sung have special significance for an academic occasion such as Commencement: Johannes Brahms, years later, incorporated the song into the climactic portion of his "Academic Festival Overture."

The form of the poem, in which every line begins with the word For, *was suggested by a portion of the long poem* Jubilate Agno, *written by the eighteenth-century poet Christopher Smart (1722–1771). The specific portion referred to was written by Smart in praise of his cat Jeoffrey.*

For this is the day of joy
   which has been fourteen hundred and sixty days in
     coming
   and fourteen hundred and fifty-nine nights
For today in the breathing name of Brahms
   and the cat of Christopher Smart
   through the unbroken line of language and all the nouns
   stored in the angular gyrus
   today is a commencing
For this is the day you know too little
   against the day when you will know too much
For you will be invincible
   and vulnerable in the same breath
   which is the breath of your patients
For their breath is our breathing and our reason
For the patient will know the answer
   and you will ask him
   ask her
For the family may know the answer
For there may be no answer
   and you will know too little again
   or there *will* be an answer and you will know too much
   forever
For you will look smart and feel ignorant
   and the patient will not know which day it is for you
   and you will pretend to be smart out of ignorance
For you must fear ignorance more than cyanosis
For whole days will move in the direction of rain
For you will cry and there will be no one to talk to
   or no one but yourself
For you will be lonely
For you will be alone
For there is a difference
For there is no seriousness like joy
For there is no joy like seriousness
For the days will run together in gallops and the years
   go by as fast as the speed of thought
   which is faster than the speed of light
   or Superman

or Superwoman
For you will not be Superman
For you will not be Superwoman
For you will not be Solomon
    but you will be asked the question nevertheless*
For after you learn what to do, how and when to do it
    the question will be *whether*
For there will be addictions: whiskey, tobacco, love
For they will be difficult to cure
For you yourself will pass the kidney stone of pain
    and be joyful
For this is the end of examinations
For this is the beginning of testing
For Death will give the final examination
    and everyone will pass
For the sun is always right on time
    and even that may be reason for a kind of joy
For there are all kinds of
    all degrees of joy
For love is the highest joy
For which reason the best hospital is a house of joy
    even with rooms of pain and loss
    exits of misunderstanding
For there is the mortar of faith
For it helps to believe
For Mozart can heal and no one knows where he is buried
For penicillin can heal
    and the word
    and the knife
For the placebo will work and you will think you know why
For the placebo will have side effects and you will know
    you do not know why
For none of these may heal
For joy is nothing if not mysterious
For your patients will test you for spleen
    and for the four humors
For they will know the answer
For they have the disease
For disease will peer up over the hedge
    of health, with only its eyes showing

* I Kings 3:16–27.

For the T waves will be peaked and you will not know why
For there will be computers
For there will be hard data and they will be hard
   to understand
For the trivial will trap you and the important escape you
For the Committee will be unable to resolve the question
For there will be the arts
   and some will call them
   soft data
   whereas in fact they are the hard data
   by which our lives are lived
For everyone comes to the arts too late
For you can be trained to listen only for the oboe
   out of the whole orchestra
For you may need to strain to hear the voice of the
   patient
   in the thin reed of his crying
For you will learn to see most acutely out of
   the corner of your eye
   to hear best with your inner ear
For there are late signs and early signs
For the patient's story will come to you
   like hunger, like thirst
For you will know the answer
   like second nature, like first
For the patient will live
   and you will try to understand
For you will be amazed
   or the patient will not live
   and you will try to understand
For you will be baffled
For you will try to explain both, either, to the family
For there will be laying on of hands
   and the letting go
For love is what death would always intend if it had the
   choice
For the fever will drop, the bone remold along its lines of
   force
   the speech return
   the mind remember itself
For there will be days of joy
For there will be elevators of elation

and you will walk triumphantly
in purest joy
along the halls of the hospital
and say *Yes* to all the dark corners
where no one is listening
For the heart will lead
For the head will explain
    but the final common pathway is the heart
    whatever kingdom may come
For what matters finally is how the human spirit is spent
For this is the day of joy
For this is the morning to rejoice
For this is the beginning
    Therefore, let us rejoice
    Gaudeamus igitur.

DEATH

I have seen   come on
slowly as rust
sand

or suddenly   as when
someone leaving
a room

finds the doorknob
come loose in his hand

LUCILLE CLIFTON

LUCILLE CLIFTON (1936–   ). *African-American poet. Clifton's
collections of poetry include* Good Times *(1969),* Good News About
the Earth *(1972),* An Ordinary Woman *(1974), and* Two-Headed
Woman, *winner of the Juniper Award in 1980. Her most recent
collection of poems,* The Book of Light *(1993), is a collection of family
portraits imbued with Clifton's warmth and wisdom and marked by her
fierce unsentimentality. She is also the author of a memoir,* Generations
(1976), and more than a dozen books of poetry and fiction for children.

THE LOST BABY POEM

the time i dropped your almost body down
down to meet the waters under the city
and run one with the sewage to the sea
what did i know about waters rushing back
what did i know about drowning
or being drowned

you would have been born into winter
in the year of the disconnected gas
and no car   we would have made the thin
walk over Genesee hill into the Canada wind
to watch you slip like ice into strangers' hands
you would have fallen naked as snow into winter
if you were here i could tell you these
and some other things

if i am ever less than a mountain
for your definite brothers and sisters
let the rivers pour over my head
let the sea take me for a spiller
of seas   let black men call me stranger
always   for your never named sake

331

LUCILLE CLIFTON

POEM TO MY UTERUS

you   uterus
you have been patient
as a sock
while i have slippered into you
my dead and living children
now
they want to cut you out
stocking i will not need
where i am going
where am i going
old girl
without you
uterus
my bloody print
my estrogen kitchen
my black bag of desire
where i can go
barefoot
without you
where can you go
without me

GHASSAN KANAFANI

GHASSAN KANAFANI (1936–1972). *Arab novelist, journalist, and
teacher. Born in Acre, Israel, Kanafani and his family fled to Damascus
when he was twelve years old. After completing his studies, he worked
as a teacher and journalist, and eventually moved first to Kuwait and
then to Beirut, where he wrote for several newspapers. Known in the
West as the spokesman for the Popular Front for the Liberation of
Palestine, Kanafani was also a talented painter and a renowned
novelist.* Men in the Sun *established his reputation as one of the
foremost writers in the Arab world; he is best known for his capacity
to universalize the experience of his characters. Kanafani's published
works include five novels, five collections of short stories, two plays,
and two studies of Palestinian literature.*

DEATH OF BED 12

My Dear Ahmad,

I've chosen you of all people to be the recipient of this letter for
reasons that may appear trivial to you, but which have become, since
yesterday, the central preoccupation of my thoughts. I've also chosen to
confide in you, because when I saw him yesterday evening, dying on a
raised white bed, I recalled how often you used the idea of death to
express extremes. Phrases of yours came back to me: "He almost died
laughing," or "I'm dead tired," and "Death can't extinguish my love"
and so on. It's true that we all use these expressions, but with you
they're a way of life. And so I thought of you as I watched him shrink
in his bed, tighten his long, thin fingers on the bed cover, go into a
convulsion, and then stare at me with dead eyes.

I suppose I should start at the beginning. You doubtless know that
I've been in the hospital for the past two months, suffering from an
intestinal ulcer. But that's not the important thing, for every time the
surgeon patches up my stomach, I have to conceal the "ulcer" in my
head about which he knows nothing. And believe me the latter is a
much more painful thing. The door of my room opens onto the main
corridor of the wing for internal diseases, while the window overlooks
the small hospital garden. And so it is that while leaning on my pillow,
I'm able to observe both the patients who ceaselessly swarm past my
door and the birds who, also ceaselessly, fly past my window. I'm sur-

333

rounded by people who come here to die under the reassuring scalpel, and whom I see arriving upright on their feet, and departing, after a few days or hours, laid out on the death trolley, wrapped in a white shroud. In the face of this, I find myself impotent to forestall the holes that have begun to open up in my head, and helpless to stop the flow of questions that relentlessly beleaguer me.

I expect to be discharged in a few days, for they've patched up my intestines as best they can. I can now walk supported by the arm of a plain old nurse, and I'm driven to do so by curiosity and instinctive motivation. The treatment's done nothing except to transfer the ulcer from my intestines to my head. Medicine here, as I told my plain old nurse, is limited strictly to physical ailments, and has never advanced sufficiently to find answers to one's mind. The crone laughed at what I said, revealing her black, gapped teeth, and led me calmly to the scales.

But enough of this talk. What really concerns me is the theme of death. And a death that one's witnessed, rather than learned of second-hand. The difference between the two is so vast that only those who've experienced the sight of someone clutching at the bed cover, holding on with all his strength to resist the terrible slide to extinction, can appreciate the difference. It's as if the bed cover could serve as an anchorage from the all-powerful one who, bit by bit, erases this life about which we know so little.

The doctors had grouped around him, and as he lay in his convulsions I was able to read the card hanging at the bottom of his bed. I'd managed to slip away from my room unnoticed, and the doctors were too preoccupied with their dying patient to notice me standing there. The card read: "Name: Muhammad Ali Akbar. Age: 25 years. Nationality: Omani." I turned the card over and read the diagnosis: "Leukemia."

Again I stared at the lean, dark face, the wide, terrified eyes, the lip fibers trembling like purple waves. In the course of their wandering, his eyes had come to rest on my face and I imagined that he was appealing for my help. I tried to think why. Was it because I used to greet him every morning, or because he read in my face a comprehension of the terror he was undergoing? He continued to stare at me, and then quite simply died.

It was only then that I was discovered, and a furious doctor dragged me back to my room, but couldn't distance me from the scene imprinted in my mind's eye. I climbed into bed and heard the nurse's voice in the corridor outside the door, saying matter-of-factly: "The occupant of Bed 12 has died."

Hearing this, I said to myself: Muhammad Ali Akbar's lost his name; he's Bed 12 now. Yet what do I mean when I personalize him and continue to use his name? Is it of any importance to him now if his name's substituted by a number? Following that train of thought, I recalled how he refused to have any part of his name omitted when addressed. Each morning the nurse would ask him: "How are you today, Muhammad Ali?" and he'd refuse to answer, for he considered his name to be Muhammad Ali Akbar, pronounced like that, all in one go, and that this abbreviation adopted by the nurse belonged to some other person.

The nurses found plenty of cause for humor in this insistence on the indivisibility of his name, but Muhammad Ali Akbar never once made concessions on this serious point. Perhaps he considered that in laying claims to his rightful name, he was realizing a possession, for he was poor, poorer than you can imagine, idling his time away in cafés. Poverty was pronounced in his face, his hands, his body, in the way he ate, and in the objects that surrounded him.

When I was able for the first time after the operation to walk by myself, I visited him. The top part of his bed was raised and he was sitting in a state of reverie. I sat on the edge of the bed for a short time and engaged in a brief and desultory talk with him. My attention was drawn to an old wooden box, firmly tied with a piece of hemp rope, that he kept next to his pillow, and on which his name was carved in a form of Persian calligraphy. With the exception of this, he owned nothing in the world apart from his few clothes hanging in the hospital wardrobe. I remember asking the nurse: "What's in that old box?"

"No one knows," she replied, laughing. "He refuses to part with it even for a minute." Then she leaned over and whispered: "These people who look poor are very often hiding a fortune. The box might have all his wealth in it."

No one visited him during his stay in the hospital. As he knew no one, I used to send him some of the sweets and cakes that my visitors so generously brought me. He received them without enthusiasm, and his complete lack of gratitude evoked a degree of passing resentment in me.

I wasn't interested in the mystery of his box, and despite his constantly deteriorating condition, his relation to it didn't change. In view of this, the nurse's opinion was that if the box had contained some kind of fortune, he would surely have distributed it by now or made provision by creating a legacy. I laughed as the young do at the apparent stupidity of her remarks; how could she expect Muhammad Ali Akbar to calmly accept and rationalize his imminent death? It was rather that the box had come to represent a symbol of permanence, and by subscribing to its durability he was insisting on the possibility of his own survival.

When Muhammad Ali Akbar finally died, with the box dutifully next to him, I considered it our responsibility to see that the unopened box was buried with him. I lodged the thought in my mind and returned to my room; but throughout that night I didn't sleep. Although Muhammad Ali Akbar had been taken to the autopsy room wrapped in a white sheet, he appeared to be sitting in my room, staring at me, or else walking the corridors of the hospital, checking his bed, and once I thought I could hear him gasp as he breathed out before falling asleep. By the time day broke over the trees in the hospital garden, I'd formed a complete story about him, for myself.

Muhammad Ali Akbar was a poor man from the western neighborhood of the village of Ibkha in Oman. A lean, brown youth, his eyes had burned with the potential of unrealized ambition. He was poor and had never known a life other than one of poverty. Everyone in Ibkha accepted their lot, and enjoyed the simplicity of life without giving thought to the acquisition of material gain. So it was that the two waterskins that Muhammad Ali Akbar carried on his shoulders, going from door to door to sell water, were the balancing scales that gave measure to his life. He was aware of a sense of displacement whenever he let go of his burden, and each morning, when he took up his load again, he would feel that his life was proceeding with tranquillity, that he was secured on a balanced path that offered no deviation from his routine habits.

It might have been possible for Muhammad Ali Akbar's life to proceed indefinitely in this organized fashion. And so it would have, had fate been as remote from Oman as civilization. Not even Oman was spared the caprices of fate, and Muhammad Ali Akbar was to prove its unwilling victim.

It happened on a scorchingly hot day. The sandy road was ablaze long before the sun had reached its zenith, and a northerly breeze from the desert dusted his face with sand. He'd knocked at a door and, from behind its crack, a dark young girl with big black eyes had peered out. It all occurred with incredible speed. He'd stood there like someone who'd lost his way, the two waterskins swaying on his slender shoulders, staring at her insensibly, wishing as a person dazed by sunstroke might that his eyes had the magic power to embrace and squeeze her. She'd exchanged looks with him out of sheer amazement; then, finding himself unable to utter a word, he'd turned around and pursued his journey home.

Muhammad Ali Akbar was noted for his shyness, even in the presence of his family, but the incident inspired him sufficiently to confide the whole matter to his eldest sister. His mother had long since died of smallpox and his father was an invalid who was paralyzed. Thus it was he asked for his sister's advice, for he was confident in a way that brooked no discussion that his sister Sabika enjoyed a degree of intelligence and balanced judgment that would enable her to cast light on his problem. She seated herself opposite him on the mat, and, enveloped in her thick black dress, remained silent until Muhammad Ali Akbar had panted out the last of his story.

Then she said: "I'll ask for her hand. Isn't that what you want?"

"Yes, yes," he replied. "Do you think there's a chance?"

His sister plucked a straw from the old mat, and replied: "Why not? You're a young man now, and we're all equal in Ibkha."

Muhammad Ali Akbar spent the night burning with anxiety, and when he rose at dawn he found his sister in a corresponding state of nervous anticipation. They agreed to meet at home at noon, so that she could present him with the results of her endeavors, and together decide on a plan to bring the matter to completion.

Muhammad Ali Akbar didn't know how he passed the intervening time, except that he wandered through the alleys with the waterskins on his shoulders. He kept on staring at his shadow, waiting for it to form a circle round his feet so that he could return home. At last it was noon and he retraced his steps back to the house. His sister met him at the door: "Her mother seems agreeable," she said, "but it has to be put to her father. He'll give his answer in five days."

Muhammad Ali Akbar felt assured that he'd succeed in his marriage proposal, and from that day on he began, in his imagination, to conceive of a future with the small, dark beauty. His sister Sabika viewed the situation with a feeling of equanimity. Experience told her that her brother was respected by the community of Ibkha, and her hopes of a successful resolution were confirmed by the importance she attached to a mother's agreement, for she was aware of how a woman can present any idea to her husband and convince him of it as if it were his own. Trusting to her conviction, Sabika felt totally reassured as to the outcome of the matter.

On the fifth day, Sabika went to the girl's house to learn of their decision. When she returned her face was marked with signs of failure. She stood in a corner of the room, unable to meet her brother's eyes and not knowing how to begin. At last she composed herself, and said: "You'll have to forget her, Muhammad Ali."

Unable to summon up words for his bewilderment, he waited for her to finish what she had to say. Sabika took advantage of his silence to continue: "Her father died two days ago, and his last wish to his family was that his daughter shouldn't marry you."

Muhammad Ali heard the words as if they'd been uttered to a stranger, but he still couldn't help asking: "But why, Sabika? Why?"

"He was told that you were a scoundrel who lived by stealing sheep on the mountain road and selling them to foreigners."

"Me?" Muhammad Ali gasped incredulously.

Sabika was unable to maintain the composure of her voice, and she trembled visibly as she said: "They thought you were Muhammad Ali. You know, the one who's a scoundrel. Her father mistook you for him."

He spread his palms out, appealing like a child forced to justify a fault he hadn't committed: "But I'm not Muhammad Ali, I'm Muhammad Ali Akbar."

"It was a mistake," his sister said. "I didn't think to tell them your full name's Muhammad Ali Akbar. I never thought it was necessary to give the complete name."

Muhammad Ali Akbar felt his chest cave in under the force of the blow, but he remained standing in the same spot, staring at his sister without really seeing her at all. Rage was blinding him, but he attempted a last shot: "Did you tell her mother about the mistake? Did you tell her I'm not Muhammad Ali, but Muhammad Ali Akbar?"

"Yes," his sister replied, "but her father's last wish was that she shouldn't marry you."

"But you know who I really am," he appealed. "I'm Muhammad Ali Akbar, the water seller."

But what use were his protestations now? Everything had, quite simply, come to an end. The issue had been decided on a misunderstanding, and his hopes had correspondingly died.

It wasn't easy to forget the girl. He found himself inexplicably hovering around her house, hoping to catch a brief glimpse of her. But in the end the realization of his failure turned the love he'd harbored into a savage rage, and finally into hatred. It got to the stage that he could no longer pass that road without the fear that he'd be driven to throw stones at the windows of her house.

From that day on he refused to be addressed except by his full name, Muhammad Ali Akbar, and he disdained to answer anyone who chose to abbreviate it, until his refusal became a habit. Even Sabika, his sister, never dared to shorten his name; he stuck unflinchingly to its full form.

But try as he might, he could never again experience happiness, and slowly Ibkha came to represent a graveyard in his eyes. He refused to marry, despite his sister's insistence, and the idea of riches came to obsess him. He wanted to avenge himself on everything, and to marry a woman with whom he could defy his native town, and thus rectify the wrong he'd suffered. But first of all he had to acquire a fortune, and it was in pursuit of this that he decided to embark for Kuwait.

The distance between Ibkha and Ras el-Khaymah was two hours on foot, and from Ras el-Khaymah to Kuwait was a further three days by sea. The fare for the journey on a dilapidated vessel was seventy rupees, but by risking this sum he had the promise of beginning a new life in Kuwait. In a year or two he'd return to Oman and swagger through the alleys of Ibkha wearing a brilliant white *aba* with a golden hem, like the one he'd seen draped across the shoulders of one of the notables of Ras el-Khaymah who'd come to his village to ask for the hand of a girl in marriage, a girl whose beauty had been heard of in his home town.

The voyage was a hazardous one. The vessel had carried its ambitious passengers across the south, and then headed up north from the straits, aiming for the corner of the gulf. They'd been constantly exposed to the dangers of the sea, but as most aboard were inured to the hardships of life, they were only too ready to cooperate with the crew in their efforts to keep the ship afloat in turbulent seas. And when at last they sighted the coast, and the masts of the boats lying moored in the quiet harbor of Kuwait, Muhammad Ali Akbar found himself responding ambivalently to a reality now divorced from the colorful world of his dreams. He searched in his mind for the key that had brought him here, and it struck him that the fantasies he'd nurtured for so long, of avenging himself on Ibkha, seemed removed and implausible. While the dilapidated vessel approached its berth, navigating a course between the ships at anchor, he was startled, for the duration of a few seconds, into a new sense of reality, and it seemed to him that the dreams he'd fabricated of acquiring wealth were simply a solace for his unrequited love and bore no practical bearing on reality.

The packed streets, the size of the buildings, the gray sky, the incandescent heat, the hot northerly wind, the streets jammed with cars, the serious faces . . . all of these things seemed to impose a barrier between himself and his dream. He wandered around aimlessly, without direction, in that ocean of people, feeling lost and vertiginous in the swim of faces, and believing with the utmost conviction that those faces which did not so much as look at him were declared enemies, that these people, and their sheer numbers, were the walls obstructing the outset of the road to his new future. Things were not as simple as he'd imagined before leaving Ibkha. Nothing appeared to have connectives here or to be sequential. It seemed the roads he walked were without end, that they circled a wall which embraced everything, and when he came upon a road at sunset that led him to the shore, where once again he found the sea, he stood staring at the distant horizon vanishing into the water. Over there was Ibkha, enveloped in a serene haze. At any rate, he assured himself, it was still there. He knew every quarter of it, how every wall bore its own distinct features, and recollecting it thus he realized that, despite everything, it was dear to his heart. The tears that quite suddenly and unashamedly scalded his face made him feel that he was drowning in a vortex of boiling water.

Muhammad Ali Akbar stood there and cried without embarrassment, for the first time since he'd grown up to be a young man, and at the same time he felt an overwhelming compulsion to have the weight of the two waterskins on his shoulders. He was still staring at the horizon as the night slowly descended around him, creating the impression that he was here in a definite place at a definite time, and that the night was no different from the night in Ibkha. People were asleep in their homes, the streets had grown silent, and punctuating it all was the rhythmic surge of the sea beneath moonlight. He felt comforted, wanted to laugh, but, finding himself unable to do so, cried again.

The dawn brought with it a renewed sense of hope, and he went back to roaming the streets. He knew in order to proceed he had first to establish contact with someone from Oman, and that sooner or later he would find this person who would prove to be a stepping stone to his new future.

As it was, Muhammad Ali Akbar took a job as cleaner in a Government office. He was issued a bicycle to run errands for his department, and it was through cycling that he came to familiarize himself with the layout of streets and buildings. He grew to establish some form of relationship with his new surroundings, but he was unable to free himself from the feeling that he was being followed by his sister's eyes, and that even here he couldn't be free of the image of the girl's latticed window and the scoundrel Muhammad Ali, who, unwittingly, had been the cause of his disaster.

The months hurried by like the rotating spokes of his wheels, and things began to grow easier. He clung to his small savings with the tenacity of one who dreads that on a sudden impulse he might lose them or have them stolen from him. This was how he first got the idea of making a strong-box in which to keep his savings.

His wealth was of a nature that couldn't be priced. Muhammad Ali Akbar had used a part of his earnings to purchase a transparent, white *aba* with a golden hem, and each evening, when he was alone with his box, he'd take out the carefully packed garment, trace his lean, brown fingers gently over the material, and spread it out before him like a map of his dreams. On it he'd trace all the streets of his village, and the low wooden latticed windows, behind which young girls peered out at the street. There, in one corner of the cloak, the past lay dormant, unrevivable, and yet its existence was what endowed the *aba* with especial significance. With the same meticulous gentleness, the lean fingers would refold the *aba* and return it to its wooden box. Only after he'd tied the box securely with a strong piece of hemp rope, could he prepare himself for sleep.

The box also contained a pair of ceramic earrings for his sister Sabika, and a bottle of perfume, gifts he would give her on his return to Ibkha, as well as a white bundle in which his money was concealed. The bundle was tied in a knot, in the hope that his savings would increase, day by day.

As for his illness, it all began one evening when he was returning his bicycle to the storeroom. He felt something burning his extremities and was shocked to discover that he could have become so weak so quickly. At first he didn't attach much significance to it, for shaking fits would afflict him whenever his longing to see Sabika or return to Ibkha proved irresistibly powerful. He'd experienced this feeling of weakness before, accompanied by an overwhelming sense of loss for the things he'd hated, loved, renounced; in short, for all the components of his past.

It was with this assumption that Muhammad Ali Akbar hurried home, but by noon the next day none of the symptoms had shown signs of abating. When he attempted to rise from his mattress, he was amazed to find that he'd slept through until noon without awakening, and what shook him even more was that his sense of weakness persisted. In a state of fear, he tried to elucidate the cause, and saw himself standing by the seashore, almost blinded by the reflected glare of the sun on the water. The two waterskins were balanced on his shoulders, and he felt a debilitating weakness. The glare of the sun increased, but he found himself unable to close his burning eyes. He went back to sleep almost immediately.

From now on, time as people comprehend it became meaningless for Muhammad Ali Akbar. Everything that took place subsequently left him with the feeling that he was floating in the air, his legs dangling above the ground like a hanged man's. He was moving past the tableau of time, and as for the latter it could only be conceived as immobile, immovable as a mountain of basalt. His role as an active participant in life had ceased, and henceforth he was to become an onlooker. He felt disassociated and connected with nothing, he was removed from a world in which actions resembled fish browsing in a glass bowl, and he felt his deflated eyes were also composed of glass.

The next time he regained consciousness he found himself being carried away by men who supported his legs and arms. He was exhausted but summoned the strength to remember that he was without something important, and managed to articulate in a weak voice: "The box! The box!"

But no one took any notice of him. In despair, he made a futile effort to return to his box, and with visible urgency, gasped: "The box!"

Again no one paid him any attention.

They'd already arrived at the door, and he clung to the door and panted in a faint voice: "The box!"

Unable to bear the strain, he relapsed into a state of trance. This time he felt the tide slowly rising round his feet; the water was intensely cold and his hands were clinging to a square rock which was pulling him down. When he regained consciousness, he found himself hugging his old box, securely tied with its hemp rope. He could see white shadows flitting to and fro; then a needle was stuck in his arm, and a face was leaning over him.

The days passed without meaning, although Muhammad Ali Akbar seemed to be frozen into the permanent severity of a pain that continued with or without his knowledge with unabating persistence. Everything merged into one: the sea with the low wooden latticed windows by the roadside, a pair of ceramic earrings with an *aba* soaked by the sea, and somewhere in the picture was a boat hanging motionless on the waves and an old wooden box.

Only once was he startled into a realization of the world, when he responded to a voice by his side inquiring: "What's in that old box?"

He looked towards the source of the voice, and saw, as if in a dream, a clean-shaven, fair-haired youth pointing at the box with insistent eyes.

But the moment of consciousness had been brief, and he'd gone back to staring mutely at the sea; yet the fair-haired youth with the clean-shaven face remained with him on the shore. After that he'd experienced a rare and sudden burst of energy. For no apparent reason everything had grown clear, and for the first time since his collapse he watched the sunrise clearly, and it seemed to him not impossible that he could leave his bed and return to doing errands on his bicycle. He felt reassured to find the box safely next to him, tied up as usual, but when he made a movement to get up, he was surprised to find himself the subject of scrutiny to a circle of white-coated men. He tried to say something, but was unable to, and felt that the tide had risen to his waist. The water had become so unbearably cold that it was numbing, and when he'd stretched out his arm to hold on to something for fear of drowning, everything had given way under his fingers. When he saw the face of the fair-haired youth again, he grew apprehensive about his box, and continued to stare at the youth's face until the water rose and obscured it from view.

"Bed 12 has died!" the nurse exclaimed.

I couldn't free myself of the image of Muhammad Ali Akbar's eyes staring at me before he died. I imagined that this man, who'd refused so resolutely to have his name truncated, might even settle for the conviction that he was Bed 12, if only he could rest assured of the fate of his box, if only he could . . .

This, my dear Ahmad, is the story of Muhammad Ali Akbar, or Bed 12, who died yesterday evening and is now laid out in the autopsy room, his body covered by a shroud. His is the lean, brown face which transferred the ulcer from my stomach to my head, and which made me write to you in the hope that you'll never again flippantly say to me: "I almost died laughing!"

Your brother

My dear Ahmad,

I'm still in the hospital. My health is progressing back to normal, and my way of finding this out is highly amusing.

Do you know how I test my strength?

I stand smoking on the balcony, and then see how far I can throw the butt into the green lanes of grass in the garden. In past weeks the butt would fall just short of the fourth lane, but now I can almost make it reach the sixth.

I understand from your letter that you don't feel the need to have witnessed Muhammad Ali Akbar's death in order to know what death is . . . you seem to feel that the event of death doesn't need all the tragic antecedents I assigned to it, and that people die with greater simplicity. The one who fell on the pavement while carrying a loaded gun, and had the bullet tear through his neck, was out at the time with an exquisitely beautiful girl. And the other one, who dropped dead from a heart attack on the road one April evening, had just got married the week before. All this is true, my dear Ahmad, I don't dispute it. However, that's not the point. The issue of death doesn't concern the dying. It's the concern of the living, who bitterly await their turn to be an example to expectant eyes. The main point of my last letter was to emphasize how necessary it is for us to transfer our thinking from the starting point of death . . . whether as in your opinion, the person dies while he's enjoying the charms of an exquisitely beautiful girl's body, or whether he dies staring at the clean-shaven face of a youth he's afraid of for the sake of his old wooden box tied up with rope. For the problem remains the problem of the end, whether it entails annihilation or immortality. Or what, my dear Ahmad?

Anyway, pouring water into a bag full of holes is a pointless exercise. Do you know what happened after I sent you my last letter? I went to the doctors' room and found them preparing a report on Muhammad Ali Akbar. They were about to open his box. . . . My dear Ahmad, how much we're prisoners of our minds and bodies! We forever ascribe our own qualities to others, and judge them through the manner of our formulated thoughts and opinions. In short, we want them to be "us," we try to conceive of them as satellites of ourselves, we hope that they see with our eyes, feel with our skins, and in addition we attempt to saddle them with our past, and our own particular way of facing life, and place them within the framework which our current understanding of time and place dictates.

Muhammad Ali Akbar was none of the things I've mentioned. He was the father of three boys and two girls, for in his country men marry young. Nor had he been a water seller, since water's abundant in Oman. A long time ago, before settling here, he'd been a sailor on a sailboat that ran a line between the gulf ports and the South.

Muhammad Ali Akbar had been in Kuwait for four years, and after unsparingly fierce efforts had finally managed, only two months ago, to open what passed for a shop on one of the pavements of the New Road. How he supported his children in Oman remains a mystery.

I read in the doctor's report that the patient had gone blind six hours prior to his death, so I'm spared the disquieting thought that he was staring at me at the moment of death. The report also mentions that the family address of the patient is not known, so burial will proceed in the presence of the hospital undertakers only.

The doctor read the report in a loud voice to his colleagues, and the technical phraseology applied only to the nature of the illness, and not the patient. It was both precise and condensed, and delivered in an elegiac tone; then, when he'd finished reading it, he began untying the hemp rope that bound the box. At this point I thought of leaving the room, for the matter didn't concern me. The Muhammad Ali Akbar that I knew had died. The one on whom they delivered a report was another person, and the box likewise belonged to that someone else. I knew only too well what was in Muhammad Ali Akbar's box, so what was the point of being inquisitive about some other matter?

However, curiosity overcame me, and I stood in a corner trembling with anticipation. The box was opened summarily, its contents examined by the doctor, and then it was discarded.

I looked apprehensively into the box. A collection of invoices relating to the shop's imported goods formed a solid wedge. In one corner there was an old picture of a bearded face, a frayed watch strap, a piece of rope, a small candle, and a few rupees scattered among the papers. To tell you the truth I was disappointed, but before I left the room I saw something that stunned me. In pushing the invoices to one side, the nurse had upturned a pair of long ceramic earrings that flashed from the bottom of the box. My head spun, but I managed to walk over to the box and pick up the earrings for closer examination. I glanced at the nurse, and was suddenly compelled to say: "He bought these for Sabika! I'm sure he did!"

She stared at me, uncomprehendingly, then both she and the doctor laughed at what they took to be a joke.

You probably know that medics like to humor their ulcer patients for fear of a relapse.

Your brother

LAWRENCE K. ALTMAN

LAWRENCE K. ALTMAN (1937–   ). *American physician and writer. Dr. Altman is one of a very few physicians working as a full-time newspaper reporter. For many years, he has been senior medical correspondent for* The New York Times, *providing memorable coverage of, among other stories, the artificial-heart insertion (performed on Dr. Barney Clark) and the AIDS epidemic. The selection that follows is from his book* Who Goes First? The Story of Self-Experimentation in Medicine *(1987).*

DON'T TOUCH THE HEART

Civilization has discarded many of the taboos of primitive societies, but some have survived into modern times. As late as the 1920s, for example, it was taboo for a doctor to touch the living human heart. By that time surgeons, aided by advances in anesthesiology, had invaded most areas of the body. They had begun to operate routinely on the abdominal organs, limbs, the face, even the brain—but not the heart. In the few instances in the preceding centuries when, in emergencies, surgeons had entered the chest to cut and sew the heart, the patient generally had died.

Well into the twentieth century, to touch the heart was to molest a sacred area of the body, its spiritual center, and most doctors feared to tamper with it. Even if they had not been afraid of incurring God's wrath, there were seemingly unsolvable physical problems. The heart constantly pumped blood; when cut, it bled profusely. How could anyone survive such a hemorrhage?

Furthermore, the heart seemed inaccessible. It lies at most three inches beneath the skin, but it is enclosed by a bony cage of ribs that protects both it and the lungs. Were a surgeon to open the chest cage to operate on the lungs or heart, air could suddenly rush in, collapsing one lung and possibly both.

By World War II, knowledge of the heart's functions and the physiology of the lungs was still rudimentary, much of the intimate physiological relationship between the two yet to be revealed. In 1628, when William Harvey discovered the circulatory system, he taught us that the heart pumps blood over and over again through a closed system of arteries and veins. But for hundreds of years that was all doctors knew. Even three centuries after Harvey's discovery, few doctors could consistently diagnose a heart condition. Physicians could rely on little more than their hands and ears as diagnostic aids. Too often, the correct diagnosis emerged only after an autopsy.

With the discovery of anesthesia in the mid-nineteenth century, surgeons experimented and devised new operations, but touching the heart remained taboo. In 1880 Dr. Theodor Billroth, the most influential European surgeon of his time, said: "A surgeon who tries to suture a heart wound deserves to lose the esteem of his colleagues." The medical profession adopted an attitude about heart surgery so fatalistic that in 1896 Dr. Stephen Paget, a noted English physician, wrote: "Surgery of the heart has probably reached the limits set by Nature to all surgery: no new method, and no new discovery, can overcome the natural difficulties that attend a wound of the heart."

By the turn of the twentieth century, surgeons had opened the chest, but not the heart. Then, in 1903, Dr. Ferdinand Sauerbruch, a famous German surgeon, performed an operation that was to make history— and it came about accidentally. One of Sauerbruch's patients was a woman with heart failure, and Sauerbruch believed it was due to constriction of the pericardium, the membrane that covers the heart. He decided to relieve this constriction. Sauerbruch, a great teacher, operated in an amphitheater before a group of observant doctors. When he cut open the woman's chest, he saw what he thought was a cyst in her pericardium and he began to cut it out. Suddenly blood spurted. Sauerbruch realized immediately that it was not a cyst in the membrane but a ballooning of the heart wall itself, known as an aneurysm, and the pericardium had become attached to it. This brutally bold, fearless surgeon quickly repaired the aneurysm and sewed the heart. The patient recovered.

Others must have tried, but failed, to duplicate Sauerbruch's success. Although these presumed failures were not reported in medical journals (surgeons prefer to report successful operations), the failures must have been known through the medical grapevine and they must have perpetuated Billroth's and Paget's earlier warnings. It would take twenty-six more years and the courage of a twenty-five-year-old surgical intern to change things.

Werner Forssmann received his medical degree from the University of Berlin in 1929, and that summer he began his internship in surgery at the Auguste Viktoria Home, a small Red Cross hospital in Eberswalde, Germany, fifty miles outside Berlin.

During his studies, Forssmann had been deeply impressed by a sketch in his physiology textbook that showed French physiologists standing in front of a horse, holding a thin tube that had been put into the jugular vein in the animal's neck and then guided into the heart. An inflated rubber balloon recorded the changes in pressure inside one of the heart chambers. The horse's heart was not disturbed by the procedure. Forssmann became obsessed with the potential value of putting a tube into the human heart. He thought that the technique could be used as an emergency measure to speed delivery of drugs to the heart of a dying patient and as a means to further understanding of the diseases of the heart and circulatory system. He could not understand why this simple technique, which would avoid the complications of opening the chest, had not already been tried on humans.

The more Forssmann thought about the horse experiment, the more he became convinced that it would work on humans as well. But he believed that neck veins would be unsuitable; patients might object because the incision would leave a scar. For cosmetic reasons, then, he focused on the veins in the elbow crease as the point of entry for the tube that would reach the heart.

Forssmann decided to wait a few weeks before asking his superior for permission to try his experiment. He would need a little time to get to know the other doctors at Auguste Viktoria, and to learn the routine.

In the 1920s, the German medical system favored those with independent financial means, and Forssmann, from a middle-class background, was at a disadvantage. His father had been killed in World War I, and he had been raised by his mother and grandmother. When Forssmann decided to emulate a physician-uncle and become a doctor, his mother worked to pay for his medical studies.

In Forssmann's time, paid medical training jobs for postgraduate medical students were rare. But Forssmann was lucky; he found a job for $50 a month—a pittance even then—as an apprentice to Dr. Richard Schneider, a general surgeon at the Auguste Viktoria Home and a friend of the Forssmann family. Then as now, the internship is an intensive training period designed to teach the accepted techniques of medicine or surgery with little or no time for devising or executing experiments. Nevertheless, not long after joining Schneider's staff as an apprentice, Forssmann approached the elder doctor and asked permission to insert a tube through the arm of a human in an effort to reach the human heart. He carefully explained to his superior that since it was too dangerous to touch the beating heart directly, perhaps a less dangerous approach would be to put a tube inside the heart.

How would he reach this vital organ that was so well protected by the ribs?

The same way the French physiologists had reached the horse's heart—through the veins. Forssmann showed Dr. Schneider the sketch from his physiology textbook. Schneider was sympathetic to Forssmann's proposal but advised the young doctor to experiment on animals first. Forssmann countered that the animal experiments by the French physiologists had already proved the technique safe. But he admitted to Schneider he did not know what would happen when the tip of the rubber tube touched the sensitive inside lining of the human heart. So he offered to do it on himself first. "I was convinced that when the problems in an experiment are not very clear, you should do it on yourself and not on another person," Forssmann recalled years later.

But Schneider refused. Forssmann then suggested doing the experiment on a dying patient. Schneider rejected this as well. He forbade Forssmann to do the experiment at all on any person, including himself. As a friend of the family, Schneider feared that Forssmann's widowed mother would have no means of supporting herself if something happened to her only child. The risk was too great, not only to Forssmann but also to Schneider's reputation. An accident would create a scandal.

Forssmann decided to do the experiment anyway—in secret. He would need equipment: sterile scalpels, sutures, and a painkiller to anesthetize the area in the elbow crease he would pierce. He would also need a long piece of sterile rubber tubing, and he knew that only the ureteral catheter, the thin tubing urologists use to drain urine from the kidneys, was long enough for his purpose. This crucial equipment was kept locked in the operating room under the care of Gerda Ditzen, a nurse of about forty-five who had a keen interest in medicine. Forssmann would need her assistance.

"I started to prowl around Gerda like a sweet-toothed cat around the cream jug," he said. He lent her medical books about anatomy and physiology and dropped by the cafeteria after she had finished lunch, ready to talk about what she had read. And each time they met, Forssmann would tell her a little more about his idea. He showed her the picture of the tube in the horse's heart and explained how the same technique could be performed on humans. She was captivated. Forssmann took her to dinner, and during the evening she asked more and more questions about his experiment. She liked the vision and passionate conviction of this young doctor, and, yes, she could clearly understand the importance of his idea. When Forssmann told her he was forbidden to do the experiment, she immediately suggested that they do it together; she would be his human guinea pig.

Forssmann had something else in mind.

A few days later, sweating from the summer heat as well as from his own excitement, he visited Nurse Ditzen in the small operating room. It was the noon break, and she was alone. He asked her to unlock the cabinet and get him a set of sterile surgical instruments—a scalpel, a hollow needle, sutures, and a ureteral catheter. Knowing no operations were scheduled for that afternoon, she asked Forssmann why he needed them. Then she realized what he was going to do. Convinced that she would be the first human to have a tube in her heart and excited by the knowledge that she would be making medical history, Gerda prepared everything Forssmann needed and willingly followed his command to climb onto the surgical table.

Forssmann strapped her arms and legs to the table, then stepped out of her view, toward the surgical workbench. He peeled the white towel from the instrument tray and examined the scalpel, the thin rubber ureteral tube, and the sutures Nurse Ditzen had sterilized. He glanced briefly across the room at the back of Gerda's head. She rested comfortably, expecting him to return at any moment with the novocaine.

Forssmann turned back to the surgical tray and briefly studied the ureteral tube. It was sixty-five centimeters long, just shy of thirty inches. Long enough, he estimated, to push through the hole in the vein in the elbow crease, slide up the arm, and twist across the shoulder, down a large vein in the chest, and into the venous connection to his heart.

His heart, not Gerda Ditzen's.

As the nurse adjusted her body to the tight-fitting straps, Forssmann worked confidently. He dabbed iodine over his left elbow crease and injected the novocaine to numb his skin. While he waited for the local anesthetic to take effect, he returned to the surgical table. Slowly and ceremoniously, he rubbed Nurse Ditzen's arm with iodine. He smiled reassuringly at Gerda, patted her arm gently and returned to the workbench, out of her sight.

Forssmann picked up the scalpel and cut through his skin. When he reached a large vein, he put down the scalpel, picked up the hollow needle, gently pushed it into the vein and left it in place. A small amount of blood spilled over his arm. Forssmann reached for the rubber tubing and pushed its tip through the hollow needle to guide it into the vein. The tube slithered along. There are valves in the veins that close when blood flows away from the heart, but because the tube was moving in the direction of the blood flow, the valves opened naturally and offered no resistance to Forssmann's tube. As he pushed the tube along the course of the vein in his upper arm, he felt a slight warmth, but no pain. Forssmann was learning that nature keeps the veins devoid of pain fibers.

When the tube reached the level of his shoulder, he stopped. Once it got to his heart, he would need documentaion, an X ray of his chest to show the tube's precise location. The X-ray machine was in the basement of the hospital. He would need Nurse Ditzen's assistance.

Just then she called to him from across the room. Was anything wrong? When would he begin?

Forssmann went over to the table. As he loosened the straps, he replied, "It's done."

Gerda pushed herself off the table and stared at the tube in Forssmann's arm. She realized immediately that she had been duped.

"She was furious," Forssmann recalled. "I told her to relax and asked her to put a handkerchief around my arm and call the X-ray technician. Then we walked together down a flight of stairs to the X-ray department in the cellar."

There, Forssmann went behind the fluoroscopic X-ray screen and ordered Nurse Ditzen to hold up a mirror so he could look over the screen and see the position of the catheter on the fluoroscope. The two were silent, completely engrossed, as they watched the tube move through Forssmann's vein. Neither noticed the X-ray technician slip out of the room.

Forssmann jiggled the catheter and inched it toward his heart; still there was no pain, only the continued feeling of warmth. On one occasion the tube hit something sensitive, for he had an urge to cough. He restrained himself.

The stillness was abruptly broken when Dr. Peter Romeis and the X-ray technician burst into the room. The frightened X-ray technician had woken Dr. Romeis from a nap. Romeis was Forssmann's friend and colleague and had expressed support for Forssmann's idea when Forssmann had first confided it to him. Now, to Forssmann's dismay, a bleary-eyed Romeis was yelling at him, telling him he was crazy.

"Romeis tried to pull the catheter from my arm," Forssmann recalled. "I fought him off, yelling, 'Nein, Nein. I must push it forward.' I kicked his shins and pushed the catheter until the mirror showed that the tip had reached my heart. Take a picture, I ordered. I knew that the main point was to get radiographic proof that the catheter was indeed in the heart, not in a vein."

The X-ray technician snapped the picture. When it was developed a few minutes later, Forssmann had his proof. The catheter was in his right auricle, the first heart chamber that he could reach through the arm vein. The tube was too short to be pushed further into the heart.

Satisfied that he had the X-ray documentation he needed, Forssmann pulled the tube out of his heart, slid it back through the veins in his chest and arm and out of his elbow crease. A few drops of blood oozed out of the hole where the tube had pierced the vein, and Forssmann put a suture or two into the wound to stop the bleeding. Then he bandaged his elbow. The incision would turn red a few days later from a mild infection. But no further complications developed.

Forssmann was luckier than he could have known. Because so little was understood about the functions of the heart, he was oblivious to the dangers that can occur when anything touches the sensitive endocardium, or inside lining of the heart wall. Abnormal, potentially fatal heart rhythms can develop. Forssmann could have died suddenly, on the spot.

Oblivious to all this, Forssmann faced a more immediate problem: Dr. Schneider. The chief surgeon summoned the young intern to his office and started to give him a lecture about disobedience.

Forssmann was deeply concerned. He knew his career was at stake. Then Schneider asked to see the X ray.

As he told me the story years later, Forssmann burst into a roaring laugh. "When Schneider saw the X-ray pictures," Forssmann said, "he agreed the experiment was a good one and decided to celebrate. That evening we went to Kretchmer's, an old-fashioned, low-ceilinged wine tavern where the waiters wore formal evening dress. We had a good dinner and several bottles of fine wine." Forssmann repeated his experiment on himself five more times over the next four weeks. Each time, he went through the same procedure, and each time he successfully pushed the catheter through his arm to his heart.

Schneider urged Forssmann to write a scientific paper describing his experiments. The older doctor knew that Forssmann's technique was revolutionary, and as the word spread he feared others would steal the idea and claim credit. Schneider also anticipated the furor that would come when the medical profession learned of the daring experiments. He told Forssmann to stress the potential therapeutic applications of catheterization and its perceived usefulness for the emergency administration of drugs to the heart, and to minimize its usefulness for research purposes. "As a method of investigation, it is too revolutionary for doctors to understand," Schneider pointed out to his young apprentice. "Say that you tried it on cadavers before you did it on yourself. The reader of your paper must have the impression that it is not too revolutionary and that it was not made without a lot of forethought. Otherwise, the critics will tear you to pieces."

Decades later, Forssmann was criticized by those who said he had pursued the catheter technique for unmerited impractical ideas and not as the valuable physiological tool it came to be. Nevertheless, Forssmann did report some of the research potential he foresaw from his experiment. In his paper, he wrote, "The method opens up numerous prospects for new possibilities in the investigation of metabolism and of cardiac function." To counterbalance this and in an effort to comply with Schneider's suggestions, Forssmann invented a story. He claimed in his report that a colleague had been with him for the experiment and had, in fact, inserted the catheter into Forssmann's arm. At that point, according to Forssmann's report, the colleague became so frightened by the whole procedure that he ran away, leaving Forssmann alone, the catheter dangling from his arm. Forssmann went on to say that he did not continue with the experiment at that time, but a few days later he decided to do it again, alone. Forssmann also claimed in his report that he had tried the technique first on a cadaver. But, as he told me much later, he catheterized a cadaver only *after* he had put the tube into his own heart. Even today, textbooks describe the fictitious, aborted first effort and the nonexistent preliminary test on the corpse.

On September 13, 1929, Forssmann sent his paper to the *Klinische Wochenschrift,* the leading German medical journal. When it appeared in November, it caused the furor that Schneider had feared. Newspaper accounts sensationalized and distorted the technique. A Berlin paper offered Forssmann a thousand marks to publish pictures of the X rays showing the catheter in his heart. Forssmann declined.

Then, Forssmann's priority in performing the experiment was challenged by Dr. Ernst Unger, the senior surgeon at another, more prestigious German hospital. In 1912, seventeen years before Forssmann's paper appeared, Unger and Fritz Bleichroeder and another colleague had published a series of papers in *Klinische Wochenschrift* in which they had reported inserting tubes into the arm and leg veins of four human volunteers. Unger now claimed that in one experiment he had pushed the catheter through an artery into Bleichroeder's heart. Bleichroeder backed him up, arguing that the stabbing pain in his chest indicated that the tube had reached his heart. But if indeed it had, they had not mentioned it in their report. Furthermore, they had taken no X rays. Without them, there was no proof.

Unger wrote to the *Klinische Wochenschrift,* charging that its editor had shirked his journalistic duties in failing to note the previous claim. Forssmann explained that because the titles of the previous papers had given no hint that they were related in any way to his project, he had not read them before publishing his own paper. The editor printed a brief note from Forssmann that explained the situation but did not yield priority.

On October 1, 1929, a month before his report would be published, Forssmann moved from Eberswalde to Dr. Ferdinand Sauerbruch's clinic at the Charité Hospital in Berlin, where he took an unpaid position in the expectation of working closely with the renowned surgeon.

Sauerbruch's clinic had become the mecca of German surgery, but from the start Forssmann was unhappy. He seldom had a chance to operate on patients, and he rarely saw Sauerbruch. When he did manage to corner him for a few minutes to outline his plans for further experiments, Sauerbruch rejected them. Sauerbruch, the great teacher and the surgeon who had performed pioneering heart operations, failed to appreciate the potential benefits of cardiac catheterization. When Forssmann's paper was published, his superiors at Charité accused him of seeking publicity. A little more than a month after he had started work, Sauerbruch summoned Forssmann to his office and fired him.

Happily for Forssmann, his old position with Schneider was vacant, and he returned to Eberswalde. There he outlined a second experiment with implications as revolutionary as his first. It was an experiment in angiocardiography, a technique in which a radiopaque substance that blocks X rays is injected into an artery or a vein so that the circulatory system can be outlined on the pictures. The areas in which the substance is present.appear white on the X-ray film.

Forssmann's proposed technique not only was different but also involved considerable risk. Instead of squirting contrast material into the arm vein so that it would disperse into the blood, Forssmann wanted to put a tube directly into the heart and squirt a different type of contrast material through it. He hoped that the contrast material would outline the anatomy of the chambers of the right side of the heart. Unlike his first experiment, this one required prior work with animals. Because the facilities at the hospital in Eberswalde were too small for this type of research, Forssmann arranged to do the studies with Dr. Willy Felix at Neukölln Hospital in Berlin. He began with rabbits, but they proved unsuitable. When Forssmann's thin catheters touched the animals' hearts, abnormal heart rhythms developed and the rabbits died.

Forssmann then tried dogs. At that time hospitals were not equipped, as they are now, with special quarters for experimental animals. Forssmann's mother cared for the dogs at her apartment. There he would inject a dog with morphine, put the sleepy animal into a potato sack and take it by motorcycle to the hospital. In experiments that recalled those of the French physiologists, Forssmann would push a catheter through a vein in the dog's neck and into its heart.

Radiopaque chemicals were just beginning to be used to help X-ray the urinary system and the stomach. Forssmann knew it would be much more difficult to use the technique with the heart, because the heart moves so rapidly. The X-ray exposure would have to be made quickly and at the precise moment. Forssmann chose an arbitrary dose of one of the radiopaque chemicals and injected it into the dogs. He took X rays, hoping that by luck he would catch a flash of the chemical rushing through one of the chambers of the heart. The first chemical he used killed several dogs, and he switched to another, sodium iodide. This proved to be safe and he managed to get the X rays he wanted. By putting about thirty of them in sequence, he showed that the heart actions could be demonstrated radiographically. Now, at least, he knew that the technique was feasible. But would it be safe on humans?

Forssmann wasn't sure. "I didn't know what the reaction of the intima [the inner lining of blood vessels] would be when the chemical was injected," he said. "I was a little anxious, more nervous than I was before the first self-experiment. You can pull a catheter out of the body, but what is injected into the heart stays in. So I experimented for a few days. I pressed the solutions of sodium iodide against my buccal mucosa [the inside of the mouth] for several hours. I also tested it with samples of blood in the laboratory. There were no reactions. Then I thought: Now I can do it on man." There was never any question in his mind who that man would be.

On the first attempt, a bent catheter tip caused the tube to deviate into a neck vein instead of going into the heart. When the tip reached the middle of the neck, it produced a dull pain in his ear. He tried again. This time the tube went smoothly to the heart. He injected the sodium iodide and felt only a mild irritation of the nasal membranes, an unpleasant transient taste in his mouth, and a slight feeling of dizziness, which passed quickly. Disappointingly, the X rays were unsatisfactory.

Forssmann repeated the experiment. At this point, he was no longer threading the catheter through the veins in his elbow crease because the most readily accessible of these blood vessels had been sewn closed after his previous catheterization experiments. Instead, he was injecting a local anesthetic into the skin around his groin and inserting the catheter into a vein in his upper leg. He would then push it up along the veins in his thigh to the abdomen and further into the main vein that drains blood from the lower half of the body and on into its connection with the heart.

Fifty years later the experience was still vivid in Forssmann's mind. As he watched one of his grandchildren crawl across the living room floor, he explained to me why he had had to be the subject of such a messy and technically difficult experiment: "Nobody else," he said, "would dirty his fingers with such experiments."

On that second try, he experienced the same fleeting light-headed feeling and a warm sensation in his mouth. Once again, the X rays were of poor quality. All that could be seen was a little cloud at the end of the catheter. The pictures were useless for diagnostic purposes. By this time Forssmann had put a tube into his heart *nine* times.

Shortly before Forssmann's report of his angiographic experiments appeared in a medical journal, he presented his findings at a scientific meeting in Berlin. Ferdinand Sauerbruch heard his paper and invited him to return to his clinic. Forssmann, believing that Sauerbruch would now encourage his research, accepted and returned to the Charité Hospital, still as an unpaid assistant. The year was 1931.

Unfortunately, it was more of the same. In the next sixteen months, Forssmann performed just three operations, about as many as he might do with Schneider in a week in Eberswalde. Sauerbruch delegated the running of his clinic to a group of subordinates who neither accepted Forssmann nor believed that he was cut out for scientific research. Forssmann was fired again. As a medical friend told him many years later, "Be happy Sauerbruch and his staff did not understand. Had they, they would have won the Nobel Prize, not you."

By 1935 Forssmann was back in Berlin, this time working with another physician, Dr. Karl Heusch, at the Rudolf Virchow Hospital. And he was ready for another self-experiment. Others had reported the technique of aortography (X rays of the aorta, the main vessel leading from the heart), but only under general anesthesia. Forssmann and Heusch wanted to learn if they could perform this technique using a local anesthetic. The two doctors decided to try it on each other. Aiming with a needle for Forssmann's aorta, Heusch pierced an area between his shoulder blade and a vertebra in his spine. Each jab at the aorta caused Forssmann excruciating pain. After the third unsuccessful attempt, Forssmann took to his bed with headaches and a stiff back.

By now Forssmann was married and had small children. When he suggested repeating the experiment, his wife, who was also a doctor, asked him not to go on. This time Forssmann listened. He had performed his last self-experiment.

To support his family, Forssmann decided to specialize in urology and general surgery. But in spite of his research successes, or more accurately because of them, he had great difficulty getting established. In one town, officials who had read his medical papers turned down his application for the job of chief surgeon. They reasoned that if he had done all these experiments on his own heart, what might he do to the hearts of his patients?

Not only did Forssmann's self-experiments create unexpected difficulties, but so would another experience. At Sauerbruch's clinic, Forssmann had been impressed by a senior staff member, a surgeon who now urged him to join the Nazi party. Forssmann's new Nazi affiliations led to an offer of the very thing his medical colleagues would not grant—the best available scientific equipment and plenty of human guinea pigs with which to carry on his research. Forssmann rejected the opportunity. "To use defenseless patients as guinea pigs," he said, "was a price I would never be prepared to pay for the realization of my dreams."

World War II broke out and Forssmann served with the German Army on the Russian front. In 1945 he avoided capture by the Russians by swimming across the Elbe River. On the other side he was taken prisoner by the American Army.

Later, because of his Nazi associations, West German officials forbade him to practice medicine. In the 1950s, when they rescinded the order, Forssmann found work as a urologist in a small German farming community, where his name was not known. It remained for others to apply his revolutionary techniques to the everyday practice of medicine.

Two of the crucial figures in that effort—Dr. André Cournand and Dr. Dickinson Richards—were based in New York City. During the early 1930s they had read Forssmann's papers on cardiac catheterization and angiography. Although they attached little value to his suggestion of using the technique for emergency administration of drugs, they saw enormous potential in catheterization as a technique to obtain blood samples from the heart in order to study the blood concentration of oxygen and carbon dioxide, the chief respiratory gases in the blood. In 1936 they began a series of experiments in which they catheterized the hearts of dogs and a chimpanzee; they discovered that the concentrations of the gases changed drastically as blood passed from the body into the lungs and back into the heart. In order to understand the physiology of the heart and lungs, doctors needed to know how much these concentrations differed in humans.

But it was four more years—1940—before Richards and Cournand felt confident enough to experiment on a human. Their first human catheterization was performed on a patient dying of cancer at Columbia-Presbyterian Medical Center; the attempt failed because cancerous growths obstructed passage of the tube through the veins. Later Richards and Cournand, working at Bellevue Hospital, used the technique experimentally in patients who were suffering from heart failure due to advanced stages of high blood pressure. By 1942 the New York team had perfected the technique for use in measuring blood components in the right side of the heart and later in the pulmonary artery that delivers deoxygenated blood from the heart to the lungs.

Neither Cournand nor Richards did what they knew Forssmann had done—neither put a tube into his own heart.

As a young man, it is true, Cournand had experimented on himself, allowing dozens of blood samples to be taken from an artery in his wrist; he had also breathed nitrogen and other gases. In an interview with me he said his superiors had rejected his offer to have his heart catheterized as a normal volunteer because of his age; he was then approaching fifty. However, a scientific paper published about those experiments, and coauthored by Cournand, lists the age range of the subjects as thirty-eight to seventy-three. That omission was to haunt Cournand for the rest of his life. "My regret," he admitted, "is from a psychological point of view—that people said, well, he did it on other people but not on himself."

In 1956 Forssmann was plucked from obscurity when he, Cournand, and Richards shared the Nobel Prize in Physiology or Medicine. At the Nobel Prize ceremonies in Stockholm, Professor Göran Liljestrand, an official of the Nobel Committee, paid tribute to Forssmann's courage in doing the "by no means harmless" experiments on himself: "It must have required firm conviction of the value of the method to induce self-experimentation of the kind carried out by Forssmann. His later disappointment must have been all the more bitter . . . Forssmann was not given the necessary support; he was, on the contrary, subjected to criticism of such exaggerated severity that it robbed him of any inclination to continue. This criticism was based on an unsubstantiated belief in the danger of the intervention, thus affording proof that—even in our enlightened times—a valuable suggestion may remain unexploited on the grounds of a preconceived opinion."

After winning the Nobel Prize, Forssmann was asked to head a German cardiovascular research institute and to perform open-heart surgery. But he recognized that he was not qualified for either position. He returned to his small farming town and continued to practice urology. "I was conscious that the others had made so much progress I could not catch up on the basics," Forssmann told me. Leaning back in a chair in his living room, glancing a little wistfully at the snowdrifts outside his picture window, he continued, "The basic sciences had become so developed that I would have needed ten years to learn the math, chemistry, and physics necessary to run an institute." Forssmann's deep voice gave way to a chuckle as he told me that even experts sometimes forget what they learn. In 1971, he said, he learned that 140 years earlier another German physician, Johann Dieffenbach, had deliberately put a catheter into the heart of a patient near death from cholera. The aim was to drain thick blood from the heart.

A few months before his death in 1979 at age seventy-four, Forssmann said what must have been on his mind for nearly half a century: "It was very painful. I felt that I had planted an apple orchard and other men who had gathered the harvest stood at the wall, laughing at me."

Today the importance of Werner Forssmann's seedling apples is universally recognized. His techniques have become standard in medical practice. Without them, birth defects affecting the heart would be irreparable and there would be no lifesaving operations on patients whose heart valves have been scarred by bouts with rheumatic fever or other diseases. Nor would heart surgeons be able to do coronary bypass operations to relieve the crushing chest pains of angina pectoris or to minimize the chances of a heart attack. Forssmann's techniques are the basis of many tests, now routine, done in coronary care units to monitor the recovery of patients from heart attacks or in cardiac catheterization laboratories to diagnose heart ailments. Without his work, it would be impossible to implant pacemakers to electronically control the beats of a heart whose rhythm is too slow or erratic. His experiments were as courageous—the results as far-reaching—as any in the annals of medicine.

RAYMOND CARVER

RAYMOND CARVER (1939–1988). *American poet and fiction writer. By the late 1970s, Carver's fiction and poetry marked him as one of the most noteworthy talents of his generation. He was a Guggenheim fellow in 1979 and was twice awarded grants by the National Endowment for the Arts. His collections of stories include* Will You Please Be Quiet, Please? *(1978),* What We Talk About When We Talk About Love *(1981),* Cathedral *(1983), and* Where I'm Calling From: New and Selected Stories *(1988). In 1993, the renowned filmmaker Robert Altman directed a major motion picture,* Short Cuts, *based on several of Carver's short stories. Carver also wrote five books of poetry, the last,* A New Path to the Waterfall, *appearing posthumously in 1989. His work has been translated into more than twenty languages.*

WHAT THE DOCTOR SAID

He said it doesn't look good
he said it looks bad in fact real bad
he said I counted thirty-two of them on one lung before
I quit counting them
I said I'm glad I wouldn't want to know
about any more being there than that
he said are you a religious man do you kneel down
in forest groves and let yourself ask for help
when you come to a waterfall
mist blowing against your face and arms
do you stop and ask for understanding at those moments
I said not yet but I intend to start today
he said I'm real sorry he said
I wish I had some other kind of news to give you
I said Amen and he said something else
I didn't catch and not knowing what else to do
and not wanting him to have to repeat it
and me to have to fully digest it
I just looked at him
for a minute and he looked back it was then
I jumped up and shook hands with this man who'd just given me
something no one else on earth had ever given me
I may even have thanked him habit being so strong

MY DEATH

If I'm lucky, I'll be wired every whichway
in a hospital bed. Tubes running into
my nose. But try not to be scared of me, friends!
I'm telling you right now that this is okay.
It's little enough to ask for at the end.
Someone, I hope, will have phoned everyone
to say, "Come quick, he's failing!"
And they will come. And there will be time for me
to bid goodbye to each of my loved ones.
If I'm lucky, they'll step forward
and I'll be able to see them one last time
and take that memory with me.
Sure, they might lay eyes on me and want to run away
and howl. But instead, since they love me,
they'll lift my hand and say "Courage"
or "It's going to be all right."
And they're right. It is all right.
It's just fine. If you only knew how happy you've made
    me!
I just hope my luck holds, and I can make
some sign of recognition.
Open and close my eyes as if to say,
"Yes, I hear you. I understand you."
I may even manage something like this:
"I love you too. Be happy."
I hope so! But I don't want to ask for too much.
If I'm unlucky, as I deserve, well, I'll just
drop over, like that, without any chance
for farewell, or to press anyone's hand.
Or say how much I cared for you and enjoyed
your company all these years. In any case,
try not to mourn for me too much. I want you to know
I was happy when I was here.
And remember I told you this a while ago—April 1984.
But be glad for me if I can die in the presence
of friends and family. If this happens, believe me,
I came out ahead. I didn't lose this one.

MARGARET ATWOOD

MARGARET ATWOOD (1939–   ). *Canadian poet and fiction writer. Atwood has won numerous prizes for her poetry as well as her fiction, which critics have dubbed "Atwoodian—for its virtuoso wit and unmistakable style." She has published eight novels, among them* The Handmaid's Tale *(1986),* Cat's Eye *(1988), and, most recently,* The Robber Bride *(1993); eleven volumes of poetry; and five collections of short fiction, including the critically celebrated* Wilderness Tips *(1991) and* Good Bones and Small Murders *(1994).*

THE WOMAN WHO COULD NOT LIVE WITH HER FAULTY HEART

I do not mean the symbol
of love, a candy shape
to decorate cakes with,
the heart that is supposed
to belong or break;

I mean this lump of muscle
that contracts like a flayed biceps,
purple-blue, with its skin of suet,
its skin of gristle, this isolate,
this caved hermit, unshelled
turtle, this one lungful of blood,
no happy plateful.

All hearts float in their own
deep oceans of no light,
wetblack and glimmering,
their four mouths gulping like fish.
Hearts are said to pound:
this is to be expected, the heart's
regular struggle against being drowned.

But most hearts say, I want, I want,
I want, I want. My heart
is more duplicitous,
though no twin as I once thought.
It says, I want, I don't want, I
want, and then a pause.
It forces me to listen,

and at night it is the infra-red
third eye that remains open
while the other two are sleeping
but refuses to say what it has seen.

It is a constant pestering
in my ears, a caught moth, limping drum,
a child's fist beating
itself against the bedsprings:
I want, I don't want.
How can one live with such a heart?

Long ago I gave up singing
to it, it will never be satisfied or lulled.
One night I will say to it:
Heart, be still,
and it will.

SHARON OLDS

SHARON OLDS (1942–   ). *American poet. A professor of creative writing at New York University, Sharon Olds is best known for the candor and eroticism of her poetry, which has been called both "purifying" and "redemptive." Olds has written four collections of poetry:* Satan Says *(1980);* The Dead and the Living *(1983), which was the 1983 Lamont Poetry Selection and won the National Book Critics Circle Award in 1984;* The Gold Cell *(1989); and* The Father *(1992).*

35/10

Brushing out my daughter's dark
silken hair before the mirror
I see the grey gleaming on my head,
the silver-haired servant behind her. Why is it
just as we begin to go
they begin to arrive, the fold in my neck
clarifying as the fine bones of her
hips sharpen? As my skin shows
its dry pitting, she opens like a small
pale flower on the tip of a cactus;
as my last chances to bear a child
are falling through my body, the duds among them,
her full purse of eggs, round and
firm as hard-boiled yolks, is about
to snap its clasp. I brush her tangled
fragrant hair at bedtime. It's an old
story—the oldest we have on our planet—
the story of replacement.

MISCARRIAGE

When I was a month pregnant, the great
clots of blood appeared in the pale
green swaying water of the toilet.
Dark red like black in the salty
translucent brine, like forms of life
appearing, jelly-fish with the clear-cut
shapes of fungi.

That was the only appearance made by that
child, the dark, scalloped shapes
falling slowly. A month later
our son was conceived, and I never went back
to mourn the one who came as far as the
sill with its information: that we could
botch something, you and I. All wrapped in
purple it floated away, like a messenger
put to death for bearing bad news.

JACK COULEHAN

JACK COULEHAN (1943–). *American physician and writer. Born in Pittsburgh, Dr. Coulehan received his B.A. from St. Vincent College and his M.D. and M.P.H. degrees from the University of Pittsburgh. He taught for a number of years at the University of Pittsburgh School of Medicine, and is now professor of medicine at the State University of New York–Stony Brook. His poetry has been published widely; collections include* The Knitted Glove *(1991) and* First Photographs of Heaven *(1994).*

THE KNITTED GLOVE

You come into my office wearing a blue
knitted glove with a ribbon at the wrist.
You remove the glove slowly, painfully,
and dump out the contents, a worthless hand.
What a specimen! It looks much like a regular hand,
warm, pliable, soft, you can move the fingers.

If it's not one thing, it's another.
Last month the fire in your hips had you down
or up mincing across the room with a cane.
When I ask about the hips today, you pass it off
so I can't tell if only the pain
or the memory is gone. The knitted hand
is the long and short of it, pain doesn't exist
in the past any more than this morning does.

This thing, the name for your solitary days,
for the hips, the hand, for the walk of your eyes
away from mine, this thing is coyote, a trickster.
I want to call, "Come out, you son of a dog!"
and wrestle that name to the ground for you,
I want to take its neck between my hands.
But in this world I don't know how to find
the bastard, so we sit. We talk about the pain.

GOOD NEWS

The first bad news is a spot on my lung
when all I came to the doctor for
was a leg that burnt like scalding water.

Then they find a hole in my spine,
right at the place my back kicked out
the day I jumped an aluminum ladder.

But no, my doctor looks at the wall
and says the black egg growing in my back
is not that, it's something new.

Today's scan shows a hole in my liver
and, strangely, though I'm still not sick,
my body begins to die.

There's Drano dripping in my vein
to scour the blood clot, and each day
brings another test and more bad news.

Toward the back of the morning paper,
I read stories of love and reunion,
tales of miraculous cures.

Mothers and children lost in the war,
sons who search, twins parted at birth,
brothers who search . . . at last they meet.

A retired butcher finds a girl
he courted in Palermo, 1946,
and they dance all night in Niles, Ohio.

Good news. That's what I need to hear,
not the next painful step
on the ladder, to the next lower rung.

Good news! If I ever get out of here,
I'll rent a bowling alley
and we'll dance all night in Niles, Ohio.

JAMES TATE

JAMES TATE (1943–   ). *American poet and educator. Tate grew up in Kansas City and now teaches at the University of Massachusetts at Amherst. A recipient of the Yale Series of Younger Poets Award for his first collection,* The Lost Pilot, *he has published eleven collections of poems; his* Selected Poems *won both the 1992 Pulitzer Prize and the William Carlos Williams Award. Tate's most recent collection,* Worshipful Company of Fletchers, *won the 1994 National Book Award for Poetry.*

ON THE SUBJECT OF DOCTORS

I like to see doctors cough.
What kind of human being
would grab all your money
just when you're down?
I'm not saying they enjoy this:
"Sorry, Mr. Rodriguez, that's it,
no hope! You might as well
hand over your wallet." Hell no,
they'd rather be playing golf
and swapping jokes about our feet.

Some of them smoke marijuana
and are alcoholics, and their moral
turpitude is famous: who gets to see
most sex organs in the world? Not
poets. With the hours they keep
they need the drugs more than anyone.
Germ city, there's no hope
looking down those fire-engine throats.
They're bound to get sick themselves
sometime; and I happen to be there
myself in a high fever
taking my plastic medicine seriously
with the doctors, who are dying.

ALICE WALKER

ALICE WALKER (1944–   ). *African-American writer. Walker is the author of the critically acclaimed* The Color Purple, *which earned her the American Book Award and the Pulitzer Prize in 1983 and was later made into an Academy Award–winning film. Critics called* The Temple of My Familiar *(1989) "a rich tapestry of human emotion woven with poetry and passion." Other books include* Possessing the Secret of Joy *(1992);* The Third Life of Grange Copeland *(1985); and* Meridian *(1976); two short-story collections,* In Love and Trouble *(1974) and* You Can't Keep a Good Woman Down *(1982); four volumes of poetry, and a biography of Langston Hughes for children. The following selection is from Walker's first book,* Once, *originally published in 1968.*

MEDICINE

Grandma sleeps with
my sick
grand-
pa so she
can get him
during the night
medicine
to stop
the pain

In
the morning
clumsily
I
wake
them

Her eyes
look at me
from under-
neath
his withered
arm

The
medicine
is all
in
her long
un-
braided
hair.

DAVID HILFIKER

DAVID HILFIKER (1945–   ). *American physician and writer. Dr. Hilfiker graduated from Yale College and the University of Minnesota Medical School. A family practitioner in a small town in Minnesota from 1975 to 1982, he then served as medical director of Columbia Road Health Services in Washington, D.C. His books include* Healing the Wounds: A Physician Looks at His Work *(1985) and* Not All of Us Are Saints: A Doctor's Journey with the Poor *(1994), a painfully honest account of the horrific state of affairs among Washington, D.C.'s poor and ill, and of Hilfiker's attempt as a physician to do something about it.*

MISTAKES

On a warm July morning I finish my rounds at the hospital around nine o'clock and walk across the parking lot to the clinic. After greeting Jackie, I look through the list of my day's appointments and notice that Barb Daily will be in for her first prenatal examination. "Wonderful," I think, recalling the joy of helping her deliver her first child two years ago. Barb and her husband, Russ, had been friends of mine before Heather was born, but we grew much closer with the shared experience of her birth. In a rural family practice such as mine, much of every weekday is taken up with disease; I look forward to the prenatal visit with Barb, to the continuing relationship with her over the next months, to the prospect of birth.

At her appointment that afternoon, Barb seems to be in good health, with all the signs and symptoms of pregnancy: slight nausea, some soreness in her breasts, a little weight gain. But when the nurse tests Barb's urine to determine if she is pregnant, the result is negative. The test measures the level of a hormone that is produced by a woman and shows up in her urine when she is pregnant. But occasionally it fails to detect the low levels of the hormone during early pregnancy. I reassure Barb that she is fine and schedule another test for the following week.

Barb leaves a urine sample at the clinic a week later, but the test is negative again. I am troubled. Perhaps she isn't pregnant. Her missed menstrual period and her other symptoms could be a result of a minor hormonal imbalance. Maybe the embryo has died within the uterus and a miscarriage is soon to take place. I could find out by ordering an ultrasound examination. This procedure would give me a "picture" of the uterus and of the embryo. But Barb would have to go to Duluth for the examination. The procedure is also expensive. I know the Dailys well enough to know they have a modest income. Besides, by waiting a few weeks, I should be able to find out for sure without the ultrasound: either the urine test will be positive or Barb will have a miscarriage. I call her and tell her about the negative test result, about the possibility of a miscarriage, and about the necessity of seeing me again if she misses her next menstrual period.

It is, as usual, a hectic summer; I think no more about Barb's troubling state until a month later, when she returns to my office. Nothing has changed: still no menstrual period, still no miscarriage. She is confused and upset. "I feel so pregnant," she tells me. I am bothered, too. Her uterus, upon examination, is slightly enlarged, as it was on the previous visit. But it hasn't grown any larger. Her urine test remains negative. I can think of several possible explanations for her condition, including a hormonal imbalance or even a tumor. But the most likely explanation is that she is carrying a dead embryo. I decide it is time to break the bad news to her.

"I think you have what doctors call a 'missed abortion,' " I tell her. "You were probably pregnant, but the baby appears to have died some weeks ago, before your first examination. Unfortunately, you didn't have a miscarriage to get rid of the dead tissue from the baby and the placenta. If a miscarriage doesn't occur within a few weeks, I'd recommend a re-examination, another pregnancy test, and if nothing shows up, a dilation and curettage procedure to clean out the uterus."

Barb is disappointed; there are tears. She is college-educated, and she understands the scientific and technical aspects of her situation, but that doesn't alleviate the sorrow. We talk at some length and make an appointment for two weeks later.

When Barb returns, Russ is with her. Still no menstrual period; still no miscarriage; still another negative pregnancy test, the fourth. I explain to them what has happened. The dead embryo should be removed or there could be serious complications. Infection could develop; Barb could even become sterile. The conversation is emotionally difficult for all three of us. We schedule the dilation and curettage for later in the week.

Friday morning, Barb is wheeled into the small operating room of the hospital. Barb, the nurses, and I all know one another—it's a small town. The atmosphere is warm and relaxed; we chat before the operation. After Barb is anesthetized, I examine her pelvis again. Her muscles are now completely relaxed, and it is possible to perform a more reliable examination. Her uterus feels bigger than it did two days ago;

it is perhaps the size of a small grapefruit. But since all the pregnancy tests were negative and I'm so sure of the diagnosis, I ignore the information from my fingertips and begin the operation.

Dilation and curettage, or D & C, is a relatively simple surgical procedure performed thousands of times each day in this country. First, the cervix is stretched by pushing smooth metal rods of increasing diameter in and out of it. After about five minutes of this, the cervix has expanded enough so that a curette can be inserted through it into the uterus. The curette is another metal rod, at the end of which is an oval ring about an inch at its widest diameter. It is used to scrape the walls of the uterus. The operation is done completely by feel after the cervix has been stretched, since it is still too narrow to see through.

Things do not go easily this morning. There is considerably more blood than usual, and it is only with great difficulty that I am able to extract anything. What should take ten or fifteen minutes stretches into a half-hour. The body parts I remove are much larger than I expected, considering when the embryo died. They are not bits of decomposing tissue. These are parts of a body that was recently alive!

I do my best to suppress my rising panic and try to complete the procedure. Working blindly, I am unable to evacuate the uterus completely; I can feel more parts inside but cannot remove them. Finally I stop, telling myself that the uterus will expel the rest within a few days.

Russ is waiting outside the operating room. I tell him that Barb is fine but that there were some problems with the operation. Since I don't completely understand what happened, I can't be very helpful in answering his questions. I promise to return to the hospital later in the day after Barb has awakened from the anesthesia.

In between seeing other patients that morning, I place several almost frantic phone calls, trying to piece together what happened. Despite reassurances from a pathologist that it is "impossible" for a pregnant woman to have four consequent negative pregnancy tests, the realization is growing that I have aborted Barb's living child. I won't know for sure until the pathologist has examined the fetal parts and determined the baby's age and the cause of death. In a daze, I walk over to the hospital and tell Russ and Barb as much as I know for sure without letting them know all I suspect. I tell them that more tissue may be expelled. I can't face my own suspicions.

Two days later, on Sunday morning, I receive a tearful call from Barb. She has just passed some recognizable body parts; what is she to do? She tells me that the bleeding has stopped now and that she feels better. The abortion I began on Friday is apparently over. I set up an appointment to meet with her and Russ to review the entire situation.

The pathologist's report confirms my worst fears: I aborted a living fetus. It was about eleven weeks old. I can find no one who can explain why Barb had four negative pregnancy tests. My meeting with Barb and Russ later in the week is one of the hardest things I have ever been through. I described in some detail what I did and what my rationale had been. Nothing can obscure the hard reality: I killed their baby.

Politely, almost meekly, Russ asks whether the ultrasound examination would have shown that Barb was carrying a live baby. It almost seems that he is trying to protect my feelings, trying to absolve me of some of the responsibility. "Yes," I answer, "if I had ordered the ultrasound, we would have known the baby was alive." I cannot explain why I didn't recommend it.

Mistakes are an inevitable part of everyone's life. They happen; they hurt—ourselves and others. They demonstrate our fallibility. Shown our mistakes and forgiven them, we can grow, perhaps in some small way become better people. Mistakes, understood this way, are a process, a way we connect with one another and with our deepest selves.

But mistakes seem different for doctors. This has to do with the very nature of our work. A mistake in the intensive care unit, in the emergency room, in the surgery suite, or at the sickbed is different from a mistake on the dock or at the typewriter. A doctor's miscalculation or oversight can prolong an illness, or cause a permanent disability, or kill a patient. Few other mistakes are more costly.

Developments in modern medicine have provided doctors with more knowledge of the human body, more accurate methods of diagnosis, more sophisticated technology to help in examining and monitoring the sick. All of that means more power to intervene in the disease process. But modern medicine, with its invasive tests and potentially lethal drugs, has also given doctors the power to do more harm.

Yet precisely because of its technological wonders and near-miraculous drugs, modern medicine has created for the physician an expectation of perfection. The technology seems so exact that error becomes almost unthinkable. We are not prepared for our mistakes, and we don't know how to cope with them when they occur.

Doctors are not alone in harboring expectations of perfection. Patients, too, expect doctors to be perfect. Perhaps patients have to consider their doctors less prone to error than other people: how else can a sick or injured person, already afraid, come to trust the doctor? Further, modern medicine has taken much of the treatment of illness out of the realm of common sense; a patient must trust a physician to make decisions that he, the patient, only vaguely understands. But the degree of perfection expected by patients is no doubt also a result of what we doctors have come to believe about ourselves, or better, have tried to convince ourselves about ourselves.

This perfection is a grand illusion, of course, a game of mirrors that everyone plays. Doctors hide their mistakes from patients, from other doctors, even from themselves. Open discussion of mistakes is banished from the consultation room, from the operating room, from physicians' meetings. Mistakes become gossip, and are spoken of openly only in court. Unable to admit our mistakes, we physicians are cut off from healing. We cannot ask for forgiveness, and we get none. We are thwarted, stunted; we do not grow.

During the days, and weeks, and months after I aborted Barb's baby, my guilt and anger grew. I did discuss what had happened with my partners, with the pathologist, with obstetric specialists. Some of my mistakes were obvious: I had relied too heavily on one test; I had not been skillful in determining the size of the uterus by pelvic examination; I should have ordered the ultrasound before proceeding to the D & C. There was no way I could justify what I had done. To make matters worse, there were complications following the D & C, and Barb was unable to become pregnant again for two years.

Although I was as honest with the Dailys as I could have been, and although I told them everything they wanted to know, I never shared with them my own agony. I felt they had enough sorrow without having to bear my burden as well. I decided it was my responsibility to deal with my guilt alone. I never asked for their forgiveness.

Doctors' mistakes, of course, come in a variety of packages and stem from a variety of causes. For primary care practitioners, who see every kind of problem from cold sores to cancer, the mistakes are often simply a result of not knowing enough. One evening during my years in Minnesota a local boy was brought into the emergency room after a drunken driver had knocked him off his bicycle. I examined him right away. Aside from swelling and bruising of the left leg and foot, he seemed fine. An x-ray showed what appeared to be a dislocation of the foot from the ankle. I consulted by telephone with an orthopedic specialist in Duluth, and we decided that I could operate on the boy. As was my usual practice, I offered the patient and his mother (who happened to be a nurse with whom I worked regularly) a choice: I could do the operation or they could travel to Duluth to see the specialist. My pride was hurt when she decided to take her son to Duluth.

My feelings changed considerably when the specialist called the next morning to thank me for the referral. He reported that the boy had actually suffered an unusual muscle injury, a posterior compartment syndrome, which had twisted his foot and caused it to appear to be dislocated. I had never even heard of such a syndrome, much less seen or treated it. The boy had required immediate surgery to save the muscles of his lower leg. Had his mother not decided to take him to Duluth, he would have been permanently disabled.

Sometimes a lack of technical skill leads to a mistake. After I had been in town a few years, the doctor who had done most of the surgery at the clinic left to teach at a medical school. Since the clinic was more than a hundred miles from the nearest surgical center, my partners and I decided that I should get some additional training in order to be able to perform emergency surgery. One of my first cases after training was a young man with appendicitis. The surgery proceeded smoothly enough, but the patient did not recover as quickly as he should have, and his hemoglobin level (a measure of the amount of blood in the system) dropped slowly. I referred him to a surgeon in Duluth, who, during a second operation, found a significant amount of old blood in his abdomen. Apparently I had left a small blood vessel leaking into the abdominal cavity. Perhaps I hadn't noticed the oozing blood during surgery; perhaps it had begun to leak only after I had finished. Although the young man was never in serious danger, although the blood vessel would probably have sealed itself without the second surgery, my mistake had caused considerable discomfort and added expense.

Often, I am sure, mistakes are a result of simple carelessness. There was the young girl I treated for what I thought was a minor ankle injury. After looking at her x-rays, I sent her home with what I diagnosed as a sprain. A radiologist did a routine follow-up review of the x-rays and sent me a report. I failed to read it carefully and did not notice that her ankle had been broken. I first learned about my mistake five years later when I was summoned to a court hearing. The fracture I had missed had not healed properly, and the patient had required extensive treatment and difficult surgery. By that time I couldn't even remember her original visit and had to piece together what had happened from my records.

Some mistakes are purely technical; most involve a failure of judgment. Perhaps the worst kind involve what another physician has described to me as "a failure of will." She was referring to those situations in which a doctor knows the right thing to do but doesn't do it because he is distracted, or pressured, or exhausted.

Several years ago, I was rushing down the hall of the hospital to the delivery room. A young woman stopped me. Her mother had been having chest pains all night. Should she be brought to the emergency room? I knew the mother well, had examined her the previous week, and knew of her recurring bouts of chest pains. She suffered from angina; I presumed she was having another attack.

Some part of me knew that anyone with all-night chest pains should be seen right away. But I was under pressure. The delivery would make me an hour late to the office, and I was frayed from a weekend on call, spent mostly in the emergency room. This new demand would mean additional pressure. "No," I said, "take her over to the office, and I'll see her as soon as I'm done here." About twenty minutes later, as I was finishing the delivery, the clinic nurse rushed into the room. Her face was pale. "Come quick! Mrs. Helgeson just collapsed." I sprinted the hundred yards to the office, where I found Mrs. Helgeson in cardiac arrest. Like many doctors' offices at the time, ours did not have the advanced life-support equipment that helps keep patients alive long enough to get them to a hospital. Despite everything we did, Mrs. Helgeson died.

Would she have survived if I had agreed to see her in the emergency room, where the requisite staff and equipment were available? No one will ever know for sure. But I have to live with the possibility that she might not have died if I had not had "a failure of will." There was no way to rationalize it: I had been irresponsible, and a patient had died.

Many situations do not lend themselves to a simple determination of whether a mistake has been made. Seriously ill, hospitalized patients, for instance, require of doctors almost continuous decision-making. Although in most cases no single mistake is obvious, there always seem to be things that could have been done differently or better: administering more of this medication, starting that treatment a little sooner . . . The fact is that when a patient dies, the physician is left wondering whether the care he provided was adequate. There is no way to be certain, for it is impossible to determine what would have happened if things had been done differently. Often it is difficult to get an honest opinion on this even from another physician, most doctors not wanting to be perceived by their colleagues as judgmental—or perhaps fearing similar judgments upon themselves. In the end, the physician has to suppress the guilt and move on to the next patient.

A few years after my mistake with Barb Daily, Maiya Martinen first came to see me halfway through her pregnancy. I did not know her or her husband well, but I knew that they were solid, hard-working people. This was to be their first child. When I examined Maiya, it seemed to me that the fetus was unusually small, and I was uncertain about her due date. I sent her to Duluth for an ultrasound examination—which was by now routine for almost any problem during pregnancy—and an evaluation by an obstetrician. The obstetrician thought the baby would be small, but he thought it could be safely delivered in the local hospital.

Maiya's labor was uneventful, except that it took her longer than usual to push the baby through to delivery. Her baby boy was born blue and floppy, but he responded well to routine newborn resuscitation measures. Fifteen minutes after birth, however, he had a short seizure. We checked his blood sugar level and found it to be low, a common cause of seizures in small babies who take longer than usual to emerge from the birth canal. Fortunately, we were able to put an IV easily into a scalp vein and administer glucose, and baby Marko seemed to improve. He and his mother were discharged from the hospital several days later.

At about two months of age, a few days after I had given him his first set of immunizations, Marko began having short spells. Not long after that he started to have full-blown seizures. Once again the Martinens made the trip to Duluth, and Marko was hospitalized for three days of tests. No cause for the seizures was found, but he was placed on medication. Marko continued to have seizures, however. When he returned for his second set of immunizations, it was clear to me that he was not doing well.

The remainder of Marko's short life was a tribute to the faith and courage of his parents. He proved severely retarded, and the seizures became harder and harder to control. Maiya eventually went East for a few months so Marko could be treated at the National Institutes of Health. But nothing seemed to help, and Maiya and her baby returned home. Marko had to be admitted frequently to the local hospital in order to control his seizures. At two o'clock one morning I was called to the hospital: the baby had had a respiratory arrest. Despite our efforts, Marko died, ending a year-and-a-half struggle with life.

No cause for Marko's condition was ever determined. Did something happen during the birth that briefly cut off oxygen to his brain? Should Maiya have delivered at the high-risk obstetric center in Duluth, where sophisticated fetal monitoring is available? Should I have sent Marko to the Newborn Intensive Care Unit in Duluth immediately after his first seizure in the delivery room? I subsequently learned that children who have seizures should not routinely be immunized. Would it have made any difference if I had never given Marko the shots? There were many such questions in my mind and, I am sure, in the minds of the Martinens. There was no way to know the answers, no way for me to handle the guilt feelings I experienced, perhaps irrationally, whenever I saw Maiya.

The emotional consequences of mistakes are difficult enough to handle. But soon after I started practicing I realized I had to face another anxiety as well: it is not only in the emergency room, the operating room, the intensive care unit, or the delivery room that a doctor can blunder into tragedy. Errors are always possible, even in the midst of the humdrum routine of daily care. Was that baby with diarrhea more dehydrated than he looked, and should I have hospitalized him? Will that nine-year-old with stomach cramps whose mother I just lectured about psychosomatic illness end up in the operating room tomorrow with a ruptured appendix? Did that Vietnamese refugee have a problem I didn't understand because of the language barrier? A doctor has to confront the possibility of a mistake with every patient visit.

My initial response to the mistakes I did make was to question my competence. Perhaps I just didn't have the necessary intelligence, judgment, and discipline to be a physician. But was I really incompetent? My University of Minnesota Medical School class had voted me one of the two most promising clinicians. My diploma from the National Board of Medical Examiners showed scores well above average. I knew that the townspeople considered me a good physician; I knew that my partners, with whom I worked daily, and the consultants to whom I referred patients considered me a good physician, too. When I looked at it objectively, my competence was not the issue. I would have to learn to live with my mistakes.

A physician is even less prepared to deal with his mistakes than is the average person. Nothing in our training prepares us to respond appropriately. As a student, I was simply not aware that the sort of mistakes I would eventually make in practice actually happened to competent physicians. As far as I can remember from my student experience on the hospital wards, the only doctors who ever made mistakes were the much maligned "LMDs"—local medical doctors. They would transfer their patients who weren't doing well to the University Hospital. At the "U," teams of specialist physicians with their residents, interns, and students would take their turns examining the patient thoroughly, each one delighted to discover (in retrospect, of course) an "obvious" error made by the referring LMD. As students we had the entire day to evaluate and care for our five to ten patients. After we examined them and wrote orders for their care, first the interns and then the residents would also examine them and correct our orders. Finally, the supervising physician would review everything. It was pretty unlikely that a major error would slip by; and if it did, it could always be blamed on someone else on the team. We had very little feeling for what it was like to be the LMD, working alone with perhaps the same number of hospital patients plus an office full of other patients; but we were quite sure we would not be guilty of such grievous errors as we saw coming into the U.

An atmosphere of precision pervaded the teaching hospital. The uncertainty that came to seem inescapable to me in northern Minnesota would shrivel away at the U as teams of specialists pronounced authoritatively upon any subject. And when a hospital physician did make a significant mistake, it was first whispered about the halls as if it were a sin. Much later a conference would be called in which experts who had had weeks to think about the case would discuss the way it should have been handled. The embarrassing mistake was frequently not even mentioned; it had evaporated. One could almost believe that the patient had been treated perfectly. More important, only the technical aspects of the case were considered relevant for discussion. It all seemed so simple, so clear. How could anyone do anything else? There was no mention of the mistake, or of the feelings of the patient or the doctor. It was hardly the sort of environment in which a doctor might feel free to talk about his mistakes or about his emotional responses to them.

Medical school was also a very competitive place, discouraging any sharing of feelings. The favorite pastime, even between classes or at a party, seemed to be sharing with the other medical students the story of the patient who had been presented to one's team, and then describing in detail how the diagnosis had been reached, how the disease worked, and what the treatment was. The storyteller, having spent the day researching every detail of the patient's disease, could, of course, dazzle everyone with the breadth and depth of his knowledge. Even though I knew what was going on, the game still left me feeling incompetent, as it must have many of my colleagues. I never knew for sure, though, since no one had the nerve to say so. It almost seemed that one's peers were the worst possible persons with whom to share those feelings.

Physicians in private practice are no more likely to find errors openly acknowledged or discussed, even though they occur regularly. My own mistakes represent only some of those of which I am aware. I know of one physician who administered a potent drug in a dose ten times that recommended; his patient almost died. Another doctor examined a child in an emergency room late one night and told the parents the problem was only a mild viral infection. Only because the parents did not believe the doctor, only because they consulted another doctor the following morning, did the child survive a life-threatening infection. Still another physician killed a patient while administering a routine test: a needle slipped and lacerated a vital artery. Whether the physician is a rural general practitioner with years of experience but only basic training or a recently graduated, highly trained neurosurgeon working in a sophisticated technological environment, the basic problem is the same.

Because doctors do not discuss their mistakes, I do not know how other physicians come to terms with theirs. But I suspect that many cannot bear to face their mistakes directly. We either deny the misfortune altogether or blame the patient, the nurse, the laboratory, other physicians, the system, fate—anything to avoid our own guilt.

The medical profession seems to have no place for its mistakes. Indeed, one would almost think that mistakes were sins. And if the medical profession has no room for doctors' mistakes, neither does society. The number of malpractice suits filed each year is symptomatic of this. In what other profession are practitioners regularly sued for hundreds of thousands of dollars because of misjudgments? I am sure the Dailys could have successfully sued me for a large amount of money had they chosen to do so.

The drastic consequences of our mistakes, the repeated opportunities to make them, the uncertainty about our culpability, and the professional denial that mistakes happen all work together to create an intolerable dilemma for the physician. We see the horror of our mistakes, yet we cannot deal with their enormous emotional impact.

Perhaps the only way to face our guilt is through confession, restitution, and absolution. Yet within the structure of modern medicine there is no place for such spiritual healing. Although the emotionally mature physician may be able to give the patient or family a full description of what happened, the technical details are often so difficult for the layperson to understand that the nature of the mistake is hidden. If an error is clearly described, it is frequently presented as "natural," "understandable," or "unavoidable" (which, indeed, it often is). But there is seldom a real confession: "This is the mistake I made; I'm sorry." How can one say that to a grieving parent? to a woman who has lost her mother?

If confession is difficult, what are we to say about restitution? The very nature of a physician's work means that there are things that cannot be restored in any meaningful way. What could I do to make good the Dailys' loss?

I have not been successful in dealing with a paradox: I am a healer, yet I sometimes do more harm than good. Obviously, we physicians must do everything we can to keep mistakes to a minimum. But if we are unable to deal openly with those that do occur, we will find neurotic ways to protect ourselves from the pain we feel. Little wonder that physicians are accused of playing God. Little wonder that we are defensive about our judgments, that we blame the patient or the previous physician when things go wrong, that we yell at nurses for their mistakes, that we have such high rates of alcoholism, drug addiction, and suicide.

At some point we must all bring medical mistakes out of the closet.

This will be difficult as long as both the profession and society continue to project their desires for perfection onto the doctor. Physicians need permission to admit errors. They need permission to share them with their patients. The practice of medicine is difficult enough without having to bear the yoke of perfection.

MELVIN KONNER

MELVIN KONNER (1946–   ). *American physician, anthropologist, and writer. Dr. Konner received both his Ph.D. and his M.D. from Harvard, and now teaches in the anthropology department at Emory University. His books include* The Tangled Wing: Biological Constraints on the Human Spirit *(1983),* Becoming a Doctor: A Journey of Initiation in Medical School *(1988),* Why the Reckless Survive *(1991), and* Childhood *(1991), which examines the cultural, biological, and psychological influences on human development from conception through adolescence. In his last two books,* Medicine at the Crossroads *and* Dear America *(1993), Dr. Konner has addressed the health care crisis and the need for reform in America from a physician's critical perspective.*

THE DAWN OF WONDER

> The most beautiful experience we can have is the mysterious. It is the fundamental emotion which stands at the cradle of true art and true science.
>
> —ALBERT EINSTEIN, *The World As I See It*

One of the most fascinating and least discussed discoveries in the study of the wild chimpanzees was described in a short paper by Harold Bauer. He was following a well-known male chimpanzee through the forest of the Gombe Stream Reserve in Tanzania when the animal stopped beside a waterfall. It seemed possible that he had deliberately gone to the waterfall rather than passing it incidentally, but that was not absolutely clear. In any case, it was an impressive spot: a stream of water cascading down from a twenty-five-foot height, about a mile from the lake, thundering into the pool below and casting mist for sixty or seventy feet; a stunning sight to come upon in the midst of a tropical forest.

The animal seemed lost in contemplation of it. He moved slowly closer, and began to rock, while beginning to give a characteristic round of "pant-hoot" calls. He became more excited, finally beginning to run back and forth while calling, to jump, to call louder, to drum with his fists on trees, to run back again. The behavior was most reminiscent of that observed and described by Jane Goodall in groups of chimpanzees at the start of a rainstorm—the "rain dance," as it has been called. But this was one animal alone, and not surprised as the animals are by sudden rain—even if he had not deliberately sought the waterfall out, he certainly knew where it was and when he would come upon it.

He continued this activity long enough so that it seemed to merit some explanation, and did it again in the same place on other days. Other animals were observed to do it as well. They had no practical interest in the waterfall. The animals did not have to drink from the stream or cross it in that vicinity. To the extent that it might be dangerous, it could be easily avoided, and certainly did not interest every animal. But for these it was something they had to look at, return to, study, watch, become excited about: a thing of beauty, an object of curiosity, a fetish, an imagined creature, a challenge, a communication? We will never know.

But for a very similar animal, perhaps ten million years ago, in the earliest infancy of the human spirit, something in the natural world must have evoked a response like this one—a waterfall, a mountain vista, a sunset, the crater of a volcano, the edge of the sea—something that stopped it in its tracks and made it watch, and move, and watch, and move, and watch again; something that made it return to the spot, though nothing gainful could take place there, no feeding, drinking, reproducing, sleeping, fighting, fleeing, nothing *animal*. In just such a response, in just such a moment, in just such an animal, we may, I think, be permitted to guess, occurred the dawn of awe, of sacred attentiveness, of wonder.

The human infant, for its first few months of life, is all eyes, in a way that no other animal infant quite is. It isn't just that its eyes are good, that it does a lot of looking; it's that it does so little else, really. It can suck, of course, and swallow, but the rest of what it does is very primitive, except for the functions of attentiveness. Even in the adult brain, one-third of all incoming signals come through the eyes. In the infant, looking and seeing are way ahead of most other functions in development, with the possible exception of listening and hearing. The infant is not a passive figure, nor an active one either, but what might be called an actively receptive one—eagerly, hungrily receptive, famished for sights and sounds, no vague, fuzzy intelligence in a blooming, buzzing confusion, but a highly ordered, if simple, mind with a fine sense of novelty, of pattern, even of beauty. The light on a leaf outside the window, the splash of red on a woman's dress, the shadow on the ceiling, the sound of rain—any of these may evoke a rapt attention not, perhaps, unlike that of the chimpanzee at the waterfall.

For most people, as they grow, that sense of wonder diminishes in frequency, becoming at best peripheral to the business of everyday life. For some, it becomes the central fact of existence. These follow two separate paths: Either the sense of wonder leads them down an analytic path, or it leads them to simple contemplation. Either way the sense of wonder is the first fact of life, but the paths are completely different in every other way. The analyst, or scientist, moved to reveal by explaining, breaks apart the image, and the sense of wonder, focusing sequentially on the pieces. The contemplator, or artist, moved to reveal by simply looking, keeps the image and the sense of wonder whole. The artist contrives to keep the attention riveted without fragmentation, by means of high trickery. This trickery involves transmuting the image into human speech—whether a literary, plastic, or musical form of speech—thus fixing in place forever the sense of wonder.

There is a photograph that has by now been seen by most people living in civilized countries. It was taken from an ingenious if crude vehicle traveling many thousands of miles per hour, across a vast expanse of space empty of air, by men who had devoted their lives, courageously and at great personal cost, to the mastery of nature through machinery. This photograph cost perhaps a billion dollars, and in one sense it is worth every penny.

It shows an almost spherical object poised against a backdrop of black. The object is partly colored a deep, warm, pretty blue, with many broken, off-white swirls drawn across it. It looks at first like a mandala, a strange symbol woven on black cloth. It looks whole, somehow, and rather small. But as we study it (it draws us in almost mysteriously), some red-brown shapes obscured among the swirls of white take on before our eyes the unmistakable images we first saw and memorized as children encountering the geography of the continents. If the space program accomplished nothing else (and I am often at pains to discern what it did accomplish), we must be grateful to it for producing that photograph.

"Got the earth right out our front window," said Buzz Aldrin. A medium-size mammal from a middling planet of a middle-aged star in the arm of an average galaxy, gazing at home. There was no excess of poetry on that mission. There was, of course, the stark poetry of aeronautics gobbledygook and the arch, well-prepared, historic *mot* of Neil Armstrong setting foot on the Sea of Tranquility, but "Beautiful, beautiful," "Magnificent sight out here," and "Got the earth right out our front window," was about the level at which these unique first views of the natural world were transmuted to human speech. This was no fault of Armstrong or Aldrin; they were chosen for other talents, which they had in full measure. But it is intriguing that such spontaneous poetry as there was was evoked by the machinery. "The Eagle has wings," one of them said as the lunar landing vehicle separated, after some difficulty, from the orbiting command station. *The eagle,* bold symbol of human hope on the North American continent and, beyond that, of the hope of humanity in the mission, *has wings,* has the means to transcend technical difficulty and to emerge, having mastered natural law.

But this stepping off the earth is an illusion. The mastery of natural law has proceeded no further than the grasp of some elementary laws of physics. Compared with the uncharted, infinitely more intricate laws of biology and behavior that govern the human spirit, this mastery is trivial, a mere conjurer's trick. The mastery of physical law can no longer save us while we are grounded in a tangle of ignorance of the natural laws that govern our behavior. In this sense, the eagle does not have wings.

When I was a young man in college, a professor took me to the American Museum of Natural History, not to the exhibits, which I had often seen, but into the bowels of the place, among the labyrinths of storage cabinets of bones and skins and rocks and impossibly ancient fossils. I was very much impressed by this chance to see the museum the way insiders, professionals, saw it.

There I met a man who had devoted most of his life to the study of the skeletal remains of archaeopteryx—the earliest tetrapod with feathered wings—embedded in a Mesozoic rock. I was introduced to him, awed by him, impressed with his intelligence and wisdom. It was obvious that he wanted to impart to me some piece of genuine, useful knowledge gained from the countless hours of squinting over that crushed tangle of bone and rock.

What he finally said was that he thought archaeopteryx was very much like people. This of course puzzled me, as it was calculated to do, and when I pressed him to explain, he said, "Well, you know, it's such a transitional creature. It's a piss-poor reptile, and it's not very much of a bird." Apart from the shock of hearing strong language in those relatively hallowed halls, there was an intellectual shock to my young mind that fixed those phrases in it permanently.

The dinosaurs ruled this planet for over a hundred million years, at least a hundred times longer than the brief, awkward tenure of human creatures, and they are gone almost without a trace, leaving nothing but crushed bone as a memento. We can do the same more easily and, in an ecological sense, we would be missed even less. What's the difference? seems an inevitable question, and the best answer I can think of is that we *know,* we are capable of seeing what is happening. We are the only creatures that understand evolution, that, conceivably, can alter its very course. It would be too base of us to simply relinquish this possibility through pride, or ignorance, or laziness.

It seems to me we are losing the sense of wonder, the hallmark of our species and the central feature of the human spirit. Perhaps this is due to the depredations of science and technology against the arts and the humanities, but I doubt it—although this is certainly something to be concerned about. I suspect it is simply that the human spirit is insufficiently developed at this moment in evolution, much like the wing of archaeopteryx. Whether we can free it for further development will depend, I think, on the full reinstatement of the sense of wonder. It must be reinstated in relation not only to the natural world but to the human world as well. At the conclusion of all our studies we must try once again to experience the human soul as soul, and not just as a buzz of bioelectricity; the human will as will, and not just a surge of hormones; the human heart not as a fibrous, sticky pump, but as the metaphoric organ of understanding. We need not believe in them as metaphysical entities—they are as real as the flesh and blood they are made of. But we must believe in them as entities; not as analyzed fragments, but as wholes made real by our contemplation of them, by the words we use to talk of them, by the way we have transmuted them to speech. We must stand in awe of them as unassailable, even though they are dissected before our eyes.

As for the natural world, we must try to restore wonder there too. We could start with that photograph of the earth. It may be our last chance. Even now it is being used in geography lessons, taken for granted by small children. We are the first generation to have seen it, the last generation not to take it for granted. Will we remember what it meant to us? How fine the earth looked, dangled in space? How pretty against the endless black? How round? How very breakable? How small? It is up to us to try to experience a sense of wonder about it that will save it before it is too late. If we cannot, we may do the final damage in our lifetimes. If we can, we may change the course of history and, consequently, the course of evolution, setting the human lineage firmly on a path toward a new evolutionary plateau.

We must choose, and choose soon, either for or against the further evolution of the human spirit. It is for us, in the generation that turns the corner of the millennium, to apply whatever knowledge we have, in all humility but with all due speed, and to try to learn more as quickly as possible. It is for us, much more than for any previous generation, to become serious about the human future, and to make choices that will be weighed not in a decade or a century but in the balances of geological time. It is for us, with all our stumbling, and in the midst of our dreadful confusion, to try to disengage the tangled wing.

DAVID RINALDI

DAVID RINALDI (1947–   ). *American physician. Dr. Rinaldi has been a practicing pediatrician for eleven years; his poetry has been published in* The Pharos *of the Alpha Omega Alpha Medical Honor Society and in the* Annals of Behavioral Medicine and Medical Education.

LET'S TALK ABOUT IT

with all the talk
about Dr Death
news-bites sandwiched
between circus and tragedy
hesitantly I say
in my confusion
"I understand him"
but still . . .
as a physician
morally and ethically . . .
and yet . . .
terminal pain . . .
and yet . . .

and surreptitiously
remember
how very secretly
I thought
thought how
Dad's castrated body
lay crooked in
prostatic pain on
his sweaty Tennessee cot
his wife's terminal phone voice
drawling out the daily news . . .
how very secretly
I calculated
how many of
those little pain-killers
it might take . . .

and silently remember
how I put it all
out of my Hippocratic mind
yet felt ashamed
for weakness . . .

and so I waited. . . .

HEATHER MCHUGH

HEATHER MCHUGH (1948–   ). *American fiction writer and poet.*
McHugh is the author of six collections of poetry, among them Dangers
(1977), A World of Difference *(1981),* To the Quick *(1987), and*
Shades *(1988), and of a collection of essays,* Broken English *(1993).*
Her most recent collection of poems, Hinge & Sign: Poems,
1968–1993, *was a 1994 National Book Award finalist. McHugh is a*
core faculty member in the MFA program for writers at Warren Wilson
College and is Milliman Writer-in-Residence at the University of
Washington in Seattle; she is currently a visiting professor at the
University of California–Los Angeles.

WHAT HELL IS

March 1985

Your father sits inside
his spacious kitchen, corpulent
and powerless. Nobody knows
how your disease is spread; it came
from love, or some
such place. Your father's bought
with forty years of fast talk, door-to-door,
this fancy house you've come home now to die in.
Let me tell you what
hell is, he says: I got this
double fridge all full of food
and I can't let my son go in.

*

Your parents' friends
stop visiting. You are a damper on
their spirits. Every day you feel
more cold (no human being
here can bear
the thought—it's growing
huge, as you grow thin).
Ain't it a bitch, you say, this

getting old? (I'm not sure
I should laugh. No human being
helps, except
suddenly, simply
Jesus: him you hold.)

*

We're not allowed
to touch you if you weep or bleed.
Applying salve to sores that cannot heal
your brother wears a rubber glove.
With equal meaning, cold or kiss
could kill you. Now what do I mean
by love?

*

The man who used
to love his looks
is sunk in bone
and looking out.

Framed by immunities
of telephone and lamp
his mouth is shut,
his eyes are dark.

While we discuss despair
he is it, somewhere
in the house. Increasingly
he's spoken of

not with. In kitchen
conferences we come
to terms that we
can bear. But where is he?

In hell, which is
the living room.
In hell, which has
an easy chair.

RONALD VALDISERRI

RONALD VALDISERRI (1951–   ). *American physician and writer. Deputy director of the Division of STD/HIV Prevention at the federal Centers for Disease Control and Prevention, Dr. Valdiserri is the author of* Gardening in Clay: Reflections on AIDS *(1994), a provocative, poignant, collection of meditations on AIDS motivated by his professional involvement with the disease as well as by the death of his twin brother of HIV-related illness. Dr. Valdiserri has spent more than ten years researching AIDS and HIV-related issues, including public health laboratory procedures and national training programs for lab workers performing HIV testing. He has written numerous scientific articles on AIDS/HIV and is the author of a book on the design, implementation, and evaluation of AIDS prevention programs.*

SUFFERING

Knowledge by suffering entereth;
And Life is perfected by Death.
—ELIZABETH BARRETT BROWNING "A Vision of Poets"

I read in the newspaper about a man whose wife and son had died of AIDS. He used to make his living as a minister but gave up his calling after his family became ill. It seems that his congregation couldn't handle "the situation" and was meager in its support and understanding. Angry and feeling unwanted, he decided to leave his church.

A woman in Chicago told me that when the organist in her church died from HIV disease, his mother was afraid to tell anyone the actual cause of death, although many already suspected it. She was fearful that if her fellow church members knew what had killed the boy, they would refuse to bury him. Instead, she told them that her son died from pneumonia.

Some religious leaders, people their followers listen to and respect, continue to describe AIDS as a righteous punishment for sinful acts. Fortunately, not all spiritual leaders follow this line of reasoning, but those who do astound me. They remind me of doctors who want to pick and choose the patients they will care for, not according to their medical training and professional responsibility, mind you, but according to personal preference and prejudice. A psychiatrist I met during my medical training, for example, told me that he wouldn't counsel clients who were obese because they made him feel uncomfortable. Even today, there are still some doctors and dentists who refuse to treat persons with HIV disease because of fear and prejudice.

I know that I am naive in my astonishment. After all, people who minister—whether they distribute medicine or the word of God—are not free of human foibles and shortcomings. Still, it shocks me when I hear about persons who are in the business of providing medical or spiritual care turning away from those who suffer from AIDS. I wonder if they aren't pushing God away, for I believe that those who suffer are closer to God's heart than the rest of us.

Undoubtedly, the way I understand suffering is influenced by my own conception of the Divinity. If I believed God's primary characteristic was omnipotence, then I might be more inclined to view suffering as a punishment. But to me, images of thunderbolts and wrathful countenances have never seemed awe-inspiring. They have always seemed like plain old human temper—raised to the nth degree. For me, what makes God God is his infinite understanding, and not just of arcane and complex facts, as if the Divinity were some kind of immense, cosmic computer. God has the ability to comprehend human feelings fully, to achieve total empathy, without the self-imposed barriers of fear, anger, and mistrust that often interfere with our human attempts to understand one another.

Because I see God as an all-knowing entity who feels and shares our pain, I don't believe that human suffering exists because of divine vengeance or spite. Nor do I believe that God enjoys our suffering. It exists because humans are neither infallible nor indestructible: we are mortal. I believe that people with serious illnesses, like AIDS, are best loved by God when they are forced to confront the painful reality that flesh was not meant to last forever. Those who are in pain come to understand the pain of others. They may not accept this knowledge with equanimity. Sometimes they are filled with bitterness even as they die. But they do understand, and to understand with one's heart the pain of others is an attribute of the Divine.

DAVID HELLERSTEIN

DAVID HELLERSTEIN (1953–   ). *American physician, novelist, and essayist. Born in Cleveland, Dr. Hellerstein received his A.B. from Harvard and his M.D. from Stanford. He trained in psychiatry at New York Hospital/Cornell Medical Center, and is now physician-in-charge of the psychiatric outpatient service at Beth Israel Medical Center in New York and assistant professor of psychiatry at Mount Sinai School of Medicine. He is the author of* Battles of Life and Death *(essays, 1987) and* Loving Touches *(novel, 1988); his most recent work,* A Family of Doctors *(1993), is an autobiographical account of changes in medical education, practice, and philosophy, as well as in patients' attitudes, from the perspective of five generations of doctors in the Hellerstein family.*

TOUCHING

"Scoot down to the edge of the table, hon," says Dr. Snarr. The small room is hot, the air stuffy. Our patient winces at the word *hon*. She is a young woman with chronic pelvic pain, the bane of gynecologists, and I can tell she doesn't like Snarr's tone. She does scoot along the table, though, and Snarr kicks a wheeled stool toward me. I sit on it, slide between her legs, ready for my lesson of the day. Feet and calves and thighs surround me, suddenly very close. Snarr positions the lamp before my chest, so light pours on her. I warm the speculum in my gloved hand and, with a twist, insert it.

"Open it up," he says. "Tighten it all the way open. Pull down to keep away from the urethra. You hit the urethra and no patient will ever come back to you."

Snarr is my teacher, a gaunt and narrow-shouldered man with a small potbelly below the belt of his corduroy pants. Before coming in here, he went over the information I had gathered and insisted it was nonsense. She couldn't possibly feel that kind of pain. I must not be asking the right questions. Hadn't I learned anything? Gynecologists traditionally have the reputation of being the dummies of medicine: surgeons laugh at their clumsiness in the operating room, internists at their ignorance of medical fact, psychiatrists at their insensitivity. And so far Snarr had done nothing to dispel that prejudice, which was too bad, considering that I was an impressionable third-year medical student, still trying to decide what field to select.

"Okay," says Snarr. "Now swab it out real well. Get some cells on that."

I swab.

"Pull that speculum out now. Get a good look at those walls."

I see pink folds as I pull, pink, moist walls bulging against the metal of the speculum—aquatic territory, the scalloped forms of submarine life. It's out. Snarr is quick next with lubricating jelly on the first two fingers of my glove. I stand up, push the stool away. I begin the manual exam.

"Aiee!" The woman screams and slides up on the table. "God! Oh God!"

"So that's . . . that's where it hurts," I say. I'm sweating. "Just . . . just a second, I'll try more gently."

I feel around again. This time she doesn't scream. She breathes deeply. I can't feel a damn thing, but with Snarr watching I can't pull out right away. For a month I've been spending afternoons in the gynecology clinic with Dr. Snarr—a month of women's bottoms on the edges of tables, of the hot lamp in front of my chest, the examining glove on my hand, powdered inside, the smells of femaleness. And the confidences of women, fascinating and at times overpowering, about their pains, their periods, their fertility, their husbands, their lovers. What gets to me, though, are the exams. The touching. Deep internal touching, feeling for the bulge of the uterus, for those small elusive olives the ovaries, exploring for tenderness, creating sudden moments of pain. Technically I'm reasonably good, as good as can be expected for a third-year medical student rotating through Ob-Gyn. But I still find it strange to be touching intimately but without passion—as a doctor.

I'm not alone in this either; the other medical students on Ob-Gyn seem just as awkward as I. We hang around in the lounge, where the pharmaceutical rep sometimes leaves free coffee and doughnuts, cracking jokes, laughing too much.

It reminds me of another situation, in the second-year physical diagnosis course, where we had to examine each other. The new idea that year was that we'd learn how to be more compassionate doctors if we practiced physical exams on one another first, before going on to patients.

We were divided into small groups, men and women together, and sent to various examining rooms. Our exams began at the head and worked down. You couldn't get too upset about looking into your medical student buddy's eyes, but by the second session, when we got down to the chest, the protests began. First the women complained and refused to be examined, but as it became clear that genital and rectal exams were also part of the required curriculum, men started to protest as well. Finally there was a full-scale revolt. A petition was circulated, meetings were hurriedly arranged with various administrators, protests were loud and vocal. The class was boycotted. We ended up learning the pelvic exam on professional models and doing rectal exams on plastic dummies. No one felt the course should be repeated.

I've always been sort of puzzled why my fellow medical students got so upset. After all, we had done just about everything together—cut open cadavers, crammed for exams, played touch football on the front lawn, dated and flirted and confided and complained. What it comes down to, I think, was that after two years together in med school, we knew each other too well, far too well for touching to be neutral. To palpate, percuss, auscultate, and probe each other's bodies brought out too many undoctorly thoughts.

We were a long way, I realize now, from learning the doctor's dispassionate touch. But the real problem came when our teachers were no better than we—when they were clumsy and awkward, too.

"All right," Dr. Snarr says, "let me try my hand." He steps in. I strip off my glove and wash my hands, ready to observe a deft exam, pinpointing the source of pain, exploring yet reassuring.

But in a second the woman is screaming, writhing on the table. Snarr is reaching way far in, clumsily it seems, pushing so hard her hips rise from the table; and she is crying, grabbing the table with her hands. I feel sick just watching. I have no way of knowing what, if anything, Snarr is finding, since he does not explain.

"All right, hon," he tells her. He pulls off his glove. "Wipe yourself off; we'll come back and see you in a minute."

"I don't know why the heck she hurts," he says when we are outside. "Give her some estrogen cream."

She'd dressed when I come back in. She's pale and woozy, and there's still pain in her eyes. I hand her the prescription.

"Come back if it gets worse," I say.

"Than what?" the woman asks.

I am embarrassed. I murmur something, that I'm sorry we didn't come up with anything. Then I hurry out after my teacher.

I find him in the side room, having coffee and doughnuts, courtesy of the pharmaceutical rep. The next patient isn't ready yet.

"Have some," he says.

I decline. I'm too jittery to eat.

"That girl," says Dr. Snarr. "What do you think her problem is?"

I consider the possibilities: pelvic inflammatory disease, endometri-osis, cysts. I talk, but I don't say what I really think: that he has no sense of what he put her through. That he's insensitive. Clumsy. A jerk. I'm disappointed, too, but I'm not sure why.

Perhaps it's that I wished he was a better doctor, a better role model. Certainly not all gynecologists are like Dr. Snarr, but at that moment it seemed as though they were. And what I needed so much was to know how to be with patients, how to deal with the feelings they evoked, how to make them feel at ease. If Dr. Snarr had been a better teacher, I might conceivably have gone into his field.

Dr. Snarr washes down the rest of his doughnut.

"So what else have we got out there?" he says.

A young black woman in a white gown looks around nervously as we enter.

"Scoot down to the edge of the table, hon," says Snarr.

Wincing at the word *hon*, the woman nevertheless scoots down. Snarr kicks the wheeled stool over toward me.

And I begin.

ABRAHAM VERGHESE

ABRAHAM VERGHESE (1955–   ). *American physician, professor, and author. Abraham Verghese is the author of* My Own Country (1994), *a compelling, heartrending, true-life account of his experience treating AIDS patients in a small Tennessee town. Dr. Verghese is a graduate of the Iowa Writers' Workshop; his writing has appeared in* The New Yorker, Granta, The North American Review, *and numerous medical journals. He is currently a professor of medicine and chief of infectious diseases at Texas Tech Health Sciences Center in El Paso, Texas.*

Excerpt from
MY OWN COUNTRY

Bobby Keller called me in the office as I was about to leave for home. He sounded shrill and alarmed.

"Doc? Ed is *very* sick! He is *very, very* short of breath and running a fever. A hundred and three. Dr. Verghese, he's turning blue on me."

"Bobby, call the emergency ambulance service—tell them to bring you to the Johnson City Medical Center."

Ed Maupin, the diesel mechanic, had had a CD4 count of 30 the previous week when I had seen him in clinic; Bobby Keller's was 500. At that visit, Ed's oral thrush had cleared up but he was still feeling tired and had been missing work. When I had examined Ed, the lymph nodes in his neck, which had been as big as goose eggs, had suddenly shrunk: I had thought to myself that this was either a good sign or a very bad sign; his immune system had either given up the fight or successfully neutralized the virus. The latter was unlikely.

Bobby, at that visit, had looked well and continued to work in the fashion store. I hoped now that Bobby's description of the gravity of the situation was just histrionics.

I was at the Miracle Center well ahead of the ambulance. Soon it came roaring in, all its lights flashing. When the back door opened, I peeked in: Ed's eyes were rolled back in his head, and he was covered with a fine sheen of sweat. Despite the oxygen mask that the ambulance crew had on, his skin was the color of lead. His chest was making vigorous but ineffective excursions.

Bobby, who had ridden in the front, was scarcely able to stand up. His face was tremulous; he was on the verge of fainting.

"Don't put him on no machines, whatever you do," Bobby begged me. "Please, no machines."

"Why?"

"Because that's what he told me. He doesn't want it."

"When did he tell you? Just now?"

"No. A long time ago."

"Did he put it in writing? Does he have a living will?"

"No . . ."

In the emergency room, I stabilized Ed as best I could without intubating him. I took his oxygen mask off momentarily and looked at his mouth. His mucous membranes were loaded with yeast again—it had blossomed in just a week. But I was examining his mouth to try to decide how difficult it would be to intubate him. His short, receding lower jaw, which the beard concealed well, could make this a tricky intubation. I asked him to say "Aaah." He tried to comply: his uvula and tonsils just barely came into view, another sign that he would be a tough intubation.

Ideally, an anesthetist would have been the best person to perform intubation. But I didn't want to call an anesthetist who, given the patient, might or might not be willing to do this procedure. Time was running out.

Ed was moaning and muttering incomprehensibly; his brain was clearly not getting enough oxygen. His blood pressure was 70 millimeters of mercury systolic over 50 diastolic. This was extremely low for him, because he had baseline hypertension. His cold, clammy extremities told me that the circulation to his arms and legs had shut down in an effort to shunt blood to the brain; even so, what blood got to the brain was not carrying enough oxygen. Ed's chest sounded dull in the bases when I percussed it; on listening with my stethoscope, he was wet and gurgly. The reason he was not oxygenating his blood was clear: his lungs were filled with inflammatory fluid. I ordered a stat chest X-ray and arterial blood gases. I had only a few minutes before I had to either breathe for him, or let him go. I needed more guidance from Bobby as to Ed's wishes.

I had an excellent nurse assisting me; she had already started an IV and brought the "crash cart." The respiratory therapist was administering oxygen and had an Ambu bag ready. I asked them to get goggles and masks in addition to their gloves, and to get a gown, mask, and gloves ready for me. They were to put theirs on and wait for me. The curtains were pulled and Ed's presence was largely unnoticed in the bustle of the ER. An orthopedist was putting a cast on an individual in the next room, and patients were waiting in the other cubicles.

I came out to the waiting room, but Bobby was not there!

I hurried outside.

Bobby and three other men and one woman were near the ambulance entrance, smoking. The men bore a striking resemblance to Ed Maupin—the same sharp features, the slightly receding chin. One of them, the oldest, wore a green work uniform. I recognized his face as a familiar one, someone who worked in an auto parts store where I had ordered a replacement bumper for the rusted one that had fallen off my Z. Bobby Keller, still trembling, introduced me to Ed's brothers, all younger than Ed. The woman was the wife of one of the brothers.

"Bobby," I asked, "can I tell them what's going on?"

"Tell them everything," Bobby said, the tears pouring down uncontrollably, his body shaking with sobs.

I addressed the brothers: "Ed is very sick. A few months ago we found out he has AIDS." (There was no point in trying to make the distinction between HIV infection and AIDS. If Ed had not had AIDS when I saw him in the clinic, he most certainly did now.) "Now he has a bad pneumonia from the AIDS. I need to put him on a breathing machine in the next few minutes or he will die. I have a feeling that the pneumonia he has can be treated. If we put him on the breathing machine, it won't be forever. We have a good chance of getting him off. But Bobby tells me that Ed has expressed a desire *not* to be put on the machine."

The assembled family turned to Bobby who nodded vigorously: "He did! Said he never wanted to be on no machines."

The family was clear-eyed, trying to stay calm. They pulled hard at their cigarettes. The smoke rose quietly around their weathered faces. They looked like a Norman Rockwell portrait—small-town America's citizens in their work-clothes in a hospital parking lot, facing a family crisis. But this situation was one that Norman Rockwell hadn't attempted, one he had never dreamed of. I felt they were fond of their oldest brother, though perhaps disapproving of his relationship with Bobby. Yet judging by how they had all been standing around Bobby when I walked out, I didn't think they had any strong dislike for Bobby—it was almost impossible to dislike him. They had had many years to get used to the idea of Bobby and Ed, the couple, and it was only the idea, I sensed, that they had somehow not accepted.

"We need to discuss this," the older brother said.

"We have no time, I need to go right back in," I said.

They moved a few feet away from Bobby and me. I asked Bobby, "Do you have power-of-attorney or anything like that to make decisions for Ed?" Bobby shook his head.

We looked over to where the family was caucusing. The oldest brother was doing all the talking. They came back.

"We want for you to do everything you can. Put him on the breathing machine, if you have to."

At this a little wail came out of Bobby Keller and then degenerated into sobs. I put my hand on Bobby's shoulder. He shook his head back and forth, back and forth. He wanted to say something but could not find a voice.

The oldest brother spoke again. His tone was matter-of-fact and determined:

"*We* are his family. *We* are legally responsible for him. We want you to do *everything* for him."

We are his family. I watched Bobby's face crumble as he suddenly became a mere observer with no legal right to determine the fate of the man he had loved since he was seven years old. He was finally, despite the years that had passed and whatever acceptance he and Ed found together, an outsider.

I took him aside and said, "Bobby, I have to go on. There is no way for me not to at this point. There's a really good chance that I can rescue Ed from the pneumonia. If I thought it would only make Ed suffer, I wouldn't do it. If this is *Pneumocystis,* it should respond to treatment."

Bobby kept sobbing, shaking his head as I talked, fat tears rolling off his eyes onto the ground, onto his chest. He felt he was betraying Ed. He could not deliver on his promise.

I had no time to pacify Bobby or try to convince him. I rushed back in. Ed looked worse. As I went through the ritual of gowning and masking (it was reassuring to have rituals to fall back on, a ritual for every crisis), it struck me that the entire situation had been in my power to dictate. All I had to do was to come out and say that the pneumonia did not look good, that it looked like the end. *I* mentioned the respirator, *I* offered it as an option. I could have just kept quiet. I had, when it came down to the final moment, given Ed's brothers the power of family. Not Bobby.

But there was no time to look back now.

I leaned down to Ed's ear and explained what I was about to do. He showed no sign of understanding. He was expending tremendous amounts of energy to breathe.

I stood behind Ed with the endotracheal tube in my right hand and the laryngoscope in the other. I put Xylocaine jelly on the tip of the endotracheal tube. We lowered the head of the stretcher, extended Ed's head over the edge.

I had the nurse now give Ed an intravenous bolus of 20 milligrams of Valium. An anesthetist might have used a curarelike paralyzing agent. In a few seconds, Ed's breathing ceased altogether.

The respiratory therapist gave him a few brisk breaths of oxygen from the squeeze bag and stepped away. I inserted the laryngoscope blade into his mouth and heaved up on the tongue. I could not see the vocal cords and could only barely see the epiglottis. I pushed the tube past the epiglottis, giving the tube some torque, hoping to steer it into the voice box and down the trachea. It went in too easily and I knew I had missed.

I pulled out and we bagged him with the squeeze bag again. I was talking to myself. *Come on Abe; hamsters are ten times as difficult as this, and you have intubated 260 hamsters at last count.* Another voice in my head replied: *This ain't no hamster.*

Ed was a deeper shade of blue now. If I didn't do it in the next try, we were going to have to call an anesthetist. Or call a Code Blue. The second time and I still did not see the vocal cords. But this time I felt the tube grate against the tracheal rings, just as with my hamsters. I listened over first one side of the chest and then the other while the respiratory therapist pumped air into the tube. I could hear good breath sounds on both sides; we had secured an airway and the tube was sitting in perfect position, just above the carina, where the trachea divides into the left and right bronchi.

It had been a while since I had intubated anyone myself; usually there were layers of interns and residents and students who fought for and did all the procedures. I was pleased with our success. The nurse patted me on the back.

"Did you know," I asked her, in the glow of my postprocedural success, "that intubation was invented by a physician named O'Dwyer as a lifesaving measure in diphtheria? It's therefore an infectious diseases procedure!"

"Yeah, right," she said, unimpressed. "I'll keep that in mind. Next time we have a trauma case that needs intubation we'll call in an infectious diseases consult."

I went upstairs with Ed to the intensive care unit. Now I wrote orders for the settings on the ventilator that would optimally oxygenate Ed's lungs. I put him on a 100 percent inspired oxygen concentration (in contrast to the 21 percent oxygen concentration we normally breathe) and dialed in the rate and the volume of each breath the ventilator would deliver. I wrote an order to have an arterial blood oxygen measurement made in half an hour to allow me to cut back on the oxygen if at all possible; pure oxygen in high concentrations is damaging in and of itself. I wrote orders for intravenous fluids and for laboratory tests. I felt better about Ed in the ICU than I had with Scotty Daws. I had inherited Scotty Daws and in retrospect it had been a no-win situation. Ed was the best sort of patient to bring to the ICU. Someone who I thought would perhaps walk out of there.

Pneumocystis pneumonia is easy to diagnose if you get a good specimen of sputum. Secretions obtained by washing out a segment of lung during bronchoscopy—so-called bronchoalveolar lavage, or BAL—are ideal, but even an ordinary sputum, as long as it is not grossly contaminated with saliva, can serve almost as well.

Since Ed had a tube going down into his trachea, breathing for him, it was simple enough to squirt some saline down it and then suck it back out with a catheter.

I carried the specimen down to the lab, made some smears of it on glass slides, then looked at them under the microscope after staining them for bacteria and TB. I saw only an outpouring of inflammatory cells and little else. To see *Pneumocystis carinii* requires a special stain called a silver stain. It would take a day for the pathology department to complete the stain and give me the definitive word on what it showed. The fact that I saw nothing but pus cells on my simple stains—no TB, no bacteria—suggested that this was *Pneumocystis.* I began Ed on trimethoprim-sulfamethoxazole, or Bactrim, the drug of choice for this organism.

The only cases of *Pneumocystis* pneumonia I had ever seen were in persons with AIDS. This was unique to my generation of infectious diseases physicians: we had all come of age in the era of AIDS.

But *Pneumocystis* had a long history before AIDS made it a household word. Epidemics of *Pneumocystis* swept through Europe in the 1940s. They occurred primarily in premature infants in orphanages, in the setting of overcrowding and malnutrition.

After the war years, the organism began to manifest only in select patients with immune-compromising conditions such as leukemia or after long-term cortisone administration. St. Jude Children's Hospital in Memphis, at the other end of the state from us, had accrued tremendous experience with this disease by virtue of their patient population—children with leukemias.

How are we to view this organism? As an invader from outside? Or an opportunist from within? To give a rat *Pneumocystis* pneumonia, all you have to do is give the rat cortisone—a potent suppressor of the immune system—and the rat then *spontaneously* develops *Pneumocystis* infection. By contrast, Betty and I had to pour staphylococci in massive doses down the hamster trachea to produce infection with staphylococci. The rat experiment suggests that *Pneumocystis* is present in low numbers in the lung at all times. The *Pneumocystis* that at this moment was filling up Ed's lungs lives in my lungs and in yours. The constant vigilance of the immune system keeps it in check. Immune suppression by steroids or, as in Ed's case, AIDS, results in unchecked multiplication of this organism.

I sought out Bobby Keller in the ICU waiting room. His eyes were red and puffy from crying. I tried to explain what I had done so far. Bobby listened perfunctorily to what I had to say about *Pneumocystis* and the amount of oxygen Ed required. It was clear he felt Ed's time had come and that we had gone beyond a threshold of intervention that Ed had not wanted to cross.

When I got home it was after midnight. Steven was in our bed. Rather than disturb them, I went to Steven's room and crawled into his bed.

It felt as if my head had just touched the pillow when my beeper went off. It was from the ICU at the Miracle Center. An intern was calling to say that Ed's heart had gone into a malignant and chaotic rhythm. A Code Blue was in progress.

"What time is it?" I asked.

"Four-thirty in the morning," he said.

"How long has the code been going on?"

"Five minutes. And there has been no sign of his heartbeat coming back."

"Keep going, I'll be right there. Ask the nurses to call in his lover and the family and have them wait in the quiet room."

In the ICU, a furious Code Blue was in progress. All the bustle and activity *around* Ed was in contrast to the activity *in* Ed's body: there was no heartbeat, and only the forceful chest compression by the intern was sending blood around. I reviewed the code chart: everything I would have done had been tried: calcium, epinephrine, bicarbonate. I waved everyone off, thanked them, and we pulled out the tube from Ed's trachea. Ed now looked peaceful, asleep.

In a few minutes there was no one in the room but an ICU nurse and myself. She was a night nurse I had seen around, but never worked with. She was picking up the debris from the code. She was dressed for a shuttle mission—gloves, gown, mask, goggles. This was not inappropriate, as during the Code Blue there was potential for splashing.

I said to her, by way of small talk, "I'm surprised that his heart should have quit so quickly. I really thought I could cure the pneumonia, wean him off the respirator, get a few more meaningful months or even years of life for him."

She stopped what she was doing, looked at me and said, affecting nonchalance: "Well they're *all* going to die, aren't they? There's not much point to this."

She left the room before I could think of an appropriate reply.

I was furious.

I wanted to ask her what the "point" was in the ninety-year-old patients that they played with in the unit for days until they were brain dead, all the while running up a huge bill that we, the taxpayers, would pay. Right at that moment there was a patient in the ICU whom we were sending up for dialysis three times a week when there was no hope of any other organ in the body recovering.

I wanted to ask her if *she* was in the same boat, would she like an extra year of life, or would she opt to leave the world right away? And for that matter, weren't we ALL going to die one day? Did she think her job was to solely take care of immortals?

I calmed myself. "Pick and choose your battles, Abe," I said to myself. In a way she had been baiting me; anything I said back to her would have been a self-fulfilling prophecy for her. It would prove my lack of objectivity. Besides, I *had* failed in this instance. Ed's corpse was proof of my failure.

When I stepped out of the room, I saw her with some other nurses at the nurses' station. She had surely finished telling them about our little encounter. I bade them all good night.

Bobby Keller and the Maupin family were in the quiet room. It was very difficult for me to go in there and tell them Ed had died. Bobby cried. His sobs were big and wrenching. Ed's brothers covered their eyes or turned their heads away from me. The eldest came over and shook my hand and thanked me. Bobby came out with, "Praise the Lord, his suffering is over," and walked alone toward the door.

The next day the pathology report of the bronchial washing from Ed's lung came back. The specimen had been loaded with the saucer-shaped, dark-staining *Pneumocystis*. At this point, of course, it hardly mattered. Ed was dead.

I thought of funerals I had been to in Johnson City where the grieving widow was escorted to the memorial service by friends and family. Tears and hugs, happy memories, casseroles and condolences. Who would comfort Bobby Keller, I wondered.

PERRI KLASS

PERRI KLASS (1958–   ). *American physician and writer of short stories and novels. Dr. Klass is a pediatrician in Boston. She has written two novels,* Recombinations *(1991) and* Other Women's Children *(1990), a collection of short stories, and a nonfiction account of her experiences as a medical student,* A Not Entirely Benign Procedure *(1988). Her most recent book,* Baby Doctor *(1992), the sequel to* A Not Entirely Benign Procedure, *recounts Klass's three years of mishaps and adventures as a pediatric intern and resident and the lessons she learned from both her patients and their families.*

INVASIONS

Morning rounds in the hospital. We charge along, the resident leading the way, the interns following, the two medical students last, pushing the cart that holds the patients' charts. The resident pulls up in front of a patient's door, the interns stop as well, and we almost run them over with the chart cart. It's time to present the patient, a man who came into the hospital late last night. I did the workup—interviewed him, got his medical history, examined him, wrote a six-page note in his chart, and (at least in theory) spent a little while in the hospital library, reading up on his problems.

"You have sixty seconds, go!" says the resident, looking at his watch. I am of course thinking rebelliously that the interns take as long as they like with their presentations, that the resident himself is long-winded and full of pointless anecdotes—but at the same time I am swinging into my presentation, talking as fast as I can to remind my listeners that no time is being wasted, using the standard hospital turns of phrase. "Mr. Z. is a seventy-eight-year-old white male who presents with dysuria and intermittent hematuria of one week's duration." In other words, for the past week Mr. Z. has experienced pain with urination, and has occasionally passed blood. I rocket on, thinking only about getting through the presentation without being told off for taking too long, without being reprimanded for including nonessential items—or for leaving out crucial bits of data. Of course, fair is fair, my judgment about what is critical and what is not is very faulty. Should I include in this very short presentation (known as a "bullet") that Mr. Z. had gonorrhea five years ago? Well, yes, I decide, and include it in my sentence, beginning, "Pertinent past medical history includes . . ." I don't even have a second to remember how Mr. Z. told me about his gonorrhea, how he made me repeat the question three times last night, my supposedly casual question dropped in between "Have you ever been exposed to tuberculosis?" and "Have you traveled out of the country recently?"

"Five years ago?" The resident interrupts me. "When he was seventy-three? Well, good for him!"

Feeling almost guilty, I think of last night, of how Mr. Z.'s voice dropped to a whisper when he told me about the gonorrhea, how he then went on, as if he felt he had no choice, to explain that he had gone to a convention and "been with a hooker—excuse me, miss, no offense," and how he had then infected his wife, and so on. I am fairly used to this by now, the impulse people sometimes have to confide everything to the person examining them as they enter the hospital. I don't know whether they are frightened by suggestions of disease and mortality, or just accepting me as a medical professional and using me as a comfortable repository for secrets. I have had people tell me about their childhoods and the deaths of their relatives, about their jobs, about things I have needed to ask about and things that have no conceivable bearing on anything that concerns me.

In we charge to examine Mr. Z. The resident introduces himself and the other members of the team, and then he and the interns listen to Mr. Z.'s chest, feel his stomach. As they pull up Mr. Z.'s gown to examine his genitals; the resident says heartily, "Well now, I understand you had a little trouble with VD not so long ago." And immediately I feel like a traitor; I am sure that Mr. Z. is looking at me reproachfully. I have betrayed the secret he was so hesitant to trust me with.

I am aware that my scruples are ridiculous. It is possibly relevant that Mr. Z. had gonorrhea; it is certainly relevant to know how he was treated, whether he might have been reinfected. And in fact, when I make myself meet his eyes, he does not look nearly as distressed at being examined by three people and asked this question in a loud booming voice as he seemed last night with my would-be-tactful inquiries.

In fact, Mr. Z. is getting used to being in the hospital. And in the hospital, as a patient, you have no privacy. The privacy of your body is of necessity violated constantly by doctors and nurses (and the occasional medical student), and details about your physical condition are discussed by the people taking care of you. And your body is made to give up its secrets with a variety of sophisticated techniques, from blood tests to X rays to biopsies—the whole point is to deny your body the privacy that pathological processes need in order to do their damage. Everything must be brought to light, exposed, analyzed, and noted in the chart. And all this is essential for medical care, and even the most modest patients are usually able to come to terms with it, exempting medical personnel from all the most basic rules of privacy and distance.

So much for the details of the patient's physical condition. But the same thing can happen to details of the patient's life. For the remainder of Mr. Z.'s hospital stay, my resident was fond of saying to other doctors, "Got a guy on our service, seventy-eight, got gonorrhea when he was seventy-three, from a showgirl. Pretty good, huh?" He wouldn't ever have said such a thing to Mr. Z.'s relatives, of course, or to any nondoctor. But when it came to his fellow doctors, he saw nothing wrong with it.

I remember another night, 4:00 A.M. in the hospital and I had finally gone to sleep after working up a young woman with a bad case of stomach cramps and diarrhea. Gratefully, I climbed into the top bunk in the on-call room, leaving the bottom bunk for the intern, who might never get to bed, and who, if she did, would have to be ready to leap up at a moment's notice if there was an emergency. Me, I hoped that, emergency or not, I would be overlooked in the top bunk and allowed to sleep out the next two hours and fifty-five minutes in peace (I reserved five minutes to pull myself together before rounds). I lay down and closed my eyes, and something occurred to me. With typical medical student compulsiveness, I had done what is called a "mega-workup" on this patient, I had asked her every possible question about her history and conscientiously written down all her answers. And suddenly I realized that I had written in her chart careful details of all her drug use, cocaine, amphetamines, hallucinogens, all the things she had said she had once used but didn't anymore. She was about my age and had talked to me easily, cheerfully, once her pain was relatively under control, telling me she used to be really into this and that, but now she didn't even drink. And I had written all the details in her chart. I couldn't go to sleep, thinking about those sentences. There was no reason for them. There was no reason everyone had to know all this. There was no reason it had to be written in her official chart, available for legal subpoena. It was four in the morning and I was weary and by no means clear-headed; I began to fantasize one scenario after another in which my careless remarks in this woman's record cost her a job, got her thrown into jail, discredited her forever. And as I dragged myself out of the top bunk and out to the nurses' station to find her chart and cross out the offending sentences with such heavy black lines that they could never be read, I was conscious of an agreeable sense of self-sacrifice—here I was, smudging my immaculate mega-writeup to protect my patient. On rounds, I would say, "Some past drug use," if it seemed relevant.

Medical records are tricky items legally. Medical students are always being reminded to be discreet about what they write—the patient can demand to see the record, the records can be subpoenaed in a trial. Do not make jokes. If you think a serious mistake has been made, do not write that in the record—that is not for you to judge, and you will be providing ammunition for anyone trying to use the record against the hospital. And gradually, in fact, you learn a set of evasions and euphemisms with which doctors comment in charts on differences of opinion, misdiagnoses, and even errors. "Unfortunate complication of usually benign procedure." That kind of thing. The chart is a potential source of damage; damage to the patient, as I was afraid of doing, or damage to the hospital and the doctor.

Medical students and doctors have a reputation for crude humor; some is merely off-color, which comes naturally to people who deal all day with sick bodies. Other jokes can be more disturbing; I remember a patient whose cancer had destroyed her vocal cords so she could no longer talk. In taking her history from her daughter we happened to find out that she had once been a professional musician, singing and playing the piano in supper clubs. For the rest of her stay in the hospital, the resident always introduced her case, when discussing it with other doctors, by saying, "Do you know Mrs. Q.? She used to sing and play the piano—now she just plays the piano."

As you learn to become a doctor, there is a frequent sense of surprise, a feeling that you are not entitled to the kind of intrusion you are allowed into patients' lives. Without arguing, they permit you to examine them; it is impossible to imagine, when you do your very first physical exam, that someday you will walk in calmly and tell a man your grandfather's age to undress, and then examine him without thinking about it twice. You get used to it all, but every so often you find yourself marveling at the access you are allowed, at the way you are learning from the bodies, the stories, the lives and deaths of perfect strangers. They give up their privacy in exchange for some hope—sometimes strong, sometimes faint—of the alleviation of pain, the curing of disease. And gradually, with medical training, that feeling of amazement, that feeling that you are not entitled, scars over. You begin to identify more thoroughly with the medical profession—of course you are entitled to see everything and know everything; you're a doctor, aren't you? And as you accept this as your right, you move further from your patients, even as you penetrate more meticulously and more confidently into their lives.

ELSPETH CAMERON RITCHIE

ELSPETH CAMERON RITCHIE (1958–   ). *American physician and military psychologist. Born in San Francisco and raised in Washington, D.C., Dr. Ritchie is a graduate of Harvard University and George Washington Medical School. Her writing has been published in a variety of periodicals including the* Journal of the American Medical Association, Military Medicine, the Journal of Clinical Psychology, *as well as literary magazines. A major in the U.S. Army, she is currently the head of psychiatry services at the U.S. Army Hospital in Seoul, Korea.*

HOSPITAL SKETCHBOOK:
LIFE ON THE WARD THROUGH AN INTERN'S EYES

On the Ward

I carry three AIDS patients, about the same as any other intern on the medicine service at my hospital. One is a young black male, one a young white female, the third a middle-aged black male. The young man received a lethal blood transfusion three years ago. The black man, married with children, has told us of his homosexual activity. The white female has known no risk factors, but we suspect IV drug use. She may simply have slept with an infected man.

A scant two years ago, in a hospital that has a high proportion of AIDS patients, an intern would average only one AIDS patient. I was a third-year medical student then. I cared for, and became close to, my intern's AIDS patient.

His name was Dave. He was attractive, very thin, and gay. He ran fevers and we could not find the cause. So we drew cultures every night, seeking the bug that shot his temperature up to 104 degrees. He would ask me late at night, while I was setting up the tubes and bottles, why I was planning to hurt him. I never had an answer I believed in. The blood cultures were always negative. We finally treated for pneumocystis pneumonia. Then he spiked fevers in reaction to the antibiotic.

At first I gowned and gloved whenever I entered his room; I hated to draw his blood, fearing needle sticks and contamination. I grew more relaxed; sometimes I almost forgot to put on gloves when I drew blood cultures.

He hated being in the hospital. He could not eat the food and seemed thinner every day. I tried once bringing him his favorite flavor of ice cream, butter pecan, from the cafeteria. He thanked me for it but I think he just let it melt.

I rotated off service. I remember his fantasies of leaving, going home to Florida, and floating downstream in a leaky canoe. I'm sure he is long since dead.

Now, with so many patients to care for, both tragedy and precautions are routine. Any patient is risky. I recently stuck myself with a needle for the first time in my life. Fortunately, the married lady had no risk factors. I sent off hepatitis screen and HTLV-3 (now called HIV) tests anyway. They are due back in two weeks. Should I sleep with my husband until then?

All of my HIV patients are sick, hurting, up here on the medicine ward. Asymptomatic ones wait for disposition on the self-care ward. They also wait for the first signs of real illness: the white thrush over the throat, the purple spots of Kaposi's, and shortness of breath of pneumocystis.

My middle-aged black man will die soon. He has cryptococcal meningitis and pneumocystis pneumonia. The titer of cryptococcus is the highest that this hospital has ever seen. Recently he has become even more short of breath and his tremor has gotten worse. He also has painful rectal herpes. Today his bronchoscopy specimens show an acid-fast bacillus, probably a special form of tuberculosis that immunosuppressed patients get. He is already on four toxic antibiotics. What do we do now?

He finally allowed me to tell his family that he is very sick. They do not know of his AIDS diagnosis. His numerous and respectable family arrived last week. They questioned me as to whether he has cancer. I hedge and talk of his pneumonia. They ask me whether he will come home soon. Not yet, he's very sick, I answer. They suspect the truth, I think, but do not ask. His wife has not called.

Interns see a lot of sickness and death. We build up protective mechanisms: she was old, he drank too much. If somebody our age is dying, our mental dams sway. It could be my best friend (who is gay), it could be my college-age brother. There, but for the grace of God, go I.

My young black male received a blood transfusion after he had a minor accident two years ago. He developed a painful throat ulcer and fevers. He was diagnosed six months ago. He did not tell his family for three more months. He is from a remote town in Kentucky and he did not know how his family would respond. They are angry that he did not tell them sooner. He is about to go home for a convalescent leave. What will his neighbors say? Will they believe the blood transfusion or suspect his morals? Will anybody enter his house?

He is still attractive and personable, if thin. This morning he told me how nice I looked. I replaced his feeding tube; his throat hurts too much to swallow. We are doctor and patient. Two years ago I would have hoped that he would ask me out.

I tell myself severely that it is no good crying for him. He has five sisters who will weep. I have other patients to care for.

The third patient, the young white female, is hostile, remote. She has end-stage renal disease and is on dialysis. You have to coax her into drawing her blood. I don't want to do it either, but the consultants recommend an antibiotic level. Of course, they are not the ones who stick her. I am her intern.

I have other patients, patients with heart, lung, liver, and kidney disease, but they come and go quickly. They die or leave. Except, of course, the elderly waiting for nursing home placement. I hope to send one to a home soon. He has been in the hospital for ninety days.

I also care for healthy HIV-positive patients. They are still working and active and only come to the hospital for staging. While here, they have their blood drawn for T-cell count and their skin pricked to see if they react to allergens. Then they return home to their jobs and families. One recent twenty-nine-year-old admission was diagnosed eight months ago. His wife was initially negative; a month ago she converted. They have two children, six and eight, who have not yet been tested.

In a year or three, they will probably be lying in a hospital bed with pneumocystis and cryptococcus raging through their brains and bodies.

Fortunately I am HIV negative. I feel lucky. My husband cooks me supper when I surface after call. My older brother and his wife just had a healthy baby. I know infected two-year-olds.

I warn my younger unmarried brother. My friends all question me. I have only moralistic-sounding statements to make. Don't sleep around!—or even occasionally. I am glad that I am married and tested negative twice. If I were single, would I insist on a blood test before sleeping with a man? I hate to sound so pessimistic when friends grill me at a cocktail party—but I don't want my friends to die that kind of death.

I wish the families of AIDS patients would come more often. You won't catch it by persuading them to eat! They need their mothers, wives, sons here. They are hurt, sick, dying. They need family. I substitute where I can. It is too little for them and too painful for me.

The Intensive Care Unit
December 25, 1985

The lady lies
surrounded by a court
of alarmed machines.
They record life:
blood pressure, pulse
and respirations.
The lady does not talk
so we read her numbers:
the language of
her failing heart.

Her daughter questions
incessantly,
her husband is mute.
Grandchildren in the waiting room
watch Road Runner.
Over the thicket of IV poles
nurses snatch glimpses
of *M*A*S*H* and *St. Elsewhere.*
Electronic Christmas carols
spew over her bed.

Once she ate, excused herself
to her powder room, breathed on her own.
Now, her body is helpless
and her mind.
Perhaps her soul
wonders at her ruined holiday.
She did not mail her Christmas cards.

I draw the bloods,
apologize for sticking her again.
She does not twitch.
Only the ventilator answers.
The Redskins' field goal
should excite her to wake.
Instead her heart throws a
crazy beat.
Then another—
time for another EKG.

I sigh; no sleep again
tonight, Christmas night.
I nibble microwave popcorn and
stale fruitcake, swig Diet Coke.
A tube bears Osmolyte for her.

The clouded moon through the window
over her busy bed, reminds me of
when I believed in Angels.
Every Christmas, when I was a child,
I searched the orange city skies
for their shining.

I seek again tonight.
No answer.
Winged men triumphantly
should bear her soul to Heaven,
bring me a festival stocking.

Yet, I hope she does not die today
(though my tasks would be fewer).
Her grandchildren should not remember
Christ's birthday and new toys
by her death.

Her blood pressure is dropping.

I will try to keep her
breathing until tomorrow.

Language Barrier

It gets hard to communicate in the old language.

When I started medical school, our courses were basically word lists. The lists were anatomy and microbiology. We memorized the eleven muscles of the thumb, chambers of the heart, classification of diseases of the colon. It was like studying French. All those nouns to memorize!

We all studied how the organs work, of course: the lungs exchange gases, the heart spins blood around, the kidney filters the waste. We peered at purple-painted bacteria, watched antibiotics scour those bugs from the petri dishes. But it was the names that we were tested on, the vocabulary that would isolate us as physicians.

In medical school we were taught never to refer to patients as a disease. To say "the gall bladder down the hall" was demeaning. We resolved always to give our patients due respect.

Back in those pre-war days, they also warned us to continue to communicate with our families, friends, and children. "Spend an hour with your child every day." "Take time out to go running." "It's important to keep up with politics."

Then came third year, the clinical years. The dicta were moot. Even if we had a free half hour it was more important, it seemed, to polish up the history and physical for presentation to our preceptors, to volunteer to hold retractors for another cholecystectomy, to scour the library for articles on esoteric aspects of lupus.

Shakespeare, botany, evolution were lost fantasies. Once, I learned how many petals adorned roses. Now, flower petals are submerged beneath liver enzymes.

The gap widened. How could our husbands know the frustrations of missing a blood draw three times, then have the intern draw pints with ease? When eating with in-laws we could not talk at dinner of the smell of melena (old blood leaking out of the rectum), nor of the skin lesions on our AIDS patients.

As time rolled by, life outside the hospital dwindles. Now I am an intern.

"How was your day, dear?" I politely inquire at home at eight P.M. after a night on call.

"Terrible. The computer went down on a very important project. I was at work from eight this morning to seven tonight. Then the bus broke down. I need a drink. Oh, yes, how was yours?"

I am silent for a minute. "Well, I was lucky last night on call. I slept from one A.M. to four A.M. Then I got a drunk hit from the nursing home with chest pain. But I slept again from six-thirty to seven-thirty. So, almost four hours." Of course that is in a cell-like call room in the bottom of a creaky bunk bed. Meal carts creaking and nurses gossiping loudly outside. Another thirty-seven-hour shift. But I got close to four hours. These days that's cause for celebration. Almost.

So, my sympathies for others' trials are slight. Unfairly, I become impatient with their tribulations. Sometimes I explode.

"Don't tell me about your difficulties with your computer. My favorite patient is dying. And one of my AIDS patients developed pneumocystis pneumonia. And you're whining because you partied too late with friends when I was on call and only got six hours of sleep."

Non-medical friends sympathize. "Oh, you poor dear." They try to help and are puzzled when I am nasty and irritable.

In cocktail conversations acquaintances say: "That's a terrible system. It should not be allowed. I wouldn't want to be cared for by somebody who had been up all night." Noses tilt. Their anger descends on me. I'm a doctor.

Thanks. I don't want to care for them either after I've been up all night. But I can't afford the energy to waste on rage at the system.

After all, it's a privilege to be a doctor.

My fellows on the battlefront become my in-arms comrades, at least until we rotate to a new service. We joke about the drunk hit. We share doughnuts and popcorn. On rounds we talk about the gall bladder down the hall and the valve in Room 4116.

We develop sexual fantasies about those in the trenches with us. At two A.M. your resident is your staff. When a patient is spurting blood out of his tracheostomy and you together insert a central line (an IV in the neck), transfer him to the unit, and save his life (at least for now), then you are brothers. Afterwards you raise Diet Cokes in companionship.

How can your husband compare to him, the man who just helped you save a life?

Marriages are made in medical school and dissolve in internship.

But the deans who pontificated in medical school about the values of outside interests were right. We—the battered products of medical school—know that to be true. It just gets harder. The gap widens.

"She didn't make it. We coded her and shocked her and put a pacemaker into her. It didn't work. Why, I'm not sure. We asked for an autopsy. What should we have for dinner?"

Hospital Spaces

Life is defined by bounds:
here, sickness and health are also sequestered.
We have the isolated rooms of infection,
and social wards of men whose
efforts are limited by chest pain.
They play spades with vigor.

Metal rails surround the beds with
air bubbling up through fluid plastic beads,
confining and relieving the comatose.

The staff have large hectic rooms
with multiple desks and phones ringing.
We report local recoveries and deaths,
call the public health department,
and field calls about AIDS and angina.

Chairs are constantly swiped from one desk
to another, as an intern dashes in to
scribble a note, feet hurting,
or to try to turf a patient to a nursing home.
This one has been in for ninety-seven days.

The hallways link the separate worlds.
Like salt sea barnacles
groups of doctors cling on the walls,
discussing their patients' potassium
(barely out of earshot),
drinking instant coffee, grateful
if a stretcher appears to perch on.
Two hours' sleep last night.
A long day's journey ahead.

The pantry is guarded by fierce ladies
microwaving the trays of hospital food.
Medical students sneak in to steal
leftover chocolate pudding.

Elevators frustrate. Waiting,
pondering my clipboard,
I can hear them ping at every floor.
Rumbling food racks are loaded.
To the lab, to x-ray, then to surgery clinic
to drop off another consult.
I wave to friends on contralateral trips.
How many romances start, and stop,
with the opening and shutting of doors?

Sometimes a patient crashes on the
seventh floor.
With cardiac monitor beeping,
and code drugs on the stretcher,
in case his heart stops,
we transport a patient vomiting blood
to the ICU on the fourth floor,
squeezing past the linen carts
in the narrow hallways,
hoping that we will make it,
before he stops breathing.

So far, so good.

More lines intersect.
The snack bar, the chapel, and barber shop,
the clinics and the morgue.
The library offers a soft chair for sleep.

My beeper is a leash,
jerking me back
to headaches and chest pain.

When I finally break out into the
winter evening,
after 38 hours of the hospital,
it is amazing that
I can remember where the car is,
and that
yellow crocuses are blooming.

JON MUKAND

JON MUKAND (1959–). *American physician, poet, and editor. Dr. Mukand attended the University of Minnesota and received his M.D. from the Medical College of Wisconsin; midway through medical school, he earned an M.A. in English literature at Stanford. He did postgraduate training in physical medicine/rehabilitation at Boston University School of Medicine, and is currently pursuing a Ph.D. in literature from Brown University. Mukand is the editor of* Sutured Words: Contemporary Poetry About Medicine *and* Articulations: The Body and Illness in Poetry *(1994).*

THE SON: RETURNING HOME
(for Sushil Kumar Eric Mukand)

Moist air crystallizes into morning, shimmers
in the sunrise, cutting my face as I leave the house,
as I leave you.
              You are the medical texts,
the pipes scattered about in empty ashtrays, the sunlight's
dull reflection from the antique brass lamp.
You are gone, resolved
in an electric moment to urned ash, leaving behind
a stray sitar note which resonates
in me with its saffron music.

The respirator's measured, regular breaths
replaced your own cigarette-scarred wheezing.
You tried to quit, but kept on borrowing
cigarettes from patients, as if a smile
was enough payment.

The peaceful hiss and sigh
of your plastic lungs
was incessantly regular.

I tried imagining the incinerator,
but during the funeral
my memory could only filter
the burned fragrance of cumin and cardamom.

Why do we need oxygen
to live or die,
for metabolism and for combustion?

Was your life
a poorly controlled chemical reaction,
and its by-product your death?

Once, under the heat
of the Indian sun, you lifted me up
to the branches
of a mango tree, caught me when I jumped down.
Now I am left with the fruit of long days,
nights away delivering babies: your heart on
crutches, arteries rusted away.
And you knew, you knew.

90 percent occlusion
of the anterior descending artery,
80 percent of the circumflex.

Hints of self-diagnosis in journal articles
you underlined: *coronary bypass, cardiac
catheters, myocardial infarctions.* Reading
your medical records, I also knew.

We can only walk so far away from home,
from our fathers, who have left us
their lives in each dying cell, each spiral
DNA staircase that ascends
or descends to the next day.

The house holds me
like a kite, reeling me in, taut
against the gusts blowing on this bamboo frame.

You will be waiting:
wire-rimmed glasses, trim moustache, smiling
with my mother, a photograph on the night-stand
before I turn off the brass lamp.

So I turn
homeward, promising to write
a *ghazal* for which you
have left behind a melody.

Someday, I will hear the *tabla,* whose rhythm
no EKG can capture and no cardiologist
can interpret. The music will
take me back to the lotus pond
at our old home in the village of Sultanpur:
then, I will drift away on the fallen petals.

ETHAN CANIN

ETHAN CANIN (1961–   ). *American physician and writer. His early fiction appeared in* Esquire, The Atlantic, *and* Best American Short Stories *(1985). Canin has won a Houghton Mifflin Literary Fellowship, the James Michener Award, and the Henfield/Transatlantic Review Award. He wrote his first book,* Emperor of the Air *(1988), a short-story collection, while attending medical school. Both of Canin's subsequent works,* Blue River *(1991) and* The Palace Thief *(1994), have met with great critical acclaim.*

WE ARE NIGHTTIME TRAVELERS

Where are we going? Where, I might write, is this path leading us? Francine is asleep and I am standing downstairs in the kitchen with the door closed and the light on and a stack of mostly blank paper on the counter in front of me. My dentures are in a glass by the sink. I clean them with a tablet that bubbles in the water, and although they were clean already I just cleaned them again because the bubbles are agreeable and I thought their effervescence might excite me to action. By action, I mean I thought they might excite me to write. But words fail me.

This is a love story. However, its roots are tangled and involve a good bit of my life, and when I recall my life my mood turns sour and I am reminded that no man makes truly proper use of his time. We are blind and small-minded. We are dumb as snails and as frightened, full of vanity and misinformed about the importance of things. I'm an average man, without great deeds except maybe one, and that has been to love my wife.

I have been more or less faithful to Francine since I married her. There has been one transgression—leaning up against a closet wall with a red-haired purchasing agent at a sales meeting once in Minneapolis twenty years ago; but she was buying auto upholstery and I was selling it and in the eyes of judgment this may bear a key weight. Since then, though, I have ambled on this narrow path of life bound to one woman. This is a triumph and a regret. In our current state of affairs it is a regret because in life a man is either on the uphill or on the downhill, and if he isn't procreating he is on the downhill. It is a steep downhill indeed. These days I am tumbling, falling headlong among the scrub oaks and boulders, tearing my knees and abrading all the bony parts of the body. I have given myself to gravity.

Francine and I are married now forty-six years, and I would be a bamboozler to say that I have loved her for any more than half of these. Let us say that for the last year I haven't; let us say this for the last ten, even. Time has made torments of our small differences and tolerance of our passions. This is our state of affairs. Now I stand by myself in our kitchen in the middle of the night; now I lead a secret life. We wake at different hours now, sleep in different corners of the bed. We like different foods and different music, keep our clothing in different drawers, and if it can be said that either of us has aspirations, I believe that they are to a different bliss. Also, she is healthy and I am ill. And as for conversation—that feast of reason, that flow of the soul—our house is silent as the bone yard.

Last week we did talk. "Frank," she said one evening at the table, "there is something I must tell you."

The New York game was on the radio, snow was falling outside, and the pot of tea she had brewed was steaming on the table between us. Her medicine and my medicine were in little paper cups at our places.

"Frank," she said, jiggling her cup, "what I must tell you is that someone was around the house last night."

I tilted my pills onto my hand. "Around the house?"

"Someone was at the window."

On my palm the pills were white, blue, beige, pink: Lasix, Diabinese, Slow-K, Lopressor. "What do you mean?"

She rolled her pills onto the tablecloth and fidgeted with them, made them into a line, then into a circle, then into a line again. I don't know her medicine so well. She's healthy, except for little things. "I mean," she said, "there was someone in the yard last night."

"How do you know?"

"Frank, will you really, please?"

"I'm asking how you know."

"I heard him," she said. She looked down. "I was sitting in the front room and I heard him outside the window."

"You heard him?"

"Yes."

"The front window?"

She got up and went to the sink. This is a trick of hers. At that distance I can't see her face.

"The front window is ten feet off the ground," I said.

"What I know is that there was a man out there last night, right outside the glass." She walked out of the kitchen.

"Let's check," I called after her. I walked into the living room, and when I got there she was looking out the window.

"What is it?"

She was peering out at an angle. All I could see was snow, blue-white.

"Footprints," she said.

I built the house we live in with my two hands. That was forty-nine years ago, when, in my foolishness and crude want of learning, everything I didn't know seemed like a promise. I learned to build a house and then I built one. There are copper fixtures on the pipes, sanded edges on the struts and queen posts. Now, a half-century later, the floors are flat as a billiard table but the man who laid them needs two hands to pick up a woodscrew. This is the diabetes. My feet are gone also. I look down at them and see two black shapes when I walk, things I can't feel. Black clubs. No connection with the ground. If I didn't look, I could go to sleep with my shoes on.

Life takes its toll, and soon the body gives up completely. But it gives up the parts first. This sugar in the blood: God says to me: "Frank Manlius—codger, man of prevarication and half-truth—I shall take your life from you, as from all men. But first—" But first! Clouds in the eyeball, a heart that makes noise, feet cold as uncooked roast. And Francine, beauty that she was—now I see not much more than the dark line of her brow and the intersections of her body: mouth and nose, neck and shoulders. Her smells have changed over the years so that I don't know what's her own anymore and what's powder.

We have two children, but they're gone now too, with children of their own. We have a house, some furniture, small savings to speak of. How Francine spends her day I don't know. This is the sad truth, my confession. I am gone past nightfall. She wakes early with me and is awake when I return, but beyond this I know almost nothing of her life.

I myself spend my days at the aquarium. I've told Francine something else, of course, that I'm part of a volunteer service of retired men, that we spend our days setting young businesses afoot: "Immigrants," I told her early on, "newcomers to the land." I said it was difficult work. In the evenings I could invent stories, but I don't, and Francine doesn't ask.

I am home by nine or ten. Ticket stubs from the aquarium fill my coat pocket. Most of the day I watch the big sea animals—porpoises, sharks, a manatee—turn their saltwater loops. I come late morning and move a chair up close. They are waiting to eat then. Their bodies skim the cool glass, full of strange magnifications. I think, if it is possible, that they are beginning to know me: this man—hunched at the shoulder, cataractic of eye, breathing through water himself—this man who sits

425

and watches. I do not pity them. At lunchtime I buy coffee and sit in one of the hotel lobbies or in the cafeteria next door, and I read poems. Browning, Whitman, Eliot. This is my secret. It is night when I return home. Francine is at the table, four feet across from my seat, the width of two dropleaves. Our medicine is in cups. There have been three Presidents since I held her in my arms.

The cafeteria moves the men along, old or young, who come to get away from the cold. A half-hour for a cup, they let me sit. Then the manager is at my table. He is nothing but polite. I buy a pastry then, something small. He knows me—I have seen him nearly every day for months now—and by his slight limp I know he is a man of mercy. But business is business.

"What are you reading?" he asks me as he wipes the table with a wet cloth. He touches the saltshaker, nudges the napkins in their holder. I know what this means.

"I'll take a cranberry roll," I say. He flicks the cloth and turns back to the counter.

This is what:

> Shall I say, I have gone at dusk through narrow streets
> And watched the smoke that rises from the pipes
> Of lonely men in shirt-sleeves, leaning out of windows?

Through the magnifier glass the words come forward, huge, two by two. With spectacles, everything is twice enlarged. Still, though, I am slow to read it. In a half-hour I am finished, could not read more, even if I bought another roll. The boy at the register greets me, smiles when I reach him. "What are you reading today?" he asks, counting out the change.

The books themselves are small and fit in the inside pockets of my coat. I put one in front of each breast, then walk back to see the fish some more. These are the fish I know: the gafftopsail pompano, sixgill shark, the starry flounder with its upturned eyes, queerly migrated. He rests half-submerged in sand. His scales are platey and flat-hued. Of everything upward he is wary, of the silvery seabass and the bluefin tuna that pass above him in the region of light and open water. For a life he lies on the bottom of the tank. I look at him. His eyes are dull. They are ugly and an aberration. Above us the bony fishes wheel at the tank's corners. I lean forward to the glass. *"Platichthys stellatus,"* I say to him. The caudal fin stirs. Sand moves and resettles, and I see the black and yellow stripes. "Flatfish," I whisper, "we are, you and I, observers of this life."

*   *   *

"A man on our lawn," I say a few nights later in bed.

"Not just that."

I breathe in, breathe out, look up at the ceiling. "What else?"

"When you were out last night he came back."

"He came back."

"Yes."

"What did he do?"

"Looked in at me."

Later, in the early night, when the lights of cars are still passing and the walked dogs still jingle their collar chains out front, I get up quickly from bed and step into the hall. I move fast because this is still possible in short bursts and with concentration. The bed sinks once, then rises. I am on the landing and then downstairs without Francine waking. I stay close to the staircase joists.

In the kitchen I take out my almost blank sheets and set them on the counter. I write standing up because I want to take more than an animal's pose. For me this is futile, but I stand anyway. The page will be blank when I finish. This I know. The dreams I compose are the dreams of others, remembered bits of verse. Songs of greater men than I. In months I have written few more than a hundred words. The pages are stacked, sheets of different sizes.

If I could

one says.

It has never seemed

says another. I stand and shift them in and out. They are mostly blank, sheets from months of nights. But this doesn't bother me. What I have is patience.

Francine knows nothing of the poetry. She's a simple girl, toast and butter. I myself am hardly the man for it: forty years selling (anything—steel piping, heater elements, dried bananas). Didn't read a book except one on sales. Think victory, the book said. Think *sale*. It's a young man's bag of apples, though; young men in pants that nip at the waist. Ten years ago I left the Buick in the company lot and walked home, dye in my hair, cotton rectangles in the shoulders of my coat. Francine was in the house that afternoon also, the way she is now. When I retired we bought a camper and went on a trip. A traveling salesman retires, so he goes on a trip. Forty miles out of town the folly appeared to me, big as a balloon. To Francine, too. "Frank," she said in the middle of a bend, a prophet turning to me, the camper pushing sixty and rocking in the wind, trucks to our left and right big as trains—"Frank," she said, "these roads must be familiar to you."

So we sold the camper at a loss and a man who'd spent forty years at highway speed looked around for something to do before he died. The first poem I read was in a book on a table in a waiting room. My eyeglasses made half-sense of things.

> *These*
> *are the desolate, dark weeks*

I read

> *when nature in its barrenness*
> *equals the stupidity of man.*

Gloom, I thought, and nothing more, but then I reread the words, and suddenly there I was, hunched and wheezing, bald as a trout, and tears were in my eye. I don't know where they came from.

In the morning an officer visits. He has muscles, mustache, skin red from the cold. He leans against the door frame.

"Can you describe him?" he says.

"It's always dark," says Francine.

"Anything about him?"

"I'm an old woman. I can see that he wears glasses."

"What kind of glasses?"

"Black."

"Dark glasses?"

"Black glasses."

"At a particular time?"

"Always when Frank is away."

"Your husband has never been here when he's come?"

"Never."

"I see." He looks at me. This look can mean several things, perhaps that he thinks Francine is imagining. "But never at a particular time?"

"No."

"Well," he says. Outside on the porch his partner is stamping his feet. "Well," he says again. "We'll have a look." He turns, replaces his cap, heads out to the snowy steps. The door closes. I hear him say something outside.

"Last night—" Francine says. She speaks in the dark. "Last night I heard him on the side of the house."

We are in bed. Outside, on the sill, snow has been building since morning.

"You heard the wind."

"Frank." She sits up, switches on the lamp, tilts her head toward the window. Through a ceiling and two walls I can hear the ticking of our kitchen clock.

"I heard him climbing," she says. She has wrapped her arms about her own waist. "He was on the house. I heard him. He went up the drainpipe." She shivers as she says this. "There was no wind. He went up the drainpipe and then I heard him on the porch roof."

"Houses make noise."

"I heard him. There's gravel there."

I imagine the sounds, amplified by hollow walls, rubber heels on timber. I don't say anything. There is an arm's length between us, a cold sheet, a space uncrossed since I can remember.

"I have made the mistake in my life of not being interested in enough people," she says then. "If I'd been interested in more people, I wouldn't be alone now."

"Nobody's alone," I say.

"I mean that if I'd made more of an effort with people I would have friends now. I would know the postman and the Giffords and the Kohlers, and we'd be together in this, all of us. We'd sit in each other's living rooms on rainy days and talk about the children. Instead we've kept to ourselves. Now I'm alone."

"You're not alone," I say.

"Yes, I am." She turns the light off and we are in the dark again. "You're alone, too."

My health has gotten worse. It's slow to set in at this age, not the violent shaking grip of death; instead—a slow leak, nothing more. A bicycle tire: rimless, thready, worn treadless already and now losing its fatness. A war of attrition. The tall camels of the spirit steering for the desert. One morning I realized I hadn't been warm in a year.

And there are other things that go, too. For instance, I recall with certainty that it was on the 23rd of April, 1945, that, despite German counteroffensives in the Ardennes, Eisenhower's men reached the Elbe; but I cannot remember whether I have visited the savings and loan this week. Also, I am unable to produce the name of my neighbor, though I greeted him yesterday in the street. And take, for example, this: I am at a loss to explain whole decades of my life. We have children and photographs, and there is an understanding between Francine and me that bears the weight of nothing less than half a century, but when I gather my memories they seem to fill no more than an hour. Where has my life gone?

It has gone partway to shoddy accumulations. In my wallet are credit cards, a license ten years expired, twenty-three dollars in cash. There is a photograph but it depresses me to look at it, and a poem, half-copied and folded into the billfold. The leather is pocked and has taken on the curve of my thigh. The poem is from Walt Whitman. I copy only what I need.

But of all things to do last, poetry is a barren choice. Deciphering other men's riddles while the world is full of procreation and war. A man should go out swinging an axe. Instead, I shall go out in a coffee shop.

But how can any man leave this world with honor? Despite anything he does, it grows corrupt around him. It fills with locks and sirens. A man walks into a store now and the microwaves announce his entry; when he leaves, they make electronic peeks into his coat pockets, his trousers. Who doesn't feel like a thief? I see a policeman now, any policeman, and I feel a fright. And the things I've done wrong in my life haven't been crimes. Crimes of the heart perhaps, but nothing against the state. My soul may turn black but I can wear white trousers at any meeting of men. Have I loved my wife? At one time, yes—in rages and torrents. I've been covered by the pimples of ecstasy and have rooted in the mud of despair; and I've lived for months, for whole years now, as mindless of Francine as a tree of its mosses.

And this is what kills us, this mindlessness. We sit across the table-cloth now with our medicines between us, little balls and oblongs. We sit, sit. This has become our view of each other, a tableboard apart. We sit.

"Again?" I say.

"Last night."

We are at the table. Francine is making a twisting motion with her fingers. She coughs, brushes her cheek with her forearm, stands suddenly so that the table bumps and my medicines move in the cup.

"Francine," I say.

The half-light of dawn is showing me things outside the window: silhouettes, our maple, the eaves of our neighbor's garage. Francine moves and stands against the glass, hugging her shoulders.

"You're not telling me something," I say.

She sits and makes her pills into a circle again, then into a line. Then she is crying.

I come around the table, but she gets up before I reach her and leaves the kitchen. I stand there. In a moment I hear a drawer open in the living room. She moves things around, then shuts it again. When she returns she sits at the other side of the table. "Sit down," she says. She puts two folded sheets of paper onto the table. "I wasn't hiding them," she says.

"What weren't you hiding?"

"These," she says. "He leaves them."

"He leaves them?"

"They say he loves me."

"Francine."

"They're inside the windows in the morning." She picks one up, unfolds it. Then she reads:

Ah, I remember well (and how can I
But evermore remember well) when first

She pauses, squint-eyed, working her lips. It is a pause of only faint understanding. Then she continues:

Our flame began, when scarce we knew what was
The flame we felt.

When she finishes she refolds the paper precisely. "That's it," she says. "That's one of them."

At the aquarium I sit, circled by glass and, behind it, the senseless eyes of fish. I have never written a word of my own poetry but can recite the verse of others. This is the culmination of a life. *Coryphaena hippurus,* says the plaque on the dolphin's tank, words more beautiful than any of my own. The dolphin circles, circles, approaches with alarming speed, but takes no notice of, if he even sees, my hands. I wave them in front of his tank. What must he think has become of the sea? He turns and his slippery proboscis nudges the glass. I am every part sore from life.

Ah, silver shrine, here will I take my rest
After so many hours of toil and quest,
A famished pilgrim—saved by miracle.

There is nothing noble for either of us here, nothing between us, and no miracles. I am better off drinking coffee. Any fluid refills the blood. The counter boy knows me and later at the café he pours the cup, most of a dollar's worth. Refills are free but my heart hurts if I drink more than one. It hurts no different from a bone, bruised or cracked. This amazes me.

Francine is amazed by other things. She is mystified, thrown beam ends by the romance. She reads me the poems now at breakfast, one by one. I sit. I roll my pills. "Another came last night," she says, and I see her eyebrows rise. "Another this morning." She reads them as if every word is a surprise. Her tongue touches teeth, shows between lips. These lips are dry. She reads:

> *Kiss me as if you made believe*
> *You were not sure, this eve,*
> *How my face, your flower, had pursed*
> *Its petals up*

That night she shows me the windowsill, second story, rimmed with snow, where she finds the poems. We open the glass. We lean into the air. There is ice below us, sheets of it on the trellis, needles hanging from the drainwork.

"Where do you find them?"

"Outside," she says. "Folded, on the lip."

"In the morning?"

"Always in the morning."

"The police should know about this."

"What will they be able to do?"

I step away from the sill. She leans out again, surveying her lands, which are the yard's-width spit of crusted ice along our neighbor's chain link and the three maples out front, now lost their leaves. She peers as if she expects this man to appear. An icy wind comes inside. "Think," she says. "Think. He could come from anywhere."

One night in February, a month after this began, she asks me to stay awake and stand guard until the morning. It is almost spring. The earth has reappeared in patches. During the day, at the borders of yards and driveways, I see glimpses of brown—though I know I could be mistaken. I come home early that night, before dusk, and when darkness falls I move a chair by the window downstairs. I draw apart the outer curtain and raise the shade. Francine brings me a pot of tea. She turns out the light and pauses next to me, and as she does, her hand on the chair's backbrace, I am so struck by the proximity of elements—of the night, of the teapot's heat, of the sounds of water outside—that I consider speaking. I want to ask her what has become of us, what has made our breathed air so sorry now, and loveless. But the timing is wrong and in a moment she turns and climbs the stairs. I look out into the night. Later, I hear the closet shut, then our bed creak.

There is nothing to see outside, nothing to hear. This I know. I let hours pass. Behind the window I imagine fish moving down to greet me: broomtail grouper, surfperch, sturgeon with their prehistoric rows of scutes. It is almost possible to see them. The night is full of shapes and bits of light. In it the moon rises, losing the colors of the horizon, so that by early morning it is high and pale. Frost has made a ring around it.

A ringed moon above, and I am thinking back on things. What have I regretted in my life? Plenty of things, mistakes enough to fill the car showroom, then a good deal of the back lot. I've been a man of gains and losses. What gains? My marriage, certainly, though it has been no knee-buckling windfall but more like a split decision in the end, a stock risen a few points since bought. I've certainly enjoyed certain things about the world, too. These are things gone over and over again by the writers and probably enjoyed by everybody who ever lived. Most of them involve air. Early morning air, air after a rainstorm, air through a car window. Sometimes I think the cerebrum is wasted and all we really need is the lower brain, which I've been told is what makes the lungs breathe and the heart beat and what lets us smell pleasant things. What about the poetry? That's another split decision, maybe going the other way if I really made a tally. It's made me melancholy in old age, sad when if I'd stuck with motor homes and the National League standings I don't think I would have been rooting around in regret and doubt at this point. Nothing wrong with sadness, but this is not the real thing— not the death of a child but the feelings of a college student reading *Don Quixote* on a warm afternoon before going out to the lake.

Now, with Francine upstairs, I wait for a night prowler. He will not appear. This I know, but the window glass is ill-blown and makes moving shadows anyway, shapes that change in the wind's rattle. I look out and despite myself am afraid.

Before me, the night unrolls. Now the tree leaves turn yellow in moonshine. By two or three, Francine sleeps, but I get up anyway and change into my coat and hat. The books weigh against my chest. I don gloves, scarf, galoshes. Then I climb the stairs and go into our bedroom, where she is sleeping. On the far side of the bed I see her white hair and beneath the blankets the uneven heave of her chest. I watch the bed-covers rise. She is probably dreaming at this moment. Though we have shared this bed for most of a lifetime I cannot guess what her dreams are about. I step next to her and touch the sheets where they lie across her neck.

"Wake up," I whisper. I touch her cheek, and her eyes open. I know this though I cannot really see them, just the darkness of their sockets.

"Is he there?"

"No."

"Then what's the matter?"

"Nothing's the matter," I say. "But I'd like to go for a walk."

"You've been outside," she says. "You saw him, didn't you?"

"I've been at the window."

"Did you see him?"

"No. There's no one there."

"Then why do you want to walk?" In a moment she is sitting aside the bed, her feet in slippers. "We don't ever walk," she says.

I am warm in all my clothing. "I know we don't," I answer. I turn my arms out, open my hands toward her. "But I would like to. I would like to walk in air that is so new and cold."

She peers up at me. "I haven't been drinking," I say. I bend at the waist, and though my head spins, I lean forward enough so that the effect is of a bow. "Will you come with me?" I whisper. "Will you be queen of this crystal night?" I recover from my bow, and when I look up again she has risen from the bed, and in another moment she has dressed herself in her wool robe and is walking ahead of me to the stairs.

Outside, the ice is treacherous. Snow has begun to fall and our galoshes squeak and slide, but we stay on the plowed walkway long enough to leave our block and enter a part of the neighborhood where I have never been. Ice hangs from the lamps. We pass unfamiliar houses and unfamiliar trees, street signs I have never seen, and as we walk the night begins to change. It is becoming liquor. The snow is banked on either side of the walk, plowed into hillocks at the corners. My hands are warming from the exertion. They are the hands of a younger man now, someone else's fingers in my gloves. They tingle. We take ten minutes to cover a block but as we move through this neighborhood my ardor mounts. A car approaches and I wave, a boatman's salute, because here we are together on these rare and empty seas. We are nighttime travelers. He flashes his headlamps as he passes, and this fills me to the gullet with celebration and bravery. The night sings to us. I am Bluebeard now, Lindbergh, Genghis Khan.

No, I am not.

I am an old man. My blood is dark from hypoxia, my breaths singsong from disease. It is only the frozen night that is splendid. In it we walk, stepping slowly, bent forward. We take steps the length of table forks. Francine holds my elbow.

I have mean secrets and small dreams, no plans greater than where to buy groceries and what rhymes to read next, and by the time we reach our porch again my foolishness has subsided. My knees and elbows ache. They ache with a mortal ache, tired flesh, the cartilage gone sandy with time. I don't have the heart for dreams. We undress in the hallway, ice in the ends of our hair, our coats stiff from cold. Francine turns down the thermostat. Then we go upstairs and she gets into her side of the bed and I get into mine.

It is dark. We lie there for some time, and then, before dawn, I know she is asleep. It is cold in our bedroom. As I listen to her breathing I know my life is coming to an end. I cannot warm myself. What I would like to tell my wife is this:

> *What the*
> *imagination*
> *seizes*
> *as beauty must be truth. What holds you*
> *to what you see of me is*
> *that grasp alone.*

But I do not say anything. Instead I roll in the bed, reach across, and touch her, and because she is surprised she turns to me.

When I kiss her the lips are dry, cracking against mine, unfamiliar as the ocean floor. But then the lips give. They part. I am inside her mouth, and there, still, hidden from the word, as if ruin had forgotten a part, it is wet—Lord! I have the feeling of a miracle. Her tongue comes forward. I do not know myself then, what man I am, who I lie with in embrace. I can barely remember her beauty. She touches my chest and I bite lightly on her lip, spread moisture to her cheek, and then kiss there. She makes something like a sigh. "Frank," she says. "Frank." We are lost now in seas and deserts. My hand holds her fingers and grips them, bone and tendon, fragile things.

ABOUT THE EDITORS

RICHARD REYNOLDS was born in Saugerties, New York, and educated at Rutgers University (B.S.) and Johns Hopkins (M.D.). His postgraduate training in medicine and allergy/infectious disease was done at Johns Hopkins Hospital. For a number of years, Dr. Reynolds was in the private practice of internal medicine in Frederick, Maryland. His academic career includes appointments at Johns Hopkins University School of Medicine, chair of the department of community health and family medicine at the University of Florida, and dean of the University of Medicine and Dentistry of New Jersey. Dr. Reynolds has written and edited many papers and a number of books, including *The Health of a Rural County: Perspectives and Problems* (with Sam A. Banks and Alice H. Murphree). He has held positions of leadership in many organizations, both regional and national, and is currently executive vice president of The Robert Wood Johnson Foundation in Princeton.

JOHN STONE was born in Jackson, Mississippi, and educated at Millsaps College (B.A.) and Washington University in St. Louis (M.D.). His postgraduate training in internal medicine and cardiology was done at Strong Memorial Hospital/University of Rochester School of Medicine and at Emory University School of Medicine. He is now professor of medicine (cardiology), associate dean, and director of admissions at Emory University School of Medicine. In addition to numerous medical papers, Dr. Stone was co-editor of *Principles and Practice of Emergency Medicine,* the first comprehensive textbook of that burgeoning discipline. His writings include three books of poetry: *The Smell of Matches, In All This Rain,* and *Renaming the Streets.* His latest book, *In the Country of Hearts: Journeys in the Art of Medicine* (1990), is a collection of essays about both the literal and metaphorical hearts.

Editorial Assistants

LOIS LACIVITA NIXON received her A.B. degree from the University of Miami (literature and nursing) and holds master's degrees from Middlebury College and Rollins College; her M.P.H. is from the University of South Florida, as is her Ph.D. in English literature. Dr. Nixon is now associate professor of medicine at the University of South Florida School of Medicine, where she teaches in the division of medical ethics and humanities. She is also chair of the Hillsborough County Hospital Authority.

DELESE WEAR was born in Louisiana, Missouri, but has spent most of her life in northeast Ohio. Since finishing her Ph.D. at Kent State University in 1981, she has taught at the Northeastern Ohio Universities College of Medicine, where she is currently associate professor of behavioral sciences and coordinator of the Human Values in Medicine Program. Her academic interests are in literature and medicine, as well as pedagogical issues in the medical humanities.

PERMISSIONS

INDEX OF AUTHORS

Abse, Danny, 222
Altman, Lawrence K., 346
Angelou, Maya, 267
Atwood, Margaret, 362
Auden, W. H., 128

Betjeman, Sir John, 126
The Bible, 20
Bontemps, Arna, 112
Borges, Jorge Luis, 99
Brooks, Gwendolyn, 166
Broyard, Anatole, 175

Canin, Ethan, 423
Carver, Raymond, 360
Chekhov, Anton, 44
Ciardi, John, 164
Clifton, Lucille, 331
Coles, Robert, 277
Cornford, Frances, 98
Coulehan, Jack, 366

Dickey, James, 227
Dickinson, Emily, 27
Donne, John, 22
Doyle, Sir Arthur Conan, 34

Eisenberg, Carola, 17

Frost, Robert, 60

Goedicke, Patricia, 298
Gonzales-Crussi, Frank, 316
Grumbach, Doris, 167

Hardison, Joseph, 311
Hellerstein, David, 395
Hemingway, Ernest, 104
Hilfiker, David, 371
Holmes, Oliver Wendell, 25
Hurston, Zora Neale, 121

Jarrell, Randall, 162

Kafka, Franz, 93
Kanafani, Ghassan, 333
Keats, John, 24
Kennedy, X. J., 287
Kirkup, James, 219
Klass, Perri, 407
Konner, Melvin, 383

Larkin, Philip, 182
Levertov, Denise, 232
Lowbury, Edward, 147

Maughham, W. Somerset, 62
McHugh, Heather, 391
Miles, Josephine, 141
Mukand, Jon, 420

Neruda, Pablo, 123

O'Connor, Flannery, 235
Olds, Sharon, 364
Osler, Sir William, 30

Paley, Grace, 217
Pastan, Linda, 307
Pym, Barbara, 142

Reynolds, Richard C., 268
Rinaldi, David, 389
Ritchie, Elspeth Cameron, 411

Sams, Ferrol, 184
Schneiderman, L. J., 299
Selzer, Richard, 251
Sissman, L. E., 249
Stone, John, 326

Tate, James, 368
Thomas, Dylan, 161
Thomas, Lewis, 149

Valdiserri, Ronald, 393
Verghese, Abraham, 399
Vonnegut, Kurt, 201

Walker, Alice, 369
Weissmann, Gerald, 288

Welty, Eudora, 133
Williams, Miller, 296
Williams, William Carlos, 68

ILLUSTRATION CREDITS

Costume of a seventeenth-century plague physician. Engraving from J. J. Manget: *Traite de la peste* . . . Geneva, 1721. Frontis to vol. 1.

Thomas Eakins, *The Gross Clinic.* Jefferson Medical College of Thomas Jefferson University, Philadelphia, Pennsylvania.

Edvard Munch, *The Sick Child.* The Tate Gallery, London.

Pieter Brueghel, *Landscape with the Fall of Icarus.* Musées Royaux des Beaux-Arts de Belgique, Brussels.

Photo of Dr. Ernest Ceriani: W. Eugene Smith, *Life* magazine © Time Warner Inc.

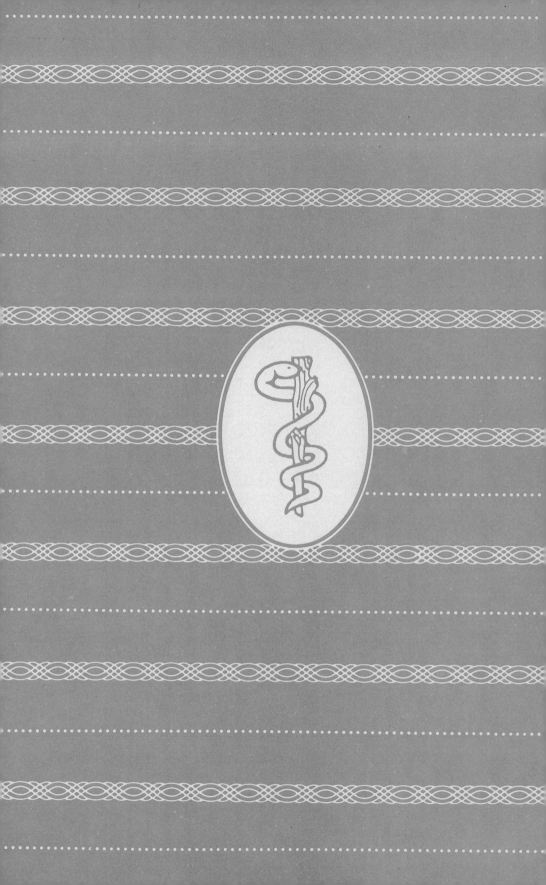